CAMBRIDGE COMMONWEALTH SERIES

General Editor: Dr E. T. Stokes

TOWARD 'UHURU' IN TANZANIA

These monographs are published by the Syndics of
the Cambridge University Press in association
with the Managers of the Cambridge University
Smuts Memorial Fund of Commonwealth Studies.

TOWARD 'UHURU' IN TANZANIA

THE POLITICS OF PARTICIPATION

G. ANDREW MAGUIRE

formerly advisor on Political and Security Affairs, United States Mission to the United Nations

CAMBRIDGE
AT THE UNIVERSITY PRESS
1969

Published by the Syndics of the Cambridge University Press
Bentley House, P.O. Box 92, 200 Euston Road, London N.W.1
American Branch: 32 East 57th Street, New York, N.Y. 10022

Library of Congress Catalogue Card Number: 75–85727

Standard Book Number: 521 07652 8

To my father and mother

Printed in Great Britain
by Alden & Mowbray Ltd at the Alden Press, Oxford

Contents

Tanzania, 1965

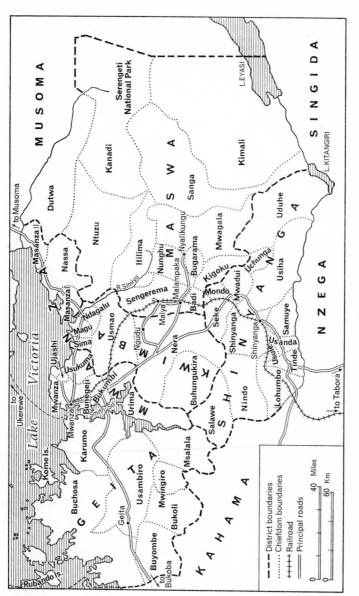

Sukumaland, 1945–63

Acknowledgements

My debts to others are many. I would like first to express my gratitude to the Government of the United Republic of Tanzania for permission to conduct the research so essential for a study such as this. I was permitted both to consult relevant government documents and to interview scores of government and party officials and Tanzanian citizens.

Special thanks are due to several ministers and junior ministers: the Honorable Paul Bomani, the Honorable S. A. Maswanya, the Honorable E. A. Kisenge and the Honorable R. S. Wambura—who were generous with their time in personal interviews. His Excellency John S. Malecela and the Honorable Chief Humbi Ziota II were the Regional Commissioners of Mwanza and Shinyanga respectively during the months of my stay. They and Area Commissioners S. Kaseko, S. Lubala, A. Madaha, S. Mohamed, T. A. K. Msonge, E. A. Nyamubi and J. K. Tosiri facilitated my work in a variety of important ways. Waziri Juma, Regional Commissioner; S. A. Kandoro, Area Commissioner; Barbara C. Johansson, Member of the National Assembly; S. P. M. Njau, Regional Administrative Secretary; and K. Z. B. Kissie and Stephen Madoshi, Deputy Regional Secretaries of TANU, were also extremely helpful. Without the patience and cooperation of these and other goverment and TANU officials the research could not have been completed.

In addition to scores of Tanzanians who gave countless hours of their time in interviews and informal discussions, a number of expatriate colonial officials were most generous and helpful. I would mention especially the late Lord Twining, Governor of Tanganyika from 1949 to 1958; former Provincial Commissioners S. A. Walden, E. G. Rowe and Sir R. de Z. Hall; and former District Commissioners Neville French, R. S. King and A. G. Stephen. I owe a special debt of gratitude to Jeffrey Ede and Michael Cook, sometime directors of the National Archives, for their assistance with documentation from the colonial period.

Robert I. Rotberg, recently of Harvard University and now of

the Massachusetts Institute of Technology, deserves my deepest
gratitude for his consistent encouragement and sound criticism
from the inception of the Tanzania research project to its conclusion. If there is merit in the present work it is due in significant
measure to my having had the fortunate opportunity and the good
sense to make myself his student. I am especially grateful, too,
to Henry Bienen of Princeton University, who read and commented
perceptively on the manuscript in its entirety, and to Rupert
Emerson, my advisor at Harvard, for his assistance with the manuscript in its dissertation phase and for his encouragement and
sound advice during the years of my graduate study.

I am also greatly indebted to Pastor Balele of Kwimba District,
Tanzania. He was a tireless and most skilful research assistant.
He conducted scores of interviews. He culled through reams of
dusty files, taking notes directly into the typewriter. He tutored
me in Swahili and translated written and spoken Sukuma when
English or Swahili did not suffice. My deep appreciation goes as
well to Yona Mwakasendo and Michael Kinunda of Tanzania,
and Lyndon Harries of the University of Wisconsin, for expert
Swahili instruction; to Marcia Wright of Columbia University
and Ralph Austen of the University of Chicago for insight and
guidance on conducting research in Tanzania; to George Bennett
of Oxford University for timely encouragement and stimulating
correspondence while I was in the field; to Joseph Nye and Martin
Kilson of Harvard University for comment and criticism during
the early stages of organization and writing; and to Gottfried O.
Lang of the Institute of Behavioral Science of the University of
Colorado for his insights into cultural change among the Sukuma
and the stimulus he has given to cross-disciplinary discussion
among those interested in Sukumaland.

I have been assisted in a variety of ways by Margaret Bates of
Smith College, J. Gus Liebenow of the University of Indiana,
Peter F. M. McLoughlin of the University of Santa Clara, Colin
Leys of the University of Sussex, Lionel Cliffe and Martin
Lowenkopf of the University College, Dar es Salaam, and the
late Derrick Stenning of the East African Institute of Social
Research, Makerere University. Mary Read Nicholson of the
University of Minnesota, Margarete Paulus of the University of
Cologne, and Colby R. Hatfield, Jr, of the University of Colorado,
shared with me for fourteen months the excitements and vicis-
situdes of research in the field.

For housing facilities and an invaluable research base at the Nyegezi Social Research Institute, I am grateful to the Mwanza Diocese of the Tanganyika Episcopal Conference of White Fathers, and personally to Bishop Joseph Blomjous and the directors of the Institute, Charles O. Noble of Goucher College and Alphonse van der Sande of Tilburg University, the Netherlands. For financial assistance during graduate school, for the generous research grant which made my field work possible, and for typing assistance, I am indebted to the Woodrow Wilson and Danforth Foundations and to the Foreign Area Training Fellowship Program of the American Council of Learned Societies and the Social Science Research Council financed by the Ford Foundation.

Elizabeth Whitson of the New York Office of Cambridge University Press encouraged me to submit my manuscript for consideration, and to her I express my gratitude. She read and commented on the text and, together with her colleagues in Cambridge, assisted me in the final preparations for publication.

My mother, Ruth, did the typing and retyping of copy and helped with the editing and indexing of the manuscript. What she knows about Tanzania she now knows more times than either she or I would be likely to admit. Her devoted assistance and critical perception have been indispensable throughout.

Finally, my wife, Meg, would like to express her gratitude to me for completing the manuscript prior to our marriage.

Abbreviations

A.C.	Area Commissioner
A.D.E.O.	Assistant Divisional Executive Officer
D.C.	District Commissioner
D.E.O.	Divisional Executive Officer
D.O.	District Officer
D.P.C.	Deputy Provincial Commissioner
E.O.	Executive Officer
FCBF	Fabian Colonial Bureau Files
GTDF	Geita District Files
KWDF	Kwimba District Files
LPF	Lake Province Files
MADF	Maswa District Files
MZDF	Mwanza District Files
P.C.	Provincial Commissioner
R.C.	Regional Commissioner
SHDF	Shinyanga District Files
SMP	Secretariat Minute Paper (Tanganyika Territory Secretariat)
SU	Sukuma Union
SUF	Sukuma Union Files
TAA	Tanganyika African Association
TANU	Tanganyika African National Union
TLC	Tanganyika Legislative Council (Proceedings)
UNVM	United Nations Visiting Mission (Report on Tanganyika)
orig. Sw.	original document in Swahili

Note on Sources

I employed four methods of gathering material. Documentary sources in the United Kingdom, Uganda, and Tanganyika were consulted. In particular, the private papers of certain British administrators and African political organizers and closed (i.e. non-current) files in regional and district government offices have been invaluable. Secondly, I personally interviewed scores of African leaders and British administrators in East Africa and in England. A few of these were important figures by any territorial or national reckoning, but most were primarily of local importance in Sukumaland. As I explain more fully in the introduction, it was my intention to discover the stuff and substance of politics at the local level by talking with those who 'made' politics at that level, rather than to limit interviews to more prominent men on what they thought happened at that level. Thirdly, I recruited several young men of the Sukuma tribe—some with previous research experience—to carry out a schedule of interviews in selected villages in the five Sukumaland districts to assess the extent of the ordinary citizen's perception of and participation in the evolving political nationalism of the postwar years. Having achieved a working fluency in Swahili, I conducted most of my own interviews with Tanzanians in that language. The Sukuma assistants, however, were able to approach and talk with even the most unsophisticated Sukuma in their own language, providing a corrective for the inevitably limited contacts (however local) of a non-African researcher. Finally, to obtain data on personal biographies and political activities of certain important persons and office-holders in addition to those directly interviewed, several hundred leadership survey questionnaires were distributed in three of the five Sukumaland districts.

Files which were available to the writer in regional and district offices in 1964 have now been transferred to the National Archives in Dar es Salaam where they have been reorganized. Notes on material from these files is therefore limited to the office of origin and citation of the specific item of documentation. A substantial portion of material in regional and district office files was in the Swahili language. All translations are by the writer. Where material quoted in the text appeared originally in Swahili, a notation accompanies the reference in the notes. Finally, all pronominal concords to African names ('Ba,' 'Wa,' 'Bu,' 'Ki,' etc.) have been dropped—except for certain inconsistencies in place names within Sukumaland.

Introduction

Tanzania is unusual in Africa today. This is not because her problems are different in kind from those of many other African nations. They are not. Indeed, some of the social, economic and political problems common to the new states of Black Africa appear more intractable in Tanzania than elsewhere. Nor does Tanzania's uniqueness depend on a particular brand of political rhetoric. While Tanzania's national leader and president, Julius Nyerere, is one of the most prominent and articulate exponents of 'African Socialism' and 'one-party democracy,' the differences between his doctrines and those of philosopher-presidents in other African states from Guinea to Zambia are less important than the similarities. But Tanzania is unique—so far—in that its political leadership, under one regime since independence, continues genuinely to attempt to give effect in practice to the mix of traditional and modern, socialist and democratic principles to which it is committed, and actually to succeed in partial but important pragmatic ways in this complex endeavor. The genius of Tanzania's leaders is that they have acted with sufficient imagination and flexibility to preserve and enhance, rather than diminish and restrict, present and future possibilities for creative political responses to old and new problems.

While a list of shortcomings is only to be expected, the list of Tanzania's accomplishments is significant in both quantity and quality, especially in comparison with other African states. Since independence Nyerere has insisted with some success on the maintenance of high standards of performance and personal conduct for the nation's leaders and civil servants and, with characteristic school-masterly humor, on circumscription of the propensity for pomposity in high places. For the most part he has maintained in practice the commitment of the nation to a non-racial attitude. This meant the admission of non-Africans to the Tanganyika African National Union beginning in 1963 and deliberate rather than hasty Africanization (later 'localization,' which made the criterion explicitly citizenship rather than race) of the administrative

B

services in the years since independence. In 1965 in an electoral innovation of perhaps far-reaching significance, Tanzania held competitive elections within the framework of the one-party system—the only African state yet to do so. While economic development has lagged behind what had been hoped for, the government has continued to elaborate thoughtfully on basic principles and to devise practical means for making the most of the available human and natural resources, as evidenced most recently in the Arusha Declaration of 1967.[1] The union with Zanzibar, while incompletely integrated structurally, has so far proved enduring. In foreign policy, Tanzania has continued to eschew dogmatic ideological identifications and to follow a principled and pragmatic policy of non-alignment.

Successful military coups d'etat have replaced more than a few of the independent African regimes so recently ushered on to the world scene. Unsuccessful coup attempts and mutinies have jolted a number of others, including Tanzania. Whether still under civilian or new military leadership, the direction in most, regardless of ideological coloration or lack thereof, has been decidedly and increasingly authoritarian. Against this background, Tanzania's short but distinctive history as an independent nation, and her perhaps all too precarious promise for the future, should be of interest to other than Tanzania-philes.

Under discussion among students of African affairs when I first visited Tanzania in 1962 were the related questions: Is African socialism a doctrine of substance? Can a one-party state be democratic? Skeptics tended to feel that ultimately there would be no alternative to choice between authoritarian and democratic styles of government. Some viewed 'one-party democracy' as but a momentary theoretical outpost on a rationalized road to an authoritarian state. Others argued that for an interim period the requirements of unity, the need for full use of limited human resources, and the exigencies and priorities of development required an enforced single-party system. This might involve the temporary sacrifice of Western liberal conceptions of civil liberties and loyal opposition, but, in the view of this sub-group of those skeptical about African socialism, the future would permit the establishment of democratic two-party or multi-party systems

---

[1] Excerpts from the Arusha Declaration are reprinted in *Africa Report*, XII (Mar. 1967), 11–13.

after the requisite economic and political bases for such systems had been attained. It is now barely a dozen years since Ghana became the first colonial black African state to achieve independence, and hence rather early to reach definite conclusions; but the authoritarian school of skeptics about African socialism seems now to have more of the preliminary evidence in its favor than do those who foresaw a trend toward parliamentary democratic systems.

Some African leaders, and a dwindling number of observers outside Africa, have elaborated the view that a third alternative exists. They believe the substance of democracy can be fostered within a single-party system. They would dispense with the outward forms of Western European and American variants of the representative system but shun also the elitist and totalitarian characteristics of communist state systems. They are confident that popular participation in government—mass membership in the party, internal discussion and criticism, true consent, even choice of political leaders—can be effected within a single-party system. For these advocates African socialism is not necessarily verbal sleight-of-hand; it is viewed as a practical possibility capable of unique innovation in the art of government.

Among the most self-conscious of the single-party regimes in Africa—and one of the few which has enshrined the one-party state in a new constitution—Tanzania has seemed for a variety of reasons to hold the most promise for the successful inauguration of something approximating to a democratic one-party state. Historically, the uniting of the country through the creation of the nationalist party, TANU, preceded for the most part the evolution of sharply differentiated and competitive social economic and political interests and groupings. Lacking historical African kingdoms and dominant individual tribes, Tanzania has largely avoided the internecine rivalries and conflicts which have rent the internal fabrics of other African states or, alternatively, led to an enforced unitary system in which important ethnic subgroups were suppressed and the people suffered markedly from widespread loss of individual liberty, lack of popular participation in party and governmental affairs, and stifling of criticism and dissent. Tanzania is alone among African states in having an African language—Swahili—as the national language. A unifying factor for Tanzania's multiplicity of tribes, the pervasiveness of Swahili is conducive to popular political participation beyond the minority of Western-educated elite. Finally, Tanzania enjoys in President Nyerere a leader of unusual intelligence, foresight, flexibility and persistence: he is one of the few in Africa, or elsewhere, to 'begin making the transition from rhetoric to reality.'[1]

But what do African socialism and one-party democracy—however they may be viewed as theoretical constructs—mean on the ground? What is the relationship between national policies and people's lives? What is the difference, if any, between what the party and the government say they are doing and what citizens at the grass roots see them to be doing, or not doing, and what they (the citizens) are willing or not willing to do as a result? Since theory and practice seldom coincide, it would seem that intensive study of administration and politics at the grass-roots level would be essential to any assessment of the successes and failures of national policies. It is no reflection on top leadership in a national capital to suggest that a complete picture of actualities in up-country localities is unlikely to derive from interviews in a ministry or departmental headquarters. Yet, it is precisely in up-country localities where doctrines of African socialism and one-party democracy do or do not achieve reality. It is only at the grass-roots level that theories about popular participation in the political system can be adequately tested and analyzed. There is a need for political scientists to study nationalist politics and problems of national political integration from below. There is likewise a need for anthropologists to study traditional societies in relation to the national political system.

The need for such research has been increasingly recognized in the past several years as the limitations on our knowledge of African politics have become more apparent. Generalizations about the rise of nationalism and studies of new elites, types of political parties and various forms of state organization have provided us with a grasp of the historical stages of the anti-colonial struggle and with an outline of the roles assumed and the structures built by Africa's nationalist leaders before and after independence. What we do not yet know enough about is how national and especially local leaders act and interact with the citizens whom they are meant both to lead and to serve; how the structures of the party and the government, especially at the local

[1] Martin Lowenkopf, 'The meaning of Arusha,' *Africa Report*, XII (Mar. 1967), 8.

level, really do function. It has become more apparent that political parties in Africa—whatever their structural characteristics and however radical their ideological underpinnings—do not and cannot rapidly or thoroughly transform the essentially rural society, even politically.

Attention thus has shifted from ideologies evolved at the center and from structural typologies of parties and discussion as to their authoritarian or democratic proclivities, toward an attempt to describe and analyze processes of national political integration. This leads in turn to more careful consideration of the nature of relationships within parties and government at all levels and between the representatives of these political institutions and the people and the problems of the society as a whole. The study of political development must perforce address itself to what actually happens when political ideas and instruments engage the environment to which they are attempting to relate and which they are, quite professedly, attempting to modify. This requires study at the grass roots. As Aristide Zolberg has pointed out: 'in order to obtain a more general understanding of African politics we must examine what occurs at the more intimate and more particular level of the local community. What is involved is less the study of local government (in its institutional sense) than the study of government locally, or, to use another phrase, the study of micropolitics.'[1]

The present work is a study in micropolitics because it is my belief that thorough and detailed case studies of selected areas within various nations are among the next necessary steps toward a fuller understanding of African politics, in both its pre-independence and post-independence phases.[2] In Africa, as in other

---

[1] Aristide R. Zolberg, *Creating political order: the party states of West Africa* (Chicago: Rand McNally, 1966), p. 153.

[2] It would be difficult, of course, to put forward generalizations about politics in Africa on the basis of a detailed study of politics in one portion of Tanzania. I have not attempted to build models or explore typologies. Nor have I attempted to make this study the vehicle for the elaboration of a theoretical framework—or even to appropriate, in what I believe could only be now an illusory and premature grasp at comprehensiveness and precision, the terminology of social theory as it has been applied to, or developed from, the African experience in the few attempts at synthesis to date. Thus, the present work does not pretend to be comparative, though it should ultimately provide, together with other micropolitical studies, the basis for useful comparative analysis. More sophisticated propositions about the development of national movements and the functioning of ruling parties could then be tested.

parts of the emerging world of new nations, problems of national political integration and economic modernization have dominated the minds of the first generation of post-independence political leaders, as well as their scholarly analysts. Especially in Africa some form of indigenous socialism—frequently espoused but seldom practiced—has been the preferred means toward the attainment of the desired ends. But the political consolidation of a fledgling nation state and the exploitation and development of its largely untapped or meager economic resources—not to mention the structuring and functioning of what is held to be a popularly based political system—require not only the acquiescence but, in some degree at least, also the active participation of a predominantly rural population. The politics of the developing nations, to be understood, must be viewed and experienced, to the extent possible, from below.

The present work is also an historical study. Current reality is shaped by today's objectives and theories. It is also shaped by the experience of the past. It would be possible to study developments in politics and administration in independent Tanzania alone; but post-independence successes and difficulties are better understood as outgrowths, at least in part, of pre-independence struggles.

The story of the development of nationalist politics in Tanzania did not even begin, as some have believed, with the formation of the Tanganyika African National Union in 1954. In some parts of Tanganyika it began at least ten years earlier, with proto-nationalist associations like the Sukuma Union and the Tanganyika African Association. Further, the rise of nationalist politics—though conforming to certain general stages of development from polite representation of grievances to protest, to incipient action, to overt organization for specified political objectives, to the consolidation of a popular mass movement bent on self-government, to post-independence administration and nation-building— varied in pace and differed in certain other respects in disparate areas depending on the impact of the colonial government's policies, on the character of traditional tribal institutions, and on the nature of the economic and social environment.

If we wish to study politics in action and government in operation, an historical as well as micropolitical approach is not only desirable but necessary. Zolberg has rightly argued that major gaps in our knowledge make it extremely difficult to reconstruct a reasonable base line from which later changes can be evaluated adequately. A more thorough examination of the period preceding independence would also afford us greater understanding of the development of political groups and cleavages, of their relationship to the non-political environment, and hence, in general, of the characteristic structures and processes which constitute the legacy which the new African states inherited.

He points out that 'tradition' in Africa 'includes the colonial experience.'[1] We must examine the African response to that experience, both before and after independence, if we wish to bring perspective to bear on political development at the level of local African society—where, as Henry Bienen has said, 'the major contributions to our understanding of African politics will be made.'[2]

While they have traditionally engaged in local studies, anthropologists have only recently begun to give some attention to the presence or absence of political linkages from within the tribal unit or sub-unit to the national party or administration, and to the evolution of such linkages through time.[3] On the other hand, as Ruth Schachter Morgenthau has observed, a generation of politically oriented Africanists saw the politics of emerging African countries from the capital cities and, on visits up-country, through the eyes of the elite—guides who, consciously or unconsciously, projected their view of the world to recipients who too uncritically accepted much of what they were shown and told.[4] Political scientists have rarely travelled up-country far enough, or focused their attention on local units long enough, to probe beneath the too readily absorbing chronology of African political and constitutional advance and, after independence, of the evolution of national governmental and party institutions and policy, to discover what was—and what was not—happening politically on the ground. This is what must now be done. It must be done

[1] Zolberg, p. 152.
[2] Henry Bienen, 'What does political development mean in Africa?' (review article), *World Politics*, xx (Oct. 1967), 136.
[3] For such an anthropological study in Sukumaland see Mary Read Nicholson, 'Legal change in Tanzania as seen among the Sukuma,' (unpub. Ph.D. diss., University of Minnesota, 1968). Nicholson analyzes Sukuma legal history, assesses the implementation of reaction to national legal change among the Sukuma, and considers post-independence retention of traditional mechanisms of dispute settlement—for example the headman's court and communal action—in conjunction with the primary courts and primary court magistrates.
[4] Professor Morgenthau made this point to a seminar of Africa scholars at New York University in the spring of 1967.

through interviews as well as documents. It requires the use of vernacular as well as of European languages. It is what is here attempted for Sukumaland.

The value of an historically oriented micropolitical case study in Tanzania derives partly from the telescoping into fifteen or twenty years of virtually the entire evolutionary process of the rise of nationalism. In Sukumaland, for example, it is possible to begin in 1945 with the first suggestions of organization by Africans for mutual aid and expression of grievances and with the first African representative in the Legislative Council (a Sukuma chief) and proceed in a very few years to the later stages of independence, the formation of a republic, and the establishment of a one-party state.

For a variety of reasons Sukumaland seemed an appropriate locale for a micropolitical historical study. The Sukuma tribe is by far Tanzania's largest, numbering over one million persons, or one-ninth of the nation's total population. It has come to be regarded as one of the more active and industrious of Tanzania's tribes. Since the war the Sukuma and neighboring peoples to the north and east have built the largest producers' cooperative movement in Africa. Because of Sukumaland's size and importance territorially, and what it deemed to be the homogeneity and malleability of the Sukuma, the British administration repeatedly used Sukumaland as an experimental area for local government reforms and economic development programs. Partly for this reason, Sukumaland (and the Lake Province generally) fostered the most active and politically oriented African voluntary associations in Tanganyika during the ten years between the end of the war and the birth of the Tanganyika African National Union in 1954. So bothersome was this penchant for political activity that the administration banned TANU from Sukumaland for four years—the only area in Tanganyika where proscriptions were so extensive in both spacial and temporal terms. It was in Sukumaland, too, that local government broke down in 1958 in the face of civil disorders—an event which, combined with external pressures, helped speed the course of change territorially toward African control and national independence.

The victory of TANU, however, did not solve the problems of modernizing politics and administration in Sukumaland. Opposition to TANU sprang up in some areas. While chiefs were replaced by administrative officers without much difficulty, the reluctance of the Sukuma to embrace voluntary 'self-help' labor, to pay higher taxes and fees, and to adopt new methods in agriculture and animal husbandry has posed since independence a continuing problem for the political leadership and for nation-building efforts.

Thus, from 1945 to 1965 Sukumaland permits an intensive study of political integration and development at the local level. This in turn provides some historical insight into the development of African nationalism generally. The view from the grass roots places both the colonial administrator and the African nationalist— before and after independence—in a new and often revealing perspective. It clarifies the contradictions underlying British policy after 1945 and elucidates the strengths and limitations of African political organization in relation to the pre- and post-independence problems of up-country. It sheds light on the successes and difficulties of an independent African government involved in the attempt to integrate and mobilize an ever larger percentage of its population. It permits some assessment of the possibilities for one-party democracy within the ideological context of African socialism.

The book is divided into four parts. Part I, 'The Setting', very briefly describes the pre-Second World War historical background and postwar constitutional development, then examines in some detail the major policies and programs of the colonial administration in the postwar period as they applied to rural life and local government. The colonial government's principal administrators and policy-makers in Sukumaland, and their approaches to economic and political development, are discussed. The traditional system of the Sukuma is outlined briefly.[1] Thus, the opening section sets forth the context which must necessarily be understood before an analysis of African political activity at the local level—to which the remainder of the work is primarily devoted—may be undertaken.

Part II, 'The Beginnings of Indigenous Politics', explores the earliest manifestations of political concern among traditional and non-traditional local elites; the development of organizational

---

[1] I treat the traditional system of the Sukuma only briefly, both because a number of other published works consider it in detail and because the subtleties of Sukuma social and political organization are not particularly significant for the development of African nationalist politics in Sukumaland or for the political administration of Sukumaland after independence.

structures with the potential for, and then a tendency toward, nationalist-oriented political activity; and finally the achievement by locally based organizations of a level of relevance and sophistication (in the two years before TANU was formed) sufficient to mobilize rural support in opposition to specific administration policies and ultimately to the administration itself. The view from below permits examination of the identity and the techniques of a politically essential—but often under-appreciated (both by scholars and by national leaders)—middle-level leadership group through whom the vital contact is made between a political organization, or government administration, and the people. The perspective of the latter on their own lives—and the extent to which they will or will not be concerned and involved with the affairs of politics and government—begins to emerge from the micropolitical study.

Part III, 'The Struggle for Power,' depicts the conflict which developed outright after 1953 between the by then clearly nationalist-oriented political movement in Sukumaland and an administration bent on the pursuit of established policies and on quarantining the increasingly vociferous, recalcitrant and well-organized political opposition. No longer was protest limited to an expression of views. Rather, protest took the form of political action: attendance at political meetings, refusal to abide by government regulations, marches, civil disobedience, telegrams to the Colonial Office and the United Nations, delegations to Dar es Salaam. Capitalizing on the weaknesses of the native authorities, on the mistakes of the colonial administration, and on their own strengths within an historical context favorable to the rapid development of African nationalism, the leaders and followers of this new brand of politics ultimately prevailed—with the assistance, of course, of external as well as internal pressures for change—in their struggle against the colonial regime itself.

While positive evidence provides the material for this section along the lines described above, negative evidence suggests something else of considerable interest: the virtual absence of influence or impact of the traditional system of political organization of the Sukuma (modified, of course, by colonial rule) on the political organization of the nationalist movement both before and after independence. I have specified the political organization 'of the Sukuma'. There is no question but that nationalist leaders and associations in Tanzania, as in other African countries, have accommodated appreciably in style, organizational structure, and even ideology to elements common to, or at least widely shared among, traditional political systems in a given area. The symbolic and ceremonial accoutrements of the charismatic nationalist leader, so reminiscent in some ways of the traditional chief; the existence of an elders' section of the party; the invocation of the African past to provide an element of 'consensus democracy' for the concept of African socialism—these are cases in point from Tanzanian politics. What is largely absent, however, is evidence to suggest that, at the local level, nationalist political institutions are shaped by or adjusted in significant ways to the particularities or peculiarities of *Sukuma* political organization.[1] This I found surprising: speculating in advance on the probable findings of an in-depth study of politics at the grass roots, I had expected the facts to be otherwise.

This is not to suggest, of course, that aspects of Sukuma traditional life were not of the utmost importance for the development of nationalist politics. Sukuma dissatisfaction with and, finally, resistance to colonial regulations which Sukuma considered inimical to established ways and to traditional economic and social organization provided the sparks for protests which eventually became overtly political. The nationalist movement capitalized on such sentiment and helped to mobilize it into organized

---

[1] Analyzed from the vantage point of the 'grass roots,' the fact seems to be that both the cooperative movement and the nationalist oriented political organizations set themselves up largely without reference to indigenous *Sukuma* institutions. When an individual decided to join one of these new associations, he paid his entrance fee, received his membership card, and entered a new world of economic or political, or both, activity and expectations—as did Tanzanians of any other tribe. Indeed, it seems to have been in areas of Sukumaland where traditional life was already most attenuated by the impact of non-traditional economic and political factors and by the ineffectiveness of native authorities that political activism prospered and that certain 'traditional' elements, who also had the requisite 'modern' traits, were enabled to play a new political role. A surprising number of lesser traditional figures were gathered into the new structures but their origins and traditional ties were incidental; it was their experience, education, qualifications, and political loyalty which counted. They worked side by side with and were directed from above by people who were implementing new ideas on the basis of new criteria. Thus, whether one is considering pre-independence economic and political associations; the elders' section, the women's section, the Youth League, or TANU as a whole; regional party conferences, district administration, or even village development committees after independence, what connections may have existed between nationalist political institutions and the traditional institutions *of the Sukuma* seem not to have resulted in the shaping of the former.

political action. The traditional associational life of the Sukuma—characterized by dance and work societies which cut horizontally across many separate chiefdoms—may also have given the Sukuma built-in receptivity to the idea of joining associations to further certain desired ends, thereby facilitating the rapid rise of economic cooperation and nationalist political institutions.[1]

Nor do I intend to suggest that traditional Sukuma political institutions were uninfluenced by the rise of nationalist organizations. TANU's attack on the traditional authority system has been, if incomplete in its effects, of such a fundamental character as to alter that system more drastically even than had the British through a combination of reformist design and unforeseen consequence. The nationalist movement before independence exploited certain dislocations in traditional life for political ends. After independence it thoroughly reorganized local political institutions in line with a uniform and non-traditional national pattern. But only in the rarest instances did the organizers of the new politics—who were mostly non-Sukuma in the first instance—attempt to adapt nationalist organizations in Sukumaland to the traditional institutions of the Sukuma. This lack of relationship posed no appreciable difficulty to the political organizers as long as the nub of politics was protest. But after independence, the nub of politics became structural change, and planned economic and political development. This has perforce raised the question of how creative and sustained political links with the conservative rural peoples—and even with the transitional middle-elites of an earlier day—are to be maintained and further developed.

Part IV, 'The New Regime', therefore analyzes the programs of the new African administration, both before and after independence, and the responses of rural Africans to the indigenous leadership. We shall discover that there are continuities and similarities in the responses to centralized control and direction, whether colonial or post-colonial, alien or indigenous. It becomes clear that political development at the local level is one of the few

[1] This is not modification or adaptation of nationalist institutions—though it may be the occasion for such for traditional institutions—so much as fortuitous assistance to their growth. See Gottfried O. and Martha B. Lang, 'Problems of social and economic change in Sukumaland, Tanganyika,' *Anthropological Quarterly*, xxxv (April 1962), 86–101; also G. O. Lang, 'Modernization in East Africa through cultural continuity: the case of the Sukuma,' unpub. essay prepared for Lang and Peter F. M. McLoughlin, eds., *Recent research in Sukumaland: essays in social, economic and political development*, forthcoming.

reliable guides to national progress in a developing state such as Tanzania. Protest against specific administration programs, discontent with the authoritarian style of local party and governmental political institutions, and even the development of opposition movements characterize the immediate pre- and post-independence period. At the same time, significant progress becomes apparent in the gradual realization of the democratic as well as the one-party aspect of Tanzania's goal for the political system. In Tanzania, as in many other nations new and old, the pursuit of 'uhuru'[1] continues.

[1] 'Freedom' is the best single English word for the Swahili 'uhuru'. In the 1950s, 'Uhuru' with a capital 'U' came to mean 'Independence', i.e. national independence. It was the rallying cry of TANU and always came first when paired with other nouns in the popular slogans of the nationalist movement: 'uhuru na umoja' (freedom and unity), 'uhuru na ujamaa' (freedom and African socialism), 'uhuru na kazi' (freedom and work), 'uhuru na afya' (freedom and health), etc. It has been used since independence to emphasize the need for continued efforts to realize a fuller measure of freedom for all Tanzanian citizens through achievement of longer-range political, economic, social, and educational goals.

PART I

THE SETTING

I

Historical Background

European penetration of the East African hinterland dates from little more than 100 years ago. Colonial administration commenced formally in 1890, but effective control in local areas required a decade or two more for its accomplishment. In its entirety the era of colonial government in East Africa comprised hardly more than half a century. The era ended with the independence of Tanganyika in 1961, Uganda in 1962, and Kenya and Zanzibar in 1963. The European presence—whatever its accomplishments or failures, advantages or drawbacks—both forced and attracted East Africa abruptly into the modern world.

I   THE SUKUMA

Details of Sukuma origins are obscure. Available evidence suggests that the tribe as it exists today is a conglomeration of disparate, indigenous, Bantu-speaking clans, overlaid with immigrant Hima (Nilo-Hamitic) stock. The migrants, who were voluntarily accepted as chiefs after their arrival, made their way around the west side of Lake Victoria from Uganda and farther north between the seventeenth and nineteenth centuries. Perhaps because it represents one geographical extreme of this migration, the Sukuma amalgam is virtually complete physically and culturally. Rigid differentiations do not exist as in some other inter-lacustrine tribes: most Sukuma believe they are at least distant relatives of former chiefs.

The individual chiefdom, rather than the tribe, was traditionally the primary focus of loyalty above the most local community of homesteads.[1] Like the Soga of Uganda,[2] the Sukuma were a

[1] Villages in the European sense do not exist in the countryside, though trading centers do. There are instead scattered individual homesteads. A *kibanda* (pl. *vibanda*) is a collection of thirty to one hundred homesteads, more or less in proximity to each other, which forms a convenient unit for community relationships and obligations.

[2] See Lloyd A. Fallers, *Bantu bureaucracy* (Cambridge, Eng.: Heffer, 1956), *passim*.

multi-kingdomed collection of more or less autonomous chieftain-cies. Approximately fifty in number, these were ruled by chiefs possessing magico-religious as well as political powers. The necessity for a fundamentally approving consensus on the part of the people, and certain privileges and sanctions enjoyed by groups within the traditional political order limited the autocratic tendencies of chiefs. Principal among these groups were electors (*bananghoma*) who were relatives of the royal line but themselves ineligible for office, leaders of the elders (*banamhala*), and leaders of the young men (*basumba batale*).

Lacking precise age-grades and associated initiation rites, the Sukuma developed their characteristic social organizations—unique within East Africa—on the basis of broader distinctions between elder and younger, male and female, married and unmarried. Within and across these categories—and often with considerable overlap—there developed a veritable plethora of cooperative cultivation groups, dancing and singing societies and special interest associations. Though generally a peaceful people, the Sukuma in the 1870s fought to turn back the Nyamwezi predator, Mirambo, who was bent on conquests to the north. In addition to occasional conflicts among themselves, they have had to guard their eastern frontiers against the incursions of Masai cattle raiders even to the present day.[1]

2   EUROPEANS, ARABS AND ASIANS

Sukumaland was an out-of-the-way area even for the nineteenth-century Arab slave traders who travelled from the coast to Tabora and then worked the area on the Tanganyika and Congo sides of Lake Tanganyika. The opening up of Sukumaland had to

---

[1] For lengthier discussion of traditional Sukuma social and political institutions see Hans Cory, *The Ntemi: traditional rites of a Sukuma chief in Tanganyika* (London: Macmillan, 1951); Cory, *Sukuma law and custom* (London: Oxford University Press, 1953), Part I; Cory, *The indigenous political system of the Sukuma and proposals for political reform* (Kampala, Uganda: Eagle Press, 1954), Part I; D. W. Malcolm, *Sukumaland: an African People and their country* (London: Oxford University Press, 1953); and J. Gus Liebenow, 'Chieftainship and local government in Tanganyika: a study of institutional adaptation' (unpub. Ph.D. diss., Northwestern University, 1955), pp. 23–65; Liebenow, 'The Sukuma,' in Audrey I. Richards, ed., *East African chiefs* (London: Faber, 1959), pp. 229–38. For invaluable unpublished material on Sukuma tribal history see the collected papers of Hans Cory in the University College Library, Dar es Salaam.

await European explorers in search of the legendary lakes and
mountains of central Africa and the headwaters of the Nile. The
first to penetrate Sukumaland was John Speke in 1858–9. From a
hill above what is today the town of Mwanza, Speke caught his
first glimpse—the first glimpse by any European—of a portion
of the vast expanse of Lake Victoria. This, the second largest
freshwater lake in the world, he correctly guessed was the source
of the Nile.[1]

The intrepid Henry Morton Stanley passed through Sukumaland in 1875 and again in 1889. As one observer familiar with
Sukumaland has noted, Stanley's descriptions of the land in
rainy season and dry season 'could hardly be improved upon
today.'[2] Stanley's taste for aesthetics and description, however,
did not stop him from a characteristically ruthless use of firepower.
He used machine guns to force his way across Nera in
1889.[3]

Answering 'Stanley's challenge to Christian England to take
the Light to dark East Africa,' the Church Missionary Society
sent a party inland from Bagamoyo in 1876.[4] Bound for Uganda,
they reached Lake Victoria near Mwanza in 1877. Several of the
party died, but Alexander Mackay and one other reached Uganda.
Mackay returned to Sukumaland ten years later. Mission stations
were opened in Usambiro in 1887 and in Nassa in 1888. Meanwhile, in 1883 the European Roman Catholic White Fathers missionary order established an outpost at Bukumbi. The White
Fathers expanded into Ukerewe in 1895, to Kome Island in 1900,
to Mwanza in 1907, and to Sumve in Kwimba District in 1911. In
1909 an American Protestant missionary society, the Africa
Inland Mission, took over the foundering C.M.S. outpost at
Nassa. The A.I.M. established stations at Kizima in Kwimba
District in 1910 and at Kolandoto in Shinyanga in 1913. In subsequent years both the White Fathers and the A.I.M. expanded
activities. They provided, in addition to religious training, most

[1] See Z. A. Marsh and G. W. Kingsnorth, *Introduction to the history of
East Africa* (Cambridge, Eng.: Cambridge University Press, 1961), pp. 61,
64.
[2] Malcolm, p. 2. Malcolm quotes two passages describing Sukumaland from
Stanley's own writings.
[3] Ralph A. Austen, 'Historical research in Sukumaland' (Paper prepared for
Sukumaland Research Conference, Philadelphia, Pa., Oct. 1965), p. 10.
[4] Marie Sywulka, *Workers together with him: a short history*, *Africa Inland
Mission—Tanganyika Territory* (Rethy, Irumu, Belgian Congo: Africa
Inland Mission Press, 1952), p. 1.

of the educational instruction and medical services then available to the indigenous population.[1]

Some Arab and 'Swahili' traders, despite a general preference for the major trade routes farther to the south, did wander north into Sukumaland in the latter part of the nineteenth century. They established outposts on the lake shore and inland (Kayenze and Lalago, for example) and are reputed to have planted the now gigantic mango trees which dot the countryside. These Arabs were not like the 'big-time' slavers of the Congo or the Sudan: they were itinerant 'little men' who dealt in cloth, oil, trinkets, native produce, skins, utensils, spices and occasionally ivory. They approximated the life-style of the Sukuma and frequently intermarried with them.[2]

Following a cue from the Arabs, the Sukuma, especially in Maswa and Shinyanga, also developed a few entrepreneurs who travelled to Lake Eyasi for salt, or to the coast for trade. In later years some Sukuma who voyaged afar took up employment on Zanzibar clove or Tanga sisal plantations. Others entered transportation and service occupations in Mombasa, Tabora, and Dar es Salaam. A few found careers in the police force or with the King's African Rifles.

The individual Sukuma, however, was never a migrant laborer by necessity or inclination. His life could be secure either at home or elsewhere. His livelihood did not require periodic alternation between wage employment and farming. Thus, the dispersal of individual Sukuma had little demonstration effect on development at home because those who left stayed away; those who didn't, stayed home. Even the potential impact of thousands of returning military servicemen and conscripted sisal plantation workers after the Second World War was attenuated by the inclination of the men to return to the health and security of Sukuma rural life and by the capacity of the society to absorb them with hardly a ripple to show for it.[3]

The first Asian traders came from Kenya and Uganda after the

[1] *Ibid. passim.* Information on White Fathers missions from the offices of the Roman Catholic diocese of Mwanza, Tanzania.

[2] Chief Majebere Masanja, interview, 17 Jan. 1965. 'Swahili' traders were Africans who spoke Swahili rather than a tribal tongue as their first language.

[3] Lake Province Annual Report, 1946, Lake Province files (hereafter cited as LPF); Mwanza District Annual Report, 1946, Mwanza District files (hereafter cited as MZDF). In 1965 most closed (non-current) files from provincial and district government offices were transferred to the National Archives, Dar es Salaam.

turn of the century. They were not very different in kind and interests from the Arabs who had preceded them. The earliest assaulters of the frontier came by foot. But the majority of the forerunners of the more wealthy trading classes followed the Kenya–Uganda railroad and crossed the lake by steamer in the years before and after the First World War. Already established with commercial houses in Kenya and enjoying connections with import–export firms doing business with India and elsewhere, these Asians opened up-country Tanganyika branches in Mwanza. With the completion of the rail line from Tabora to Mwanza in the late 1920s, Mwanza became Tanganyika's hub of trading activity on the lake and an inter-territorial *entrepôt* which attracted yet more Asian investment, then branches of European concerns. Until shortly before the Second World War, the German-built administration buildings at the edge of the lake and the massive hill-top home of Mwanza's senior administrator dominated the architecture of the town. As the town grew, permanent British-built constructions were required to take care of the expansion. Mwanza Asians, hitherto content with mud-wall construction, moved to multiple-storied cement structures which are today the occasionally colorful and utilitarian—if unimaginative—hallmarks of Asian enclaves throughout East Africa.[1]

3 GERMAN AND EARLY BRITISH ADMINISTRATION

The race of 1889–90 between British and German soldiers of political fortune, bent on collecting enough chiefs' signatures to rationalize an East African seizure of power by their respective governments, never found its way to Sukumaland. While in the capitals of Europe in 1889 and 1890 British and German statesmen delineated the boundaries of German East Africa (later Tanganyika), British East Africa (Uganda, Kenya and Zanzibar), and British Central Africa (Rhodesia and Nyasaland), the Sukuma remained relatively isolated and immune from the first incursions of administrators until some years after the partition.[2]

[1] Interviews: C. K. Patel, 26 Jan. 1965; D. K. Shah, 25 Jan. 1965; H. N. Virji, 28 Dec. 1964. For a fuller account of Asians in Tanganyika see George Delf, *Asians in East Africa* (London: Oxford University Press, 1953), chaps. I, V and IX.

[2] For a fuller account of this early period in East Africa see Kenneth Ingham, *A History of East Africa* (London: Longmans, 1962), chaps. IV–VI. For details on developments at the south end of Lake Victoria in 1889–90 see Ralph A.

In the late 1890s, after subduing a few recalcitrant native authorities, the Germans took the first steps toward establishing a coherent administration in their new African territory.[1] The character of their relationship with traditional authorities then inclined as much toward what has come to be known as the indirect rule model of administration as to that of direct rule, the style of administration more usually associated with German colonialism. The latitude given to Sukuma native authorities by the Germans did not arise from any fondness for African tradition or hope for the stable long-term evolution of African local government institutions; it was due rather to shortage of staff and other exigencies of the earliest 'bush-bashing' phase of colonial rule.

So, in the first instance, was British practice. Indirect rule, which had its origins in the administrative arrangements of nineteenth-century British India was adapted as an imaginative expedient by Lord Lugard in Nigeria. It became a theory of administration only with the writings of Lugard and his disciples. Eventually, it became a mystique through association with Victorian conceptions of the white man's burden and with an anthropologically inspired twentieth-century reverence for African tribal tradition.

When, after the defeat of Germany in 1918, German East Africa was awarded to Britain under a League of Nations mandate and renamed Tanganyika, British Administration was as yet unaffected by notions of indirect rule. Ironically, in Sukumaland for example, British administration was, if anything, more direct than its German predecessor. Provincial and District Commissioners often deposed or installed native authorities without regard for local tradition. They amalgamated or divided traditional tribal units with an eye toward efficiency and convenience. They imported Ganda 'akidas' from Uganda to oversee groups of chiefdoms. Mission-trained schoolboys without ties to ruling families were as likely to be made chiefs as any legitimate heir.

Austen, 'Native policy and African politics: indirect rule in Northwest Tanzania, 1889–1939,' (unpub. Ph.D. diss., Harvard University, 1965), chap. III.
[1] Austen has shown that the advent of German administration encountered more resistance in Sukumaland than others, notably Cory, have suggested. See Austen, 'Native Policy,' chap. IV, but cf. Cory, *Sukuma law*, p. 3. The discussion of German and early British administration in this chapter is indebted to Austen's work as well as to my own findings. See also Austen's more recent *Northwest Tanzania under German and British Rule: Colonial Policy and Tribal Politics, 1889–1939* (New Haven, Yale University Press, 1968).

Even where a traditional ruling family was preserved, matrilineal succession gave way under colonial duress to the more 'rational' patrilineal form.

4 INDIRECT RULE: SUKUMALAND VARIATIONS

The arrival from Nigeria in 1925 of Sir Donald Cameron as governor signalled the beginning of a conscientious effort to effect principles of indirect rule.[1] In Sukumaland in the late 1920s and early 1930s, administrators endeavored to meet the wishes of the people by re-establishing traditional ruling lines in some areas where they had been ousted previously. Cameron's Secretary for Native Affairs, Charles Dundas, reported that in Mwanza Province there were 'all too many Chiefs who have in the past been appointed without right or title.'[2] He urged in several localities the re-institution of indigenous authorities. These changes were most frequently implemented, however, in areas where the alien chiefs had proven to be personally unsuitable or where strong local opposition, as in Usmao or Kanadi, made them ineffective. Elsewhere, as in Geita (known as 'Uzinza' before 1950) where no suitable alternatives seemed available aliens were allowed, for the sake of efficient administration, to remain. In fact at times, as in Ntuzu, non-traditional chiefs were not only preserved but also placed in office by Cameron and post-Cameron Lake Province administrations.[3]

Although Cameron's policy sought in theory to foster traditional native authorities as a basis for the evolution of local administration, in practice the changes wrought did as much to transform as to consolidate tradition. Even indigenous chiefs, who had depended upon electors, elders, leaders of young men's societies and the people themselves for their initial selection and subsequent exercise of authority, found themselves increasingly estranged from this traditional context as they became simultaneously tied to and empowered by an alien colonial superstructure. The power of the chief increased in relation to these other traditional groups.

[1] For discussion of the Cameron period see Ingham, pp. 294–305, and Margaret L. Bates, 'Tanganyika under British Administration, 1920–1955' (unpub. Ph.D. diss., Oxford University, 1956), *passim*.

[2] Report by the Secretary for Native Affairs on His Tour of Tabora, Mwanza, and Bukoba Provinces, June–July 1927, Secretariat Minute Paper (hereafter cited as SMP) 10952, former Tanganyika Territory Secretariat, National Archives, Dar es Salaam.

[3] See correspondence in SMP 11170, 11208, 12793, 13314/2, 26166.

At the same time, the chief lost the position of preeminence which his new employer, the British government, now enjoyed. In the eyes of both chief and people, the local incarnation of alien rule, the District Commissioner, assumed an aura of authority and the prerogatives of power.[1]

A further departure from traditional forms was the attempt to establish federations of chiefs. The first federation in Shinyanga in 1926 was followed by others in Maswa and Kwimba. Smaller sub-district federations were set up in Mwanza; and, in November 1932, all the chiefs of Sukumaland met together for the first time. After debating at length the virtues of paramountcies versus federations, the administration decided to permit no paramount chief. The 'most influential' of the chiefs, however, occupied a 'somewhat nebulous position as *primus inter pares*.' Even the federation idea itself was alien to Sukumaland's pattern of autonomous multiple chiefdoms. This, together with the burden of disagreement within the administration and other preoccupations of the 1930s, meant that little of substance was accomplished before the war. Nonetheless, the concentration of power in the hands of chiefs and initiatives in the direction of federation illustrated that the doctrine of indirect rule was elastic enough to support radical modification of traditional political structures.[2]

5   DEVELOPMENT

Development in Tanganyika as a whole had suffered between the wars because of the change-over from German administration, the paucity of administrative personnel, and a continuing uncertainty as to the future of a mandated territory. This anomalous status inhibited both private and governmental expenditure. Britain did not know that the territory would not some day revert to German administration, and was, in any case, more devoted to the improvement of her colonies. The depression further stalled development during the final decade of the inter-war period.

Within Tanganyika, the Sukuma, though populous and wealthy by subsistence standards, received less attention than, say, the

---

[1] For an analysis of the changing role of the chief in the colonial context, see Lloyd A. Fallers, 'The predicament of the modern African chief: an instance from Uganda,' *American Anthropologist*, LVII (Apr. 1955), 290–305; and Fallers, *Bantu bureaucracy*, *passim*.

[2] On early attempts at federation see SMP 10923, 13927, 21052, 23461, and Austen, 'Native Policy,' chaps. XI, XIV.

Chagga or the Haya. The indifferent fertility of the cultivation steppe did not attract the European farmer who preferred the volcanically rich soil of the Kilimanjaro slopes and the more familiar European environment of the highland areas.

Though Catholic and Protestant missionary outposts in Sukumaland dated from the end of the nineteenth century, Christianity did not rapidly take hold. Even missionaries were subject to European preferences: they were often less inclined toward the disease-ridden shore areas and the vast expanse of open land stretching to the south and east from Mwanza than they were to the verdant cliffs and sandy beaches of Bukoba, or to the fragrant atmosphere and bracing climate of Moshi or Tukuyu.

Characteristics of the people and the economy were important factors, too. The Sukuma's very life depended upon the cultivation of food crops. Drought and famine were ever-present possibilities. To prevail against the inevitable vagaries of climate and soil in the cultivation steppe required the sustained labor of men, women and children during several stages of the yearly agricultural cycle. Usually appraised by the critical European eye as a hard worker (in other repects he was disparaged as 'dull' and 'unimaginative'), the Sukuma found that the daily and seasonal requirements of his mixed agricultural and pastoral economy left little leisure for the luxuries of European education and religion. While he and his wife (or wives) and his older children tilled the fields, the younger children, even the smallest, took the family's few head of cattle, sheep and goats, out to graze.[1] Even the construction of a home required long treks into the few remaining forested areas and laborious transport of poles back to the homestead site. Availability of water, too, was a problem during the dry season when rivers disappeared beneath the sandy soil.

In contrast, the Haya and Chagga lacked cattle. Even their staple nutrient, bananas, was available with a minimum of toil in the fields. Coffee cash-cropping—again with relatively little labor required—provided revenue. Material for house construction was readily available, as were water supplies. Leisure and funds for the indulgence of European-inspired pursuits were available, especially to men and to school-age children. European missionaries proliferated in the 'progressive' context of Moshi and Bukoba.

[1] Actually, only about half of the Sukuma were cattle owners. Averages of cattle owned per homestead varied from a few head in some areas to several dozen head in others (Cory, *Sukuma law*, pp. 4–5).

In Chaggaland farmers as well as missionaries prompted and accelerated African evolution toward modern European skills and values. Further, the paucity of land encouraged competition for status within the two tribes in spheres other than land holding and cultivation. The Sukuma, on the other hand, were able to push outward in several directions from their home areas. They felt no pressure of land other than waning fertility—a malady which was corrected with a further move and reapplication elsewhere of the methods of shifting extensive cultivation.

Yet the Sukuma were more favorably endowed with current resources and economic potential than many other tribes. With agriculture as well as stock, they were more sedentary and more wealthy than the purely pastoral Masai. The Gogo and other tribes of the arid central Tanganyika plain shared with the Sukuma a mixed agricultural–pastoral economy, but only at the most meager subsistence level. In contrast to them, the Sukuma enjoyed the high quality and more diverse soils and additional rainfall of the cultivation steppe.

Cotton cash-cropping began between the wars to foster the beginnings of a monetary sector as coffee had done earlier among the Chagga and the Haya. Rice, ground nuts and a variety of root crops, vegetables and grains varied the agricultural possibilities. In the 1940s, too, gold and diamonds were discovered in Sukumaland. Though under private European and government control, minerals, added to the wealth in stock and agricultural produce, made Sukumaland (and the Lake Province as a whole) the largest and richest area in the territory, both in actual and potential terms.

Even between the wars—despite the stagnation generally characteristic of the Tanganyikan administration—Sukumaland elicited the attention of forward-looking officials and researchers. Initiative in the direction of federation groupings was one result. Investigation of the people and of the economy with a view toward rehabilitation of the land, development of the economy and long-range political stability was another. The government hired Hans Cory, an Austrian immigrant turned anthropologist–sociologist, to investigate secret societies among the Nyamwezi and the Sukuma. In particular, he was directed to discover whether such societies might be potentially subversive organizations.[1] An agricultural officer, N. V. Rounce, and an administrative officer,

---

[1] Chief Secretary to P.C., 1 Dec. 1936, MZDF.

D. W. Malcolm, embarked on extensive studies of the land and the economy.[1] They both took the view that soil erosion and exhaustion from the overpopulation and depredations of people and livestock threatened to make Sukumaland a desert. In a matter of decades, plans would have to be made and strong measures taken to reclaim the land already lost and to prevent the loss of additional land and forest areas which would accompany the continuing Sukuma thrust into contiguous areas.

Thus, Sukumaland stood about midway on an imaginary continuum between Tanganyika's 'productive' and 'unproductive' regions; the Sukuma people about midway on a scale of Tanganyika's 'advanced' and 'backward' tribes. To the enterprising colonial administrator, Sukumaland seemed an area of challenging problems, yet an area where solutions might successfully be effected. A situation neither hopeless nor sanguinary, Sukumaland seemed a place where the genius of European knowledge and technology might usefully confront the most typical and pervasive problems of African life and development.

6   CONSTITUTIONAL ADVANCE

In contrast to some of the more precocious African states which can date the organizational origins of nationalist politics to the inter-war or even pre-First World War years, Tanganyika was a late starter. In part, this is because Tanganyika was one of the United Kingdom's most neglected territories until after the Second World War. With even less educational and economic progress than in many other African territories, a middle-class African elite and a nationalist political consciousness were slow to emerge. Paternalism and gradualism characterized the approach of the colonial administration to the question of progress toward self-determination and self-government—an attitude acquiesced in by the League of Nations.

Unlike the Trusteeship agreement of the United Nations after the Second World War, the mandate did not require the administering power to give urgent attention to African participation in government and administration in preparation for the day when the inhabitants of the territory would achieve independence. Both the League and the mandatory power judged this to be a

[1] N. V. Rounce, *The agriculture of the cultivation steppe* (Cape Town: Longmans, 1949), *passim*; Malcolm, *passim*.

long way off indeed—as did most Africans themselves. There were no visiting missions (as there were later under the United Nations) to effect on-the-spot checks of administration and political development in the territory and to provide, thereby, a catalyst for change. Pressures for change from the international community and from within Britain herself were virtually non-existent, and internal pressures in Tanganyika itself were scarcely greater.[1] In the 1930s some suggestions of political activity were encountered in Dar es Salaam and Tanga and among the relatively advanced Haya and Chagga; but for the most part, Tanganyika was virgin territory for nationalist politics until after the Second World War.

While the British—as with all their colonies—regarded self-government as the ultimate goal for Tanganyika, they pursued, after the Second World War as before, a policy which limited African participation in government to modified traditional institutions. They anticipated that Africans would take a direct part in national politics only at an unforeseeable future date.[2] Thus, the administration projected into the post-war period a policy of indirect rule plus gradual progress toward parliamentary government. In the 1950s, however, when attempts were made finally to give effect to this policy in local government institutions, its inherent inconsistencies became manifestly apparent.

At the same time, international interest in the political development of trust territories (now under the United Nations) increased dramatically. Pressures for rapid political advancement toward self-government and independence came from the United Nations, from within the United Kingdom, and—as dependencies in Asia and then in Africa achieved independence—from Africans themselves, both outside and inside Tanganyika. Beginning in 1948, United Nations visiting missions toured Tanganyika every three years and reported to the international community on administration and political development in the territory. The Trusteeship Council periodically discussed the progress which was or was not being made and passed resolutions calling for steps toward early self-government on a democratic rather than a racially weighted basis.

The colonial administration, too, became more concerned

---

[1] See B. T. G. Chidzero, *Tanganyika and international trusteeship* (London: Oxford University Press, 1961), pp. 115–32.
[2] *Ibid.* p. 117.

with constitutional advance. The first African members of the Legislative Council were appointed in 1945. Beginning in 1947— the same year that Tanganyika became a Trust Territory under the United Nations and that India became independent—memoranda urging political and economic reform in the United Kingdom's overseas territories emanated from the Colonial Office in London. Of particular importance for Tanganyika—which had not yet undertaken, as had other British territories, the partial application of principles of parliamentary democracy to local government—was a recommendation from the Secretary of State for the Colonies, Arthur Creech Jones, for the revamping of native administration (chiefs supervised by expatriate District Commissioners) to allow democratic local councils and the establishment of institutional relationships between central and local government.[1]

Following his arrival in the territory in 1949, a new governor, Sir Edward Twining, appointed the unofficial members of the Legislative Council a Committee on Constitutional Development and charged it with the task of reviewing both territorial and local constitutional structures and making recommendations. The Committee rejected Twining's suggestions for an unofficial majority in the Legislative Council to select, through an electoral college system based on provinces, an equal number of African and non-African members. It rejected, too, his proposal for immediate local elections. The Committee favored instead the continuation of an official majority in the Council with parity representation of Europeans, Asians and Africans on the unofficial side. It accepted in principle the idea of elections, but the further appointment in 1952 of a Special Commissioner on Constitutional Development was required for specific recommendations. Eventually a plan was developed for a hierarchy of local government councils which, at least down to the district level, were eventually to become multi-racial in composition. Between 1953 and 1955 the new councils, territorial and local, came into being. They were a curious and internally inconsistent blend of semi-traditional native authority structures, of principles of parliamentary democracy and of the expedient of parity representation which gave each of the three races—vastly disproportionate in their percentages of the total population—equal representation.

[1] Margaret L. Bates, 'Tanganyika,' in Gwendolyn Carter, ed., *African one-party states* (Ithaca, New York: Cornell University Press, 1962), p. 413.

In the meantime, Africans interested in more rapid political change had begun to organize more purposefully and effectively. The Tanganyika African Association, founded with the help of British civil servants in Dar es Salaam in the late 1920s, became increasingly politically oriented after the Second World War. It petitioned United Nations visiting missions and colonial commissions on matters pertaining to the political development of the territory and gradually established a number of units, largely independent of each other, in other parts of the territory. Tribal unions among the Haya, the Rangi, the Chagga, the Meru, and the Sukuma took on, at times, the characteristics of political organizations in the early 1950s. In 1954 a school teacher and university graduate named Julius Nyerere transformed the Tanganyika African Association into the Tanganyika African National Union—the organization which, in a few short years, became the vehicle for a national movement calling for an end to colonial rule and the early achievement of self-government and independence.

During the years when Nyerere and a few lieutenants toured the country to organize TANU branches, he also 'discovered the possibility of utilizing United Nations pressure and began systematically to utilize this weapon in an attempt to influence the administration.'[1] TANU delegations all over Tanganyika petitioned the United Nations visiting mission in 1954. Nyerere himself travelled to New York to address the Trusteeship Council in 1955, and again in 1957. Committed to achieve independence and to establish a democratic form of government through constitutional means, TANU placed itself in opposition to Twining's policies of parity multi-racialism, to the administration's continuing commitment to native authority structures, to the refusal of the administration to set a target date for independence and, when elections were projected, to a qualitatively restricted franchise.

The administration reacted defensively, arguing that TANU was not representative of African opinion, was racialist, and entirely too radical. It proscribed government servants from joining political organizations in 1953 and passed legislation under which branches of TANU were banned after 1954. Though he had earlier been appointed for a short period to the Legislative Council, Nyerere himself was prohibited from addressing public meetings in 1958. In an attempt to counteract TANU, the

[1] *Ibid.* p. 420.

administration inspired the creation in 1956 of the United Tanganyika Party with members recruited from all races, a party dedicated
to principles of multi-racialism and deliberate rather than accelerated constitutional advance. The UTP, however, found little
support among Africans and disappeared altogether when TANU-
supported candidates of all three races were returned by substantial
margins in all contested constituencies in Tanganyika's first
territorial elections in 1958–9.

By 1959 the administration, under a new governor, Sir Richard
Turnbull, radically altered its policies for the political development of the territory. This turnabout was the result of a combination of internal and external pressures. There was widespread
discontent with the administration's natural resources conservation
policies and its attempts to institute local multi-racial councils.
Discontent, which evolved into civil disobedience, became focused
—through the medium of TANU—in nationalist demands for
more rapid decolonization and an early date for independence.

Such demands and their urgency seemed reinforced by developments elsewhere in Africa. Ghana achieved independence in
1957, and rapid constitutional progress was apparent in Nigeria.
By way of contrast, however, political disturbances in neighboring
Kenya and Nyasaland had led to the proclamation by the British
administering authorities of states of emergency. Unlike the
West African states, Kenya and Nyasaland (especially when the
latter was considered part of the Federation of Rhodesia and
Nyasaland) had significant proportions of non-African, including
white, populations. To those at the United Nations, in London
at Whitehall and in Parliament, in Dar es Salaam and throughout
Tanganyika who were concerned about the future course of
constitutional and political change in Tanganyika (which had a
preponderance of Africans, but some white settlers and a substantial number of Asians), 1958–9 was the time for watershed
decisions. While both the administration and its critics felt that
the ultimate goal of political development in Tanganyika could
only be self-government and independence on the West African
model—perhaps with some guarantees for Tanganyika's non-
African minorities—there was no measure of agreement as to
timing until the overwhelming TANU electoral victory of 1958–9.
This victory was repeated in 1960, and under the leadership of
Governor Turnbull and TANU President Nyerere, Tanganyika

moved rapidly toward responsible government, internal self-government, and independence in December 1961.

The struggle to achieve 'uhuru' in its fullest sense continued of necessity after independence had been achieved. No longer was the struggle against an alien colonial regime, but against 'poverty, ignorance, and disease' and to achieve national unity, political integration and economic development. More specifically, Tanzania (Tanganyika united with Zanzibar in 1964) has attempted, with a flexibility and persistence unique among the new nations in Black Africa, to build a society and a political system both socialistic and democratic, as Tanzania interprets these terms.

2

The Administration: Postwar Political and Economic Development

In the post-Second World War years the administration of Tanganyika emphasized throughout the territory the introduction of English-style local government institutions and the development of subsistence economies into cash-productive units. A host of factors prompted change: Tanganyika's status as a United Nations Trust Territory under British administration, independence for India and reform pressure from the new Secretary of State for the Colonies, the availability of Colonial Development and Welfare funds, and an influx of new men and new ideas into the Tanganyikan administration itself. Especially during the governorship of Sir Edward Twining (1949–58) colonial administration in Tanganyika reached its high watermark of imagination and activity.

Within Tanganyika, the administration devoted an unusual degree of attention, effort, skill and money in attempts at political and economic transformation of Sukumaland.[1] Sukumaland

[1] A thorough study of the administration of Sukumaland in the postwar years would require a book in itself. The most that can be attempted in this introductory chapter is a summary of the principal directions of policy and practice to provide the necessary background for the more detailed study of African politics which follows.

In addition to published material and documentary sources, this chapter is based on personal interviews which included the following: Lord Twining (Governor of Tanganyika, 1949–58), 23 Apr. 1965; James Cheyne (P.C., Lake Province, 1946–7; Secretary for Native Affairs, 1947–49), 15 Apr. 1965; Sir R. de Z. Hall (P.C., Lake Province, 1947–9; Member for Local Government, 1949–53; and subsequently Governor of Sierra Leone), 14 Apr. 1965; E. G. Rowe (P.C., Lake Province 1949–54; Member for Local Government, 1958–9), 14 Nov. 1963; S. A. Walden (P.C., Lake Province, 1954–9), Nov. 1963, and Apr. 1965; G. T. Bell (P.C., Lake Province, 1959–61), 8 Apr. 1965; F. H. Page-Jones (Member for Local Government, 1953–8), Nov. 1963; J. E. S. Griffiths (D.P.C., Sukumaland), 20 Apr. 1965; J. W. T. Allen (D.P.C., Lake Province), Dec. 1963; C. C. Harris (Acting P.C., Lake Province), 14 Apr. 1965; A. W. J. Eyers (Provincial Security Officer), 6 Apr. 1965; K. B. A. Dobson (D. C., Mwanza), 2 Dec. 1963; Neville French (D.C., Geita), 2 Dec. 1963; R. S. King (D. C., Geita), 6 Dec. 1963; A. G. Stephen (D.C., Kwimba), 20 Nov. 1964; Gavin Green (Cooperative Officer), 13 Nov. 1964; Charles Allen (Agricultural Officer), 4 Mar. 1964; Vincent Allen

became a prime experimental area for the implementation of the government's new programs. The pan-tribal Sukumaland Federal Council (1946–60), the multi-racial Lake Province Council (1949–55) and its larger statutory successor, the South East Lake County Council (1955–60), were each respectively the first institutions of their kind in the territory. The attempt to establish a coherent hierarchy of local representative councils from village to federation or county was nowhere more zealously prosecuted than in Sukumaland. Finally, the Sukumaland Development Scheme (1948–55)—the first of its type and scale in postwar sub-Saharan Africa—expended approximately two million pounds in an effort to maximize agricultural and veterinary development through careful land usage, livestock control, and improved agricultural methods.[1]

If there are instances in history where the findings and ideas of research-oriented individuals have influenced policy, postwar Sukumaland is one of those instances. If there are instances where—in addition to secular historical trends—the attitudes and personalities of powerful men have shaped events, Sukumaland provides also one of those. The prominent research figures were three already mentioned—Malcolm, Rounce and Cory. This triumvirate, however, does not exhaust the list of experts who participated in the often elaborate and detailed process of planning for change in Sukumaland.[2] The most decisive administrative figures were Provincial Commissioners, E. G. Rowe and S. A.

(Agricultural Officer), 2 June 1964; W. D. Gibbons (Agricultural Officer), 30 Jan. 1964; Arthur Jenkins (Agricultural Officer), Mar. 1964; Justin Mecer-Wright (Agricultural Officer), 21 Feb. 1964; A. C. A. Wright (Research Officer), 13 Apr. 1965; Dick Curtis (Settlement Officer), Mar. 1964.

For a scholarly discussion of post-war administration in Sukumaland, see Liebenow, 'Chieftainship,' *passim*; Liebenow, 'The Sukuma,' in *East African chiefs*, pp. 238–59; Liebenow, 'Responses to planned political change in a Tanganyika tribal group,' *American Political Science Review*, L (June 1956), 442–61; Liebenow, 'The Chief in Sukuma local government,' *Journal of African Administration*, XI, No. 2 (Apr. 1959), 84–92; Liebenow, 'Some problems in introducing local government reform in Tanganyika,' *Journal of African Administration*, VIII (July 1956), 132–9; and Bates, 'Tanganyika under British administration,' *passim*.

[1] John D. de Wilde, assisted by Peter F. M. McLoughlin, Andrew Guinard, Thayer Scudder, Robert Maubouche, *Experiences with agricultural development in tropical Africa* (Baltimore: John Hopkins Press, 1967), II, 419 (n.).

[2] Government files are replete with lengthy papers and reports on topics ranging from traditional methods of beer preparation to prospects for mechanical cultivation to proposals for the improvement of rules of procedure in local native authority council meetings. Not merely administrative ephemera, these documents played a role in the process of policy formulation. Some of the more important papers are listed in the bibliography.

Walden. Men of radically different temperament, they implemented and formulated, shaped and directed, initiated and rescinded policy and program during the most critical decade of colonial rule in Sukumaland—the 1950s.

As we have noted, the idea of a federation for Sukuma chiefs dated from 1932 and even earlier. Also, experiments in land rehabilitation and stock control were tried on a limited scale in the 1930s. The Second World War, however, delayed any major departures, political or economic. Several chiefs asked in 1942 for a resuscitation of Sukumaland-wide meetings, but they were told that wartime demands argued for the postponement of any new initiative until peace had been restored. Nor did available staff or funds allow the launching of large-scale economic programs other than the campaign—directly related to the war effort—for the slaughter of cattle to supply beef for Britain. Not until after the war did the administration embark on dynamic and wide-ranging programs for political and economic advance.

I   THE SUKUMALAND FEDERAL COUNCIL

Malcolm was the most persistent advocate of a federal council of chiefs for Sukumaland. His ideas for political federation were closely linked with his assessment of the problems and potentialities of the land and his conviction that concerted efforts by the administration were needed to reverse the quickening trend toward desiccation. He viewed the Sukuma as an industrious but unwittingly destructive people. In Malcolm's view, only a supra-district organization—sensitive to the particular characteristics and molded to the special needs of Sukumaland—could adequately meet the challenge to rational planning which this large and important portion of the territory posed. In 1945 on taking up the post of District Commissioner of Maswa, he was asked to select a suitable site for a Sukumaland federation headquarters.

First Steps

After the war the administration moved ahead with Malcolm's proposals. Preliminary work on dam construction and general lay-out began on the new Malya site, ten miles north of Malampaka railway station, in late 1945. In October 1946 all the Sukuma chiefs met together for the first time. Lord Hailey laid the foundation stone of a federation council hall in September 1947, and Acting Governor Surridge officially opened the new council hall a year later. As a Senior Provincial Commissioner wrote before his departure from Sukumaland in 1946:

This great federation of Sukumaland is perhaps one of the most important federal developments of local government in Africa, embracing as it does a population of over three quarters of a million in an area of about the size of Switzerland...It is essential for the greatest care and fore-thought to be exercised in laying the foundations of what may well become an African tribal unit of no small importance.[1]

From the beginning, the federation was associated with plans for the development and rehabilitation of Sukumaland. As the federation took its first steps in the three years after the war, the first of what were later to become a 'team of officers' began to arrive and a 'preliminary plan for land utilization in Sukumaland, for the first three years of limited staff,' was prepared.[2] Beginning with the 1946 meeting, the federation council, uniting all of Sukumaland's fifty-two chiefdoms, met twice yearly. A select executive committee of twelve chiefs met four times a year.

In his opening speech to the first plenary session in 1946, the Provincial Commissioner stressed the developmental problems of Sukumaland and the government's plans for attacking them. He cited the advantage of the larger unit which would allow uni-formity of administration throughout Sukumaland, encouraging both good government and economic progress. Judicial, adminis-trative, legislative and financial aspects of the federation were hammered out. With the guidance of the administration, the chiefs agreed on a partial amalgamation of existing native treasuries, on administrative and legislative prerogatives for the federation with regard to matters of general interest to Sukumaland and on the establishment of a limited court of appeals.

Items for discussion at Sukumaland Federal Council meetings usually originated with European administrative or develop-mental officers. Chiefs infrequently suggested items of their own, but these were circulated first to District Commissioners who discussed them with chiefs at district level before approving them for general consideration. Final agenda for federation meetings were drawn up in consultation with the permanent chairman, Chief Majebere Masanja, but the administration pulled most of the weight. Chiefs were briefed before their arrival, and District Commissioners chaired all functional committees. Occasionally, a presiding European officer would absent himself

[1] Lake Province Annual Report, 1945, LPF.   [2] *Ibid.*

so that freer discussion might take place on a particular item. But in essence the chiefs—both because of their own relative unsophistication and because of the administration's formidable devotion to the soundness of its plans—found themselves acting as ratifiers of policies, programs, rules, and orders initiated from above.

Development Efforts

By 1948 the administration appointed a full-time Coordinating Officer (later made a Deputy Provincial Commissioner) to oversee the progress of the federation and of the development scheme. Discussions at Federal Council meetings expanded to include virtually every aspect of administration and development. Customary law, agriculture, animal husbandry, medicine, education, welfare, courts, markets, publications, native administration, development and research all came within the purview of the council. To implement development schemes, the Federal Council formulated rules and orders which grew in such bulk and complexity by the early 1950s that they impinged on virtually every aspect of a Sukuma's life and work.

While the chiefs enjoyed relatively little leeway in relation to the plans and projects of their European superiors, it must not be assumed that they served simply as grudging and recalcitrant tools of the administration. The administration succeeded in convincing some chiefs, especially the more educated ones, that its programs were farsighted and progressive. The chiefs, too, achieved an added measure of status through their involvement in the superior deliberations and special affairs of the Federal Council, and they became more powerful in relation to their constituents. Lord Hailey noted with considerable prescience— for this is precisely what happened in the middle 1950s:

The educated minority of the community will gain increasing power over the uneducated masses, of which the result will inevitably be seen in the growth of a general spirit of opposition to the constituted Native Authorities.[1]

Chiefs and Councillors

The administration fostered attempts to forestall such an unhappy eventuality through the application of democratizing measures. In 1947 the Secretary of State for the Colonies, Arthur Creech

[1] Lord Hailey, *Native administration in the British African territories*, 1: *East Africa* (London: H.M. Stationery Office, 1950), pp. 234–5.

Jones, pressed for the development of more representative institutions in African local government. A dynamic and idealistic young Provincial Commissioner, R. de Z. Hall, set out to convince the chiefs that people's representatives, or councillors, should be added to the Federal Council. In Maswa, Malcolm was partial to the selection of *basumba batale*, the village leaders of the young men's organizations, 'as more independent representatives of popular sentiment than the village headmen.'[1] Maswa chiefs had found them 'of enormous value in enlisting the support of the people' for development measures.[2] The majority of chiefs, however, refused to accept *basumba batale*, who had sometimes in the past acted to check their authority.[3] Noting that the tasks of the *basumba batale* were traditionally 'to assist with problems in the countryside and not to attend meetings of the chiefs,' the latter insisted that the *basumba batale* would be 'irresponsible' and 'destructive' in any council.[4]

In 1948 various schemes were proposed in the several districts for the selection of representatives. It soon became clear, however, that most of the chiefs opposed not just the *basumba batale* but the very idea of representation. They rightly foresaw an inevitable diminution of their own powers. After noting 'that there was no public demand for representation at Malya,' the chiefs ultimately acquiesced to the administration's rationalization 'that it was better to have the machinery ready in advance of the public demand, rather than to appear to make reluctant concessions to it when it became too strong to resist.'[5]

Thus, beginning in 1948, each chief came to meetings of the Federal Council accompanied by one or more councillors whose task it was to represent the views of the people. In reality, however, many of the councillors were never more than *protégés* of the chiefs. No satisfactory system of election was ever devised. Chiefs and subchiefs made their own selections. The councillors participated only marginally, if at all. Though the administration tried various devices to instill a more independent spirit into the councillors, these met with scant success. Most of the councillors, like some of the chiefs, were too unsophisticated to play a significant role and came to Malya primarily for the ride and the overnight

---

[1] *Ibid.* p. 235.   [2] Malcolm to P.C., 23 June 1947, LPF.
[3] See Malcolm, pp. 35–6.
[4] Minutes of the Sukumaland Federal Council, 3–4 Dec. 1947, LPF.
[5] D.C. to P.C., 31 July 1948, MZDF.

allowances. In the formalized and sometimes frighteningly large federation context European officers and educated chiefs tended to dominate.

2 A PYRAMID OF REPRESENTATIVE COUNCILS

While Sukumaland's first contingent of people's representatives were testing their wings at Malya, Provincial Commissioner Hall and the government sociologist, Hans Cory, prepared the ground for an even more audacious innovation in local government. Cory, fresh from Bukoba where he had concluded two years of research on Haya history, law and custom, embarked in 1948 on a study of Sukuma law and custom with a view toward its unification and codification. By 1949 he was ready to move on to a study of traditional Sukuma political organization preparatory to its reformation along democratic lines 'from the parish council upwards.'[1] The report, which he submitted to the administration in 1950, served as the administration's basis for an attempt over the next five years to establish an elaborate hierarchy of representative councils.[2]

Indirect Rule—Democratic Style

The new council scheme superseded indirect rule of both the early pragmatic and later doctrinal varieties. No longer a holding operation requiring but minimum administration, the aggressive colonialism of the postwar era asked of its officers maximum effort to effect rapid political change. With the dogmas of Western liberalism standard parlance throughout the world, even a devotion to the development of indigenous political structures had to share the spotlight with newer commitments to democracy.

'After a minute scrutiny of the Sukuma tribal structure,' Cory held that 'none of the existing institutions could be used as a base for the building up of an effective and modern political system.' He recommended 'complete emancipation from traditional institutions, with the exception of the executive,' because the offices of the great commoners and of chiefdom and village elders 'differ considerably in different areas as to their functions and powers'

[1] Lake Province Annual Report, 1949, LPF.
[2] The report, with an additional section entitled 'The constitution in practice,' was later published (Cory, *The indigenous*).

and because 'the old institutions were based, almost without exception, on conceptions and ideologies which have lost, or are in the process of losing, all hold on the people.'[1] He judged, nevertheless, that the Sukuma 'had an indigenous political system in which democratic ideas were present as well as the usual autocratic ones.' This made it 'possible to design a constitution which employed latent conceptions to satisfy modern requirements.'[2]

Though alleged 'latent conceptions' and the retention of 'the executive' allowed the British—still partial to indirect rule—to rationalize the innovations as based to some extent in indigenous culture and practice, the truth was that English local government was being imported virtually intact into the African context. In line with a model proposed by Creech Jones, Cory suggested the election of village (or parish) councils, then indirect election of two members from these to higher councils at subchiefdom or chiefdom level. These, in turn, were to elect representatives from among their own number to district federations and to the Sukumaland Federal Council. With regard to this ascending pyramid of indirectly elected councils, Cory argued that 'there is no reason why this system should not be extended ultimately to the Legislative Council level.'[3]

Implementation

Sukumaland, however, was a large enough project for the next few years. With 47 chiefdoms and some 795 villages, the completion of the pyramid from village to federation required the incredible total of 907 separate council entities. With strong leadership from Provincial Commissioner E. G. Rowe and the continuous efforts of Cory and administrative officers in the field, over 100 village councils were established in 1951 in selected experimental areas. Another 130 were set up in 1952. In 1953 attention turned to higher councils: 18 chiefdom councils, 37 subchiefdom (and divisional) councils, and 375 additional village councils were established.

By 1955 district advisory councils met three or four times a year in all districts. All had some non-African membership by 1956. By that date, too, the entire pyramidal hierarchy of lower councils (each of which met monthly) was virtually complete from village upwards in all districts.

[1] Cory, *The indigenous*, p. 96.   [2] *Ibid.* p. 124.   [3] *Ibid.* p. 107.

Difficulties

Until the pyramid of councils was completed, a decided gap existed between the Sukumaland Federal Council at Malya and the people in the villages. Even after the pyramid became a fact, the Federal Council, because of its extraordinary size, tended toward 'irresponsibility and unwieldiness.' Representing as it did a joint meeting of the five district federations (47 chiefs, 92 councillors) rather than a council where the principle of delegated representation was recognized, the Federal Council 'apex' was viewed in 1954 as 'out of alignment with the subsequently created base.'[1] There was, however, considerable reluctance on the part of the chiefs and councillors—characteristic of vested interests in legislatures anywhere in the world—to entertain a motion for the council's reduction in size. Only after considerable prompting from the administration did the council agree to reduce its numbers from 139 to 99, then to 75 members on the formula of 7 chiefs, 7 commoners, and 1 nominated unofficial from each district.

The effectiveness of the lower councils varied. The administration quickly discovered that continuous supervision of established councils was necessary in most cases for their continued functioning. Only those councils under especially effective chiefs or subchiefs developed any momentum of their own, and even these required periodic guidance. It was obvious that the limited European staff could not continuously supervise the monthly meetings of hundreds of councils, and other schemes were attempted. Supervision by unofficial members of chiefdom and subchiefdom councils proved a failure, but African council supervisors employed by the district office proved somewhat more successful.

Village councils, however, continued to languish. Where the village councils were most active, initiative came from chiefs rather than from the local units themselves. Moreover, the substance of the activity was most likely to be with regard to implementing policies set at higher levels. In Shinyanga, for example, 'the Chiefs, on their own initiative and through the Parish Councils, set about the over-stocking problem in a most determined manner and it speaks well for the usefulness of the Parish Councils.'[2]

[1] J. V. Shaw, 'The development of African local government in Sukumaland,' *Journal of African Administration*, VI (Oct. 1954), 171–8.
[2] Lake Province Annual Report, 1956, LPF.

In essence the government used the councils as instruments to implement and enforce unpopular land, agricultural and animal husbandry legislation. The inherent contradiction between democratic representation of the people and control of all policy from above by the government through the chiefs was never resolved. This difficulty was aggravated by the fact that the people relied upon the chiefs to make decisions, a pattern enforced by tradition and by the educational differences between the chief and his people. Even Cory recognized that 'the present political set-up...has been reformed according to our own pattern before it is ready to fulfil many of its primary conditions' (e.g., 'civic spirit,' a 'general high level of culture and morals'). He noted 'the lack of control...by any party or constituency' to permit councillors to express their personal views, making it 'impossible to assume that the councillors are representative of public opinion.'[1]

Finally, Cory and the administration generally failed sufficiently to sense the dangers inherent in the isolation of the rurally based councils from the more vocal economic and political interests developing independently in the urban and semiurban areas. Representation of voluntary associations on native authority councils was not permitted. The arrangement allowed appointment of individually qualified Africans to higher level councils and permitted direct elections at village level, but these devices proved insufficient to bridge the widening gap when the administration and the chiefs so clearly dominated the entire authority system, and the voluntary organizations so clearly existed and functioned outside that system. When the final assault on the colonial administration, and with it the native authority system, came in the late 1950s, the active and vocal segments of the population reacted against the councils because they embodied more of alien control and unpalatable legislation than they did of the democratic representation which was the avowed justification for their existence.

3   THE SUKUMALAND DEVELOPMENT SCHEME

Neither the Sukumaland Federal Council nor the elaborate pyramid of representative councils below it were designed simply as intriguing experiments in local government. They were designed also to enlist the support of the people for policies related to the

---

[1] Cory, *The indigenous*, p. 123.

rehabilitation and development of Sukumaland and as instruments for the most efficient implementation of those policies. If anything, political advancement was regarded as secondary in importance. Describing the government's plans for Sukumaland as 'the first great step taken towards the regeneration of your country,' the Acting Governor told the Federal Council of chiefs in 1948:

I also advise you that, in however important a light you regard your own political aspirations, these must take second place to your people's agricultural, social and economic progress. It must be remembered that there can be no sound political advancement unless the social and economic framework is secure.[1]

Rounce and 'The Team'

In addition to the work of Malcolm, the research into land utilization in the cultivation steppe conducted by Rounce provided the basis—both in terms of factual data and in terms of psychology—for the government's development plans in Sukumaland. Rounce's findings were published 'with the object of assisting those who are to extend the improved methods to the people.'[2] Among administrative and developmental officers in Sukumaland, Rounce's book became known as the 'Sukumaland Bible.' Both a formidable compendium of factual data on land, crops, livestock and people, and an elaboration of proper principles for application in the field, the book provided the starting point for land usage planning in Sukumaland. After the war Rounce himself served as Regional Assistant Director of Agriculture in the Lake Province and gave the added force of his personality to laying the foundations of the Sukumaland Development Scheme.

European officers, posted on special assignment to the Sukumaland Development Team at Malaya, began to arrive in 1946 and 1947; but it was not until the early 1950s that Sukumaland felt the full impact of the Development Scheme. In essence the Scheme was designed to maximize the possibilities for productive use of the land by redistribution of what appeared to be surplus populations of people and livestock. Then, applying as rationally and consistently as possible what were believed to be sound principles of cultivation and animal husbandry, Rounce's famous 'Sukumaland Equation' outlined an optimum population density of 100

[1] Minutes of the Sukumaland Federal Council, Nov. 1948, LPF.
[2] Rounce, p. ix.

per square mile and estimated water requirements per 30 square miles of inhabited area.[1]

As with the contemporaneous attempts to establish pyramids of representative councils, the aims were laudable and idealistic. The difficulty was the extent to which the implementation of the aims might require undesirable controls and restrictive legislation. Argument over the virtue of techniques of compulsion versus those of example and persuasion was to remain lively throughout the history of the Sukumaland Development Scheme and beyond. Rounce, the most influential figure in the field, argued that 'the African must be compelled to help himself.' Since 'agriculture...is the foundation of the prosperity...of the greater number of Africans and as such should be uppermost in the minds of the administrators,' Rounce pleaded for more emphasis by the administration on agriculture, and suggested 'an understanding by those who govern that in place of the stress which forces Europeans to do things, the African must be compelled—and forceably too—to improve the conditions under which he lives, with his own hands.'[2]

Though Rounce and others would have desired it, the Tanganyikan administration did not agree to legislation permitting the forcible removal of people from overpopulated areas. Dar es Salaam ruled that the number of persons could be restricted in any new areas opened up by the clearing of bush and provision of water supplies, but only encouragement could be used to diminish the populations already over-concentrated in the heavily settled areas. Refusal to admit new persons to already overcrowded areas was permissible, but eviction of trespassers could not be countenanced. They could, however, be prosecuted and fined according to prevailing practice.

Legislation of various sorts was already on the books of the individual district federations before the Development Scheme was effectively launched. Native authority orders dating from 1946 and 1947 required every farmer yearly to plant one acre of cotton, to tie-ridge one acre of cultivated area for conservation of top-soil and to uproot and burn cotton stalks after harvest for prevention of insect infestation in the subsequent year's crop.

[1] *Ibid.* p. 105.
[2] Rounce to Dr Rita Hinden, 2 Mar. 1945, in the 'Tanganyika' file of the Fabian Colonial Bureau (hereafter cited as FCBF), London. I am indebted to the Fabian Colonial Bureau for permission to consult relevant documentation in their files.

In 1948, after the Federal Council was established as a superior native authority, the chiefs decided 'that the power to make rules under the Native Authority Ordinance shall only be exercised by them jointly, together with the power to make orders in respect of matters appertaining to agriculture, forestry, and animal husbandry.'[1] In 1949 consolidated sets of orders with regard to tie-ridging, planting of cassava, interplanting of cotton and food crops, manuring, ploughing, soil conservation and forestry were approved by the Federal Council. While Dar es Salaam dallied with the fine points, the first instalments of compulsory legislation were already on the books in Sukumaland.

Land Usage Councils

After protracted negotiations with Dar es Salaam, the substance of the land usage legislation advocated by Rounce and Provincial Commissioner Rowe was passed by the Sukumaland Federal Council in May 1950, approved by the Governor in December, and signed into law by resolution of the Federal Council in May 1951. Unlike existing legislation which sought to limit soil erosion and increase crop yields, the new Sukumaland Federation Land Settlement Rules and Livestock Restriction Rules were designed to attack the underlying problem of human and stock densities in relation to available land. The legislation established a hierarchy of land usage councils to administer the new rules.[2] Village and area land usage councils, composed of native authorities and popularly elected representatives, were supervised by advisory councils staffed by provincial and district administrative personnel. The councils determined maximum population densities for villages and labelled villages as 'open,' 'restricted,' 'reserved,' 'closed' or 'bush-edge' units depending on the desirability of and conditions for further settlement. Prospective immigrants were required to apply for entry permits. The councils also ordered the sale or removal of stock from overcrowded areas—the first compulsory destocking in Sukumaland since the Second World War—and all stock movements from one land usage area to another required a permit. Persons convicted of offenses against the rules were subject to fine or imprisonment.

The administration soon discovered that land usage councils could be set up effectively only in areas where the political 'Cory

---

[1] Lake Province Annual Report, 1948, LPF.
[2] These rules are reproduced in Cory, *Sukuma law*, Appendix III, pp. 173–6.

councils' were already functioning. In spite of the desire of agricultural officers to have a separate set of councils based on rationally determined land units and devoted entirely to land problems, it was too much to expect the administration successfully to inaugurate, or for the people simultaneously to accept and operate, two new council hierarchies which dealt with different matters and had different yet overlapping geographical boundaries. In 1953 the administration and the Federal Council decided that 'political councils...must assume responsibility for the implementation of land usage policies as one of their more important functions.'[1]

Seeds of Dissatisfaction

This dove-tailing of institutions and responsibilities unquestionably gave the political councils work of substance, but it also further enforced the tendency to implement policy from above rather than to represent the people from below. African politicians of the 1950s were not slow to recognize this fact and to place the onus of undesired legislation on the native authority system and the councils as well as on the European administration. Unwittingly, the latter abetted the trend. To make the new laws more palatable, the administration consciously designed to have controversial measures enacted by native authorities rather than directly legislated by the central government. This approach backfired since native authorities, as well as the laws themselves, came increasingly under attack.

By 1953 or 1954 the Sukuma peasant felt that he was being pushed around. The tribulations of the present, not administrative-sponsored visions of the future, interested him most. Everywhere new rules, regulations and taxes seemed to require this, prohibit that, or take a few more shillings yearly from his pocket. He had to tie-ridge and manure certain portions of his fields, plant specified minimum acreages of cassava (as an antifamine measure) and cotton, plant at certain times and pull out cotton stalks by certain dates for burning after harvest, refrain from cultivating near gullies, cutting trees or transporting cattle without a permit, have his cattle dipped or inoculated against disease, slaughter or sell a certain percentage of his cattle each year and produce on request certificates indicating sale or attesting that the hides from slaughtered beasts had been seen by the appropriate government

[1] Shaw, *Journal of African Administration*, VI (Oct. 1954), 174.

officer. These were but a few of the more salient examples of literally scores, if not hundreds, of specific natural resources measures which had begun to accumulate by 1952. In addition local rate, including the cattle tax, and the levy on cotton seemed to the Sukuma to deprive him of his due while providing nothing visible in return. A number of officials felt at the time that the bulk and complexity of Sukumaland legislation was getting out of hand. Many agree in retrospect that Sukumaland was over-legislated and over-regulated. Governor Twining has said, 'Quite frankly, this led to the breakdown of indirect rule.'[1] The councils were unable to survive the fact of their use as Rounce's legislative arm.

While the schemes advanced by Rounce looked good on paper, they failed to appreciate sufficiently the laborious work which conservation measures implied for a people who worked with their hands and hoes in the field. Further, compulsory cattle destocking ignored what some have termed a Sukuma 'mystique' with regard to cattle. The Sukuma did not want their cattle to be touched. Not only were cattle the currency of bride price and one of the Sukuma's few capital resources; they were also very specially regarded as almost members of the family.[2]

Traditional tribal attitudes toward methods of cultivation and the status of cattle were not the only stumbling blocks, however. More recently, experts have questioned the rationality even of the general lines of agricultural and veterinary development planning during the 1950s. Apparently the provision of additional land areas for habitation vitiated attempts to replace traditional extensive with modern intensive methods of cultivation. Even determinations of optimum human and cattle population densities have been called into question. Objectively, it appears that Sukuma resistance to the content of specific measures, as well as to methods of enforcement, may have been inspired as much by rationality as by ignorance, as much by economic considerations of self-interest as by politics.[3]

[1] Lord Twining, interview, 23 Apr. 1965.
[2] I owe this point to Charles Noble of Goucher College. Lord Twining has spoken of this mystique (Twining, interview), as have various anthropologists.
[3] I am indebted for this perspective on development planning in Sukumaland to Peter F. M. McLoughlin of the University of Santa Clara, California. He served as a District Officer in Sukumaland in the 1950s and returned in 1964 on a research study for the World Bank. His analysis and critique of development policy in Sukumaland appears in chap. 6 ('Tanzania: agricultural development in Sukumaland') of de Wilde, II, 415–50.

4   MULTI-RACIALISM AND REGIONAL COUNCILS

Post-Second World War constitutional developments in Sukumaland involved even more substantial departures from the theory of
indirect rule than the Sukumaland Federal Council and the Cory
pyramid of subordinate representative councils. The desire of the
government that democratization should provide a role for the
non-African as well as the African (at least at higher levels of local
government) produced a multi-racial policy of territorial political
development which can be regarded in retrospect only as the
principal blunder of the Twining regime. Together with a felt
need for decentralization of government from Dar es Salaam to
appropriate subordinate units, this led in 1949 to the formation
of the Lake Province Council, by 1954 to multi-racial district
advisory councils, and in 1955 to the establishment of a statutory
South East Lake County Council.

The Lake Province Council

A non-statutory advisory council with some executive control
over the administration of development funds, the Lake Province
Council was the first of its kind in the territory. Stretching from
Bukoba in the west to Musoma in the east and encompassing
one-fourth of Tanganyika's population and half of its productive
wealth, the province seemed a likely place to launch the multi-
racial experiment. Divided equally between nine *ex officio* and
nominated senior officials of the provincial administration and nine
unofficial members (including two Europeans, two Asians and
five Africans), the Council met for the first time in June 1949.
The language of debate was English rather than Swahili, which
sharply limited the possibilities for African membership. Chief
Shoka Luhende of Uduhe in Shinyanga District was the only
Sukuma appointed at the outset. Eustace Kibaja, a Tanga-born
government clerk who received the first nomination as unofficial
African representative of Mwanza township, was replaced in 1952
by Paul Bomani, a Sukuma and the leader of the cotton cooperatives. Following English patterns of local government organization
and procedure, the council divided into functional committees.
The full council met three times yearly. Its agenda customarily
included official response to questions of public interest; examination of reports on the work of departments and on development
schemes; consideration of recommendations from the three
council committees; and debate on formal motions.

This was the first multi-racial local government body of any size in Tanganyika (outside the Legislative Council itself and a few township councils). It was explicitly designed to be 'the forerunner of similar and equally significant political developments in other parts of the Territory.'[1] Provincial Commissioner Hall (himself an unusually progressive exponent of African constitutional advancement) felt it necessary to explain the rationale behind the multi-racial form to the first meeting of the Council. Noting that in the neighboring countries of Uganda, Northern Rhodesia and Nyasaland 'the present tendency is to create Provincial African Councils,' he explained that:

This is not intended in Tanganyika, since it is considered that the interests of immigrant races and of Africans are so closely interlocked, and that the contribution which immigrants can make to the development of Tanganyika is so great that it would be unrealistic and indeed against the interests of the indigenous people to aim at purely African institutions at so high a level as the Province.[2]

Governor Twining elaborated Hall's thesis:

Your members are drawn from the three principal races which make up the people of this Territory. You will thus have the opportunity of demonstrating, in a local setting and in contact with practical problems of administration, that cooperation between the people of different races on which the future destiny of Tanganyika Territory depends.[3]

A policy was here launched which was to be perpetuated through various commutations and permutations until the breakdown of multi-racial district councils in Geita and elsewhere in 1958 and the victory of TANU at the polls in 1958–9. It was being launched despite the fact that Asians, as important as they were to the economy, constituted only a fraction of the African population and despite the fact that Europeans, other than government personnel and missionaries, were numerically negligible. If anything, Tanganyika had as strong a case as Uganda and a stronger case than Northern Rhodesia to be classed along with the West African colonies as an African territory.

Some identified this anomaly at an early date and saw dangers ahead. Kidaha Makwaia, a Sukuma chief and the first African appointed to the Legislative Council, spoke repeatedly of the

---

[1] Minutes of the Lake Province Council, June, 1949, LPF. The statement was attributed to Governor Twining by P. C. Hall in the latter's opening speech to the first meeting of the Council.

[2] *Ibid.*   [3] *Ibid.*

E

primacy of African interests in the late 1940s. In 1950 a leading
European unofficial member of the Lake Province Council, J.
Bennett of Bukoba, sharply questioned the implications of multi-
racial trends. Favoring elections to the Legislative Council only
for Africans, he argued:

Surely there is no doubt as to the declared policy of the British Government...That policy is very simply the paramountcy of African interests
...It would seem impossible to reconcile an electoral system involving
alien races with a completely objective advance toward the goal of
African independence. At the risk of being declared a reactionary, I
must say that the more deeply the alien races become implicated in
elected representation to central legislature the more will disinterested
leadership of the African give way to considerations of racial interests.
Electoral representation on a racial basis, with emphasis increasingly on
racial interests, leads all too easily to segregation, and is in the mind of
the writer to be avoided at the level of central legislature. That way
lies 'apartheid' in a situation where 'Eendrag' (unity through teamwork)
is essential to solution.[1]

The government decided, on the contrary, that Tanganyika
was so backward educationally, economically and politically that
only the multi-racial formula offered hope for competent and
responsible territorial and sub-territorial governing units. The
Lake Province Council, however, had little impact on Sukumaland. Coinciding in time with the major organizational and
developmental efforts of the Sukumaland Federal Council and
the Sukumaland Development Scheme, the Provincial Council
remained of marginal concern to Sukumaland native authorities
and European administrators who were involved with local council
hierarchies and development plans. Most ordinary Africans knew
nothing of the council other than (after 1952) that Paul Bomani
was a member.

The multi-racial idea, however, went forward at the district
level where Cory made provision for the inclusion of non-Africans
on the district advisory councils in 1954 and 1955. These councils
remained stepping stones to the Sukumaland Federal Council
rather than to the Provincial Council. True, the Governor and
others envisaged an eventual multi-racial hierarchy with indirect
selection from district to province to territorial Legislative Council.
No sooner did the Lake Province Council get under way, however,
than discussions were opened at higher levels of government with
regard to the institution of sub-provincial regions or counties

[1] Bennett to the Chairman of the Lake Province Council, 4 Oct. 1905, MZDF.

which would be more manageable in size and more rationally related to enthnographic divisions and natural economic units than the existing provinces.

The South East Lake County Council

Again the Lake Province—specifically Sukumaland—was designated as an experimental area for the proposed innovations. It became apparent, however, that an implicit conflict with the existing Sukumaland Federation was involved. An entirely African institution of chiefs and councillors, the federation had been built up by the administration over a number of years and with some fanfare. The only federation of its type in the territory, it also constituted what was regarded by the administration as the essential indigenous legislative prop for the ambitious Sukumaland Development Scheme. The federation as a whole could not readily be absorbed into the proposed Sukumaland County Council because the latter would be a multi-racial unit of local government, not a native authority. Further, the county council would need to be limited in numbers to achieve any degree of effectiveness. Though Governor Twining was disenchanted with the Federal Council and was soon to disband the entire Malya development operation in favor of strengthened provincial and district development teams, he could not abruptly abolish the Federal Council. He decided, finally, that for both economic and political reasons the new county council should be expanded beyond Sukumaland to include the cotton-growing districts of the eastern portion of the Lake Province. His move side-stepped direct conflict with the existing federation, but weakened the new county unit.

The South East Lake County Council, officially established in 1955, included eight districts stretching over some 25,000 square miles from Shinyanga in southern Sukumaland to North Mara on the Kenya border. Members nominated by the provincial administration, together with councillors selected by district councils, numbered 54. Meetings were held twice a year. The new council replaced the Lake Province Council, but its role was more difficult to define than had been that of its predecessor. Writing to the Member for Local Government, the Deputy Provincial Commissioner described his perplexity with the anomalous and impractical nature of the new experiment:

It has been the view of many members that the County Council will duplicate too much of the work already done by the comparatively highly organized Native Authorities and that done by the Central Government. In this Province, where we have few non-African farmers, and where most non-natives are resident in Towns, Minor Settlements and Trading Centers, the real local government is performed by the Native Authorities. The matter is too involved for any solution to be found just yet but after a year or two of a County Council working, many adjustments will have to be made. For the present anyway it will be a matter of trial and error with effort concentrated on winning over the Native Authorities to delegate more and more of their powers to the County Council.[1]

The Council was 'too unwieldy,'[2] and was ultimately dissolved in 1959 after it became clear that multi-racial conceptions of government in Tanganyika were no longer tenable.

5   EFFECTING CHANGE

Innovations: Rowe

Provincial Commissioner Rowe (1949–54) presided over the most creative and experimental years of local government administration and development in Sukumaland. He built on the ideas and initiatives of Malcolm and Hall before him. He relied extensively on Rounce and Cory during his five years in the Lake Province. Rowe combined the sort of concentration and dedication to his office which made him the master of every detail with an historical sense which placed Sukumaland and Tanganyika in the wider context of Africa and the world. He was a tireless proponent of and negotiator for the political and economic development schemes in which he believed. He sometimes wearied officials in Dar es Salaam but seemed always in Mwanza to speak with a voice which identified the historic tasks of the postwar era and which exhorted his junior colleagues to greater efforts. Rowe was an imposing administrator who believed that he had a mission to accomplish and the means with which to make a most significant beginning.

More than Rounce, Rowe saw that the problem of development had a human dimension. Addressing the Lake Province Council in 1952, he quoted a British journal, *The Quarterly Review*, to the effect that 'no theory could be termed practical unless it made

---

[1] D.P.C. to the Member for Local Government, 18 Feb. 1955, LPF.

[2] As Cranford Pratt has noted, the Council "broke almost every maxim of successful local government." See R. C. Pratt, "Multi-Racialism and Local Government in Tanganyika," *Race*, II (Nov., 1960), 42.

proper allowance for the temperament of those expected to carry it out.' He emphasized the necessity of associating 'individual men and women, with all processes of Government action or organized work—from conception of the idea and early planning to the final stages.' Development had to be understood as a social as well as a material process. Quoting from a review in *The Economist*, he suggested a 'double rule-of-thumb test' for the acceptability of development projects: 'Does it meet a want which the people concerned actively feel? Is it a job in which the people concerned can actively participate?' Rowe saw that the tasks were great and that Sukumaland and its problems offered 'complexities enough for a lifetime.' Though provided with 'makeshift weapons' and lacking 'enough supplies,' Rowe felt that 'mutual understanding,' 'tolerance,' 'generosity,' 'sheer dogged persistence,' and 'sharing of common interests between individual members of all communities in interracial organizations' would point the way to economic, social and political progress.[1]

Questions

The problem of involving the people in the changes proposed for Sukumaland exercised the talents of yet another research officer seconded to Sukumaland in 1951. The administration asked A. C. A. Wright, a former administrative officer in Uganda, to investigate land tenure, stock holding, and the Sukuma social outlook and to propose techniques for the implementation of economic and social development programs. Rowe wrote to Wright:

For some considerable time it has been felt that although many Chiefs and other enlightened persons have understood the necessity for new methods in agriculture and animal husbandry, few tribesmen have appreciated the urgency of the matter, despite some four years of preaching by the Government with the result that comparatively little progress on the ground has been made, except in those areas where there has been a sufficiency of European staff to insist on improved methods. It has been further noticed that where this pressure has been withdrawn the tribesmen return to their erstwhile apathy. It is now felt that probably the methods used may have been wrong and a study of these methods together with the reactions of the peasants is necessary in order to evolve a new approach, e.g. through indigenous social groupings and societies as well as through the Native Authority.[2]

[1] Minutes of the Lake Province Council, Nov. 1952, LPF.
[2] Rowe to Wright, 28 Aug. 1951, LPF.

With the research results of Cory, Malcolm and Rounce at hand, plus three months of his own in the field, Wright concluded:

The problem is now one of procedure—how to apply the agricultural and sociological knowledge already available in such a way as to achieve the desired objective of a well-balanced mixed husbandry with the minimum use of compulsory sanctions during the period of change.[1]

Yet, when Wright laid his proposals before the Provincial Council a year later, they were too thorough-going even for Rowe. Starting, to be sure, with the problem of how to achieve rapid economic and social change in Sukumaland, Wright moved from finer points of procedure to a radical re-assessment of the entire direction of postwar policy for political and economic change. He argued for a vastly improved substructure of transportation and communication as prerequisite to significant advance. He urged fundamental changes in customary land tenure to permit security of individual holdings as the necessary prelude to agricultural innovation and household improvement. He advocated model villages and pilot projects with demonstration effect as the techniques most likely to win the support of the people. He decried the restrictive legislation and compulsory techniques associated with massive agricultural schemes.

On the political side, Wright found native authorities corrupt and inefficient. In his view the indirect rule ideas of the 1930s were inappropriate for the postwar period because chiefs were unequal to the tasks required for economic development. At the same time, he judged political modifications in the direction of representative democracy premature. Elected councillors as individuals, and the pyramid of councils as a system, would be even less capable of efficient and progressive administration than the chiefs. Wright argued that the real need was for trained African local government officers gradually to supplant the chiefs. Some chiefs might well be included in the new cadres, but most would not. He proposed rigorous instruction of qualified candidates, then selection for posts on the basis of merit.[2]

Whatever the strength of his arguments—and they foreshadowed quite remarkably some of the policies adopted in Tanganyika after independence—Wright was too radical for his time and too sweeping in his criticism. Even the most enlightened and

[1] Wright, 'Note on Progress: October–December 1951', LPF.
[2] Wright's analyses and proposals were contained in a series of papers. The most important titles are listed in the bibliography.

progressive minds in the Tanganyikan administration found his proposals indigestible. Despite his previous administrative experience, he was regarded as an impractical idealist, as a man who sparked ideas rapidly but without sufficient appreciation of the exigencies of time and place. Conceding that 'while there may be grounds for holding such a drastic overhaul to be needed and while it may be difficult to set bounds to your fundamental and vigorous approach towards our present situation and its remedy,' Rowe suggested that Wright limit his presentation to the Lake Province Council to a two-page summary of non-controversial items. Other matters pertaining to 'high policy' could be discussed confidentially within the central government at provincial and territorial level, allowing a possible later installment for the Council 'in a form which they can assimilate.'[1] The Rowe administration in the Lake Province and the Tanganyikan administration territorially were committed to change; but directions and policies, and even procedure, were deeply set by 1952. Alterations of the radical nature which Wright proposed could not be entertained seriously.

Malcolm's and Rounce's schemes for radical transformation of peasant agriculture (through application of the most stringent measures if necessary) appropriated the psychology of the white man's burden to the economic sphere in a postwar era characterized by impatience with the doddering half-measures of the past. The Sukumaland Development Scheme was, after all, a contemporary of the Groundnut Scheme.[2] While the latter failed to consider the intractability of the soil itself, the former considered the land with great care but failed sufficiently to allow for the intractability of the people. Being a man of foresight and of independent mind but insufficiently appreciated in his time, Wright would have spent more money on material infrastructure while taking more time to convince people by persuasion and example of the value to them of economic and social change.

On the political side Cory's system of councils seemed responsive to world-wide demands for democracy at the same time

---

[1] Rowe to Wright, 3 Nov. 1952, LPF.
[2] The Groundnut Scheme was a £25,000,000 agricultural development project with supporting port and railway facilities launched in the Kongwa-Mpwapwa region of Tanganyika in the late 1940s. It failed primarily from 'a grave lack of preliminary planning and experiment' and was characterized by a 'tone of extravagance and even of fantasy' until its abandonment in 1950 (Ingham, pp. 379–80).

that it meshed with previous structures of native administration.[1]
Wright's proposed cadre of professional African administrators
accommodated to neither.

An Authoritarian Approach: Walden

Provincial Commissioner Walden (1954–9) could hardly have
provided a more stark contrast to Rowe. Walden was the tight-
fisted, hard-nosed, administrator's administrator. A pragmatist,
he was suspicious of schemes of any sort. With funds for the
Sukumaland Development Scheme running out about the time
of his arrival as Provincial Commissioner, Walden agreed with
Governor Twining that the entire development headquarters at
Malya was an unrealistic, ivory tower operation which should be
disbanded. Thus, senior staff and training schools were relocated
in Mwanza and remaining financial assets divided among provincial and district administrations. In Walden's view, too, the
Sukumaland Federal Council seemed to serve no worthwhile
function. He reduced the number of yearly meetings from two or
three to one. Even the South East Lake County Council, which
was instituted during his tenure (the result of planning which
stretched back to 1951), took second place under Walden to more
traditional methods of administration through provincial, district
and native authority structures.

Both Rowe and Walden were able and decisive administrators,
but with a difference. Where Rowe tended to be diplomatic and
circumspect, Walden tended to be abrupt and caustic. Rowe utterly
devoted himself to the accomplishment of programs which he
believed were in the best interests of the populace, but during his
final years in the province he suffered heightened criticism of
his administration from politically minded Africans. He seemed,
nevertheless, still willing to explain and to educate—albeit paterna-
listically—those who opposed him. Walden, on the other hand,
was less interested in idealistic programs but more outraged by
criticism. He seemed to regard criticism as directly threatening
to his, and the government's, authority. Where African political
leaders felt it possible to talk with Rowe, they could not talk with
Walden, who adopted Twining's refusal to see Mwanza leaders of

[1] Demands for democracy were focused specifically on Tanganyika by virtue
of its peculiar status as a United Nations Trust Territory and more generally,
through the medium of policy-makers in London, on Tanganyika and all
British African territories as a result of the independence of India and then
the rapid constitutional advances undertaken in the Gold Coast.

the Tanganyika African Association in February 1954 as the model for his own attitude.

While continuing to press forward with economic development and local government reform, the Walden administration committed itself to the fundamentally conservative task of strengthening native authorities against the politicians. With the exception of the dubious commitment to multi-racialism, there was no sense of new ideas or of purpose during the Walden years. Of course, Rowe might have done many of the things Walden did later had he stayed. But it seems clear that the Twining–Walden attitude, which treated emerging political leaders as irresponsible subversives, sharpened the conflict as much as anything that was said or done on the other side. In essence the Walden regime was a holding operation, which, despite a Sukumaland-wide ban on the Tanganyika African National Union (TANU) from 1954 to 1958, could not ultimately be successful. It disintegrated during an unsuccessful attempt to institute a statutory multi-racial district council in Geita in 1958. After outbreaks of civil disobedience spread to other districts in late 1958, the entire regimen of restrictive legislation from the years of the Sukumaland Development Scheme was abolished at a special meeting of the Sukumaland Federal Council in November. The administration lifted the proscription on TANU, elections were held, and the transition to independence began.

Denouement

Walden stayed on until July 1959, but by that time the victory of TANU in Sukumaland was all but complete. The South East Lake County Council was dissolved in 1959, and despite a final attempt by the chiefs to reconstitute the Sukumaland Federal Council with new powers and responsibilities, it too disappeared in 1960. The Cory pyramid of representative councils lingered on, but TANU, despite protestations to the contrary, gradually undermined the remaining vestiges of the power and prestige of native authorities. Cory deliberated with TANU leaders over African district councils which replaced the multi-racial councils, but he was able to salvage only temporarily any role for traditional native authorities. With independence, statutory district councils were constituted almost entirely on elective lines. The TANU government set up an entirely new administrative organization in place of the old native authority structure.

Assuredly, the redirection of colonial policy in Tanganyika owed at least as much to external pressures for decolonization—from the United Nations, from critics and policy-makers in London, and from the sheer pace of changes already effected in the Indian subcontinent and developments well under way in the British West African territories—as to internal events like those in Sukumaland. Nevertheless, pressures from below—though they cannot be regarded as having been *the* determinants of policy changes—were essential catalysts in the redirection of policy, both as to substance and timing.

While to many who had labored the colonial efforts in Sukumaland seemed to turn too quickly to dust, on reflection a balance may be struck. Modified native authority structures and particular proposals for economic and political development came to naught. Even directions of policy in the 1940s and 1950s were questionable in important respects. Yet nothing can be more certain than that much of the organization, style and method of British administration has remained. In addition to setting administrative standards, the British identification of problems needing solution aided the post-independence government of Tanzania in defining some of its principal tasks. Finally, through the language of political liberalism and experiments with representation—if not always through actual behavior and successful implementation of sometimes ambitious and sometimes misguided plans—the British left Tanzania a legacy of some value.

PART II

THE BEGINNINGS OF INDIGENOUS POLITICS

3

Incipient Political Activity

While the colonial administration contributed immeasurably to the history of Tanganyika, it could never create more than a part of that history. In the perspective of centuries, the dominating presence of Europeans was brief; the tenure of Africans will be lengthy. Even at the height of the colonial period, policies and programs designed by the British in London, Dar es Salaam or Mwanza had ultimately to be implemented among Africans in the territory which was their homeland.

Although the main thrust of nationalism was associated with the activities of manifestly political organizations (principally TANU) in the 1950s, there were less dramatic—but no less remarkable— beginnings before then. From the earliest days of European penetration, traditional native authorities—in so far as they were able—acted to serve the interests of themselves and of their people as they understood those interests. Later, when a few African leaders—usually chiefs in the first instance—were appointed to important positions within the colonial structure, they were able to criticize and to represent even without the aid of nascent political associations. But the future lay with emerging non-traditional educated elites and with the voluntary associations which they founded in the years following the Second World War.

Nationalist organizations, however, did not spring full-blown from the turbulent political context of the 1950s. Associations, which later struggled to replace Tanganyika's European adminis- trators and traditional African authorities, concerned themselves in an earlier day with a variety of more specific economic and social needs and grievances. True, among leaders and members a political sensitivity was present from the beginning, a political posture always implicit. But people act politically only when certain conditions are fulfilled. Circumstances must first be felt to be intolerable enough to prompt diversion from the routines of daily life and work. A favorable readjustment of those undesired

45

circumstances must seem to be a real possibility. Finally, leadership must emerge to galvanize the inchoate political sentiments of potential followers into organized political action.

Before 1950 Africans in Sukumaland had complaints and grievances, but these seemed—if not marginal—less than vital to their lives. For the more sophisticated town elite, politics was an extracurricular activity to be indulged in leisure hours. Meetings produced discussion and occasionally a petition, but little else. For the farmer in the countryside, politics—except for the most local variety—remained an unknown quantity. A man's family, his stock, the agricultural cycle, and enough income from cash-crops to purchase some household amenities were his principal concerns. In these early postwar years militant leaders failed to emerge because likely candidates for the role were still in school or too hampered by inadequate salaries to jeopardize their jobs with outside political undertakings. Moreover, taking the risks of leadership made little sense where there would have been few followers. Indeed, might-have-been leaders probably made no such conscious calculations as these. A myriad of contributing factors—education, economic and social development, political consciousness, internal pressures from the colonial administration and external pressures from a world which had impact perforce on the ideas and institutions of administrators and administered alike—had not yet effected in Sukumaland an historical context which could make either militant political leadership, or the following of such leadership, a live option.

Nevertheless, the anticipatory stage of proto-politics was vitally important. In Sukumaland, as elsewhere, men built on the accomplishments of their predecessors. Early leaders, however ineffectual, prepared the way for their more effective successors. The structure and program of early associations, however insubstantial, provided the necessary groundwork for the more forceful organizations of a later day. Whatever the unique factors which acted as special catalysts to the militant politics of the 1950s, the politics of those years appears also to have grown from the soil of the more moderate politics of the 1940s.

I.   CHIEFS AS POLITICIANS

As in some other parts of Africa, the first politicians in Sukumaland were the chiefs. The chiefs talked with the first European explorers and fought or bargained with the first European administrators. Chosen to be the executive arm of native administration by German and British colonial rulers, the chiefs and their sons were among the first Africans to receive the rudiments of Western education and instruction in the art of government. Albeit caught in an ambiguous position between the traditional expectations of their people on the one hand and the new demands of alien rulers on the other, the chiefs had an opportunity to achieve new positions of power and influence. Given their unique position within the colonial administrative scheme, they became increasingly independent of customary tribal political controls. In the absence of an independent educated elite, they were able to assume in part as well a new political role. In addition to administrative duties and indulgence of dynastic intrigue (a political pastime typical of chiefs), they registered grievances and represented at least some needs of the people to higher authority.

Makwaia to London

Chief Makwaia of Usiha chiefdom in Shinyanga traveled to London in 1931 to testify at hearings on the question of closer union for the East African territories. Elected by a joint meeting of Sukuma and Nyamwezi chiefs, he was the most representative of the three African witnesses selected by the Tanganyikan administration to put forward African views. Before leaving for London, he 'traveled extensively around Mwanza and Tabora Provinces requesting the opinions of other chiefs on questions relating to Closer Union.' Unlike the other delegates, Makwaia spoke no English and had to rely on a Sukuma interpreter. Even so, 'as senior member and therefore official spokesman of the Tanganyika group he was able to utilize his sense of ceremony and articulate expression of local interests to good effect and emerged from the hearings with considerably enhanced honor.'[1] United with the Tanganyikan administration and the 'Cameron–Lugard–Oldham group' in opposing any sort of political union with white-settler-dominated Kenya, Makwaia spoke for African interests. Even today he is remembered by one Sukuma political leader as Sukumaland's first 'great politician.'[2]

Attempts at Federation

After the transfer of Shinyanga District to the Lake Province in

[1] Austen, 'Native policy,' p. 438.   [2] Lameck Bogohe, interview, 25 Jan. 1965.

1932, Sukuma chiefs made their first attempts to join in a unified federation. Makwaia became the acknowledged spokesman. Though the government initially proclaimed the October 1932 meeting of the Sukuma chiefs 'an important event in the evolution of the Native Administration in the Lake Province,'[1] enthusiasm on both sides soon diminished and in 1934 the conferences were discontinued. While some attention was paid to substantive economic problems such as cattle marketing and to troublesome matters of native law and custom, the chiefs seemed most interested in the 'protection of material prerogatives lost in both the conversion to indirect rule and the retrenchment measures of the Depression.'[2] For its part the administration, wary for political reasons of any trend toward large-scale federation, was not overwrought when the project lapsed.

In the 1930s other chiefs, notably Masanja of Nera and Majebere of Mwagala, emerged as leaders of the chiefly federations in their own districts of Kwimba and Maswa. Chief Balele, who followed Masanja as chief of the extensive and populous Nera chiefdom, studied in England at an agricultural college and traveled in the Middle East to visit African troops during the Second World War. Exercising the only real political leadership in Sukumaland in the years before 1945, these influential chiefs worked to enhance the status of Africans by learning to master what they could of what the West had to offer and turning it to the advantage of themselves and their people within the structures of the colonial context.

The historical situation was not yet ripe, and the chiefs themselves were not personally inclined toward the sort of agitation for economic and political advance which characterized the post-Second World War years. Occasionally in the later 1930s, provincial officers suggested that discussion among the Sukuma chiefs might be useful on some issues. The Governor, however, feared that such meetings might become 'foci for political agitators.'[3] It is of some interest that the administration used the same

---

[1] Press release on a 'Meeting of the Sukuma chiefs of the Lake Province,' 12 Nov. 1932, SMP 23461.
[2] Austen, 'Native policy,' p. 440. The chiefs were interested in such matters as their salaries, tribute rebate from the administration's hut and poll tax, abolition of tax on plural wives, the right of the chiefs to ivory collected within their domain, and the claim of local treasuries to a certain portion of the profits derived from minerals mined in Sukumaland.
[3] File note on a meeting held at Government House, 29 Nov. 1935, SMP 23461.

language here that it was to employ twenty years later against anti-chief, nationalist politicians. Fearing that combined meetings would increase 'the danger of the smaller and less vocal chiefs being led into spurious and ill-considered agreement with the leaders, without the support of their people' and raising the spectres of 'oppression' and 'chaos,' Dar es Salaam advised that any joint discussions should be arranged by the chiefs themselves rather than by government officers and that any such meetings should be kept 'as informal as possible.'[1]

Kernels of Protest

At times, too, particularly those chiefs who were less influential and sophisticated than some of their more prominent colleagues, struggled against the high-handedness and indignities which unhappily seem everywhere to have been a part of the colonial experience. In 1932 the Mwanza chiefs petitioned the Chief Secretary in protest against a district officer who not only refused to consult with them before taking action in the name of the native authority, but also on occasion entered chiefs' houses without permission, abused them verbally, and assaulted them physically, even in front of their own people. The chiefs asked that the offending officer not be permitted to remain in Mwanza.[2] Though the administration had 'no doubt [the assaults] did occur' and that 'they do definitely make the position of righteous indignation a rather difficult one to assume,' it held that the complaints had not been 'brought to the notice of the Provincial Commissioner in the proper form,' that 'the whole thing is a great piece of impertinence...definitely an engineered attack on a District Officer,' and that 'if any notice were taken of it, the effect on authority would be deplorable.'[3] The officer in question continued to be posted in Mwanza. The petitioners were simply informed that his Excellency the Governor had seen the petition and that any complaints they might wish to make to the Provincial Commissioner in the presence of the offending officer would be considered.[4]

Physical assault, of course, was not typical of the relations

[1] File note, W. E. Scupham to the Chief Secretary, 18 Mar. 1936; Scupham for the Chief Secretary to P.C., 31 Mar. 1936, *ibid.*
[2] Chiefs of Mwanza District to the Chief Secretary, n.d. (orig. Sw.). An English translation of the petition may be found in SMP 21058.
[3] Mitchell to the Chief Secretary, 15 June 1932. *ibid.*
[4] Chief Secretary to P.C., 15 Sept. 1932. *ibid.*

F

between the chiefs and administrative officers. One of the main purposes of indirect rule was to develop chiefs into efficient administrators to forward the government's programs. This was a difficult enough task where chiefs were capable, influential and amenable to change; it was virtually impossible where, as in Mwanza, the chiefs were less distinguished, at least in the eyes of the administration. Whether the recalcitrance of chiefs was due more to change as such or to the high-handed way in which certain government officers effected change, is at times difficult to determine. Whether exasperation on the part of officers was due more to the 'backwardness' and incompetence of the native authorities or to an objectionable sense of racial superiority which precluded even the rudiments of courtesy, is equally difficult to assess.

Whatever the case, the Mwanza chiefs, for example, expressed in 1937 their concern, confusion and dissatisfaction with the efforts of a district officer to amalgamate the native chiefdom treasuries into a federation treasury. In a petition to the Provincial Commissioner, they combined a conservative harking back to the known and comfortable past with an insistence on respect and rights for Africans. While not yet sharing an awareness that national self-government could provide the only final answer (which is characteristic of the political impulse of later years), it was notable that the chiefs adopted (as they had in 1932) the essentially political means of the petition.[1]

On Behalf of African Interests

After the Second World War when Tanganyika became a trust territory under the United Nations, the petition became an even more potent political weapon. For the first time there arose the possibility of appeal to an authoritative body outside (and with some possible jurisdiction over) the colonial administration. The Colonial Office, too, began to take a more personal interest in Tanganyikan affairs. When the then Under-Secretary of State Creech Jones visited Mwanza, Malya and Shinyanga in 1946, 'the African community was especially pleased to have the opportunity of discussing some of their thoughts and problems with a member of the British Government and full advantage of this opportunity was taken by the Sukumaland Chiefs.'[2]

[1] Chiefs of Mwanza District to P.C., 15 Jan. 1937 (orig. Sw.). An English translation of the petition may be found in SMP 26229.
[2] Lake Province Annual Report, 1946, LPF.

The first United Nations Visiting Mission to Tanganyika in 1948 received a lengthy petition from the Sukumaland Federation of Chiefs. The chiefs lobbied for exemption from any form of taxation for themselves on the grounds that this was 'an ancient rule.' They asked for an immediate increase in the number of schools and hospitals, and requested that 'for the benefit and interest of the public' a certain percentage of revenue from gold and diamond mining in Sukumaland be turned over to the Sukumaland native treasury.

What seems surprising is that the chiefs moved beyond an exposition of parochial interests and of ever-present desires for more funds, better education and increased social services to frame a set of more radical and specific economic and political demands. These may be summarized as follows:

1. African representation in the Legislative Council be increased through the nomination 'by the Public' of one non-official member from each province.
2. Africans be given the opportunity for training as administrative cadets with a view toward their appointment as Assistant District Officers.
3. 'Immediate consideration' be granted of possible ways of developing African cooperative societies, trading companies, and agricultural enterprises.
4. No land be alienated by lease or sale in rural areas without the consent of the native authorities concerned.
5. 'When the Tanganyika Government sits together with world merchants to consider the produce prices, the Native Authority should be given opportunity of attending such meetings.'[1]

These representations by the chiefs were in some respects more sophisticated and far-reaching than those of a provincial conference of the Tanganyika African Association held in Mwanza in 1947; they were more specific than the pleas of a Shinyanga TAA petition to the same United Nations Mission in 1948.[2] Voluntary associations, initiated after 1945, were not yet in a position to play a sustained and vocal political role. On the other hand, they had made beginnings, and these doubtless served as an indirect stimulus to the more enlightened chiefs.

For its part the Federation was able and willing to assume the progressive posture, at least on paper, which the 1948 petition suggests. Chiefs were not yet alienated from their people, as they

---

[1] Petition from the Sukumaland Federation of Chiefs to the United Nations Visiting Mission, Aug. 1948, LPF. Quoted phrases are from the petition.
[2] See below, pp. 62–9; 72–4.

later were to be, by excessive and restrictive development legislation; nor were they yet wholly at cross-purposes with an emerging non-traditional educated elite. Because of the perpetuation
of a native authority local government structure which allowed
little opening for town-oriented critics, chiefs in 1948 still spoke
for what many Africans believed to be general African interests.
Leading chiefs were still—though for but a year or two more—
the most prominent politicians.

2 KIDAHA MAKWAIA

After 1945 the most prominent of all the chiefs was David Kidaha
Makwaia, son of the great Chief Makwaia of Usiha and a distinguished student at Makerere College in Kampala where he studied
for a diploma in agriculture. Later he spent a year at Oxford.
On the death of his father, Kidaha became chief of Usiha in
1945. The same year Governor Battershill appointed him one of
the two first African members ever to sit on the Tanganyika
Legislative Council. From the outset Kidaha took a leading role
and for ten years he was the acknowledged ranking spokesman
for African interests in the territory.

In Legislative Council

In his maiden speech to the Legislative Council, Kidaha emphasized the need for 'coordinated policy' of the government's natural
resources and social services departments in tackling the country's
problems and he stressed that education of the African masses
was essential to long-term development.[1] At a Legislative Council
meeting in July 1946, Kidaha put no less than thirty-seven formal
questions to the government. This was the first time that an
African in Tanganyika had ever queried the highest levels of the
administration officially and publicly. The questions were penetrating, at times embarrassing to the government, and adequate
responses from the members concerned were not always forthcoming.[2]

[1] Tanganyika, *Proceedings of the Leglislative Council* (hereafter cited as TLC),
15 Dec. 1945.
[2] Kidaha probed the government's intent with regard to the consolidation and
printing of tribal laws, the translation into Swahili of government publications
on native administration, and increased African representation in the Legislative Council and on other government bodies. He queried differentiation on
the basis of race with regard to transportation, accommodation, prison diet,

From the first years of his tenure on the Legislative Council, Kidaha not only urged the acceleration of development efforts of every sort and improvement of the quality and efficiency of native administration, he also consistently elaborated the view that African interests should be 'paramount,' that Tanganyika was 'primarily an African country.'[1] While acknowledging the useful role played by Asians already resident in the country, he sharply opposed land alienation to non-natives. He supported immigration legislation designed to limit the further influx of Asians. In 1951, while Julius Nyerere was still at the University of Edinburgh, Kidaha spoke on constitutional development in a manner which anticipated in some respects the stance of the leader of the Tanganyika African National Union a few years later.[2]

Until the mid-1950s in fact, Kidaha was regarded by many Tanganyikans as the most logical candidate for national political leadership should the opportunity for an African to assume such leadership afford itself. One of Tanganyika's first college-educated Africans, he was also one of her most prominent chiefs. Nomination as the first African member of the Legislative Council in 1945 was followed in later years with other prominent appointments: to the Tanganyika Executive Council in 1950, to the Central Legislative Assembly of East Africa in 1950, to the East African Post and Telegraph Advisory Board in 1952, and to the East African Royal Commission on Land in 1953.[3]

Kidaha resigned his position as chief of Usiha in 1954 partly because his wider involvements kept him away from his chiefdom. Also, he was weary of the intramural rivalries within the Sukumaland Federation of Chiefs, of the ascendancy of the conservative

salary scales in the medical services, permission to run sweepstakes or to engage in mining operations and recruitment and appointment to administrative cadres of the government service. He emphasized the need for education, and for agricultural, medical and public health training. He asked that native authorities be permitted to engage in trade and that they receive a certain percentage of the revenue from mining operations carried out in their domain. He questioned the introduction of tax on cattle in some parts of the territory. In later sessions, he opposed government proposals to control the market prices of stock. Finally, implicitly supporting the status of Tanganyika as a United Nations Trusteeship Territory, he pointedly inquired: 'Is Government aware that Africans are utterly opposed to any proposal that Tanganyika should become a Colony?' (TLC, 25 July 1946).

[1] *Ibid.* 26 Aug., 10 Dec. 1947. [2] *Ibid.* 14 Nov. 1951.
[3] *Who's Who in East Africa* (Nairobi: Marco Surveys, 1964), Part II, p. 20. Kidaha became Assistant Minister for Land in 1957. For details see J. Clagett Taylor. *The political development of Tanganyika* (Stanford, California: Stanford University Press, 1963), p. 153.

Majebere, and of being an agent of local district and provincial administrators who zealously pressed forward with what he regarded as 'arbitrary measures.' These related to local government and natural resources legislation, and, more especially, to compulsory destocking, which he opposed. Kidaha preferred to concentrate his efforts on territorial problems.[1]

Reluctant Politician

By the early 1950s, however, a distinction was developing between Africans who wanted to lead within the establishment and those who felt that the path to African advancement lay with the voluntary political associations. Kidaha had been only marginally involved with the Tanganyika African Association. Regarding it as more of a social club than a political organization, he met from time to time with TAA members in Dar es Salaam. He recalls some 'very useful meetings' where 'one got additional points about occurrences elsewhere in the country.' He purposely refrained from referring to TAA in the Legislative Council. He felt that up-country branches were organizationally weak because most of the members were civil servants. As such, they were at the mercy of the administration which could and did transfer at will those who became involved in political activities. Further, he felt that TAA in the late 1940s was not truly representative of the population. Kidaha felt he could make stronger points in the Legislative Council by speaking more generally of the views of Africans.[2]

In the early 1950s, however, and most particularly in the Lake Province, TAA developed from a politically oriented discussion group into an active political organization. Kidaha was outside Tanganyika for a considerable portion of 1953 and 1954 while serving with the East African Royal Commission on Land. Still, in 1954 or 1955, he could have shifted gears. It is reported that before he made his decision to resign his teaching position at Pugu, Nyerere suggested to Kidaha that he might assume the presidency of the fledgling Tanganyika African National Union.

[1] Kidaha Makwaia, interview, 20 Nov. 1964; Kidaha to the leaders and people of Usiha, published in Swahili by the Government Printer, n.d. (1954), Shinyanga District files (hereafter cited as SHDF). See also Judith Listowel, *The making of Tanganyika* (New York: London House and Maxwell, 1965), p. 134.
[2] Kidaha, interview; TLC, 14 Nov. 1951. But cf. George Bennett, 'An outline history of TANU,' *Makerere Journal*, No. 7 (1963), p. 1.

Nyerere, who seems not to have committed himself to politics as a full-time occupation until September 1955,[1] may have felt that Kidaha, who had resigned the chiefship of Usiha in 1954 to devote himself to wider interests, was in a better position than he to assume a territorial leadership role. If in fact the offer was made, Kidaha declined it for reasons which are not known. Perhaps unsure of his leadership capabilities in the proffered role, but at the height of his prestige within the establishment, he may have calculated that his political contribution could be greater if he remained where he was.[2]

The personality factor is difficult to weigh, but may be important. Kidaha has been described by some as indecisive. An American missionary who knew Kidaha well has observed that he had a definitely conservative bent.[3] An evangelistically inclined Roman Catholic convert from Islam, Kidaha seemed to combine a religious conservatism with a political distrust of radical democracy or socialism. While insisting always that a primarily African state was the goal for Tanganyika, Kidaha was cautious as to the specific constitutional steps to be taken in that direction. Between 1951 and 1956 he seemed to adopt much of the language and some of the philosophy of multi-racialism.

Kidaha and Nyerere

In 1951, for example, in the same speech in which he castigated 'those who believe that the African's role is to play second fiddle in politics,' Kidaha argued for the retention of an official majority in the Legislative Council in the following terms:

Because we still have to learn to trust and have confidence amongst the members of the different races, I think it highly desirable and appropriate that we should retain an official majority in the Legislative Council. This is the only reliable safeguard for both minorities and the African

---

[1] After resigning his teaching position at Pugu, Nyerere returned to his home in Musoma. For several months he taught the Zanaki language to an American Maryknoll missionary. He did not move permanently to Dar es Salaam until late September or early October 1955 (The Rev. Arthur Wille, interview, 22 May 1964; also Bennett, *Makerere Journal*, No. 7 (1963), p. 6).

[2] See, however, a different version and interpretation in Listowel, pp. 135–9, 198–9. Listowel's account sets a much earlier date—1947, at the time of the controversy over closer union for Kenya, Uganda and Tanzania—for the political estrangement of Makwaia and Nyerere. Her version would appear to place in doubt the reliability of the report that Nyerere later offered Makwaia the leadership of TANU.

[3] The Rev. Alan Smidlein, interview, July 1964.

racial majority...The greatest political tragedy that could ever happen in this country would be the granting of full political rights to some races and denying them to the others. All sensible men of all races are willing to share political rights with their brethren of other races on a basis of genuine partnership.[1]

It is not that the sentiments were not noble. Rather, in Tanganyika in the early 1950s, these notions of racial harmony and the sharing of political rights 'on a basis of genuine partnership' implied specific governmental policies which gave Europeans and Asians political parity or even preponderance in spite of an overwhelmingly African population. But the merits of the policy of multi-racialism—or even Kidaha's views—need not be argued here; it is sufficient to indicate the extent to which Kidaha's stance then differed from that later adopted by Nyerere.

Though Kidaha inveighed against racial discrimination in hotels, pushed persistently for more education, development and services, warned against the imposition from above of local councils (though not against their multi-racial character), and asked that Swahili be permitted for Legislative Council speeches, he generally took a more conservative view on some other issues which charged the emotions of nationalist politicians. He supported government policy as set forth in a White Paper at the time of the Meru land controversy. He felt that non-racial development, which allowed for African and non-African private enterprise as well as for cooperative societies, would be in the interests of the Lake Province cotton industry. In 1954 he supported the Registration of Societies Ordinance and, in 1955, the Penal Code Amendment Bill. Both laws were designed to curtail the political activities of what the government (and Kidaha) regarded as irresponsible persons.[2] He was cautious about the introduction of elections:

We are not ready for elections...Some people would like to have self-government today...Self-government, like democracy, is one of those fashionable catch phrases and political slogans that one hears all over East Africa these days, but do these people really know what it would mean if we have so-called self-government tomorrow, if we had democracy—whatever democracy means.[3]

[1] TLC, 14 Nov. 1951.
[2] See speeches by Kidaha in the Legislative Council: TLC, 14 Nov. 1951; 18 Feb., 27 Aug., 24 Nov. 1952; 1 Oct. 1953; 4 April 1954; 3 Nov. 1955.
[3] TLC, 1 Oct. 1953.

Eight months later Nyerere, appointed temporarily to fill
Kidaha's seat in the Legislative Council while the latter toured
with the East African Royal Commission, took the opportunity
to raise the matter of elections. He asked for 'elections for the
Members representing Dar es Salaam and a panel of names from
the Provinces, from which the Governor should make his appointment.'[1] Though as Kidaha had, he supported a continuing official
majority, his emphasis was different. As he wrote to Marjorie
Nicholson of the Fabian Colonial Bureau after the formation of
TANU:

Most thinking people in Tanganyika believe that time is ripe for a real
constitutional change...but Government, and the majority of Unofficial
Members of the Legislative Council are too obstinate to change their views
...We have been accused of racial politics, of aiming at a policy which is
contrary to the declared policy of the Government; of wanting independence in five years; of starting self-government campaigns...Our
aim is certainly self-government; when to attain it the people of Tanganyika will decide. We are not racial; but I have emphasized that we
must aim at a democratic Tanganyika, and those who fear democracy
need not come or remain in the Territory.[2]

While Nyerere pushed ahead with the formation and organization of TANU and while the political temperature rose, Kidaha
emphasized more frequently the need of the administration to
develop better 'public relations,' to interpret more carefully
to the people its 'intentions and aims':

There is a real need for people to identify themselves with the Central
Government instead of the contrary situation that one observes at
present...The masses of the people are still very gullible and are subject
to all sorts of rumors.[3]

What we need very urgently in the Territory are better public relationships...to sell Government to the people who at present appear to regard
it as being too impersonal and remote...As long as this state of affairs
persists one cannot help feeling that Africans will continue to feel the
administration as being a sort of alien Government.[4]

Eventually, Kidaha found that the problem was deeper than
public relations. He concluded that the doctrine of multi-racialism
'is clearly outmoded.' He criticized the substitute slogan '"non-
racialism" which seems to have stealthily been brought to the

[1] *Ibid.* 25 May 1954.   [2] Nyerere to Nicholson, 15 Sept. 1954, FCBF.
[3] TLC, 17 Nov. 1953.   [4] *Ibid.* 15 May 1956.

field of political acrobatics to replace the unpopular slogan of "multi-racialism".[1] Briefly a member of the administration-fostered United Tanganyika Party, Kidaha resigned in 1956 when it became clear that the party would not declare Tanganyika to be a primarily African country—a position on which Kidaha had insisted since 1945 and a stance which he rightly regarded as a 'precondition to African support.'[2]

By late 1956 Kidaha supported elections on a common roll. In a letter to the Fabian Colonial Bureau he expressed concern that election proposals under consideration were too restrictive of African interests. He noted that Nyerere's 'views on the matter are the same as mine,' he spoke of Nyerere as a 'friend,' 'sincere and a person one should trust,' and said that he shared 'most of Mr. Nyerere's political beliefs.'[3] Kidaha did not join TANU until 1964, but he continued through the 1950s to assist Nyerere in a variety of ways and the relationship between the two men apparently remained friendly. Because of his position, Kidaha was able to supply Nyerere with some information about what was going on inside the government and the multi-racial United Tanganyika Party which opposed TANU. On at least one occasion he was instrumental in arranging a meeting between Governor Twining and Nyerere.[4]

Nyerere must be regarded as having influenced Kidaha considerably, despite Kidaha's conservative inclinations. For the most part, however, whatever similarities of view may have developed, Kidaha lacked a taste for the more activist and nationalistic forms of politics. He seemed to have been uncomfortable with the politically oriented men who gathered around Nyerere in the middle 1950s. Though Nyerere apparently defended Kidaha against some of the latter's more virulent African critics, Kidaha was not respected by nationalist politicians and remained associated with the administration in the minds of most.[5] In the later 1950s the rift grew. For a while just after independence, Kidaha even assumed the mantle of opposition leader for some who found themselves disenchanted with TANU.[6]

[1] Kidaha to Lady Selwyn Clarke, 20 Sept. 1956, FCBF.
[2] Kidaha, interview. Kidaha was one of the original signatories of the manifesto of the United Tanganyika Party (Taylor, pp. 137–8).
[3] Kidaha to Clarke, 20 Sept. 1956, FCBF.
[4] Kidaha, interview.
[5] See Listowel, pp. 237, 244, 279, 287, 299.
[6] See below, pp. 353–7.

3 NEW ELITES AND NEW ASSOCIATIONS

In the post-Second World War years, chiefs in Sukumaland began to lose their monopoly on leadership. African products of mission schools and Swahili-speaking townsmen with a sophistication born of travel, trade, and perhaps a smattering of Koranic education, began to emerge as distinctly non-rural, non-traditional elites. It was not long before younger men with primary school education, together with a few worldly-wise older men in rural areas, began also to think and act for themselves in a manner independent of traditional categories and of native authority structures. Such men as these were to provide the 'transitionals'— the middle level local elite so critically important to the early stages of the development of nationalist organizations.

The Educated African and Local Government

The administration recognized in principle that new elites posed a problem and an opportunity. A territorial conference of Provincial Commissioners considered the issues in 1945. A subsequent secretariat memorandum stated:

> There can be but little doubt that during the years immediately preceding the war a number of factors, amongst which may be included the growth of a semi-educated class and the illiteracy of many Native Authorities, has fostered in the minds of some members of the younger African generation a belief that they were at least the mental equals of some of the chiefs who ruled them and that they themselves were becoming entitled to a share in the general administration of their chiefdoms.

> It may be stated with certainty that this process has been hastened during the war years by the temporary return to their homes of many thousands of African troops on leave and the pending demobilization of the latter demands that the whole question should receive early and serious consideration.

The memorandum observed, however, that:

> It does not appear that there is any general desire on the part of African tribesmen in the Territory to agitate for the removal of their chiefs or for any great divergence from the present system of native administration. They merely feel that the educational level which many of them have achieved entitles them to a greater share than they possess at present in the administration of their country.

Provincial Commissioners were requested, nevertheless, to 'give thought to this problem' with particular attention to the possibility of including 'younger intelligentsia on advisory councils.'[1]

[1] Memorandum on the Problem of Relations Between Native Authorities and the Younger African Generation, 12 May 1945, SMP 33136.

The problem of the place of the educated African in local government became a controversy when, in August 1947, Elspeth Huxley, after a tour of Tanganyika, was quoted in the *Tanganyika Standard:*

Speaking of native administration she said the indirect system in Tanganyika had remained static for twenty years. How to fit in the young educated man had not been solved or even tackled in Tanganyika.[1]

She compared Tanganyika unfavorably with Kenya and Uganda where African majorities were directly or indirectly elected to local councils. In correspondence with the Tanganyika Secretariat, she claimed that in Tanganyika 'the educated element has not been drawn in organically...He may be consulted and coopted on to councils, but there is no real electoral system as yet.' She noted that 'amalgamation' and 'stream-lining' (as with councils in Chaggaland and Sukumaland), however necessary,

do not solve the fundamental problem of how democratic ideas are to be blended with a hereditary system of chieftainship, of how privilege is to be curbed without the collapse of discipline, or, for instance, how the new towns of technicians envisaged by the groundnut planners fit into any system of local government that one can imagine arising out of the rather feudal set-up of the present system of indirect rule.[2]

The government rejoined with vigorous disclaimers to the effect that Mrs Huxley's impressions were 'incorrect,' that in fact 'increasing opportunity was being given to younger Africans of the educated class to sit on councils.'[3] A conference of Provincial Commissioners

considered that there may well be a place for [advanced Africans] as observers or advisors to the non-indigenous institutions of councils of chiefs or headmen. It was desirable as far as possible that Africans should be placed on committees and boards as well as on their own councils, with a view to inculcating ideas of voluntary service and financial responsibility.[4]

In July 1948, however, the Acting Governor stated clearly the limits beyond which the administration was not prepared to go:

It is not, in present circumstances, possible to take special steps for the previous training of Africans for participation in local government...

[1] *Tanganyika Standard*, 11 Aug. 1947.
[2] Huxley to the Chief Secretary, 28 Sept. 1947, SMP 33136.
[3] *Tanganyika Standard*, 11 Aug. 1947. See also correspondence in SMP 33136,
[4] Extract from Minutes of Provincial Commissioners' Conference, June 1948. SMP 33136.

Every effort is, however, made to associate the more intelligent unofficial Africans with local government bodies, e.g. Chiefs, Councils, etc.[1]

That these efforts were not to prove sufficient to provide the answers to the dilemmas so accurately formulated by Mrs Huxley was for the history of the 1950s to prove. The systems of modified native authority councils adopted in Sukumaland and elsewhere eventually brought in 'elected' representatives, but they were often informally designated lieutenants of the chiefs and were rarely 'advanced' or 'educated.' Africans in the latter category were sometimes included in advisory councils in towns and at provincial and county levels; but these bodies were never more than artificial creations which failed entirely to resolve the disparities between town and rural, non-traditional and traditional, educated and uneducated, democratic and feudal.

In 1950 Lord Hailey warned that unless the native authority structures could 'find a place for' and 'engage the interest of' the 'educated and progressive elements of the community' those structures would 'fail to constitute a training ground for the political institutions of the country.' He warned that if they failed, they 'may indeed (if the experience of West Africa is to be repeated in East Africa) run some danger of being popularly decried as obstacles to political advance.'[2] But warnings did not bring solutions. The native authority system—even in modified form—remained remote from the independent interests centered in but not limited to the towns. Eventually to be inspired by the conscious articulation by leaders throughout the continent of the demands of African nationalism, and assisted by insistent international pressures for decolonization, it was these interests—when linked with a more pervasive rural discontent—which were to prove powerful enough to undermine within ten years the entire system of colonial and native administration.

Associations

In Mwanza in 1945—and later in other districts—an informal approach to the problem and the opportunity posed by new African elites resulted in the initiation by a handful of European officers of an interracial group for discussion of a wide variety of topics. The discussion approach, however, held no promise for those desiring real activity. It could in no way substitute for the

[1] Acting Governor to the Secretary of State, 22 July 1948, *ibid*.
[2] Hailey, p. 352.

lack of training for administrative posts of potentially capable Africans, appease an increasingly strong desire for effective representation of the interests of the new elites, or forestall the postwar development of a variety of all-African voluntary associations bent on more radical solutions to fundamental problems. By 1947, in addition to several Asian associations and the European–African discussion group already mentioned, the roster of African associations in Mwanza included six tribal unions, Roman Catholic and Muslim religious associations, a tailors' union (the first and, still by 1950, the only trade union in Tanganyika), a traders' cooperative society, a social–cultural club and the Tanganyika African Association. Night school English instruction of Africans by Africans, the buying of household supplies at local traders' shops, religious observances, social and athletic pursuits and the proximity enforced by shared occupations or neighborhoods—all brought Africans together in the hot-house atmosphere of the new town.

Hodgkin's characterization of the new associations in the new towns of postwar Africa has meaning for Mwanza as well as for the larger, wealthier, and more highly differentiated West African examples with which he was more familiar.

It may be argued that these associations are many of them unstable and short-lived; their aims confused or utopian; their financial basis precarious; their methods sometimes brutal, sometimes ineffective; their discipline feeble; their philosophy incoherent; their leaders frequently corrupt, self-seeking, ignorant, irresponsible, and at war with one another. Precisely the same criticisms were levelled against the popular organizations thrown up by the new towns of early nineteenth-century England. Their importance, however, lies partly in their rich variety, reflecting the range of interests and aspirations of the Africans who created them; partly in the evidence they provide that African vitality— far from being crushed by the squalid surroundings and crude discipline of these colonial towns—has been stirred to new forms of expression. The associations of contemporary Africa are democratic, not in the sense that they can serve as models of democratic organization; but in the older sense that they have been constructed by a *demos* which is slowly discovering, by trial and error, the institutions which it requires in order to live humanly and sociably in the urban world into which it has been thrust.[1]

What was notable, at least in Mwanza, was that the African associations, while clearly sharing to a greater or lesser extent

[1] Thomas Hodgkin, *Nationalism in colonial Africa* (New York: New York University Press, 1957), p. 91.

the characteristics mentioned, seemed to avoid the more disastrous of the alternatives. Though unstable, financially insecure, often feeble and ineffective, the more important of the Mwanza-based associations proved astonishingly durable. These would include the Tanganyika Africa Association, the Sukuma Union, the Mwanza African Traders Cooperative Society and the Lake Province Growers Association. Seldom characterized by brutality, they suffered from less corruption than might have been expected and were relatively free of internecine rivalries. For the most part, too, they were led by the more articulate, responsible and socially concerned Africans rather than by those who were less so.

Discussing the contribution the new associations made to the development of national movements in African countries, Hodgkin argues, once again with applicability to the Sukumaland context:

First, they have made it possible for Africans to recover, within the new urban context, the sense of common purpose which in traditional African society was normally enjoyed through tribal organization. Second, they have given an important minority valuable experience of modern forms of administration—the keeping of minutes and accounts, the techniques of propaganda and diplomacy. In this way they have made it possible for the new urban leadership to acquire a kind of informal professional training—rather in the way that Nonconformist and working-class associations trained the new Labour leadership in nineteenth-century Britain. Third, in periods of political ferment and crisis, these associations provide the cells around which a nation-wide political organization can be constructed.[1]

Urban and Rural Discontents

Though the only urban center in Sukumaland and the third largest town in the entire territory, Mwanza's population numbered no more than 10,000 in 1945. In the fifteen years after the Second World War it more than doubled in size. A polyglot of mixed African tribes constituted a considerable majority numerically, but several thousand Asians and several score Europeans dominated the commercial and administrative affairs of the town. Located at the south end of Lake Victoria at the hub of the Lake Province, Mwanza had been an administrative headquarters since the days of German control and a commercial center after steamer and rail connections linked it to the Kenya railroad in the north, then to the central Tanganyika line in the south. An expanding economic base, better communications and increasing opportunities for education gave rise to a larger salaried African work

[1] *Ibid.* pp. 84–5.

force and to the development of a more sophisticated African elite.

The process was similar, though on a much smaller scale, in Shinyanga, the only other center large enough to be reckoned in official parlance as a township. An administrative outpost built in 1927, Shinyanga became a trading center of some importance after the discovery of diamonds at nearby Mwadui in 1940. Other minor settlements of a few hundred and trading centers of a few score persons dotted the Sukumaland landscape. They appeared especially in the vicinity of district government offices and mines or on the rail line and principal roads.

Primarily a conservative rural area, Sukumaland posed as much of a problem for the politically oriented townsmen of the new associations as for the European administration. Although the struggle for control and power between British administrators and nationalist politicians became in the 1950s a struggle for the countryside and its people, support for the associations in the early postwar period came principally from the towns and a few prominent centers outside the towns. But in Sukumaland, as throughout predominantly rural Tanganyika, political protest, to be widespread and successful, had to be based on rural, not just urban discontent. Associations limited to the towns could not but be weak. The associations' leaders realized this but were only marginally successful in their halting and intermittent attempts to extend the bases of their support into non-urban areas. Nonetheless, their efforts, and the organizational structures they established, in part prepared the way for the more effective political undertakings of a later day.

4   THE TANGANYIKA AFRICAN ASSOCIATION

The Tanganyika African Association (TAA) was founded in Dar es Salaam 'sometime between 1927 and 1929.' Despite some 'modest forays' into politics in the 1930s it remained more 'a social rather than a political organization.' Members were mainly civil servants, teachers and traders with activities centered in Dar es Salaam.[1]

Politically, the local branch of the association was the most important of numerous African-led associations, unions and

---

[1] Ralph A. Austen, 'Notes on the pre-history of TANU,' *Makerere Journal*, No. 9 (1964), p. 23. See also Bennett, *Makerere Journal*, No. 7 (1963), p. 1.

welfare groups which operated in Mwanza in the late 1940s. Frequently dismissed by Africans and Europeans as TANU's mild predecessor, TAA was never in Mwanza reducible to civil servants giving tea parties. Unhampered by tribal, religious or occupational prerequisites to membership, TAA bridged a diversity of parochial interests. From its formation in February 1945 the Mwanza branch concerned itself with the rights, welfare and advancement of both urban and rural Africans. The beginning of African nationalist politics in Mwanza, and therefore in Sukumaland, may fairly be said to have predated by nearly ten years the formation of TANU in 1954.

Mwanza: Beginnings

TAA's first set of office-bearers[1] reflected the composition of Mwanza's postwar African elite. Generally, non-Sukuma, Christian civil servants with secondary-school educations held the positions which required most in reading, writing and financial skills. Muslim towndwellers of little education, but with prestige based on trading, crafts and religious leadership, represented a larger proportion of TAA membership and took the figurehead offices of president and vice-president.[2]

TAA's first president was Amri Mgeni, a respected shop-owner, landlord and teacher of the Koran. However, it was the first secretary, Joseph Chombo, who directed the activities of TAA from 1945 until his civil service transfer from Mwanza in 1948. In Dar es Salaam as a clerk in the Medical Department, he became a member of TAA in 1938. After transfer to Mwanza, he opened the Mwanza branch of TAA in 1945. Chombo is remembered by his contemporaries as an activist who also led the Catholic Association and ran evening adult classes at the Mwanza town school.[3]

The beginnings of the branch in Mwanza were modest. Like

---

[1] TAA to P.C., 20 Apr. 1945, LPF.
[2] Three Sukuma and one well-educated Muslim varied the pattern. Of the three Sukuma officers, one belonged to the poorly educated Muslim town group. The others—a civil servant and a teacher—received middle-school education, one by virtue of his relation to a chiefly family, the other through a close connection to the town mission school. The Sukuma did not attract missionaries, or accept European education, as quickly as did some other tribes in East and Central Africa. As a result, secondary education was a rarity among the Sukuma in 1945.
[3] Interviews: Saidi Ali, 3 Dec. 1964; Joseph Chombo, 28 Nov. 1964; Eustace Kibaja, 30 Nov. 1964; M. I. Kitenge, 27 Jan. 1965.

G

fledgling voluntary associations anywhere, TAA lacked a permanent headquarters and full-time staff. Meetings were held about once a month with an average attendance of some thirty persons. The entrance fee was one shilling with one shilling monthly subscription.[1] Roughly a third of the members were civil servants, the rest a miscellany of traders, clerks, and others employed in the town. Membership may have reached 100 or more by the end of the first year. At meetings social problems and mutual aid and benefit activities were discussed, occasionally with government officials invited, but in general there were 'no very important things at that time.'[2] During 1945 TAA helped in 'supporting the African Night School.'[3] Consulted by the government on social and welfare rules proposed for the town, TAA held special meetings so that the rules could be 'corrected by the members of the African Association.'[4] A TAA request for permission to collect money throughout the township for the African Association's 'Building Fund' (to establish a permanent TAA headquarters) was refused when the Provincial Commissioner ruled that 'only members of the Association may be canvassed.'[5] As yet without links to the countryside or to TAA branches elsewhere in Tanganyika, Mwanza TAA's first year activated few concerns beyond township affairs and the mechanics of running a voluntary association.

At the outset, the administration officially considered TAA a desirable medium for the development and expression of African opinion. The Provincial Commissioner addressed the inaugural meeting of Mwanza TAA in February 1945, and wished the fledgling success. An incident later in the year, however, revealed that misunderstanding was an everpresent possibility. The Provincial Commissioner, apparently suspecting TAA of unauthorized collection of money, asked Isaac Msowoya, a TAA officer who was also a clerk in the provincial office, to investigate. Msowoya, a Nyasa who had served for some years with the Tanganyika Civil Service, reported that meetings of TAA and other groups had

---

[1] Msowoya to P.C. 30 Oct. 1945, LPF. TAA fees varied at different times and in different places. See below, p. 138, and Bennett, *Makerere Journal*, No. 7 (1963), p. 2.
[2] Chombo, interview.
[3] Government Inspector of Schools to TAA, 7 Feb. 1945, MZDF.
[4] Msowoya, to P.C. 30 Oct. 1945. LPF.
[5] Handwritten note by P.C. on a letter from Chombo to P.C., 19 Jan. 1946, MZDF.

taken place in the town, but that as far as he could discover no money had been collected. Unsettled by the incident, Msowoya wrote: 'As now I am aware that Government seem to be against Government employees becoming members [of TAA] I would like to assure that I am deleting my name from this Association.' He nevertheless argued that African government employees throughout Tanganyika 'are conductors of this Association so as to run it smoothly to satisfy Government, otherwise if it were left to the leadership of town people alone, Government would be receiving many unnecessary representations or complaints.'[1]

The Provincial Commissioner assured Msowoya that 'there is no objection at all' to his continued membership in TAA.[2] Clearly, however, TAA depended upon the approbation of the administration and there were limits beyond which that approbation might not extend. In the event of suspicion the Provincial Commissioner was willing to use his clerk as a special investigator. In the event of conflict which might prejudice his government job, the clerk was willing to sever his relationship with TAA. Militant nationalist politics was still some years away.

Issues Defined: A Provincial Conference

In 1946–7 an initial, if ephemeral, political bridge from town to countryside was fashioned in Ukerewe where a local TAA branch undertook 'independent weighing' of African-produced cotton in an effort to obtain fair prices from Asian buyers.[3] By 1947, in addition to Mwanza and Ukerewe, seven other TAA outposts existed in the Lake Province. Because of its size, central location and the prior existence of goverment provincial offices, Mwanza was a natural choice for a provincial TAA headquarters. In early 1947 Mwanza sent Msowoya to Zanzibar for the annual meeting of territorial TAA. On his return Chombo called a provincial conference in Mwanza.

Inspired now by a feeling that the activities of Africans in Mwanza were part of a larger effort of TAA territorially, Chombo wrote to all TAA secretaries with a passion and a sense of identity and direction which marks this—despite the explicit emphasis on education and economic advancement—as the first political manifesto of Mwanza's postwar years:

[1] Msowoya to P.C., 30 Oct. 1945, LPF.
[2] Handwritten note by P.C. on Msowoya's letter of 30 Oct. 1945, LPF.
[3] See below, pp. 88–9.

Let us Africans unite and push forward...Education indeed is the key. It makes no sense for Africans of one part of Africa to progress if those in another part are still sheathed in overwhelming ignorance. And no one else will liberate us from this plight other than we ourselves...You yourselves know the importance of THIS ASSOCIATION AND IF SOME- ONE DOES NOT KNOW EXPLAIN IT WELL TO HIM...TELL HIM IT IS AN ASSOCIATION TO UNITE AFRICANS THAT THEY MAY ACHIEVE MORE IN EDUCATION, TRADE, AGRICULTURE AND ALL THINGS PERTAINING TO TRUE CIVILIZED LIFE FOR THE ENTIRE RACE OF AFRICANS.

Chombo lamented that members had not often enough in the past gathered to discuss and act in unity through TAA, 'the great voice of all we Africans.' Though TAA had the largest membership of any association in the area, he emphasized that TAA's impor- tance was not recognized and respected by many Africans and that TAA was weak because it lacked paid officers and a permanent headquarters.

Chombo hoped also for the sympathy and participation of native authorities. He asked branch leaders of TAA to consult with their chiefs to invite native authorities to attend the conference. Unity with native authorities was indispensable and necessary. The voice of TAA should know no 'boundary' but be that of 'every African.'[1]

Representatives from eight TAA branches stretching from Bukoba to North Mara attended the May conference. Other associations in Mwanza town, including the Sukuma Union, sent representatives. The president, Selemani Panda, called for all Africans to unite through TAA to 'fight for our race.' Chombo, as provincial secretary, set the specific task: 'You yourselves are the African Association, and every one of you must use this meet- ing to consider the best means of ridding ourselves of all the hard- ships which beset Africans.'[2]

Forty-five separate items appeared on the agenda and over thirty were vigorously discussed during the two-day meeting. Here already in embryo were the issues of 1950, of 1953, of 1958: fear, suspicion and resentment of non-Africans who monopolized the marketing of crops and trade and took African land; opposition to specific tax levies combined with dissatisfaction and misunder- standing regarding the use of native authority revenues; opposition

[1] Chombo to 'Honorary Secretaries' of TAA in Biharamulo, Bukoba, Missungwi (in Mwanza District), Musoma, Ngara and Ngudu (in Kwimba District), 25 Apr. 1947, LPF. (orig. Sw.)
[2] Minutes of a Provincial Conference of TAA held in Mwanza, 17–18 May 1947, LPF (orig. Sw.).

to specific natural resources measures combined with growing distrust of administration intentions regarding African well-being and advancement; and dismay at the increasing identification of native authorities with the administration. The demand for self-government was not yet explicit and TAA still hoped to enlist the support of native authorities in the rural areas. Still very much a compilation of grievances, the minutes of the conference were presented to the Provincial Commissioner by African leaders who were assuredly still more suppliants than revolutionaries. As yet the pressure of undesired governmental programs was not sufficiently great, nor African sentiment sufficiently aroused, to galvanize a miscellany of complaints into focused opposition to the colonial system itself.

The Politics of Response

Though exhilarated by the conference, TAA's grander plans for a permanent headquarters, full-time staff, and recruitment of rural Africans appear to have slipped quickly into the background. These were full-time tasks for full-time politicians. Lacking the latter, TAA returned to the more pedestrian role of raising an occasional objection or periodically forwarding a complaint. For its part, the administration cooperated with TAA by notifying it in advance of the visits of important government personnel, by meeting its objections with careful explanation, and by consulting with TAA regarding African appointments to the township authority.

An incident in September 1947 illustrated TAA's strengths and weaknesses in a crisis situation. After receiving news of labor strikes in Dar es Salaam and Tabora, '200 Africans of many occupations' held a mass meeting in Mwanza. They asked Chombo, as provincial secretary of TAA, to urge upon the government their case for wage increases. He did so, asking that the matter be given priority consideration and that a reply be made within the week—failing which, the workers would strike.[1]

Chombo, however, was tactically undercut by the workers who left their jobs the same day. In the face of this calamity, Chombo the following day agreed at the behest of the Provincial Commissioner to arrange a meeting to explain to the strikers the necessity of returning to work before their demands could even be

---

[1] Chombo to P.C., 15 Sept. 1947, MZDF.

considered.[1] By the third day, however, most workers had returned to their jobs, and the administration told Chombo to cancel the meeting.[2] Of sufficient status among township Africans to be an appropriate mediary for both the dissidents and the government, TAA lacked the organizational strength either to discipline the tactics of the former or to resist being used by the latter.

An official account of the incident suggests an unfortunate administrative tendency either to underplay the importance of expressions of dissent or to deal with disturbances purely in terms of law and order. According to the administration's report:

> Rumours gathered strength locally as to a general strike being arranged for Monday 15th September and on that date a handful of Railway employees refused duty at Mwanza Port. The local township 'riff raff' and strong-arm gentlemen took advantage of this fact and having armed themselves with sticks, proceeded to intimidate Government employees and domestic servants. Prompt Police and Administrative action landed most of the ringleaders before the Resident Magistrate within a few hours and as they were all promptly and suitably dealt with under the law the joy was taken out of the proceedings which fizzled out in the afternoon.[3]

This account may well have described some of the events which took place during the week in question; but the clear implication, which was fallacious, was that a handful of riff raff had produced the entire incident. With a scapegoat selected, the administration could indulge its unfortunate penchant for self-congratulation. With certain critical facts omitted (the meeting of 200 workers, the representation by and intermediary role of TAA, the continuation of the strike over a three-day period), no consideration needed to be given to the possibility that legitimate grievances may have existed, that those involved may not all have been undesirable self-seekers, that the government should perhaps have given some attention to underlying causes. The administration compounded this error in subsequent years, a fact which of itself helped bring the time when 'prompt police and administrative action' would no longer suffice.

The administration was solicitous, however, as long as TAA remained 'on good behaviour.' In February 1948 the District

---

[1] Chombo to the *Liwali* of Mwanza, 17 Sept. 1947, MZDF. (Orig. Sw.).
[2] D.C. to Chombo, 17 Sept. 1947, MZDF.
[3] Mwanza District Annual Report, 1947, MZDF.

Commissioner informed TAA that the Chief Secretary to the Tanganyikan government would be visiting the Lake Province in March. TAA leaders requested an interview. Reflecting its preoccupation now with township problems, TAA's memorandum to the Chief Secretary agreed in general on the need for town planning but argued that new zoning laws and housing specifications required such large and expensive structures that Africans would not be able to build according to their wishes and capacities and would, without sympathetic support from the government, be forced to leave the township.[1] In May Provincial Commissioner Hall, while stressing there could be no claim by any Association to be represented as such on the township authority, granted a consultative role for TAA and, in 1949, nominated a TAA-suggested candidate to the authority. In 1950 all three Africans appointed by Provincial Commissioner Rowe were TAA members. With the advent of elections to ward councils and the township authority in 1952, TAA members provided both the majority of candidates and the preponderance of winning candidates.[2]

Even had they wished to, Mwanza's Provincial Commissioners, and later the voters, would have been hard-pressed to find alternative candidates of sufficient education and/or status who were not members of TAA. The Provincial Commissioners, however, could afford indulgence of TAA's special standing among township Africans because TAA as yet posed no direct threat to the administration's preoccupation with rural development and its commitment to the gradual transformation of native authority structures. The administration never consulted TAA with regard to authorities or councils other than those in Mwanza and Shinyanga townships. At the same time, the rule that there would be no representation of associations as such was adhered to without modification in subsequent years.[3]

---

[1] TAA to D.C., 10 Mar. 1948, MZDF.

[2] Africans were first nominated to the Township Authority in 1947: the *Liwali* of Mwanza and Joseph Mzigaba, a translator at the Resident Magistrate's Court and a member of TAA. In 1950, TAA members Paul Bomani, Mzigaba, and Idi Faiz were appointed. In 1952, Mzigaba, Faiz, Moses William, Isaac Munanka, S. E. Mdachi, Henry Chasama, Amiry Maftah, Abedi Kazimoto, and Jeremiah Cleophas—all TAA officers at one time or another—were elected to township ward councils.

[3] In the early 1950s the government turned down requests of the Sukuma Union and the Lake Province Growers Association for representation on the Sukumaland Federal Council. A request by TAA for representation on the proposed county council was also refused.

Shinyanga: A Petition to the United Nations

The Tanganyika African Association in Shinyanga began in 1940 under the leadership of a Bemba artisan and trader, Juma Issa. After four years of Koran studies, Issa took up carpentry in 1911 and worked in the Tabora area until 1925. The government's need for literate Africans brought Issa into the civil service in Mwanza where he served from 1925 to 1929 as accountant, assistant town headman, and *liwali*. Eventually, he resigned his post, but the government persuaded him to serve again during the war as a special police constable in Tabora, then in Shinyanga. At the end of the war he returned to his private building trade, this time in Shinyanga.[1]

Though Issa recalled attending a conference of the Tanganyika African Association at the coast in 1928, it was not until after his arrival in Shinyanga in May 1940 that he became a local TAA leader. As in Mwanza, the beginnings were quite modest. Issa's house served as headquarters; there were few members, and, at best, infrequent meetings. TAA operated a small 'African Association shop' which sold sugar, rice, piece goods, etc. during a time of high prices and shortages caused by the war. Eventually, TAA's membership grew to 92, including about a third from outside the township. Issa himself was president, with Ali Makani, a non-royal *protégé* of Chief Makwaia, as vice-president.[2]

In 1948 Issa and twenty-one other African residents of Shinyanga township presented a lengthy petition 'on behalf of the Shinyanga District' to the first United Nations Visiting Mission to Tanganyika.[3] This was remarkable if one considers that only ten petitions were presented from all of Tanganyika; and of these only three others—from the Dar es Salaam headquarters of TAA, the Chagga Council, and the Bahaya Union—were concerned in any significant way with African aspirations.[4] Though the

---

[1] Issa, interview, 18 Feb. 1965.

[2] Interviews: Issa and Makani, 18 Feb. 1965; Joseph Petro, Nov. 1964.

[3] The petition, dated 20 Aug. 1948, was reproduced in full in United Nations, Trusteeship Council, Official Records (Supplements), *Visiting Mission to Trust Territories in East Africa: Report on Tanganyika* (hereafter cited as UNVM), 1948 (T/218).

[4] The Dar es Salaam headquarters of TAA reported the existence of 39 branches and 1,780 members. Their petition, however, was not as remarkable for political content as the Shinyanga petition. The Dar es Salaam petition dealt with social, economic, educational and labor problems, asking simply for steps toward the education of Africans for self-government (UNVM, 1948, p. 202).

Shinyanga petition did not identify itself as a TAA petition, Issa's name, reflecting his position as president of Shinyanga TAA, appeared at the top of the list of petitioners and all, or almost all, of the signatories were TAA members. Two-thirds of the petitioners were government servants; more than half a dozen tribes were represented.

The Shinyanga petition began with a note of appreciation and 'heart-felt thanks' for 'all the British people have so far done' and an acknowledgment that the British government 'to whom the United Nations have entrusted our care, will do all in its power 'to help us get through the darkness before us.' The petition pleaded eloquently for more education, greater participation of Africans in legislating, administering and governing, a higher standard of living, increased opportunities for African traders in town commerce, full African control of trade in rural areas, higher wages for mine workers and greater share in revenues earned from Tanganyika's mineral wealth. The petitioners asked for 'full freedom in speech...in publications of all sorts and in public life.' Finally, they pleaded for an end to the 'heart-breaking... colour bar...if good social relation and mutual agreement between the different Nationalities [in the territory]...are to be put into practice.'

More than Chombo's passionate appeal for unity, more than the compilation of grievances by the Mwanza provincial TAA conference of 1947, the Shinyanga document set forth keenly and clearly that African advancement required for its accomplishment fundamental changes in the relation between rulers and ruled. The petitioners understood that alleviation of specific grievances would not be sufficient, that an equality in rights, opportunities and status *generally* would be required.

Nor did the Shinyanga document wince at the crux of the matter—the exercise of political power. While acknowledging that changes would take place 'in accordance with the supervision of the British Government,' the petitioners expressed 'thanks and gratitude to the United Nations *for securing us freedom*' (italics mine) and, though not stating explicitly the goal of independence, they pointed unmistakably toward self-government.[1]

Not yet aware that the democracy for which they called would require nothing less than the departure of the colonial rulers, or that Africans themselves might disagree over the means and

[1] Shinyanga petition, UNVM, 1948 (T/218).

structures of enhanced African participation, the Shinyanga group nevertheless posed the fundamental political questions of power, authority, consultation and consent which were to underlie the specific controversies and dominate the political struggles of the 1950s. The Shinyanga petition was a most unusual document in the Tanganyika of 1948. It clearly stated the essential issues between mature colonialism and aggressive nationalism years before nationalism itself had come of age.

As in Mwanza, the administration afforded TAA a consultative role with regard to African appointments to the township authority. TAA-recommended unofficials were sometimes appointed. The president of TAA, Issa, was himself appointed in 1950.

An Appeal to the People

As Chombo and other leaders recognized, the strength of TAA would depend on rural support. In fact, links with the countryside remained more talked about than achieved during Chombo's tenure. In mid-1948, however, TAA's vice-president, Selemani Mahugi, made a written plea for wider support in a lengthy letter addressed to all citizens of Mwanza District and distributed through the chiefs. Himself an uneducated Sukuma tailor originally from rural Nassa, Mahugi's homespun combination of exhortation, argument, wit, analogy and story-telling may have held more attraction for the ordinary Sukuma than appeals from the more sophisticated Chombo.

Mahugi cited a saying of African elders: 'One stick is easy to break, but many sticks bound together are not easily broken.' He emphasized that the government approved of TAA and its purposes, and that TAA was the logical instrument of the unity he envisaged.

While Mahugi at times interpreted the relation between colonial rulers and African ruled in somewhat paternalistic terms, his was nevertheless a forward-looking, political message:

Many will say that we are only black people...we will accomplish nothing even if we try...

It is by our own efforts only that we will progress...Quick discouragement yields nothing, but persistence and hard work reap reward.

Since the war, wise Africans have established TAA branches in almost all the large towns of Tanganyika and Zanzibar. In April leaders met in Dodoma to further build and strengthen TAA. Every African is a child of TAA; there is no division of tribe or religion. TAA is to build unity, to speak out about our problems, to seek our rights. TAA is not for two days only or for two years. Those who come after us, being more knowledgeable, will build TAA better than we. Do not be discouraged even if the road is long and difficult. Let us begin now to fashion a path for our children.[1]

The letter was one of TAA's earliest attempts to interpret *directly* to rural people the facts about and purposes of TAA as an organization.

5 THE SUKUMA UNION

Sukuma associations existed in some form between the wars, if not before, in parts of Tanganyika, Kenya and Zanzibar. Separated from their homeland because of trade, travel, military service or other employment—and from the traditional tribal culture by education and religious differences—Sukuma *'emigrés'* joined with their fellows in associations for maintaining cultural contact and mutual aid.[2] Even in Mwanza township, a Sukuma Union was attempted some years before the end of the Second World War, but it failed to survive for reasons somewhat obscurely laid to 'ill-feeling' and 'obstructions.'[3] One may surmise that, as with so many ephemeral African voluntary associations, it disappeared for want of leadership, membership, funds or sustaining purpose.

Beginnings

The founding meeting of the post-Second World War Sukuma Union brought together eighteen Sukuma from Mwanza on 12 December, 1945. Moses William, a teacher–clerk of the township mission school who had been elected a secretary of TAA at its formation nine months before, acted as secretary for the first Sukuma Union meeting. The minutes of the meeting recorded the names of all those present 'so that we will remember them always, because they have brought great benefit to all Sukuma people.'[4] The discussion pointed out that Sukuma lived in Mwanza without knowing or caring about each other. Often they spoke Swahili or other languages, and even pretended to be from

[1] Mahugi to 'All citizens' of Mwanza, 5 June 1948, MZDF. (Orig. Sw.).
[2] Interviews: Paul Bomani, 4 Feb. 1965; Fabian Ngalaiswa, 20 Feb. 1965.
[3] Minutes of a meeting of the Sukuma Union (hereafter cited as SU), 29 Jan. 1945, Sukuma Union files (hereafter cited as SUF), privately held, Mwanza, Tanzania. (All minutes originally in Swahili unless otherwise noted.)
[4] Minutes of SU meeting, 12 Dec. 1945, SUF.

foreign parts. The purpose of the new Union was to encourage
Sukuma to care for each other and to help each other with life's
difficulties: old age, sickness, death and accidents.

One of the principal founders, Fabian Ngalaiswa, a teacher at
Tabora School home on leave, wrote to the District Commissioner
elaborating a somewhat more ambitious scheme. Ngalaiswa
envisaged an association which would enlist the support of the
chiefs and attract Sukuma in the rural areas as well as in the
township. Dues would be graduated according to ability to pay.
A special voluntary monthly collection, modelled on wartime
collections which had the administrative help of District Commissioners, would provide a development fund for hospitals and
schools. Other aims included preservation of Sukuma customs,
of the Sukuma language and acquainting the government with
Sukuma problems. A branch of the association would be for
women to bring their particular problems for consideration.
Ngalaiswa asked that the District Commissioner assist the new
association by informing the chiefs 'so that all Sukuma' may join.[1]

The District Commissioner noted to his superior that the
scheme would 'provide some means of expression to the inarticu-
late peasant (for whom it is intended especially to cater), whose
opinions thus expressed could then be represented to the council
of chiefs in federation.' He pointed out, however, that the scheme
might 'duplicate the intentions of Government as expressed in
the proposed Sukumaland Federation' and that the collection of
money might be viewed as 'just another tax,' or even as one to
which contributors might give 'precedence over the official tax.'[2]
When, fearful of the 'disasterous' implications of the growth of
an independent authority outside the already weak native authority
system, the Provincial Commissioner forbade collection of
funds, Ngalaiswa returned to his teaching post at Tabora and the
first year of the new Sukuma Union's life was directed by men
with less imaginative goals in mind.

The Union's first general meeting was held in late December.
A local township carpenter, Kipande Kishiba, was elected presi-
dent. The secretary–treasurer of the Mwanza native treasury, John
Lugaila, became treasurer. The key post of secretary went to
Moses William. The Union divided Mwanza township into
seventeen sections or wards and appointed headmen and

[1] Ngalaiswa to D.C., 12 Dec. 1945, LPF. (Orig. Sw.).
[2] D.C. to P.C., 12 Dec. 1945, LPF.

headwomen to oversee the activities of the Union in their own localities. General meetings were to be convened once a month; meetings of the officers, twice a month. The entrance fee was one shilling with monthly dues set at one shilling for men and a half shilling for women.[1]

Mutual Aid

In January 1946 the Union outlined its policy on the mutual aid matters which were to absorb a major portion of its time and energy in the first year of its existence. A February meeting was the occasion for the collection of dues from new members. President Kishiba expatiated on the theme of cooperation, arguing that 'unity is strength' and that the Union 'even if it does not profit us, it will profit our children and grandchildren.'[2]

Monthly general meetings and bi-weekly committee meetings were held more or less regularly throughout 1946. Two officers attended a meeting of TAA in March. For the most part, however, the Union was absorbed in its own affairs. Every request for assistance—in cases of death, sickness, accident, fire, etc.—involved a determination by the officers of its merit, then a collection of contributions. The system seemed to work reasonably well, but those whose requests were denied were inevitably disenchanted. To others it may have seemed that the entrance fee, monthly dues and special contributions required more input than they, as individuals, were likely to receive in benefits.

Consequently, monthly dues were reduced and fines were instituted for absence or tardiness at meetings. President Kishiba directed headmen and 'headwomen' to hold meetings for propaganda and recruiting work because 'many people do not yet know that there is a Sukuma Union here in town.'[3] But attendance lagged and financial problems increased.

At the start of 1947, plans for a grand public celebration kindled new enthusiasm but it was vitiated when lack of funds required cancellation of the project. The possibility of opening a cooperative shop also absorbed the attentions of the Union. Fabian Ngalaiswa, who was now in Mwanza and again active in the Union, pointed out that the Chagga and the Haya had improved themselves by

[1] Minutes of SU meetings, 12 Dec. 1945; 12, 19, 26 Jan., and 2, 16 Feb. 1946, SUF. Information for the remainder of this chapter was obtained from the minutes of these and subsequent SU meetings. Only quoted material will be specifically cited.
[2] Minutes of SU meeting, 2 Feb. 1946, SUF.   [3] *Ibid.* 23 Feb. 1946.

capitalizing on a local crop, coffee. Rather than engaging in competition with Asian shops by selling miscellaneous products, Ngalaiswa recommended that it would be best in Mwanza to concentrate entirely on its local product, fish. He undertook to arrange with the Mwanza African Traders Cooperative Society to sell fish through them to a company in Uganda. However, the Uganda concern would not pay the price asked and no motorboats were available in Mwanza to make the deliveries, so this proposal, too, never materialized.

An interesting attempt at what one might call pan-tribal provincialism was made under the new activist leadership of Ngalaiswa and Moses William who again assumed the Union's top posts in late 1947. Leaders of the Union met with leaders of the local Haya, Kerewe and Zinza tribal associations to form a new association to coordinate representation of the interests of all the tribes of the province. Two months later, however, after some disagreements between the Haya secretary and Sukuma members of the new body, the Union decided not to cooperate with the new Lake Province Local Tribes Union, but to concentrate entirely on Sukuma Union affairs. Like the Tanganyika African Association, the Union became involved in the discussion of town planning and zoning problems in 1947 and 1948, but little of substance resulted from Union representations to the administration's township executive officer. In any case, the Union had virtually disintegrated, with only a couple of meetings to its credit in 1948. It became entirely moribund in 1949 but was to be reopened under new leadership in 1950.

Frustrations and Failure

With the single exception of its brief participation in the abortive Lake Province Local Tribes Union, the Sukuma Union in this first phase of its postwar history concerned itself entirely with the affairs of Sukuma residents of Mwanza township. Its interests were most narrow and its membership apparently highest in its first year, 1946. With eight officers and some sixty ward leaders providing the nucleus of the Union, total dues-paying membership probably reached well over a hundred. The Union and its membership were concerned entirely with the doctrine of cooperation and the practicalities of mutual aid. The Union was, in fact, an attempt to re-create in the town context a sense of tribal community and a network of communal obligations. It sought to provide some of the services for town-locked individuals which they would have enjoyed had they lived in traditional rural communities. By its very nature, however, a heterogeneous town society encouraged the breakdown of old loyalties and the formation of new social alignments based on geographical proximity, religious ties, occupational commitments and a variety of extra-curricular interests. This, plus logistical problems which mutual aid schemes encountered in the town situation and the monetary outlays which alone could make assistance to individuals meaningful in an urban context, combined to make the obstacles to success formidable indeed.

When people saw that they were likely to get less than they gave, interest flagged and little more than a hard core of officers and a handful of headmen remained active. The only solution to the withering away of the Union appeared to be higher dues or special fund-raising schemes—first for a public celebration, then for the formation of a Sukuma Union shop, then for a fish co-operative society. All failed just as repeated attempts to expand membership and keep current the payment of monthly dues had failed. When attendance at any Union meeting involved the assessment of fees, dues, and special contributions (which made it more expensive to belong to the Union, for example, than to TAA), it was not surprising that people demurred, then stayed away altogether. The Union failed even to foster the Sukuma language—one of its original aims. From the outset, minutes were kept in Swahili and Ngalaiswa himself noted that 'the time for writing in our own language has not yet arrived.'[1]

On the other hand, the hard core were committed, persistent, generous of their time and money and at times imaginative. It should be appreciated that they began and continued literally 'from scratch.' Meetings were held in people's homes and most of the office supplies were donated—a pen, a bottle of ink, ten sheets of lined paper, five sheets of carbon paper, a ruler, a file book, etc. The care, precision and fidelity with which the minutes were kept and notations made is worthy of admiration. What few funds the Union had were kept at the Roman Catholic town mission so that they would be available at any hour. This seemed more important to the officers than earning interest at the bank where the money would have been less readily available.

In the final analysis, however, the efforts of the small core of

[1] Minutes of SU meeting, n.d.

leaders were for naught. They could not overcome the economic and sociological factors in the town which tended to undermine the success of an enterprise whose chief characteristic was an appeal to traditional tribal values. Nor did they yet have a message for rural Sukuma.

4

Traders, Cotton Cooperatives and Politics

In the period after the Second World War cotton became the principal cash crop of Sukumaland and one of the primary products of the Tanganyikan economy. From small beginnings during the years of German administration, cotton output, less than 3,000 bales in 1922, rose gradually to 25,000 bales by 1948 and 38,000 bales by 1953. After the formation of cotton cooperative societies, production leaped to over 100,000 bales in 1955, to 150,000 bales in 1957 and to 235,000 bales in 1963. The number of cotton cooperative primary societies increased from 38 in 1953 to 450 in 1963. Membership in the early 1960s approached 200,000 growers. Primary societies grouped themselves into 19 unions which united in 1955 to form the massive Victoria Federation of Cooperative Unions, the largest African-owned and -operated cooperative organization on the continent and the single largest enterprise in the Tanganyikan economy.[1]

Arising out of discontent with the Asian-controlled monopoly buying system, which both exploited the grower by legal means and cheated him through corrupt and illegal methods, the cooperatives had captured 13 per cent of the total crop by 1953,

[1] Statistics from: Minutes of a meeting held to consider methods whereby the present system of cotton marketing might be improved, 11 Jan. 1949, MZDF; Draft speech to be delivered by Mr C. K. Patel (President) at the Lake Province Ginners' Association's party on 24 Nov. 1955; LPF; 'Cooperative movement in the Lake Region, Tanganyika, East Africa' (Cooperative Department, Mwanza, 1963), p. 1 and Appendix A (mimeographed). I am indebted to Margarete Paulus of the University of Cologne, Warren J. Roth of the Maryknoll Seminary, Glen Ellyn, Illinois, and Peter McLoughlin for general information on the cooperative movement in Sukumaland. A. Mbelwa, Regional Cooperative Officer, Mwanza, and Gavin Green, of the Ministry of Commerce and Cooperatives, Dar es Salaam, were most helpful in personal interviews.

For an informative study of, *inter alia*, cooperatives in Sukumaland and the Lake Province, see Margarete Paulus, *Das Genossenschaftswesen in Tanganyika und Uganda: Möglichkeiten and Aufgaben* (Berlin: Springerverlag, 1967). Paulus discusses cooperatives with attention to the political context within which they operate.

60 per cent by 1956 and 100 per cent after 1959. In 1956 the Victoria Federation opened its first ginnery, completed a second in 1958 and opened four more in 1960. After 1962 the Federation launched a program to buy out privately owned Asian ginneries. By 1965 it ginned about 65 per cent of the total crop. In every year since 1959 African growers have received in excess of twenty million dollars for their seed cotton crop.[1]

The rise of the cooperative movement in Sukumaland (and in neighboring Ukerewe and Musoma) must be understood in political as well as economic terms. In the years immediately following the war, economic and political grievances were not clearly distinguishable. The proto-political associations—TAA and the Sukuma Union—first interested themselves in the general welfare and advancement of Africans rather than in clearly defined political objectives such as greater African representation or self-government. Their specific complaints were often economic.

The cooperative movement, on the other hand, found that most economic issues had political overtones. The economic dominance of Asians and their exploitation of the African grower provided the starting point. Developing 'emotional, national and racial pressures'[2] coincided with the movement's attempt to secure administration approval for its activities. In the years before 1954, the cooperatives, like TAA and the Sukuma Union, became a forum for the airing of political grievances. When the government decided to move decisively against the political associations in 1954, it forced the cooperatives to insulate themselves from politics. The move succeeded partly because Nyerere, the president of TAA (and subsequently of TANU), and Paul Bomani, the leader of the cooperatives, decided then to accept the tactical and strategic value of a distinction between economic and political activity. But Bomani, with his various cooperative schemes, had already led the penetration of the rural reas by organizers in the early 1950s. The groundwork he laid in 1951 and 1952 hastened the impact of TAA and the Sukuma Union outside the towns in 1953 and 1954. As George Bennett has noted, 'politics, by definition the occupation of city-dwellers, needed, in the great spaces of Tanganyika and the slight growth of its towns, contact

---

[1] 'Victoria Federation of Cooperative Unions Limited' (Victoria Federation, Mwanza, 20 Aug. 1964), pp. 1–5 (mimeographed).
[2] 'Cooperative movement,' p. 1.

with the countryside.'[1] In Sukumaland that contact came first through the cooperatives.[2]

I BOMANI AND THE MWANZA AFRICAN TRADERS

Beginnings

Before the end of the war, African traders in Mwanza, with the assistance of the government, joined to form the Mwanza African Traders Cooperative Society. It was the beginning of the cooperative movement in Sukumaland. Originally designed to reduce costs under war and postwar conditions of scarcity and economic control of retail prices, the society benefited African traders who were hard-pressed to compete against their more affluent Asian counterparts. Though by 1946 the Registrar of Cooperative Societies was skeptical of its possibilities for continuing success, the Mwanza administration reported that channeling the rice quota through the Traders eliminated all complaints from consumers. 'In addition supplies of cassava, millet, sugar and oils, and 5 per cent of piece goods have been given to the cooperative society and it is apparently the most popular shop in the town, for African consumers allege that it is about the only shop in which they can be sure that they will be charged the correct prices.' Critical of Asian intransigence, the administration decided to assist the African traders:

Despite statements in newspapers by Indian leaders of their great desire and hope to promote both welfare and commerce among Africans, each time the African cooperative society is given a very small share in the available trade the Indian merchants, without exceptions, raise a howl of protest...It is intended to start slowly to increase the African share in trade despite the protests of the Indians.[3]

In 1947 Paul Bomani, a young Sukuma hired as treasurer-accountant, discovered a shortage of stock and loss of funds. He called in all receipts, exposing the forgeries of the acting secretary of the Traders, who was then jailed. Bomani earned the plaudits and respect both of the traders and of the provincial administration. Idi Faiz, a clerk in the provincial administration and a

---

[1] Bennett, *Makerere Journal*, No. 7 (1963), p. 1.
[2] However, a branch of TAA was active in Nassa and adjacent rural areas as early as 1949. See below, pp. 113–22.
[3] Mwanza District Annual Report, 1946, MZDF.

84 *The Beginnings of Indigenous Politics*

TAA leader, became the new secretary. He remained until 1949 when Bomani acceded to the top post.[1]

Despite a lack of capital, the Traders succeeded in re-establishing a sound financial position and under the leadership of Bomani and Faiz, memberships increased to 95 by 1950.[2] From the outset Sukuma and non-Sukuma had joined the society, but prior to Bomani's arrival leadership had tended to devolve on the more sophisticated and educated non-Sukuma such as Isaac Msowoya, who had been the Traders' first manager, or Faiz. With Bomani's elevation to the post of secretary in 1949, more Sukuma traders from outside the town were attracted into membership. A second Sukuma, Francis Bujimu, took the post of assistant secretary. Within three years the Traders extended their concerns to the marketing of native produce. Ultimately, Bomani concentrated his attention on problems of cotton marketing where, it was felt, African producers were most flagrantly exploited by Asian middlemen.[3]

Paul Bomani

The story of Bomani's meteoric rise to a position of national power and prominence is pre-eminent among Sukuma success stories. Only Chief Kidaha Makwaia and Dr Wilbert Chagula, now Principal of the University College, Dar es Salaam, have career histories which approach Bomani's.[4]

Bomani's father Lazaro—who played an important role himself in the history of the cooperatives and of TAA—had attended a Seventh-day Adventist mission school in Maswa, and for more than twenty years taught and preached at schools and missions from Ikizu in Musoma District to Kwimba in Sukumaland.

[1] Paul Bomani, interview, 4 Feb. 1965; Mwanza District Annual Report, 1947, MZDF.
[2] Mwanza District Annual Report, 1950, MZDF.
[3] Interviews: Bomani; Bujimu, 21 Dec. 1964. Bujimu, a graduate of the White Fathers' Seminary at Nyegezi outside Mwanza, gave up plans for the priesthood to apply for the Traders' post. In subsequent years he went on to high positions with the Lake Province Growers Association, the Victoria Federation, and the Mwanza District Council.
[4] Other remarkable Sukuma include: Mark D. Bomani, now Attorney-General of Tanzania; Peter C. Walwa, who has served as Junior Minister in the Ministry of External Affairs and as a Regional Commissioner; Chief Charles Masanja, of Nera, who has served as Principal Assistant Secretary for Regional Administration in the Office of the President; and Mbuta Milando, who has served as an Area Commissioner and as Private Secretary to President Nyerere.

Born at Ikizu in 1925, Paul attended primary and middle school there, then completed a one-year teacher training course. In 1944 he desired to continue his education at Tabora Secondary School, but the Seventh-day Adventists wanted him to follow his father's foot-steps as teacher and pastor.

Both Paul and his father wanted him to continue at Tabora. His admission, however, was apparently blocked by the Seventh-day Adventist pastor at Ikizu. The Bomanis believe he wrote directly to the Tabora Headmaster and to the Education Department in Dar es Salaam to intervene. Paul made application to other schools, received the support of teachers at Bwiru Government School outside Mwanza for a special memorandum to the Director of Education, but it was all for naught. The elder Bomani angrily resigned his position with the Adventists. In 1945 he took a job as storekeeper in charge of provisions at the Mwadui diamond mine in Shinyanga and took Paul with him as clerk at the company store.

After the shake up in the leadership of the Mwanza African Traders Cooperative Society in 1947, the society called Paul from Mwadui to assume the post of treasurer–accountant. Members of the society from the progressive Nassa area—where the Bomanis were widely known—felt they could use Paul's acquired skills as a clerk in the Traders' Mwanza office. The committee of the society, under the chairmanship of Kasim Kisesa (a Manyema Muslim trader in Mwanza town), agreed to offer Paul the vacant post.[1]

2 THE COOPERATIVE MOVEMENT

Bomani's earliest attempts to extend the Traders' activities beyond the wholesale supply of piecegoods and household items to retail traders met with failure. In 1949 he cooperated with a Nassa branch of TAA to appeal for an option on the supply of emergency foodstuffs to the Nassa area in time of famine. In 1950 he made attempts to enter the sisal market at the time of a sisal boom. The following year, in cooperation with a similar traders' coopera- tive society based in Maswa,[2] he presented to the Sukumaland

[1] Interviews: Paul Bomani; Lazaro Bomani, Sept. 1964.
[2] The Maswa African Traders Cooperative Society was founded in late 1946. By the end of 1947 it listed more than sixty members, and by the end of 1949 seventy-five members. Operating on the same principles as the Mwanza group, it never became as active or as influential and eventually disintegrated as a result of desuetude and financial insolvency. Maswa District files (here- after cited as MADF).

Federal Council a request for a sisal buying monopoly for the two societies. As late as 1952, Bomani contracted on behalf of the Traders to supply a thousand bags of sunflower seed to a European concern, but he succeeded in filling only half the order.[1] By 1952, however, the energies of Bomani and of other leading traders had shifted almost exclusively to cotton. Other experiments had failed because Asian competitors were better equipped and they had the backing of the government for reasons of alleged efficiency and skill. With cotton, however, Africans had the force of numbers, a prime crop, and the possibility of sustained effort on one problem through time—advantages which had been lacking in the earlier attempts with emergency food provisions, sisal and sunflower seeds.

With cotton, too, the government, as well as African leaders and farmers, knew that Africans were being systematically cheated by unscrupulous Asians. The unsalaried Asian buyer, who received a commission of something like one shilling and a half per hundred pounds of seed cotton, had been long accustomed to cheating the grower to make his profit. This corrupt system pitted the wits of the buyer against the illiterate grower. One government source estimated that growers were defrauded at a consistent average of 15 per cent of the value of their crop.[2] The business was so lucrative that buyers paid ginners as much as 10,000 to 12,000 shillings for a purchasing option! The buyers were adept at such sharp practices as hiding the scale reading from the grower, short-weighting, taking the benefit of surplus fractions of a pound, or deducting too much for the weight of the container.[3] It is not surprising that African growers eventually became anxious to assure a fair return for their year of labor in the fields.

Approach to Producers

Bomani's first initiative in the direction of producers' cooperatives came in late 1950. In December he and the chairman of the Mwanza African Traders, Kisesa, held meetings in Bukumbi chiefdom in Mwanza District and on Ukerewe island to the north of Mwanza. After one unsuccessful trip to Bukumbi, Bomani subsequently arranged in advance with the respective chiefs,

[1] United Africa Company, Ltd. to the District Cooperative Officer, 10 Dec. 1952, MZDF.
[2] Gavin Green, interview, 13 Nov. 1964.
[3] Interviews: Green; Justin Mecer-Wright, 21 Feb. 1964.

taking care to explain to them the purposes of the proposed organization. In return he received the full support of both chiefs. They arranged for the Traders delegation to address public meetings, and they spoke on behalf of Bomani's proposals.

In Bukumbi the people were Sukuma, and Bomani himself addressed them in the Sukuma language. In Ukerewe, where the language was foreign to him, a Kerewe-speaking trader spoke on his behalf. Addressing the people, Bomani or his representative started with the proposition:

I think every one will agree when I say that the farmer's biggest problems and gravest doubts arise at the time of selling his produce because being cheated is a common thing in this land.

He argued that this state of affairs did not exist everywhere, that 'it is only we who are harassed because many of us do not know how to read...and to handle figures.' He pointed out that more schools were needed, but that this required money. Money, in turn, came only from the sale of crops:

If our crops do not bring a fair price, when *will* we get money enough to build our schools?...At present there is only one way...'UNITY.'

He emphasized that coffee cooperatives had helped the Haya and the Chagga to advance and that their example should be emulated. The purpose of a cooperative organization, he explained, was to enrich the members themselves by eliminating cheating by buyers, getting a fair market price for crops and distributing second payments from surplus funds after the year's expenses had been met. Not concentrating yet entirely on cotton, Bomani spoke about crops in general in Bukumbi and about rice in particular in Ukerewe.

At the 1950 Bukumbi meeting, the deputy chief, Otto Richard, noted that earlier attempts with a sort of cooperative society had foundered but that 'today is our chance to launch our organization with ease due to the assistance of these gentlemen.' The meeting agreed: 'We want unity; we are tired of doing our work for the [profit of] Asians.' The meeting decided that entrance fees of one or two shillings would be insufficient but delayed collections until another time.[1]

In Ukerewe in answer to questions about transportation and financing, Bomani proposed buying trucks and stores from

---

[1] Minutes of the First Meeting of Growers—Bukumbi, 7 Dec. 1950, MZDF. (Orig. Sw.).

subscription fees, registering the society with the Cooperative Department, and carefully administering funds from a bank in Mwanza. The meeting unanimously endorsed Bomani's proposals and the chief of Ukerewe closed the meeting with the words:

> If our country be compared with those of others, you will note that we are better off than many of our neighbors. Therefore let us not be ignorant. There are many profitable possibilities in our country such as this union of farmers, health and cleanliness, and good farming. Let us not try to oppose such things because it is these indeed which will improve our country.[1]

Independent Weighers

While Bomani's extension of the interests of the Mwanza African Traders into the realm of produce marketing eventually provided the necessary leadership for the growth of cotton cooperative societies and the formation of the Lake Province Growers Association, the history of the 'independent weigher' and, subsequently, of village controlled weighing checks on the cotton buyers, provided an equally essential touchstone for the successful inauguration of the cooperative movement. As early as 1946 an official Agriculture Department report stated: 'The African considered he was being "done down" and many were desirous of obtaining for themselves scales and ready reckoners in order to check the weights and cash received.'[2]

In August 1946 a small Ukerewe branch of TAA, led by Mustafa Mabenga (a Kerewe farmer who later became a principal architect of the Victoria Federation of Cooperative Unions), sought to formalize an arrangement whereby TAA members could oversee the weighing of their own cotton. The senior agricultural officer in Mwanza, N. V. Rounce, refused the request but suggested any complaint of improper weighing could be reported for investigation.[3] In July 1947, however, instead of checking the scales of the buyer as he weighed the cotton, TAA decided to provide separate scales of its own to weigh each member's cotton *before* it was taken to the buyer, thereby providing an independent verification.[4]

This system of independent weighing worked reasonably well

---

[1] Minutes of the First Meeting of Rice Growers—Ukerewe, 30 Dec. 1950, MZDF. (Orig. Sw.).
[2] Mwanza District Annual Report, 1946, MZDF.
[3] TAA to Rounce, 23 Aug.; Rounce to TAA, 29 Aug. 1946, MZDF.
[4] TAA to the Regent of Ukerewe, 19 July 1947, MZDF. (Orig. Sw.).

with TAA's weighers handling more than 200,000 pounds of seed cotton in 1967.[1] The task of servicing all growers was beyond their capabilities, however, so TAA encouraged individuals to register with the government as independent weighers, who then charged a small fee, usually –/05 per load.[2] The system spread from Ukerewe, or developed independently, first in the Mwanza chiefdom across the Speke Gulf and then beyond.

As had been the case in Ukerewe, problems inevitably resulted. Buyers developed new types of fraudulent practice, and often buyer and grower haggled over the exact weights

for three hours or more with hundreds of people waiting. Then when the last hours of the day came, all would sell at the buyer's prices just to get home for something to eat. Still another trick was for the Asian buyers to close down completely and thus force the people to take their cotton and go home or to sleep out in the open with the cotton until the next day.[3]

With an unusually large crop in 1948 delays, congestion, cheating and conflict rose to the point where 'irritable and unmanageable' growers on occasion pushed down the flimsy metal storehouses, stole cash from the buyers, and refused to 'obey orders of Agricultural Staff.'[4]

In the following years village groups bought or rented scales, appointed their own watch-dog committees, and reserved certain market days for cotton from designated villages. The village movement was especially strong in Nassa where a high proportion of primary-school-educated farmers and traders gave a progressive tone to the community.

Formation of the Lake Province Growers Association

Bomani did not capitalize on his initial trips to Bukumbi and Ukerewe and on the nascent village organizations in Bukumbi and Nassa until 1952. By early 1952, however, he decided that the village weighing system was inadequate to meet the needs of the

[1] This probably included also the cotton of non-members, who may have paid a small fee.
[2] The East African shilling—equivalent in value to the English shilling—was divided into 100 cents. Thus, one-twentieth of a shilling, or five East African cents, would be written: –/05.
[3] Paul Bomani in an interview with the Rev. Warren J. Roth, 1962. I am indebted to Father Roth for making available to me the notes from his interview.
[4] Minutes of a meeting held to consider methods whereby the present system of cotton marketing might be improved, 11 Jan. 1949, MZDF.

growers. He raised funds in Nassa sufficient for a trip to Uganda for himself and two Nassa leaders, Ndaki Italicha, an elder, and Stephano Sanja, who had originated the Nassa branch of TAA in 1949.[1] The three visited the headquarters of African-operated cotton cooperatives in Uganda, and Bomani returned to Mwanza in February determined to concentrate his efforts on cotton producers' cooperatives.

Also at the beginning of 1952, Bomani had been nominated by Provincial Commissioner Rowe to a seat on the Lake Province Council. Active in township affairs and reasonably proficient in the English language, Bomani was a natural selection. Returning from Uganda in time for the February meeting of the council, Bomani used this as a forum to press on the administration his interest in cooperatives and the need for a cooperative officer to be posted to Mwanza if this were to be—as the administration insisted—a necessary prerequisite to the commencement of cooperative organization. The administration agreed that a cooperative officer would be desirable, but some officials doubted that producers' cooperatives would work. Others wanted evidence that the farmers themselves wanted the societies. In any case, no sense of urgency on the matter seems to have developed until after Bomani began in earnest to organize.

In March Bomani toured various parts of Sukumaland to build support for the cooperative idea. His father, Lazaro (by then a trader in Magu), lent Paul his Chevrolet truck and the two, from their own pockets, covered the expenses of the trip. Bomani wrote in advance to native authorities, traders, school teachers, pastors and outstanding farmers asking people to come to the meetings. Receptions varied. In Magu he found no support. In Nassa where Italicha had spread the word, some two hundred persons appeared and the meeting was 'a tremendous success.' Bomani collected two shilling entrance fees and shares at ten shillings each. A local committee was selected. Bomani warmed to his theme, arguing that cotton buyers became rich in three months (the length of the cotton buying season) while the growers worked a whole year and remained poor. He pointed to the success of the Haya and Chagga in enriching and elevating themselves through coffee cooperatives. He argued that if the Ugandans could do it with cotton, then so could the cotton growers of Tanganyika.

---

[1] Paul Bomani, interview. For details on Nassa TAA, see below, pp. 113–22.

The Nassa meeting may be considered the founding of the first cotton cooperative society. Official registration by the Cooperative Department was more than a year away; but it would not have come then if Bomani had not made his beginnings when he did. From Nassa he moved on to Ntuzu in Maswa where the meeting was also a success. The powerful chief of Ntuzu, Ndaturu, himself joined the society; he gave it unstinting support because he too was angered by Asian buyers' treatment of growers. At neighboring Itilima, traders supported the idea of the cooperative, but there was little support initially from farmers. Itilima was to become, though, a cooperative stronghold by 1953. At Bukumbi and Ukerewe, where Bomani had held meetings in 1950, he again received the support of the local authorities. Ukerewe, in fact, had 'the most enthusiastic crowd of all.' In Geita, which Bomani had visited on several occasions in late 1951 on behalf of the Sukuma Union, he also received support though conflict was to develop with a strong, independently initiated cooperative movement in Buchosa.[1]

In early April Bomani received unexpected assistance from the government: he was asked by the Chief Secretary to attend a meeting in Dar es Salaam of the Lint and Seed Marketing Board for discussion of cotton prices. Bomani wrote to supporters in Bukumbi asking them to continue organizational work during his absence. He indicated a hope that his representations on prices might achieve positive results and that, on his return, 'we will call a general meeting to gather together all [cooperative society] representatives.'[2] Back in Mwanza, Bomani wrote his supporters in Nassa, Masanza I, Ntuzu, Ukerewe, Bukumbi and Buchosa. On 29 and 30 April the first meeting of the Lake Province Growers Association convened in Mwanza. In addition to reports on Bomani's March–April tour of Sukumaland and his trip to Dar es Salaam, the agenda included the formation of new local cooperative societies, consolidation of funds and membership lists, discussion of the uniting of all the individual societies into one body (which was effected with the formation of the Growers Association), preparation of by-laws, determination of organizational procedures and selection of secretaries and committees.[3]

---

[1] Bomani, interview with Roth.
[2] Bomani to Bukumbi members, 25 Mar. 1952, MZDF. (Orig. Sw.).
[3] Bomani to all cooperative society representatives, 21 Apr. 1952, MZDF.

3   NEGOTIATIONS WITH THE ADMINISTRATION

Aware of the ground swell for cooperatives then developing in Bukumbi, a far-sighted District Commissioner, K. B. A. Dobson, had written the Deputy Provincial Commissioner as early as February 1951:

I would like to suggest that the Registrar be contacted even at this stage, as the situation in Bukumbi will require action by the time correspondence with the Registrar reaches the pitch of being decisive as to whether we can have a Cooperative Officer for Sukumaland or not.

The Waziri [Regent] at Bukumbi, on my instructions, is busy collecting names and signatures of persons who certify that they know what they want, who understand what a cooperative society is and who are prepared to form one when it is agreed to, by us. We have already stated that we will not start one until we have a Cooperative Officer in Sukumaland. He is therefore a *sine qua non*, and I suggest that the application for his posting might well go forward now, as I am expecting a long petition and vigorous demand from Bukumbi in the immediate future.[1]

The District Commissioner noted also 'signs of a similar movement in Nassa.'[2]

Restrictions

After the Growers Association meeting in Mwanza in April the administration became very much concerned. A district officer reported:

Paulo Bomani of the African Traders Co-operative Society has apparently held a public meeting in the Welfare Centre attended by representatives from all over Sukumaland... at which he stated that the Trading Co-operative had been closed down and that it was now a producers cooperative only.

The district officer had discovered ten books of printed receipts for cooperative society membership while visiting the native authority headquarters at Bukumbi. Membership fees were five shillings and apparently eighty shillings in all had so far been collected. Otto Richard, the regent, had supported Bomani from the outset, and the district officer concluded correctly that 'the implication was that the Native Authority was helping in the collection.' He prohibited any further activity in this regard and impounded the receipt books.

Reporting to the District Commissioner, he noted that 'the three

[1] D.C. to D.P.C. 22 Feb. 1951, LPF.
[2] Handing-over Notes, July 1951, MZDF.

promoters in Bukumbi of this collection are African traders not cultivators.' He questioned the suitability of the Mwanza African Traders Cooperative Society for the task of organizing producers, whether money raised from farmers for a cooperative should be deposited in the Traders' account, and whether Bomani should be told to cease collecting money until the arrival of a cooperative officer. He judged:

It is extremely suspect that erstwhile members of an active traders co-operative should suddenly...[be] promoters of a producer co-operative, when there is no suggestion that they are to become servants of such co-operative.

He urged that the arrival of a cooperative officer 'be expedited as this whole matter has a strong political background.'[1]

The Mwanza District Commissioner noted that similar 'preliminary propaganda' for the cooperatives had occurred also 'in Nassa and Massanza I and doubtless all over the district.'[2] The Deputy Provincial Commissioner, too, in a confidential letter to District Commissioners suggested that 'the unguided development of these cooperatives may have serious political repercussions.' He urged the Provincial Commissioner 'to press for the early appointment of a Cooperative Officer, as it is clearly a matter of urgency.'[3] Fearing that the movement might go off 'half-cocked' with 'undesirable repercussions,' the Provincial Commissioner did press the government for the appointment. Although he acknowledged that 'attempts by producers to form Cooperative Societies for the marketing of cotton may well cause some embarrassment this season...[and that] there are signs that some producers are (very understandably) becoming impatient and may start "cooperation" on their own without waiting for guidance of any sort,' he had to report that 'the Commissioner for Cooperative Development cannot provide an Officer until 1953 at the earliest.'[4]

Meanwhile, late in May, Bomani approached the director of

---

[1] Safari Report, 14–17 May 1952, MZDF. The D.O. was R. E. S. Tanner. Tanner, a scholar as well as administrative officer, has published extensively on the Sukuma. See Warren J. Roth, 'The Wasukuma of Tanganyika: an annotated bibliography,' *Anthropological Quarterly*, XXXIV (July 1961), 162–3. Tanner became Director of the East African Institute of Social Research, Kampala, Uganda, in 1965.
[2] D.C. to D.P.C., 11 June 1952, LPF.
[3] D.P.C. to D.C.'s of Mwanza, Maswa, and Geita, 16 June 1952, LPF.
[4] P.C. in a monthly letter to D.O.'s, Apr.–May, 1952, LPF.

the Tanganyika Cotton Company, Ltd., and asked that the company's Ukerewe affiliate permit the Mwanza African Traders Cooperative Society to take over cotton buying for the ginnery in place of the usual Asian agents. They met with the District Commissioner of Ukerewe to discuss the proposal.

In a subsequent letter to the Provincial Commissioner, the company stated its 'sympathy with African aspirations in this matter' but noted that 'before it can be committed to any practical applications of what, at the moment, is a revolutionary change, there are many points which must be clarified from the Government side.' Specifically, the company inquired as to the legal status of the Traders with regard to cotton buying outside Mwanza District. Concerned over the need for proper handling of and accounting for large sums of money, the company asked if defalcations could be recovered through civil actions against guilty parties or, alternatively, if the government itself would underwrite possible losses. Noting that there might be political implications of a change from Asian to African buyers, the company nevertheless implied that there were sound financial and administrative, as well as moral, arguments for such a change:

[We] are fully aware of the malpractices which obtain during the season, and which they wish to see eliminated. The Native Grower himself is becoming more astute and is not, in these days, so easily defrauded. Consequently, Buyers are not so keen as they once were to buy in the Native Buying Posts as the rate of commission which on the face of it does not give them a great return after all the expenses have been paid.

If the government could give the proper assurances, the company seemed prepared to 'experiment in 1953 with one Buying Post in cooperative hands.'[1]

Like everything else to do with cooperatives, further negotiations toward any such innovation required, in the administration's view, the prior presence of a cooperative officer. Bomani, however, continued to organize. By June, a month before the 1952 buying season was to open, Bomani recalls having collected about 30,000 shillings. The Growers Association bought a truck, a duplicating machine, and rented an office. The administration, anxious to forestall Bomani's activities until the following year when a cooperative officer presumably would have arrived, 'warned him against having further meetings.' Bomani relates that he was told not to travel outside Mwanza without special permission from

---

[1]   Tanganyika Cotton Co., Ltd. to P.C., 2 June 1952, MZDF.

the Provincial Commissioner. He went anyway to Bukumbi and Ukerewe. He was followed by security officers; but the administration took no action, he believes, because of possible 'political effects.'[1]

Leaders of the Association in various rural areas were also subjected to the interference, in some cases harassment, of unsympathetic native authorities. Members of the Masanza II Growers Cooperative Society, for example, found it necessary to appeal by letter to their chief asking him not to be 'doubtful' about the incipient local organization which was not designed 'to break laws of the government [but rather to] fight for our African wealth.'[2] Begging for the chief's sympathetic cooperation in a manner which implied his previous opposition, the Masanza group outlined plans for selling their cotton *ensemble* at specific buying posts on designated days using the scales they had purchased.

Delegations to Dar es Salaam and Moshi

Bomani, meanwhile, headed a delegation to Dar es Salaam to appeal directly to top levels of the administration for recognition and registration of the, as yet, unofficial Lake Province Growers Association. He pressed again for the posting of a cooperative officer to Mwanza. Unsuccessful, he returned to Mwanza. With the onset of the buying season only weeks away, he told the Provincial Commissioner that if the Association were not registered forthwith, he and his organization would do what they could to boycott the markets for the season. Growers would simply stay at home and allow their cotton to rot in the fields.

Bomani feels his ultimatum was decisive in securing a letter of introduction from Acting Provincial Commissioner Bone to the Commissioner for Cooperative Development in Moshi.[3] Bone recorded that the Bomani delegation 'went to Moshi on their own initiative with a letter of introduction from me.'[4] Whatever the nuances, Bomani led a delegation of five to see the Commissioner in early July. The Commissioner pointed to several reasons why African growers, even if organized in cooperatives, might not receive higher returns than under the existing system. The

[1] Bomani, interview with Roth.
[2] Masanza II Growers Cooperative Society to the Chief, 7 July 1952, MZDF. (Orig. Sw.).
[3] Bomani, interview with Roth.
[4] Bone to the Regional Assistant Director of Agriculture, *et al.*, 31 July 1952, MZDF.

delegation contended, however, that even under the price structure imposed by the Cotton Board, producers' cooperatives were possible and desired by the growers. They argued that 'even if no visible monetary advantage accrues to members the removal of fear of being cheated over weights would be a sufficient reason for the formation of societies.' The delegation indicated that many growers were already willing to pay for independent weighing and that some had formed village organizations to safeguard their interests. In fact, five of these local groups had already subscribed funds to the Growers Association. They pointed out that 'applications have been made to the administration from time to time since 1949 for assistance in forming societies but without result.' Now they had come in person to inquire what the Co-operative Department could do for them. They cited the successful experience of Uganda Africans with cotton cooperatives. The Commissioner seemed to agree that this was relevant despite 'slightly different circumstances.'

The Commissioner reviewed cooperative staff and postings. He made it clear that nothing could be done for the 1952 season, 'but that if staff permitted, a Cooperative Officer would be posted to Mwanza as early as possible in 1953.' So far, this was no different from the position taken by the administration in Mwanza.

He made one concession, however, which reversed the entire tone of the negotiations: he was prepared to permit interim organizational activity pending the arrival of the cooperative officer. He wrote to the Provincial Commissioner:

In the meantime no harm would be done by tentative selection of potential officers and honorary secretaries and by framing and discussion of bye-laws for registration at a later date.

He also indicated he was prepared to train and employ up to four African cooperative inspectors from Sukumaland. Each candidate would have to have completed secondary school; he welcomed recommendations of suitable individuals from the delegation.

The Commissioner's proposals allowed the anxious organizers of the cooperatives a positive forward look. They served also to curtail the administration's attempts to throttle altogether Bomani's activities and to avert the threatened boycott. Restraint, nevertheless, was emphasized. The Bomani delegation met with the Managing Committee of the Kilimanjaro Native Cooperative Union, and, according to the Commissioner for Cooperative

Development, 'the dangers of starting operations without sound advice and assistance were stressed by me and also by the meeting with the K.N.C.U. Committee.'[1]

The Bomani delegation regarded the outcome of their talks with the Commissioner a 'victory,' as indeed it was. They returned to Sukumaland inspired to foster the formation of additional societies. In August, Christopher Kyaze, a leader of the cooperative movement in Uganda, returned Bomani's February visit to Uganda with a visit to Sukumaland. Kyaze joined Bomani in a tour to launch additional primary societies.[2] The still unofficial Lake Province Growers Association held monthly meetings in Mwanza, and by October some thirty prospective local units sent better than sixty representatives to attend.[3] With the movement growing at such a rate, the administration hastened the arrival of the promised cooperative officer. He arrived in October 1952 several months before even the most optimistic prognostications of the Commissioner had suggested.

A Cooperative Officer: Green

Because of the government's concern with the political overtones of the burgeoning cooperative movement, an administrative officer, Gavin Green, was seconded to the Cooperative Department especially for the Mwanza assignment. Over the next several years—despite occasional sharp disagreement over method and pace—Green worked closely with Bomani to establish the cooperatives on a secure foundation. An indefatigable worker and a brilliant administrator, Green also combined fluent Swahili with an unusual capacity to relate personally to African leaders and emotionally to their aspirations. Often regarded by his British compatriots as an 'empire builder' devoted as much to the aggrandizement of his own interests as to the advancement of cooperative principles and sound administration, Green endured the side-long glances of lesser men jealous of his success and

[1] Commissioner for Cooperative Development to P.C., 10 July 1952, MZDF. From Moshi, Bomani went on to Kenya to study cooperatives there. In Nairobi he talked also with leaders of the Kenya African Union and the Kikuyu General Union. Bomani was, at this time, also secretary of the Sukuma Union. In Mombasa he found Sukuma who were 'ready to form' a Sukuma Union branch there. (Bomani to the Kikuyu General Union, 30 Sept. 1952; Minutes of 20 July 1952, SUF.)

[2] D.C. to D.P.C., 26 August, 1952, MZDF. Also Bomani, interview.

[3] Minutes of the Seventh Meeting of the Lake Province Growers Association, 23 Oct. 1952, SUF. (Orig. Sw.).

suspicious of the maverick qualities which allowed him to identify, in their view, overmuch with African interests. What cannot be gainsaid, however, is that Green stands second only to Bomani himself among architects of the cooperative movement in Sukumaland. The Victoria Federation of Cooperative Unions is a monument to Bomani's leadership and to the cooperative spirit of the Sukuma people; it is also a testament to the skill and dedication of Green.

Green quickly saw that the cooperative movement had arisen out of the legitimate economic grievances of growers and was originally 'defensive not aggressive' in character. He held, however, that under Bomani's leadership the movement had 'become the vehicle for political expression which has obscured its essential motive force':

Racial animosities and political discontent were used to increase membership and gave a more effective rallying point...Greater strength was given to the marketing grievances by attention of the [Lake Province Growers] Association to political matters, such as the follow up of supposed injustices in the Native Courts, stock reduction, appeals to the Chief Secretary, and latterly the two cents [cotton] cess.

While admitting that the 'political [leadership's] vociferousness achieved recognition of the movement by Government and was almost entirely instrumental in the setting up of the Cooperative Department in the Lake Province,' Green set out to redirect the movement in line with sound economic and cooperative principles toward 'the formation of registered and legal Cooperative societies.'[1]

The growth of the cooperative movement in 1953 and 1954 was astonishing. Since not all areas where embryo societies already existed could be handled simultaneously, Green concentrated his initial efforts in selected chiefdoms in Mwanza, Maswa, Kwimba, Geita and Ukerewe Districts, leaving other chiefdoms and all of Shinyanga and Musoma Districts to a later time.[2]

To assist the fledgling societies, the Lint and Seed Marketing Board advanced loans for purchase of capital equipment. In early 1953 the Registrar of Cooperative Societies officially recognized

[1] Notes on Cooperative Development in Maswa and Mwanza Districts, 1953; notes on Cooperative Development in the Cotton Areas of the Lake Province, 1953, MZDF.
[2] The selected Sukumaland chiefdoms were those where the cooperative movement had already made the most extensive beginnings: Nassa, Masanza I, Ntuzu, Itilima, Magu, Sima, Buchosa, and Karumo.

thirty-eight primary societies and during the 1953 buying season these collected 12.5 per cent of the total crop. Nassa, Geita and Ukerewe—at once the heaviest cotton-producing areas and the most politically inclined—emerged as the strongholds. In Nassa over 90 per cent of the cotton was collected by the new societies which boasted membership of 70 per cent of the taxpaying population. In 1954 twenty-seven new societies were registered, making sixty-five in all. Membership totalled 32,000, but thousands more affiliated themselves with societies which were awaiting registration. In 1954 registered societies handled one-third of the total crop, a 300 per cent increase in percentage terms, and a 600 per cent increase in terms of bulk, over 1953.[1]

4 THE POLITICS OF ECONOMICS

Issues

In setting up the cooperatives the administration did encounter what it considered to be political problems. Bomani, for example, had organized his local societies on what he held were cohesive chiefdom units.[2] Green insisted they should be broken down into smaller units of 500–600 members correlated geographically with existing buying posts. In addition to arguments in favor of local control and economic efficiency, the administration feared that an alternative bureaucracy within the political and administrative boundaries of chiefdom units would weaken the native authority structure by encouraging the already incipient political tendencies of the cooperatives.[3] The Growers Association, however, regarded the administration's view as typical of 'divide and rule' tactics.[4] The administration's position, of course, prevailed. The Association, though, continued to press for government acceptance of larger units—a success achieved in 1955 with the registration of Unions and of the Victoria Federation of Cooperative Unions which drew together under one central administration all the cotton societies in the Lake Province.

The second item on the agenda of political contention was a cotton cess of 2 cents per pound imposed by the Sukumaland

---

[1] Lake Province Annual Report, 1953, 1954 LPF; Mwanza District Annual Report, 1953, MZDF.
[2] Bomani, interview.   [3] Green, interview.
[4] Notes on Cooperative Development in the Cotton Areas of the Lake Province, 1953, MZDF. See also Liebenow, 'Chieftainship' p. 276.

Federal Council in late 1952. In April 1953 the Growers Association wrote a letter of complaint to the Chief Secretary with copies to all chiefs and government officials in Sukumaland. The Association argued that the legislation was passed without consulting the people; that chiefs were threatened by District Commissioners with loss of their posts if they did not agree to the cess; that chiefs, in any case, were exempt from local rate, destocking and the cotton cess and should, therefore, not take it upon themselves to legislate these burdens on others.[1]

The Shinyanga chiefs drew up a memorandum refuting the charges. Aside from the fact that some Shinyanga chiefs were among the most powerful in Sukumaland, such a bold and independent statement on their part may also have been related to the absence, as yet, of any appreciable cooperative impact in Shinyanga. The Shinyanga chiefs pointed out that chiefs *were* subject to cotton cess and destocking. Since 1947, too, new chiefs appointed were liable for local rate. Denying that the administration had used constraint, they held that the decision on cotton cess was 'agreed by the meeting...at Malya by the Councillors of Malya who are the Chiefs and Bagunani who are citizens chosen by the people in order that they may be their voice at the Malya meetings and who explain to the people what happened at Malya when they return home.' The Shinyanga chiefs asked: 'Have you and your association given any opinions to your people's representatives?'

This raised once again the vexatious question of representation of a voluntary association at the Federal Council. The Shinyanga memorandum argued: 'Had you sent your case to Malya first [it] would have been considered and seen whether [it] were just or not.' The chiefs went on to invite Bomani and two others to attend the June meeting of the council 'so that we may explain at length.'[2]

Members of the provincial administration, however, viewed the matter differently. Commenting to the Provincial Commissioner on the memorandum of the Shinyanga chiefs, the Deputy Provincial Commissioner pointed out that for the Growers Association 'there was no opportunity to send "your case to

[1] Lake Province Growers Association to the Chief Secretary, 6 April 1953, cited in a draft memorandum by the Shinyanga chiefs to the Lake Province Growers Association sent to the D.C., May 1953, LPF.

[2] Memorandum by the Shinyanga chiefs to the Lake Province Growers Association, May 1953, LPF.

Malya first," as the cess was announced at the October meeting, without prior discussion.'[1] This interpretation is supported by J. Gus Liebenow who was conducting research in Sukumaland at the time:

At the initial suggestion of a cotton cess as a new source of revenue, the chiefs were enthusiastic about the idea...However, in the face of opposition from the cotton growers to the cotton cess, a number of the chiefs began to reverse themselves and withdraw their support for the cess. The administration acted quickly, and—in the opinion of a number of administrative officers—practically presented the chiefs with a 'sign or else' situation.[2]

The administration admitted—at least to itself—that there had been no real opportunity for prior consultation of the people or even preliminary discussion in council before the cess was announced.

The point, of course, was that the administration had decided a cess was necessary: therefore, there would be a cess, pretensions toward representative local government notwithstanding. When the Growers Association asked the administration to allow it to send representatives to attend the June council meeting as the Shinyanga chiefs had suggested, Provincial Commissioner Rowe wrote Bomani:

I regret that it is not permissible for deputations to take part, as such, in the formal meetings of statutory and constitutional bodies, whether of Central or of Local Government, since this would amount to syndicalism, which is not acknowledged by law or Government policy... Meetings...are usually open to individual members of the public and as such any person may listen to the proceedings—provided he does not attempt to interrupt them or take part in any way.[3]

As Liebenow noted with regard to the administration's actions on the cess, 'the hostility...engendered among the cotton growers made it plain to the administrative officers and chiefs alike that new political forces had arrived on the Sukuma scene.'[4] Cognizant of this fact, Rowe suggested to Bomani various 'more effective ways of meeting your Association's stated desire for general knowledge as to what is going on in the country.' He pointed out that if members of the Association wished to protest against particular regulations, 'the proper constitutional course is either for such persons to offer themselves for selection as [councillors]...or,

[1] D.P.C. to P.C., 28 May 1953, LPF. [2] Liebenow, 'Chieftainship', p. 266.
[3] Rowe to Bomani, 4 June 1953, LPF. [4] Liebenow, 'Chieftainship,' p. 266.

failing this, to brief an appointed [councillor] to raise the matter and represent the desired views.'[1] He proffered also interviews with himself or with the Deputy Provincial Commissioner at Malya, and even informal meetings with chiefs at district federation headquarters which might be arranged with the relevant District Commissioner's assistance.

Despite the government's inflexibility on the question of providing an opportunity for the Association formally to address its views to the Federal Council, Bomani seemed appreciative of Rowe's positive suggestions and the generally solicitous tone of the letter. He thanked the Provincial Commissioner 'for your sound advice' and added. 'I am now fully aware of the constitutional inappropriateness of such deputation to such body as Malya in formal meetings.' He said, however, that the Association would send some observers to the June meeting 'because the need by the growers to know what is happening at Malya is so pressing that their mere attendance will appease them quite considerably.'[2] He indicated that he would make appointments with the Provincial and Deputy Provincial Commissioners as suggested.

The cotton cess, nevertheless, remained for some time a point of contention. The issue was picked up as well by the Sukuma Union, and especially by the Tanganyika African Association in late 1953 and 1954. In 1954, when the Lint and Seed Marketing Board raised the price for cotton by twelve cents from −/50 −/62 per pound, controversy over the cess itself diminished. However, the larger issues of dissatisfaction with the Sukumaland Federation, suspicion of the administration and of the chiefs, and the felt lack of popular consultation among those associated with various voluntary organizations remained.

At another level, the understandable impatience of unregistered local societies, which had to wait a year or two before officially beginning operations, sometimes resulted in political difficulties. These societies continued with independent weighing, charging the standard −/05 per load. Often, however, they collected an additional illegal −/05 for the society itself—a practice which the growers generally supported. In Masanza II one such society ran afoul of an unsympathetic chief after trying to collect the extra fee from him as well. Four leaders were prosecuted, convicted and sentenced to twelve months for illegal collection of funds,

---

[1] Rowe to Bomani, 4 June 1953, LPF.
[2] Bomani to Rowe, 6 June 1953, LPF.

conspiracy, extortion, making false accusation against the chief, and, finally, failing to obey an order of the chief to appear before the District Commissioner (who had come to try to sort out the difficulties).[1]

In general, Provincial Commissioner Rowe encouraged a more flexible approach to this particular brand of illegality:

It is requested that no difficulties be placed in the path of societies which wish to open subscriptions for share capital with a view to ultimate registration...If unauthorized subscriptions take place, transgressors should not, in the first instance, be arrested but should be advised of the proper procedure. Criminal prosecutions should only be initiated if advice to obtain your permission to hold a public subscription is wilfully disregarded.[2]

Tensions nevertheless persisted at the local level where chiefs and would-be cooperative organizers sometimes found themselves at odds. Difficulties arose especially in those areas where native authorities were least sophisticated, most resistant to change, and most suspicious of any independent activity which threatened to undermine their personal control of affairs. In a few areas, too, cooperative organization intertwined with activities of the political associations. The administration approved of the first and disapproved of the second, but for native authorities in the countryside it was sometimes difficult to draw a clear distinction.

The Mweli Farmers in Geita

A further difficulty appeared in Geita District where embryo cotton societies arose previously to and independently of the Lake Province Growers Association. Dating from July 1950, the Buchosa Farmers Union was led by Paul Misoji, a former agricultural instructor. At once a consumers' and producers' cooperative, the Buchosa Union concentrated its attention on cotton marketing. In April 1951 members queried the government about choosing representatives of the union to be appointed 'quality clerks' at Asian buying posts, about buying their own scales and arranging to sell members' cotton on special days and about the possibility of being registered as a cooperative. In September they sent a lengthy memorandum to the Sukuma Federal Council complaining about the unjust practices of Asian buyers and their Ganda clerks. They asked, too, that a representative of the Buchosa Farmers sit on the Mweli (Geita) Federation Council of chiefs. By February

[1] Mwanza District Annual Report, 1954, MZDF.
[2] Rowe to D.C.'s 30 July 1954, MZDF.

1952 the union numbered about 330 members in Buchosa, and another group had formed in neighboring Karumo with some 60 members. By July the two groups—united as the Mweli Farmers Union—had a combined membership of 1,700 and a bank balance of 4,000 shillings. In addition to cotton marketing, they now proposed to build a school, a soap factory and a hospital. By mid-August the union had banked a total of 40,000 shillings. By January 1953 the District Commissioner reported phenomenal growth in membership to a total of 5,000![1]

Bomani had made visits to Geita on behalf of the Sukuma Union in 1951. When he began to appear after March 1952 on behalf of the incipient cooperative movement based in Mwanza, conflict with the existing groups in Buchosa and Karumo immediately arose. The Mweli Farmers Union strongly identified with its own independent beginnings and refused to follow Bomani's lead. Bomani, however, went ahead to organize where he could. He drew the ire of the Farmers who accused him of stirring up trouble in their areas. Bomani was successful in Karumo and in other parts of Geita, but the Farmers held their stronghold of Buchosa intact. The Farmers also disassociated themselves from what they and the government believed to be the political intentions of Bomani. Misoji relates that he once turned down Bomani's suggestion that he head a Sukuma Union branch in Geita because his interest lay entirely with cooperatives, not with politics—especially in multi-tribal Geita where an organization such as the Sukuma Union could only be divisive.

In any case, suspicious of what seemed to them a Bomani-led, Mwanza-based, economic imperialism with questionable political overtones, the Mweli Farmers refused to deposit their funds in the account of the Lake Province Growers Association. Ultimately, they registered themselves in September 1954 as a separate union—the first union of societies (as distinct from the individual primary societies themselves) to be registered in Sukumaland. With the formation of the all-embracing Victoria Federation of Cooperative Unions in mid-1955, however, the Mweli Farmers had no choice but to join lest they founder alone and unassisted. The Federation placated the Mweli group by electing the chairman of the Mweli Farmers, Masanja Shija, president of the new

[1]   Paul Misoji, interview, 19 Aug. 1964; D.P.C. to D.C., 15 Sept. 1951; Buchosa Farmers to D.C., 3 Feb. 1952; D.C. to P.C., 23 Feb. 1952; D.C. to Green, 14 Jan. 1953, Geita District Files (hereafter cited as GTDF).

Federation and by permitting all unions to maintain separate financial accounts.

Bomani: To England and Back

At the end of the 1953 cotton season the Growers Association decided to send Bomani—by then an influential leader even in the eyes of the Provincial Commissioner—to England to study cooperative methods. A government bursary provided half the needed funds and informal, personal subscriptions from members of the societies the other half. Even then, the administration seems to have attempted to deter Bomani from his independent path by absorbing him into the establishment. Before Bomani left for England the government offered him a job at a high salary and in the senior staff scale—a post for which Bomani says he had no qualifications. He went to England as planned and spent a year at Loughborough College.[1]

Returning to Sukumaland in October 1954, Bomani pushed ahead with plans for the formation of unions of cooperative societies and of an over-arching federation of unions. Previously the administration, which had been loath to permit the centralizing power which such a scheme implied, had opposed the larger unit. Economic and administrative necessities dictated the unit nevertheless. The Cooperative Department announced its acceptance of the federation idea at a general meeting of all registered societies of the Lake Province Growers Association in November 1954. The department registered eight unions in early 1955, and the Victoria Federation of Cooperative Unions was formed in July.

Bomani's return from England was, in itself, a major political event. Francis Bujimu, the secretary of the Growers Association, wrote all cooperative societies and political associations of Bomani's September date of return. With the government's permission, the Association collected funds for a special delegation of fifty to receive Bomani at the airport in Dar es Salaam and to escort him back to Mwanza—by train to Tabora, then by bus through Sukumaland. At Shinyanga, Missungwi and Nassa, Bomani was greeted by large crowds.[2]

A month after his return, Bomani, who had served previously on

[1] Bomani, interviews with Roth and with the author.
[2] An account of Bomani's return is contained in the Sukuma language newspaper, *Lumuli* (No. 68, 1954), published by the Roman Catholic Diocese, Mwanza. Material appearing in *Lumuli* was translated for the author by Pastor Balele.

the Lake Province Council, was appointed by Governor Twining to the Legislative Council. He took over the absent Chief Kidaha's seat for the December 1954 meeting of the council, then was seated in his own right under the multi-racial formula adopted in 1955 providing for a European, an Asian and an African representative from each province. Though chosen primarily because of his economic leadership of the burgeoning cooperative movement, Bomani was the first representative of the new politics to find a voice in the higher councils of the Tanganyikan administration.

Ideas and People: Activation of the Countryside

While the activities of the cooperative movement became more strictly economic, the attitudes of those involved ranged widely over an entire spectrum of economic, social and political affairs. At a March 1954 meeting of the Growers Association, Liebenow recorded the views of delegates on a wide range of matters pertaining to 'development in Sukumaland.' He summarized their remarks as follows:

Economic Activities

1. There should be more freedom as far as trade is concerned. People should be allowed to sell their cattle, ghee, and other products wherever the prices are highest. We are prohibited from selling our ghee in Uganda or our cattle in Bukoba, and this is causing great poverty in Sukumaland.
2. People in my area have to pay Shs. –/50 for the local rate, no matter what the age of their cows.
3. Why should we cultivators be forced to work on dam construction without pay? I understand there is money in the Native Treasury for such work, and the people should be paid.
4. Government has imposed a system whereby people have to buy land from the headmen in order to settle in Geita. This is unjust. (An executive officer of the Tanganyika African Association interrupted at this point to state that this was untrue. He had investigated the charge and found individual corruption, not Government policy to be responsible.)

Education

5. Why has Government changed the middle school curriculum in favor of having our sons and daughters work all day long on the school *shambas* (fields)? We want our children to go on to higher education; they can't do that if they spend so much time on agriculture.
6. Government should build more secondary schools. It harms our

children if they are not permitted to go beyond Standard IV or Standard VIII. They are only slightly educated when they get that far and they cannot find good jobs.

Medicine

7. The hospitals are very low standard when it comes to treating African patients. The food is bad, there are no mosquito nets, they are short of drugs, and they practice discrimination. If an African can pay, why shouldn't he have a private room just like the Europeans?

Political

8. Efforts should be made to have people other than chiefs on the Legislative Council so that cotton growers and the ordinary people may be heard.
9. Why aren't members of the cooperative societies represented on the chiefdom and parish councils? These councils are of no use to the people since only the chiefs and their house-boys sit there. (Four statements were made to this effect.)
10. Swahili should be used on all councils in Tanganyika so that the ordinary people can understand what is happening and so that they can express their views.
11. The deposition of chiefs is all wrong. Government asks the people to elect their chiefs, but they have nothing to say about whether they should be deposed. This should be done by the courts or by the people; but not by the D.C. [District Commissioner] alone.
12. The British Government is much more of a dictatorship than a democracy. This we know because UNO (United Nations) said that the Wameru had been cheated out of their land, but the Tanganyika Government ignored the fact that UNO judged against it. (Actually, only the Fourth Committee of the Assembly indicated that the Administering Authority was at fault. No critical resolution was ever passed by the General Assembly as a whole.)
13. Cattle destocking was forced upon the people without discussing it with them before-hand. (Three comments were made along similar lines.)
14. Government doesn't give the chiefs a chance to consult their people. The chiefs do not know what the agenda of the Sukumaland Federal Council will be until they reach Malya. There they are forced to sign agreements without being able to consult the people.
15. Why should we have multi-racial councils in Tanganyika? The Africans are in the majority in this country, but a minority on the councils. Our people cannot keep up with the Europeans and Asians in debate. (Two comments along this line.)

Liebenow pointed to the 'preponderance of remarks of a political character,' noting that 'even the remarks placed under the rubrics of education, medicine, and economic activities indicated a general attitude of hostility to the activities of Central

Government and of Native Authorities.' He went on to point out that 'the political attitudes expressed...have frequently been the source of conflict between the cooperatives and the chiefs' and he described a varying pattern of relationships:

In Nassa and other chiefdoms of the Victoria Nyanza littoral, where membership in cooperatives is very high, the chiefs and the cooperatives are antagonistic towards each other. In Maswa, on the other hand, the large societies and the Native Authorities have established a cordial relationship. In Geita the Native Authorities are indifferent to the whole movement.

We have noted that the native authorities of Bukumbi, Ukerewe and Ntuzu were especially approving of the initiation of the cooperative movement. The chief of Nunghu in Maswa and the chief and subchiefs of Nera in Kwimba are also known to have been sympathetic and helpful. Elsewhere, indifference or outright opposition (as in Masanza II) seems to have been characteristic; there is not the slightest doubt that the predilection of many cooperative society leaders was toward criticism of the chiefs.[1]

It is of particular interest also that Liebenow found explicit opposition to multi-racial councils expressed as early as March 1954. The only multi-racial council in the area at the time was the Lake Province Council, though a few Europeans and Asians were beginning to be added to advisory district councils in line with multi-racial adaptations of the 'Cory pyramid.' A county council was projected and reforms in Legislative Council composition anticipated—both along multi-racial lines. Multi-racial councils became a celebrated issue in 1958 when the government attempted unsuccessfully to institute a statutory multi-racial council in Geita District. At that time the government argued that multi-racial councils were acceptable to the people; that agitation was whipped up in Geita by professional 'agitator' types. Liebenow's finding suggests that multi-racial councils were a subject of controversy, if not also of focused opposition, as early as 1954. If so, the government should have had ample opportunity to anticipate some of the difficulties it was later to face.

[1] Liebenow, 'Chieftainship,' pp. 273–5. Liebenow related: 'At the meeting... I asked the following question: "Which chiefs in Sukumaland are, in your opinion, doing a good job?" There were immediately cries of "None! None!" The chairman, who was nudged by his secretary, was apparently made aware of the fact that at least one sub-chief and a headman were represented at the meeting, and he suggested that that sub-chief as well as the Chiefs of Nunghu and Ntuzu were the only ones who were doing good jobs. Doing good jobs apparently meant cooperating with the cooperatives.'

The attitudes expressed at the March 1954 meeting of the Lake Province Growers Association were typical of persons involved in any of the principal voluntary associations operating in Sukumaland in 1954. It should be understood, too, that the remarks recorded were made in response to a general question put by Liebenow and not as part of the actual business meeting of the Association. The wide ranging discussion in this unusual situation should not obscure the fact that the Association by this time was concentrating its activities more or less exclusively on cooperative matters. During his year and a half as cooperative officer in the Lake Province, Green had made an impact. Also, as will be seen later, the cooperative societies became even more strictly apolitical after the government moved decisively against the political associations a few months later.[1]

But the political impact of the cooperatives was considerable before 1954. In terms of statistics alone, the cooperatives by 1954 had something like ten times the number of members (approximately 30,000) of either TAA or the Sukuma Union (approximately 3,000 each).[2] While TAA and the Sukuma Union attracted some membership from rural areas before 1952, their impact was greatest in 1953 and 1954 *after* the cooperatives were already well under way. Bomani's extended tour of rural areas in March 1952 preceded by a year and a half the first strenuous efforts of Lameck Bogohe and A. S. Kandoro on behalf of the Sukuma Union and TAA. Without doubt, Bomani's tour softened up the rural areas for the later incursions.

For the activation of the countryside, it did not much matter which issue or which group came first. What did matter was that people involved themselves in an association because they felt the association would help them alleviate certain of their grievances which the government and/or the chiefs would not, or could not, alleviate. The flagrant abuses of Asian cotton buyers and the years of attempts by farmers to mitigate their difficulties through various independent weighing schemes made fertile ground for the cooperative movement. It appealed quickly to a large number of people over wide areas. It was particularly strong along the lake littoral where cotton production was highest and where economically and politically motivated trader and farmer groups tended to be most educated, most numerous and most ambitious for their own advancement. It flourished also where chiefs gave

[1] See below, pp. 183–6.   [2] See Liebenow, 'Chieftainship,' pp. 270, 277, 280.

their support or where the depredations of local ginnery owners and their subsidiary buyers were most severe.

With regard to technique, Bomani and a core group of able assistants made use of whatever friendly contacts they had in each area. Bomani's leadership was skilful in style as well as in content. Green has spoken of Bomani's 'admirable and attractive lack of arrogance [and his] persuasiveness.'[1] Sometimes Bomani worked with native authorities, more often with traders and ambitious cotton farmers, and sometimes, too, with traditional village leaders such as the *basumba batale* (leaders of the young men's societies) or the *banamhala* (elders). Local residents of a variety of backgrounds had apparently been involved in the village weighing organizations which preceded the cooperatives proper. Whatever the case, Bomani usually succeeded in mobilizing support from a diversity of elements. The committees of the earliest primary societies indicated, for example, wide ranges in the ages of members. While the secretary was often a young man with some education, the majority of any committee were usually senior members of the community.[2] The cooperatives, therefore, were never simply collections of discontented and vociferous young men. The new societies responded to a need felt throughout the community and they engaged the efforts, leadership and membership of many segments of any community in which they were active.

To the Sukuma, whose fondness for their chiefs had never been excessive (especially with the plethora of restrictive legislation imposed in the postwar years), the cooperatives must also have seemed attractive because chiefs, headmen and other traditional status figures were not permitted to assume prerogatives beyond those of simple membership unless specifically asked to do so. Egalitarian pressures within Sukuma society have been remarked by both administrators and anthropologists. Observers have also noted among the Sukuma a decided independence of character combined with a propensity to form powerful collective units when there seemed sufficient need or cause. As Gottfried and Martha Lang have pointed out, traditional patterns of cultural and social association, which united individuals across political

[1] Green, interview.
[2] Information giving the names and ages of the committee members of primary societies at the time of their registration is contained in the official Register of Cooperative Societies, Ministry of Commerce and Cooperatives, Dar es Salaam.

and administrative boundaries, may have facilitated the rapid spread of the cooperatives.[1] One prominent Sukuma leader has said: 'The Sukuma are always ahead of others on joining if they agree that something is good.'[2]

In any case, the Sukuma (and neighboring peoples in Ukerewe and Musoma) demonstrated in the early 1950s an astonishing capacity for coordinated cooperative organization. Bomani and the Lake Province Growers Association brought new ideas into the conservative rural areas. They awakened thousands to a conscious definition of their economic and political plight. They offered concrete machinery for the alleviation of latent grievances and the achievement of new aspirations. The gateway to mass politics was opened.

[1] Lang and Lang, *Anthropological Quarterly*, xxv (April 1962), 93–4.
[2] Lameck Bogohe, interview. See also Liebenow, 'Chieftainship,' p. 267.

5

Politics Achieved: TAA and the Sukuma Union

While Bomani built the foundations of the cooperative movement, the Mwanza branch of the Tanganyika Africa Association was far from idle. In rural areas specific grievances relating to Asian and Arab domination of the economy and a general dissatisfaction with native authorities and the European administration combined to launch political activity in the countryside. In the early 1950s TAA in Mwanza transformed itself under new leadership into a thoroughly activist, even militant, organization. Bent on mobilizing a variety of existing discontents into a potent political force, TAA broadened its base of support and intensified its efforts to articulate African views to higher authority. The new brand of politics angered the administration. Misunderstandings compounded a widening gap in loyalties and outlook. Denied the political leverage it sought, TAA turned its attack on the colonial regime itself. By early 1954—some six months before TANU was born—government administrators and TAA politicians in Sukumaland had already reached the point of impasse.

The Sukuma Union also became in the early 1950s a full-scale political movement under an organizer who sought a mass basis of support in the rural areas. Unlike TAA, which Sukuma Union leaders felt had a continental or territorial focus and was concerned with the problems of Africans in general, the Union was first intended to deal with the problems of Sukumaland in particular. The Development Plan and the Malya Federation were programs and institutions particular to Sukumaland. They gave rise to particular problems. The most suitable vehicle for dealing with these problems appeared to some to be an all-Sukuma political association which would, like the federation of chiefs, deal in a unified but exclusive manner with the Sukuma and Sukumaland. However, as the Union became a more powerful political force in the countryside and, like TAA, developed a strong anti-chief, anti-administration complexion, it became less distinguishable from TAA and all but assumed, somewhat paradoxically perhaps, the character of a nationalist movement. In March 1954 the administration added the Sukuma Union to the list of political associations proscribed for government servants. As TAA was the only other African association listed, the Union became unique among Tanganyika's multiplicity of tribal associations in being so designated—a testament to its rather unusual political characteristics.

Within the wider context of Tanganyika, these developments were unusual indeed. In the years after the Second World War the Haya and the Chagga, among whom political consciousness had become apparent in the 1930s, remained preoccupied with parochial tribal concerns. Elsewhere, only in the Kondoa District in 1951 and among the Meru in 1951–2 did voluntary political activity by Africans on behalf of African interests achieve an incipiently nationalistic focus.

In Mwanza, however, the activities of TAA—and simultaneously of the Sukuma Union—made the Lake Province the acknowledged focal point for political activity in Tanganyika between 1952 and the formation of TANU in 1954. While TAA in Mwanza was becoming a forceful political organization with militant leadership, regular meetings and extensive membership, the territorial headquarters of the association in Dar es Salaam 'was without a president, and no meetings were held during the second part of [1952].' Julius Nyerere became TAA's president in 1953, but 'the next year was spent in drawing up a new constitution and in seeking the support of the tribal authorities for the new organization.'[1] Meanwhile, without help from Dar es Salaam, Mwanza TAA became perhaps the single most powerful, anti-colonial, political force in Tanganyika.

I   TAA: A RURAL FOOTHOLD

Late in 1947 TAA's secretary, Joseph Chombo, left Mwanza on a civil service transfer. Henry Chasama, a Nyamwezi from Msalala chiefdom in west Mwanza (Geita), took over as provincial secretary. Schooled at Bwiru near Mwanza, Chasama worked for the township authority as a market clerk. Ironically, it was the newcomer Chasama, rather than Chombo, who presided over the inauguration—in 1949 at Busega in

[1] Taylor, p. 95.

K

Mwanza District—of the first active TAA branch in rural Sukumaland. Chombo, who had hoped to build TAA in the rural areas, never really succeeded. Chasama's success, however, was probably due less to efforts of his own than to the rise at this particular time of an articulate and aggrieved non-traditional local leadership in Busega. It was in Busega that the issues and conflicts which were to wrack other parts of Sukumaland in later years first crystallized.

The three small chiefdoms of Masanza I, Nassa, and Masanza II—which together constitute the area known as Busega— lie on the south shore of Lake Victoria. Nassa, the central of the three, the most populous, and the acknowledged capital, is about seventy miles east of Mwanza town. Busega is separated from the rest of Mwanza District by the northern chiefdoms of Kwimba District, but more importantly, by the Simiyu River which, until a large bridge and all-weather approaches were constructed in 1963, was impassable except by canoe or ferry for much of the rainy season. At the edge of Sukumaland, Busega thrived with a vitality characteristic of independent-minded Sukuma immigrants living in a frontier context. New opportunities combined with a minimum of traditional obligations and restraints. There was competition among a mixture of tribes and an unusual number of semi-educated farmers and traders anxious to extend themselves beyond the usual bounds of rural conservatism. Thrust in upon itself by physical barriers—yet liberated by an inner vitality which was enhanced by cross-currents of influence from Mwanza, Maswa, Ukerewe and Musoma—Busega became in the late 1940s and early 1950s one of the most active centers of economic and political activity in Sukumaland.

Initiatives

Led by a Sukuma farmer and trader, Stephano Sanja—who, like most of the Busega leadership, was subsequently active in the cotton cooperative movement and in the Sukuma Union—local supporters of TAA opened a branch office at Nassa in May 1949. An immediate letter to Chasama asked for a meeting with the chiefs of Mwanza and for a TAA delegate to attend the Sukumaland Federal Council meetings at Malya. It proposed a large public meeting in Nassa on 26 June to introduce TAA to the people, queried the right of non-Africans to immigrate to villages and, finally, expressed the desire of the Busega branch to be called the 'Sukuma Union, Busega.'[1]

These proposals suggested some confusion in the minds of Busega leaders. Yet here were the seeds of what were to become persistent political motifs. Requests for meetings with the chiefs implied rejection of government as the exclusive domain of native authorities. This, together with the direct approach to the people through a large public meeting and with the ambivalence over TAA versus the Sukuma Union, suggested an attempt by critics of the administration to exploit *any* possible alternative channels of expression. Here were ambitious Sukuma dislodged from the cocoon of traditional political loyalties and all but disenfranchised under the government-controlled native authority system. Here, too, in the objection to non-African immigration into villages, was the embattled small African trader seeking politically a leverage which was otherwise denied him.

In his reply to the letter of the Busega branch, Chasama pointed out that TAA was the 'father' of all Africans and united them regardless of tribe, whereas the Sukuma Union could be divisive and discriminatory. Meetings with the chiefs would not be of any particular usefulness because TAA had power independent of the chiefs and could meet with the government directly. Chiefs, as Africans, could be helped by TAA, but TAA did not in any way depend on the chiefs. TAA, however, had a right to send someone to attend meetings of the Federal Council if it wished to do so.[2] These propositions were soon to be tested.

In August, the Busega branch presented its first set of written representations to the government. Somewhat chastened, perhaps, by a more realistic grasp of what might be accomplished, TAA confined itself to the request that the government look into several matters which provoked and irritated Busega citizens: (1) that

[1] Details contained in Chasama to Busega TAA, 15 June 1949, in Yakabo Sagala, selected papers privately held (hereafter cited as Sagala papers), Nassa, Tanzania. I am indebted to Mr Sagala for making available to one of my research assistants papers of historical importance from his personal files.

[2] *Ibid.* Chasama's letter was somewhat misleading. His argument that TAA 'had a right' to send someone to the Federal Council glossed over the fact that this was something any citizen could do—but only as an observer. TAA was not given any sort of representation on the council. Also, Chasama's assurance that TAA's power was independent of the chiefs, though accurate so far as he knew at the time, turned out to be somewhat premature, as the subsequent events in Nassa demonstrate.

cotton growers were not being paid for weights registered in fractions of a pound and were suffering from over-deductions for containers; (2) that bus fares showed no relation to miles travelled and people were packed in far beyond the legal limit; and (3) that wild animals from the Serengeti Game Reserve regularly destroyed crops in bordering areas.

The Administration's Reaction

The disposition of the specific complaints is less important than what the sequel demonstrated concerning the relations between the government, the chief and the new branch of TAA. Three months passed before TAA was informed by the District Commissioner that all representations to the government had to be forwarded to the district office through the appropriate native authority, i.e., the chief of Nassa. The government clearly did not want TAA to consider itself an alternative to the existing local government hierarchy. The *raison d'être* of a rurally based TAA branch, however, was precisely to effect such an alternative. Regretting very much the District Commissioner's ruling, TAA replied:

The strength of the Tanganyika African Association resides in consultation with the government because it is the government which exercises power. To consult via the chief is the same as to say that TAA is weak and useless...

We agree to consult with the chief...but many concerns of the African Association cannot be dealt with by the chief, but only by the District Commissioner himself. If we continue [to consult via the chief]...it will indicate that this association has no authority with the government...

The committee and all members ask that you give TAA full authority. If this is not possible it will be a great calamity for us as many chiefs see no value in this association. We will simply disintegrate.[1]

Again in January the District Commissioner assured TAA that cooperation with the chief would add to, rather than detract from, the strength of the association.

With policy on proper procedures thus established, the District Commissioner undertook, now five months after the original letter, to respond to the specific complaints made therein. After providing a rationale for the *status quo* in each instance, he concluded that if TAA still felt certain policies to be unjust, it should send a representative to talk with the relevant provincial officials.

[1] Busega TAA to D.C., 13 Dec. 1949, Sagala papers. (Orig. Sw.).

Its only opening, TAA grasped this suggestion and sent two of its members to Mwanza. When the delegates arrived to see the provincial agricultural officer, they were told: 'Go back home; I will send you an answer by letter.' Two months later no answer had yet been received, and Busega TAA again wrote to the District Commissioner that members would be 'pleased to receive an answer.'[1]

Traders, Politicians and Chiefs

The Busega branch frequently concerned itself with the problems of African traders during 1949 and 1950. This reflected the fact that a substantial core of the branch's members were traders. Moreover, there were specific interconnections between Bomani's Mwanza African Traders Cooperative Society and Busega TAA.[2]

In general, the overriding issue was the one raised more than two years previously at the Mwanza provincial conference: that non-Africans should be barred from trading in the villages; that petty trade, especially foodstuffs, should be reserved to Africans. Late in 1949 famine developed in Busega due to failure of the long rains some months before. According to the administration, the problem of food shortage was 'simplified in that Sikh ginners offered to act as wholesalers.'[3] For Busega's African traders, however, and for TAA, the crisis served both to dramatize their plight and to give them an opportunity strongly to state their views.

Writing in November to the District Commissioner over the signature of Bomani as 'Honorary Secretary, Busega TAA,' TAA argued that the Sikh ginners had not provided sufficient

[1] Busega TAA to D.C., 8 May 1950, MZDF. (Orig. Sw.).
[2] Similarly, in Maswa a TAA branch was opened in August 1949 with offices at the headquarters of the Maswa African Traders Cooperative Society (formed in late 1946) at Nyalikungu. There was also a branch in Kanadi under one of the cooperative society members. Nothing much, however, seems to have come of this beginning and TAA in Maswa had to await Stanley Kaseko's initiatives in Malampaka in early 1954. (See below, pp. 171–8.) The still positive attitude of the administration toward TAA in 1949 was exemplified in the D.C.'s acknowledging letter: 'I am pleased to note this sign of progress and will do whatever is in my power to assist the local branch if they need anything. I shall be glad to be informed of the activities of the branch as and when they occur.' (Chasama to D.C., 25 Aug. 1949; D.C. to Chasama, 1 Sept. 1949; Secretary–Treasurer, Sukumaland Federal Council, to Provincial TAA, 24 June 1951; membership list Maswa African Traders Cooperative Society, MADF.)
[3] Mwanza District Annual Report, 1950, MZDF.

food, nor had they established the food reserves which they had promised to the government before being granted the wholesale option. Contending that the ginners 'have no sympathy for Africans,' TAA reported that the meeting could see no reason why the option was given to the Sikh ginners to distribute food to Africans when an African cooperative society could handle the work much more effectively. TAA requested that emergency provisions be distributed through the Mwanza African Traders Cooperative Society as quickly as possible before the short rains disrupted communications and made further distribution impossible.[1]

The Mwanza Traders did not get an option for distribution of foodstuffs in Busega, but the Busega branch continued in 1950 to press the case of small African traders to the point of open conflict with the local chief.

In line with the policy laid down by the District Commissioner, representations by TAA were forwarded first to the chief for his comments. In this case the chief commented that he was not yet satisfied that Africans could be efficient traders on their own, that they still had much to learn from Asians whom they imitated in order to learn, and that he could see no reason to prohibit Asians from local trading and force them to move away. The District Commissioner then replied to TAA that it was not the government's practice to give monopolies in trade to one group or another and that anyone could trade in any goods on the basis of free competition. Conflict between TAA and the chief then became pronounced. In a letter direct to the District Commissioner, TAA said it could not forward its letters via the chief because the chief did not want to cooperate with TAA. TAA would agree only to send him copies. Under the heading 'Chief Oppresses Africans,' TAA charged that the chief unjustifiably delayed and refused to grant trading licenses to Africans, had even on one occasion given preference to an Arab, and asked that licenses henceforth be granted from Mwanza rather than by the chief. TAA protested that it was an organization independent of the native authority and renewed its earlier argument that on matters relating to the

[1] Busega TAA to D.C., 6 Nov. 1949, MZDF. Bomani wrote a letter on behalf of Busega TAA as early as June 1949. Bomani lived and worked in Mwanza, but he travelled periodically to Nassa. He was, of course, a member of TAA in Mwanza, but the fact that affiliations were stretched to the point where he could sign a letter on behalf of Busega TAA, asking for an option for the Mwanza African Traders, reflected the close interconnections which existed.

leadership of the District Commissioner himself TAA had the right to approach the government directly.[1]

Scandalized, the chief wrote to the District Commissioner to claim TAA's contentions were lies. By law he, the chief, was responsible for giving licenses and this required investigation of applicants' reputations, permission from local headmen for land, certification of sufficient capital and assessment of the need for additional shops in given areas. He defended his grant of a trading plot to an Arab on grounds of superior and efficient service to the people of the area.

In more general terms, the chief castigated TAA for trying to set itself up in opposition to local government authority and he warned that trouble would develop if this continued. Recalling the difficulties that TAA had caused the district office during the famine, the chief indicated that TAA had now turned its attack on him. He viewed the traders in question as stupid, illiterate, uncivilized people who believed that native authorities no longer had any power; they were self-seeking individuals who had no proper understanding of what their association should do.[2]

With feelings at such a pitch, the District Commissioner took a more conciliatory tone, noting that he would talk things over both with the chief and with a TAA representative on his next visit to Nassa. On the question of the Arab trader, however, he elaborated the theory of free competition buttressed by the need to consider the needs of individual areas on their merits, not on the basis of racial discrimination. This was maddening for TAA, which retorted that only very recently Sikh ginners had been given exclusive rights to food distribution at the expense of African traders. The District Commissioner replied that during the famine the Sikh ginners were the only organization with boats and lorries sufficient to handle properly the distribution of emergency food supplies.[3]

Differing Perspectives

A sisal boom in mid-1950 illustrated further the felt identity of interests between traders and TAA in Mwanza and Busega. In the process of attempting to extend the activities of the Mwanza

[1] D.C. to Busega TAA, Mar. 10; Busega TAA to D.C., 28 Feb., 18 Mar. 1950, MZDF. (Orig. Sw.).
[2] Chief Kapongo to D.C., 27 Apr. 1950, MZDF.
[3] D.C. to Busega TAA, 13 May, 7 July; Busega TAA to D.C., 16 May 1950, MZDF. (Orig. Sw.).

African Traders Cooperative Society into sisal buying in rural areas, Bomani held his meetings in Busega in the office of the African Association. At the same time Chasama, on behalf of TAA, took on the sisal campaign as a matter of importance and worked to get the support of chiefs for a plea to the government to prohibit Asians from dealing in sisal.[1]

Though trading interests dominated the activities of Busega TAA in 1949–50, the association did not make trading problems its sole concern.[2] In any case, TAA's strength as an organization was based in part on its flexibility; it could and did adapt at different times and in different places to a variety of needs and aspirations.[3] Most particularly, the story of Busega TAA's first two years was important because it detailed the first outright conflict between a chief and politicians in postwar Sukumaland; it anticipated, in miniature, the sort of conflict between native authorities and non-traditional political leaders which became widespread in the ensuing decade.

The conflicting perspectives of the chief, the government and the new politicians should be clearly understood. Chief Kapongo of Nassa, in office since 1923, had more taxpayers and received a higher salary than any other chief in Mwanza District. Though not one of the great chiefs of Sukumaland, and in spite of only a Standard VI education, Kapongo was regarded by the administration as the most capable and progressive chief in the district. From the royal line in Nassa, and elected in the traditional manner, he certainly regarded himself as the pre-eminent figure in his chiefdom. To him, as traditional leader and as the highest-ranking

---

[1] Bomani to the traders of Magu, Masanza I and Nassa, 9 June; Chasama to Busega TAA, 25 June 1950, Sagala papers. A further instance of cooperation between the Mwanza Traders and TAA in mid-1950 concerned the expulsion of persons from Ukerewe Island. Bomani wrote to Chasama that one man had come to the Traders' office complaining that his farm had been forcefully sold by the native authority, but 'since I have little influence on this matter compared to the African Association, I send this complaint along to you so that you may assist him as you deem appropriate...Please keep me informed.' Chasama then followed up with the P.C. and the D.C. of Ukerewe. (Mwanza Traders to TAA, 26 May 1950, Sagala papers; Chasama to P.C. and D.C., 4 Aug. 1950; D.C. to Chasama, 11 Aug. 1950, MZDF.)

[2] In addition to the cotton weighing complaints as already noted, Busega TAA made representations at various times asking for the abolition of cotton zones; that 'enemy' (presumably German) land be given to Africans; that Europeans, Asians and Arabs not be given preference over Africans when ferry boats were crowded. (Busega TAA to D.C., 31 May 1951, and 15 Aug. 1951, MZDF.)

[3] See below, pp. 139–42.

government officer in the area, all deference was due. From this perspective, the young activists who took independent initiatives in economic and political matters could only be viewed as troublesome, self-seeking upstarts.

From the point of view of the new politicians, the chief represented a conservative, perhaps decrepit *status quo*. There were new initiatives to be taken and new battles to be won, and this seemed possible only through actions independent of the chief, through representations direct to the district administration. The administration, though, seemed to pose a constantly shifting target; somehow the issues could never be joined. If it were not that correspondence had to be forwarded through the chief, then it was that a delegation might be sent to see the agriculture officer— but, in the event, only to be rebuffed. There seemed always some new procedure to be implemented, some other channel to be followed before points raised could be answered on their merits. Each time a fresh piece of paper and the composition of a new letter would be required, together with another exercise in patience as a long wait for an answer was sure to follow. Even when the answer finally came, it would be in the inimitable language of British officialdom: terse, legalistic, but fundamentally unhelpful, often ignoring or sidestepping the underlying complaints, even at times the specific issues raised in the initial appeal. Somehow, in the end, there was always some regulation or some ruling which, though 'non-discriminatory' and 'in the interests of the Africans themselves,' meant, in fact, that Africans could not do or be whatever it was that they desired to do or be.

The administration, for its part, gave its approbation to TAA in the abstract but viewed the Busega activists as particularly vociferous types who would need some watching if they were not to get out of hand. There was no question at this point of deliberately squelching the association, but the administration probably did design to dampen TAA's enthusiasm on the grounds that a certain firmness on the government's part, and an insistence on proper procedure, would be beneficial to the maturing of the association and its leaders. Accustomed to the less troublesome operations of TAA in the township under the paternal eye of the Provincial or District Commissioner, the administration discovered that the paternal eye could not extend as easily to rural Busega. The chief, however, was on the spot and he was the arm of government in the area. Further, it would be instructive for all associations to become accustomed to the prospect of working their ideas upward through the hierarchy of native authorities—just as any citizen would need to do. The native authority system, after all, *was* local government.

So the reasoning went, and so the estrangement of native authorities and new politicians was made inevitable. So, too, the estrangement of the politicians from the colonial administration —to which, interestingly enough, they had first applied directly for relief and assistance when they found themselves critical of, and in conflict with, native authorities. One can only speculate as to how the political history of the 1950s might have been different had the administration anticipated more fully the limitations of reliance on native authorities and from an early date adopted a more sympathetic and constructive attitude toward the new politicians.

2   THE SUKUMA UNION: BEGINNING AGAIN

The initiators of the revitalized Sukuma Union were Philip Kilala, a carpenter with primary school education, and James Bubele (educated at St Andrews College, Minaki, near Dar es Salaam), an employee of the East African Railways and Harbours. Kilala was a student in Bubele's evening English class in Mwanza. In 1949 and 1950 the two often discussed African problems. Bubele was sufficiently travelled and sophisticated to realize that in terms of general development Sukumaland was behind Uchagga and Uhaya, not to mention Kenya and Uganda. He and Kilala discussed the need for an association to 'raise up' Sukumaland. Doubtful about taking the problems of Sukumaland to TAA, which dealt with 'the difficulties of Africans which relate to all Africa,' they decided it would be necessary to form an association to deal with the problems particular to Sukumaland, 'like our chiefs who have united and come together at...Sukumaland Malya.'

To launch the new endeavor, Kilala and Bubele recruited other interested Sukuma in the Mwanza area—notably Tito Budodi and Henry Chasama (formerly the provincial secretary of TAA) who were market clerks; John Lugaila, the clerk of the Mwanza native treasury; and James Malongo, head teacher of Bwiru School. The group decided to ask Henry Chagula, a graduate of Makerere teaching at Bwiru School, and Paul Bomani, the secretary of the Mwanza African Traders Cooperative Society, to join. The initiators looked for leadership to these prominent and successful Sukuma: Bomani 'has been secretary of an association for a long time and doubtless he will say much that will be of profit to us since he knows a great deal,' and Chagala 'knows a lot because of his education.'[1] Chagula became president and Bomani secretary. Other officers were those of the initial core group already mentioned. All Sukuma and Nyamwezi living in Sukumaland were welcomed as members, from the highest chief to the humblest peasant. General meetings and committee meetings were held monthly, but attendance was low, generally less than a dozen. By-laws stressing the need for self-reliance and outlining the Union's concerns for improved education, health and agriculture were submitted to the government which found them 'quite in order.'[2]

Despite its ambitious initial plans, the Union in its 1945–9 phase had concentrated in practice primarily on mutual aid for Sukuma living in Mwanza. After 1950, the reconstituted Union addressed itself to more fundamental problems of economic and, later, political development. Chagula has argued that Sukumaland should have been the richest area in Tanganyika. Like Katanga in the Congo, Sukumaland boasted the greatest wealth and diversity of natural resources in the territory—gold, diamonds, hedge sisal, cattle and other livestock, cotton, rice, maize, groundnuts. Yet, said Chagula, Sukumaland remained—because of 'bad administration'—one of the poorer areas of the territory. Like Bomani, he felt a passion for improvement and a desire for rapid change born of the feeling that the government and non-Africans exploited Africans. A primary reason for reactivating the Sukuma Union in 1950 was to achieve for the African people of Sukumaland the prosperity which Chagula and others felt they properly deserved.[3]

Chiefs and Critics

According to Chagula, the Union intended (and the by-laws

---

[1] 'How the Sukuma Union began,' by James M. Bubele, n.d. (1951), SUF. (Orig. Sw.) In portions of this chapter, as in Chapter 3, I rely heavily on materials from the Sukuma Union files. I am indebted to former officers of the Union for their cooperation in locating the files and in affording me access.
[2] D.O. to Chagula, 14 Dec. 1950, MZDF.
[3] Chagula, interview, 1 Dec. 1964.

confirmed this) to cooperate with the government in all fields pertaining to development. In any case, cooperation rather than opposition to or interference with government programs was to be recommended if the Union wished to continue in operation. However, as with TAA after 1949, penetration of rural areas inevitably meant conflict with native authorities and, consequently, with the colonial administration. Like TAA, the Union sought to take the grievances of people directly to the government rather than through the chiefs, initiating a rival independent channel which the chiefs opposed. Further, the Union in particular often received complaints against the chiefs themselves. Under British administration, chiefs and native authorities had become much more powerful than they were in traditional Sukuma society. For years there had been no outlets—as there were traditionally—for the expression of dissent. Nor was there any longer an opportunity for circumscribing a chief's powers, which were now established and guaranteed by an alien authority.

The Union found that discontent focused on communal labor turn-outs, on the implementation of natural resources legislation, and on the services rendered directly to the chief himself—cultivation of his fields, provision by local residents of food and services for the chief and his large entourage when on safari, the slaughter of a cow at the behest of the chief whenever a government officer arrived. Traditionally, these services were accepted, but the relationship of service was reciprocal. For example, the chief was expected to provide food and services for his people in case of famine or special need. An unsalaried magico-religious authority in the traditional Sukuma order, he accepted tribute both to sustain himself and his family and to provide a sort of savings banks in kind for the chiefdom at large. A chief who failed to produce the needed rain for crops and who ran out of stores could be turned out of his job by discontented subjects.

Not so under the British. The chief became a civil servant entirely dependent on an alien regime for his authority, his tenure and his salary. Traditional forms of tribute made little sense when the chief no longer needed tribute to sustain himself, and when his subjects were themselves moving into the cash sector of the economy and no longer required insurance deposited with the chief in the form of foodstuffs. Many chiefs, however, continued to press the traditional requirements on their subjects. The latter —particularly those who had received a few standards of primary education or who were trying to earn money themselves in cotton, cattle or small trade—resented the impositions of the chief. In the post-Second World War era, these impositions appeared to be anachronistic and increasingly authoritarian. Citizens resented, too, the fact that the chief's salary, plus the exactions in kind which he continued to extract, gave the chief every advantage over his more lowly competitors in the modern cash sector. It was not unusual for a Sukuma chief to own an automobile or a truck, a conspicuous demonstration of affluence which could not fail—even among his own people—to aggravate at least the aspiring few.

Many, of course, regarded the administrative and economic preminence of the chief as the natural order of things. Considered 'shauri la Mungu' (the will of God), it was a *de facto* situation simply to be noted rather than opposed. Uneducated and less wealthy members of the community were not subject to the same scale of frustrations and deprivations due to chiefly hegemony as were their more educated, wealthy and ambitious counterparts. Discontented, the latter tended to move from the inner bastions of Sukumaland in Maswa, Kwimba and south Mwanza to frontier areas in Geita and Busega where they could nurture their ambitions in relative freedom. Where such men collected, as in Nassa and Karumo-Buchosa, economic and political associations were not slow to arise. But there were still, even in these border-land areas, grievances to be enunciated and native authorities—albeit weaker ones than those from whence the discontents had come—to be reckoned with.

The uneducated and less wealthy majority remained quiescent, however, only up to a point. When the occasional aggravations of the chiefs' personal requirements became compounded with the regimen of rules and restrictions associated with the implementa-tion of the Sukumaland Development Scheme, the more ordinary Sukuma found that he was being told what to do with his land and livestock by chiefs, headmen, agricultural instructors or veterinary assistants, and that if he didn't do what he was told, he was hauled into court and fined. Though the detested regulations were conceived and drawn up by the British, they were legislated into force through the Federal Council of chiefs and the district chiefly federations. After peasants joined with already disen-chanted semi-educated and local trading elites to resist the en-croachments of native authorities and the unwanted regulations, the ground was prepared for town-based elites to penetrate the countryside with a message which attacked not only the chiefs but the alien administration which controlled them.

The Struggle for Indentity and Program

Thus, in the early 1950s the Sukuma Union became a focus for the increasing number of Sukuma in rural areas who felt that the existing native authority regime not only failed to satisfy their aspirations, but positively militated against those aspirations. Individuals brought complaints against particular chiefs. Leaders denounced the excesses of the entire system. The Union, of course, favored development—and it was particularly active in attempts at educational advancement—but it held that the development schemes of the administration and the native authorities were pushed forward without consultation or consent of the people whom the schemes were intended to serve. A cardinal complaint was that the so-called 'people's representatives' were not truly elected. The chief held a *de facto*, if not a legal, veto; and the Union found that in practice it was impossible to achieve what it regarded as its due portion of representation on the councils at any level.

The Union then sought for itself a formal constitutional role. In April 1951 it requested representation on the Sukumaland Federal Council so that its members might learn more in detail about the development schemes and bring their views directly to the Council on development and native authority matters.[1] But no more than with TAA would the administration tolerate this sort of initiative. In the eyes of the administration, not only did the particular representations of the Union threaten the development schemes, but the very fact of a separate organizational hierarchy—against which the Provincial Commissioner had warned in 1945—seemed calculated to undermine established local government. The government replied (in a decision consistent with its earlier rulings on township authorities and procedures to be followed by the TAA branch at Busega) that no voluntary associations—not even the Sukuma Union—could be represented in the Sukumaland Federal Council; that the views or requests of the Union must be taken initially to the local chief. The chief would first discuss a matter with other chiefs and councillors in the district. If it were felt that the matter warranted consideration

[1] SU to the Secretary, Sukumaland Headquarters, Malya, 5 Apr. 1951, MZDF.

at the Council, it would be presented to the District Commissioner for consideration for the agenda.

Dissatisfied, the Union made further inquiries. The administration then pointed out that anyone might attend meetings of the
Federal Council as an observer, but that he would have no right
to speak or vote.[1] Meetings of the Council were held two or three
times a year. Beginning with the November 1951 meeting, Bomani
and other Sukuma Union representatives observed the proceedings
and lobbied between sessions with the councillors.[2] They made
notes on items of special interest. One marginal comment beside
a section of the November 1951 minutes, outlining the plans for
destocking measures to be instituted the following year, read thus:
'This is dangerous. Let's be awake!'[3]

At the end of 1950 the Sukuma Union had only thirty-five
members on its rolls. Most lived in Mwanza town—a dozen
clerks, half a dozen teachers, half a dozen traders, a few artisans
and medical dressers and two students at Makerere College in
Uganda. Though they lived or worked in the town, most of the
members, being Sukuma, had contacts with the areas in which
they were born and raised—in Maswa, Kwimba, Geita, or
elsewhere in Mwanza District itself. In the rural context they
stressed the close relationship of the Union with farmers' and
traders' organizations. Late in 1950 and early in 1951 members
began to sign up from rural centers, and the nuclei for later
branches appeared. By the end of the year there were nearly one
hundred dues-paying members. More than a fourth were farmers
and traders based in rural areas.

The Union succeeded in opening branches in several outlying
areas in 1952. Where interest in a locality seemed to warrant a
branch, a local representative was selected to enroll members.
At other times a delegation of Union officers from Mwanza
arranged to make the trip to hold a special meeting for the opening
of a branch. Sometimes membership in a local branch was—at
least at the outset—insufficient to provide a full battery of officers
and committee-men. Branches were not yet numerically impressive units and most did not quickly develop an independent local
program. Membership and committee meetings in Mwanza,

[1] D.P.C. to SU, 16 Apr. 1951, SUF; D.C. to SU, 17 Oct., 1951, MZDF.
[2] Interviews: Chagula; Bomani, 4 Feb. 1965.
[3] Handwritten marginal comments on Minutes of a meeting of the Sukumaland
Federal Council, 30 Oct.–2 Nov. 1951, SUF. (Orig. Sw.).

held every several months and attended usually by some leaders from outlying branches, remained the principal forums for discussion of issues. Not until late in 1953 and early 1954 did leaders from headquarters devote themselves to lengthy tours through rural areas.[1]

Leaders in Mwanza, meanwhile, increasingly felt the need for a permanent office building and for full-time salaried officers, but with some more obvious connections to the countryside. Some argued that a permanent headquarters should be located outside the township, where people would be more interested in the activities of the Union, and staffed by non-civil servants not subject to transfer. Others countered that the work of the Union was most easily carried out in town where qualified men—not simple farmers—had quick access to government officials. The second view prevailed, but the Union agreed to hold more of its public meetings outside of the township limits.

Chagula left Mwanza on transfer in January 1952—apparently a confirmation of the widely held belief that the government deliberately transferred politically minded civil servants to other areas when they became too actively involved locally. In Chagula's case he and other teachers were accused of fomenting a student strike at Bwiru School (which Chagula denied). At the Union's farewell for Chagula, Bomani hailed him as the courageous father of the Union who, unlike other well-meaning but more fearful souls, never hesitated to jeopardize himself, his job or his reputation in working for the well-being of his tribe.[2]

With Chagula's departure, the leadership of the Union fell to Bomani and to the newly elected president, Dominick Kipondya,

[1] Register of branches and membership lists, SUF. One of the more active branches of the Union, dating from mid-1951, opened in Geita and by mid-1952 claimed 129 members in Buchosa chiefdom. An area of heavy Sukuma immigration since the war, Buchosa still was ruled by a non-Sukuma chief. Under the leadership of a farmer, Methusela Goyi, the Union came quickly into conflict with Chief Paulo Rugagaza. Chief Paulo complained that members of the Union refused to turn out for communal labor and warned the D.C. that the purpose of the Union was to oppose the government and the native authorities. The Union pressed the view that the slaughter of one cow for fifty persons who had worked ten days each was not sufficient pay for communal turnouts. The Union asked for wages in money, not meat. The Union insisted that it did not oppose the government but only wished to represent the rights of the Sukuma people. It planned to collect funds for an independent school and a hospital as well as a Union office. (Minutes, 14 Mar. 1953; SU to D.C., 26 Feb. 1952, SUF.)

[2] Speech by Bomani, 2 Jan. 1952, SUF. (Orig. Sw.)

a secretary of the Mwanza native treasury who had studied for some time in England. For Bomani, as for previous leaders, the significance of the Union lay in collective organization; but Bomani had a practical understanding of organization—based in part on his work with cotton growers—which earlier leaders had lacked. He travelled into the rural areas in 1951 and 1952 on behalf of the incipient Lake Province Growers Association and, in his capacity as secretary of the Sukuma Union, recruited for the Union as well. He pointed out that the quality of self-reliance characteristic of the individual or of local groups of Sukuma in the past profited nothing in the contemporary world; the Sukuma was still backward in comparison with other tribes. Only an effective association could make its voice heard. Bomani told his followers that it was thrilling to see that very Sukuma, who was sufficient unto himself in the past, showing today 'a desire for cooperation with his fellows so that he will be listened to.'[1]

Having had its appeal for representation on the Sukumaland Federal Council denied by the government the previous year, the Union found itself in 1952 increasingly critical of the Council. It claimed that the so-called people's representatives were lackeys of the chiefs, with no voice and no power. Bomani urged the Union to call a separate general meeting of all Sukuma, but the Union rejected the suggestion in favor of a more gradual and moderate propaganda approach: newspaper articles and speakers to tour the districts.[2] Aware of the need for publicizing its activities, the Union selected one member to write regularly in the only Sukuma-language publication extant—the *Lumuli* newspaper published by the Roman Catholic Mwanza Diocese. At general meetings held in Mwanza in 1952, the Union addressed itself principally to problems of education, destocking and taxation.

Education was a primary interest of the elite who realized that the long-term progress of the Sukuma would depend on more and better education. In October 1951 the Union made an attempt through the town elders to inspect the township schools and in 1952 raised questions about school fees. By mid-1952 they decided that they should raise money to establish an independent middle school. The need was great because many children were unable to find places to continue after completing the four years of primary school. The Union considered secondary and even

[1] *Ibid.*
[2] Minutes of a meeting of SU, 20 Jan. 1952, SUF. All minutes orig. Sw.

L

university education a future possibility for the proposed school and some hoped the Union might eventually establish bursaries for overseas education.

The officers of the Union made the first financial contributions and personally subscribed donations of thatch and mud-brick. In September the District Commissioner was notified of the Union's intentions with regard to two possible locations for the proposed school. The Union planned to collect funds for the school by a house-to-house canvass in Mwanza. Julius Nyerere, asked to be principal of the independent school, declined the post but gave the project his blessing.[1]

The project was ambitious but far beyond the available or potential resources of the Union, so the idea was dropped after nearly two years of intermittent efforts. The sustained interest of the Union in the school dramatized, however, the feeling of many elite Africans that educational services were inadequate in Sukumaland. It also demonstrated a desire for opportunities other than those dictated and directed by the government.

Proposals for compulsory destocking of cattle drew the attention of the Union in 1951 even before the new destocking rules were promulgated. After the new regulations had come into force, the Union discussed the matter at great length and appointed a special committee to examine it more closely. Returning from a trip to the Northern Province on cooperative society business, Bomani reported to the Union that Africans in Arusha had asked, 'Are you those Sukuma who agreed to destock their cattle because of a government order?' In late 1952 the Union strenuously objected to destocking and to the tax imposed on cattle sold at the markets: not only were cattle owners forced to sell, but they were then taxed as well! It was felt that the low prices offered at cattle markets made compulsory destocking in practical fact intolerable, that cattle prices should be increased substantially so that the farmer could buy European hoes and tractors and further improve his land, and that the formation of a cattle cooperative was a possible solution to the price problem. The Union designated its president and secretary to write a letter to the Sukumaland Federal Council, firmly objecting to the onerous measures related to cattle. They were charged also to request an explanation of the disposition of all taxes collected in Sukumaland.[2] In fact, cattle destocking and

[1] *Ibid.* 4 Apr. 1953; SU to D.C., 8 Sept. 1952, MZDF; Bomani, interview.
[2] Minutes, 2 Mar., 20 July, 24 Aug., 1952; 14–15, Mar. 1953, SUF.

cattle tax were to become the dominant political issues of the middle 1950s.

3   TAA: MOBILIZATION OF DISCONTENT

Through the early 1950s the interests of the administration and of African politicians seemed increasingly to polarize. The latter became more numerous, and both sides became more aggressive and less flexible. New ideas, which had emerged at higher levels of the administration after the war, were being felt on the ground as implemented policies. The administration pursued with fervor its dream of a pyramid of representative councils from village to federation and prosecuted with diligence its schemes for transforming the economy. The administration forced or cajoled the people to accept unpopular legislation (e.g. cattle destocking, cotton cess, cattle tax, tie-ridging) through the Sukumaland Federal Council. Committed to a policy of strengthening constituted native authorities for the new tasks of local government, it turned a deaf ear to the complaints of political leaders and their appeals for representation of political associations.

As it became clear that the administration did not intend to give the educated elite of the towns a significant role in the reformed and 'democratized' structures of local government, the new politicians turned still more to the rural areas where they found another more receptive audience. Between 1951 and 1954 the cooperative societies, the Sukuma Union and TAA extended their organizations rapidly and dramatically into the countryside. Under vigorous African leadership, these associations combined new economic and political ideas with a capacity to articulate the accumulating grievances of the peasant and to cater to his needs in a world molded more and more by non-traditional as well as traditional forces.

Because of their obvious identification with the administration, chiefs and other native authorities fell ever further into disrepute. When the ideas and activities of the new associations—spurred on both by rising African political consciousness and by the excesses of administrative development schemes—spread from the towns and prominent rural centers into the homesteads and villages of the Sukuma farmer, the native authority system directly confronted the challenge of the new politics. In the countryside the bread-and-butter issues were oppressive agricultural and veterinary legislation, grievances against chiefs and payment of various taxes and fees to central and local governments. Amidst the maze of rules and orders then pertaining in Sukumaland, it was not a difficult task to link the aspirations of the more sophisticated elite for freedom from colonial rule with the desires of the ordinary rural Sukuma to be free from rules which prevented him from cultivating his land as he saw fit. Only partly modified and still supported by the colonial administration, the native authority system found, once rural discontent had become pervasive, that the challenge of a nationalist-oriented politics was one with which it was finally unable to cope.

Thus it was that intense and highly organized political activity existed in Sukumaland for at least two years before TANU was formed. The advent of TANU in mid-1954 required little more than a change of letterhead. TANU in Sukumaland was basically TAA under a new name. With assists from the cooperative movement and the Sukuma Union, TAA had by 1954 already achieved—in leadership, membership, organization, style and ideology—the status of a full-scale political movement.

A Petition to the United Nations

A petition submitted by the Mwanza branch of TAA to the 1951 United Nations Visiting Mission framed the more urgent demands which characterized the pre-TANU period. Asking that the Mission consider the views of Africans as well as of the administration, the Mwanza unit stated:

The Africans must now have a big say over the rule and public funds of the Territory in order to enable them to acquire independence in the near future. In fact it is high time that Africans should be given an opportunity to start shouldering the rule of the country.[1]

Specifically, TAA requested increased African representation in the Legislative Council; immediate introduction of the elective principle in all public bodies (e.g. Provincial Council, Land Utilization Board, Cotton Board, etc.); responsible posts for Africans in administrative and technical *cadres*; abolition of 99-year leases of Crown Lands to non-Africans and restriction of European settlement; a single educational system with Swahili rather than English the medium of instruction; more education

---

[1] United Nations, Trusteeship Council, Official Records, *Petitions from Tanganyika*, T/Pet. 2/103, Oct. 1951 (mimeographed).

for Tanganyikans including overseas training in countries other
than England for lawyers, engineers, doctors and teachers (perhaps with direct financial assistance from the Trusteeship Council);
and finally, in the economic sphere, encouragement of African
cooperatives, loan banks for Africans, a percentage of mining
and estate revenues to go direct to local native treasuries and free
trade with the rest of the world so that imported goods would
be less expensive and reduce the cost of living.[1]

The petition of the Mwanza branch was more strongly worded
even than the petition of TAA headquarters in Dar es Salaam.
Though the Dar es Salaam petition made some similar and some
additional points, there was no language comparable to Mwanza's
explicit: 'to acquire independence in the near future.'[2] A contrast
may also be drawn with the petitions presented by Sukuma
chiefs, who had made such strong representations to the U.N.
Visiting Mission in 1948. The Shinyanga chiefs now contented
themselves with a plea for better education. The Kwimba chiefs

[1] *Ibid.* A separate petition from a TAA branch, which located itself at Ngudu
in nearby Kwimba District, asked for loans for Africans, better wages, a
hospital, a college, telephone service and eight African representatives in the
Legislative Council (T/Pet. 2/108, Oct. 1951). There is no evidence to show
that Ngudu, any more than Maswa, developed an active TAA organization
of its own. No traces of branch activity appeared in available government
files and people living in the Ngudu area do not remember TAA as having
been active there as people inevitably do remember wherever TAA was really
active. Nonetheless, Ngudu TAA representatives appeared from time to
time: at the 1947 Mwanza provincial TAA conference; with this 1951 petition
to the United Nations; in 1954 on provincial TAA or TANU committee
lists. M. I. Kitenge knew personally a Hehe tailor who lived in Ngudu and
was a member of TAA (Kitenge, interview). The writer believes that a civil
servant or a trader or two in Ngudu at various times were TAA members,
but that there was never an ongoing branch activity as there was in Busega,
and later in Geita and Malampaka.
   The Government Employees Association of Mwanza also presented a
strongly worded petition to the 1951 United Nations Visiting Mission.
They criticized discrimination in employment, asked for higher wages and
pressed for nomination of African government servants to the Legislative
Council. They made the point that discrimination against Africans 'holds
back progress to self-government' (T/Pet. 2/102, Aug. 1951).
[2] *Ibid.* T/Pet. 2/120, Sept. 1951. *Inter alia*, the Dar es Salaam petition asked
for more than parity representation for Africans in the territorial government
and for a permanent United Nations liaison officer in every Trust Territory.
The petition criticized the Tanganyika European Council and opposed an
East African High Commission; it made a miscellany of points about African
rights, education, land and the civil service. Besides the Dar es Salaam,
Mwanza and Ngudu TAA petitions, the only other TAA petition in the
territory was from Dodoma—a mild document which pleaded only for better
education for Africans (T/Pet. 2/111, Oct. 1951).

asked for a secondary school, a technical school and a maternity hospital with the usual phraseology about 'under the good guidance of the excellent British Government...[which is] teaching us how to administer our country in the right way.' The Maswa chiefs, somewhat more importunate, asked for a college with degrees, a railroad from the Northern to the Lake Province, and eight African representatives in Legislative Council.[1]

Six years had not significantly altered the sociological description of Mwanza's African elite.[2] The percolation of grievances and aspirations, however, and an expanding political consciousness did bring what was essentially the same group that had led TAA since its formation in Mwanza in 1945 to a more sophisticated, insistent and focused expression of views in the 1951 petition. Yet however eloquent, language is never the whole of politics. The truly decisive change in TAA leadership was to come a year later with the advent of *full-time* political organizers—men who differed from their predecessors not as much in background as in singular vocational commitment to politics as a way of life.

The mounting anxieties of the chiefs—who evinced increasing concern over the need for all associations and citizens to 'cooperate with their rulers' in 'progressive measures' for the improvement of Sukumaland[3]—were shared by the administration. In 1951 the Provincial Commissioner noted 'a progressive lessening in tribal discipline.' In 1952 he observed that 'the growing political consciousness of many elements in the African population... demands the closest attention.' And in 1953:

The most significant aspect of the year has been the development and spread of a local political 'opposition'...with a vocal and ambitious few soliciting the support of the multitude with promises of successful opposition to authority in any convenient field.[4]

---

[1] *Ibid.* T/Pet. 2/106, 107, 110; Oct. 1951.

[2] Only the names had changed. The president, like Mgeni before him, was a long-time resident of Mwanza town, an artisan and a religious leader in the Muslim community (Amiry Maftah). The secretary, in terms of background an almost identical replica of Chombo, was a Catholic secondary-school-educated Bonde employed in the Medical Department (S. E. Mdachi). As in 1945, other officers included a non-Sukuma Christian clerk in the provincial administration, a well-educated Muslim holding an office of secondary importance, and a Catholic middle-school-educated product of Sukumaland (though a Nyamwezi) having connections with a local chiefly family. (Interviews, and MZDF.)

[3] Secretary–treasurer, Sukumaland Federal Council, to provincial secretary of TAA, 24 June 1951, MZDF.

[4] Lake Province Annual Report, 1951, 1952, 1953, LPF.

In Sukumaland by 1953, there was many a 'convenient field' for political opposition, especially natural resources legislation enacted in conjunction with the Sukumaland Development Plan. As early as 1946 the administration required tie-ridging, a new cure for soil erosion, of at least a half acre of land by every cultivator, a regulation received skeptically even by certain government officers.[1] In 1948 a former government officer who had served in the Mwanza area for six years complained that 'ever-changing Agricultural Officers plague and bewilder the Natives with ever-changing decrees' and decried the mounting restrictions on farming, land, forests, housing, prospecting and mining, hunting, and marketing, which were enforced by fines and imprisonment.[2] In 1951 the Provincial Commissioner himself warned of 'a disturbing sign of dangerous accumulation of legislation impossible of thorough enforcement.'[3] After 1951, however, the situation was further aggravated with the introduction of compulsory destocking, cattle tax and land settlement rules designed to control the movements of people and stock. By 1953 the Provincial Commissioner's 'local political "opposition" ' was in full bloom.

Of course, the new politics was not simply a reaction to restrictive legislation. Other more secular trends were at work, and the Provincial Commissioner pointed to some of them in his annual reports: increased wealth and mobility, improved communications, immigration from outside of 'both men and ideas.'[4]

What he did not say—and almost certainly could not then see—was that the colonial era was beginning to end in Sukumaland as throughout Africa. Regardless of what the administration might have done or not done, political changes which led inevitably to independence could not, by their very nature, have been contained by an administration whose departure from the scene ultimately would be required. However grand the design and noble the conception for the planned political and economic development of Sukumaland, the restrictive legislation deemed necessary for the attainment of that development carried the seeds of its own

[1] 'Apparently the new cure for soil erosion is tie-ridging and this is being encouraged by propaganda among African tillers... Until the African Agricultural Inspectors realise that their job is instructing and not persecuting they will not have much support from the African population.' (Mwanza District Annual Report, 1946, MZDF.)
[2] United Nations: T/Pet. 2/40, 15 Oct. 1947.
[3] Lake Province Annual Report, 1951, LPF.   [4] *Ibid.* 1951, 1952.

destruction: it both galvanized and gave a foothold to the 'political opposition.' When on the one hand repression of this 'opposition' was deemed necessary to save both the legislation and the plans for development, and on the other, external pressure for constitutional change began to be felt from London, the United Nations, and elsewhere in the 'Third World,' the dislodgement of the entire administrative structure became but a matter of time. Peasants who wanted to be left alone, politicians who wanted a place in the sun for both themselves and their people and the trend of the times toward self-determination, self-government, and independence were to prove a compelling combination.

The New Leadership: Bomani, Munanka and Kandoro

The architects of the envigorated Lake Province TAA of the early 1950s were Paul Bomani, Isaac Bhoke Munanka and Saadani Abdu Kandoro. All three embarked on political careers which were to carry them to important party and government posts both before and after independence. At the time of writing, these men were, respectively, Minister of Economic Development, Minister of State (President's Office) and Area Commissioner (Bagamoyo) in the government of Tanzania.

Bomani's leadership of the cooperative movement has been discussed. A member also of TAA and of the Sukuma Union, Bomani became president of the latter in 1951 and of TAA in 1952. One of Mwanza's outstanding figures, he also served in those years on the Township Authority and the Lake Province Council.

Munanka, a Kuria from North Mara District to the east of Lake Victoria, completed Standard X and a two-year clerical course at Tabora School. Posted to Mwanza as a government clerk in 1948, he became a member of TAA but did not become prominent until after his resignation from government service in January 1952. Never happy as a civil servant, Munanka found his *forte* in active politics. He was elected vice-president of TAA in January 1952 and president after Bomani went to the United Kingdom to study in October 1953.

Kandoro, son of a Manyema trader–farmer and a native of Ujiji, completed teacher training school at Bwiru in 1944 before taking up a post in the native treasury at Uyui, Tabora. He resigned his government post in 1946 to become a trader. The initiator of various associations of a semi-political or political nature in the Ujiji–Tabora area (including a branch of TAA in 1944), he took his political predilections with him on trading trips, travelling sometimes as far as Mwanza, Musoma and even Nairobi. He sold chairs, oil and utensils at the town markets where he traveled, but he also talked politics and met Bomani and Munanka in Mwanza. He recalls addressing a large meeting on one occasion in the Mwanza community center where people were 'surprised to see a man who sold chairs at the market wanting to govern.' He claims to have questioned the validity of alien rule as early as 1947 and to have pushed for the reorganization and re-christening of TAA in early 1952. In 1952 Bomani and Munanka asked him to become provincial secretary of TAA in Mwanza and in 1953 he moved his home to Mwanza from Ujiji the better to devote his efforts to his new post.[1]

With Kandoro's election as provincial secretary in mid-1952, the top leadership of TAA was for the first time in the hands of men who were not civil servants. Kandoro had resigned from government service to go into trading and then abandoned trading for politics. Munanka resigned from the civil service to devote himself to politics and to the establishment of an African-owned and -operated transport and trading company. Bomani worked only briefly as a clerk before switching to cooperatives and politics. No longer was TAA to be the avocational interest of men whose major energies were absorbed elsewhere; TAA was to be one of the products of men who served as full-time political organizers, who dedicated the major portion of their energies to the fostering of African enterprises and associations with an economic or political cutting edge. No longer would TAA simply register grievances or present petitions or organize in *ad hoc* response to a particular need in a particular area; TAA would become a full-scale political movement led by men motivated by a singular passion for the most fundamental political change of all—self-government. From the time of their first all-night political discussions in Mwanza in 1951–2, Bomani, Munanka and Kandoro defined their goal explicitly, simply, powerfully: 'to search for ways to release the country from enslavement...to work for an end to alien rule.'[2]

---

[1] Kandoro, interview, 21 Nov. 1964; also S. A. Kandoro, *Mwito wa Uhuru* (The Call of Freedom) (Dar es Salaam: Thakers, 1961), *passim*.

[2] *Ibid.* p. 19. (All quoted material from Kandoro originally in Swahili unless otherwise noted.)

Organization of the Party

In January 1952, Kandoro, Munanka and M. I. Kitenge,[1] another of the politically active core group in Mwanza, wrote to TAA headquarters in Dar es Salaam proposing that TAA's name be changed to signal its transformation into a more clearly political organization which 'stands unequivocably for the rights of the citizens of this country.' They proposed several alternative designations, including 'Tanganyika African National Union'— the name adopted by TAA at its eventual reorganization in July 1954.[2]

In February Bomani, Kandoro and Joseph Petro, the district secretary of TAA in Shinyanga, met with three representatives of a branch of TAA at Bukoba to decide on by-laws for a refurbished Lake Province organization. The by-laws, which were to serve temporarily until by-laws for Tanganyika as a whole should be established from Dar es Salaam headquarters, required that general provincial meetings be held four times yearly, that officers be elected annually and that entrance fees and annual subscriptions be six shillings and four shillings respectively. A permanent provincial office in Mwanza would be staffed by a full-time salaried secretary who could not accept part-time employment elsewhere. No provincial officers could be government servants or work for Europeans or Asian concerns—a consideration dictated certainly by the felt need to make politics itself a full-time occupation, but also, perhaps, by a desire to avoid untoward influence or pressure from employers who might not be entirely sympathetic with the activities of the association. All money collected by district branches would be turned over to the provincial headquarters, and the needs of each branch would be met by an allotment of 200 shillings. Contributions from members of any race would be accepted, but only Africans could be members—and race, not birthplace, was to define

[1] Kitenge, a Manyema Muslim born in Mwanza township, attended primary school in Mwanza and middle school in Bukoba. He worked as an agricultural instructor for four years before taking up trade and tailoring independently after 1949. Involved in a multitude of trading and political associations in Mwanza in the 1950s, he was one of the 'activists' whose name will appear from time to time, but who never became one of the pivotal figures. He epitomized the young, vigorous, imaginative, but only moderately well-educated 'Swahili' townsman who plied the political trail of the fight for independence but never reaped the reward of personal advancement to a position of status or responsibility outside his own locality.
[2] Kandoro, pp. 2–3.

'African.' There was no delineation of the political aims of TAA as such, but it was specifically stated that 'the Provincial Branch has the right to appeal to the United Nations if the Colonial Office or the Dar es Salaam Secretariat are unwilling to listen, to give assistance, or to forward representations to higher authority.'[1]

Munanka led 'the next attack' (as the Deputy Provincial Commissioner characterized it) in January 1953.[2] He headed a TAA delegation which met with Provincial Commissioner Rowe to urge that destocking and livestock taxation be abolished and that the people themselves—rather than native authorities alone—be more thoroughly consulted on legislative questions. The outcome of the meeting was unsatisfactory from TAA's point of view: aside from reiterating the necessity for the legislation in question, the Provincial Commissioner maintained that the people were properly consulted through public meetings held by native authorities and increasingly through new local councils. These were the established constitutional channels through which TAA should register its views. In somewhat schoolmasterly fashion, Rowe assured the deputation that the government did not 'despise' TAA and that 'if your intentions [are] good, you can help.' Admitting that it was difficult for citizens to keep accurately informed, he said: 'If you trust Government and Native Authorities to raise the people, the country will progress, but if every false sermon [is] believed, trouble follows.'[3]

Branches outside Mwanza: a Variety of Interests

The branch of TAA in Shinyanga also became increasingly active in the early 1950s. Joseph Petro, a civil servant who became TAA's district secretary, asked the United Nations Visiting Mission in 1951 to permit Tanganyika Africans to select an African to attend United Nations meetings on behalf of Africans and the following year recommended to the government in a 'Memorandum on Constitutional Development' that Shinyanga should

---

[1] Minutes of a meeting to draft by-laws for TAA, Lake Province, Feb. 1952, SUF. The by-laws also contained several provisions more typical of a mutual aid society than a political association: assistance for members when sick, oppressed or killed either because of their connection with the association or for other reasons.
[2] TAA to P.C., 16 Jan. 1953, including handwritten comments by D.P.C., LPF.
[3] 'Notes on meeting between the P.C., Mwanza, D.P.C., Malya and the African Association on Friday, 13 Feb., 1953,' LPF.

have ten official and ten unofficial African representatives on any new county council. These were to be 'selected by Africans themselves and *not* by the Government itself.'[1] TAA lobbied, too, for the use of Swahili in the Legislative Council and other government councils, and for greater African representation in government bodies at all levels.[2]

Though a branch of Lake Province TAA, the Shinyanga branch operated quite independently of Mwanza. In contrast to Mwanza and Nassa where *former* government servants and small retail traders provided the core of TAA leadership after 1951, Shinyanga's core group remained currently employed civil servants plus local cattle traders. Much smaller and less important than Mwanza, Shinyanga was not the sort of place to induce a civil servant to abandon his job for full-time work with nascent African economic or political associations. African retail traders were lacking because in Shinyanga Indians and Arabs dominated retail trade. Cattle traders were present because Shinyanga was the heart of Sukuma cattle country. TAA meetings were planned to coincide with the once or twice monthly cattle markets held in the township so that cattle traders from outlying areas could participate.

A Geita branch of TAA opened at Katunguru in the northern part of the district near the lake in mid-1952. TAA's leader was a Sumbwa Muslim, Rashidi Shiza by name, a tailor by trade. In October 1950, Shiza had formed at Katunguru a branch of the Mwanza-based Lake Province African Tailors Union—the only registered trade union in the territory at that time. After organizing a strike for fewer hours and higher wages in May 1951, he was convicted of unlawful activities and sentenced to five months in jail and a 300-shilling fine. Released from jail in June 1952, he returned immediately to Katunguru and three days later formed a local branch of TAA.[3]

Katunguru then became the headquarters of TAA in Geita District and, after Busega, the second strong rural branch of TAA in Sukumaland. Shiza established sub-branches in other parts

---

[1] United Nations: T/Pet. 2/118, Aug. 1951; TAA memorandum, 5 Mar. 1952, LPF.

[2] Joseph K. Petro, 'Political history of TAA Shinyanga,' a paper prepared for Kivukoni College, Dar es Salaam, 1964; Petro, interview, Nov. 1964.

[3] D.C. to Labour Officer, Mwanza, 16 Oct. 1950; 17 Apr. 1951; Labour Officer to D.C., 23 Oct. 1950; 20 Apr. 1951; 3 Aug. 1951; 23 Apr. 1951, GTDF. Shiza, interview, 20 Feb. 1965.

of the district where he could find local men to lead them. As elsewhere in Sukumaland, resentment against destocking and natural resources regulations provided the springboard for some of Shiza's representations and led to disputes with local native authorities and government officials. Desire for improved boat service to Mwanza and the need for a new market at Katunguru also concerned the association. By the end of 1952 Geita TAA had 96 members and by the time of the ban in 1954, perhaps 200.[1] In addition to their TAA activities, Shiza and other local TAA leaders took prominent roles in local cotton cooperative societies.[2]

The branch of TAA at Busega best reflected the mounting resistance in rural areas against increased pressure from above with regard to enforcement of natural resources legislation and prosecution of offenders. Owning itself 'dumbfounded by the sudden change...since 1951,' the Nassa-based branch complained in 1953 that senior government officers and native authorities were seeking out prosecutions as they had never done before. If the District Commissioner and the chief themselves became prosecutors, who then would act as magistrate? Or had procedures been changed so that cases would go directly to a high judge rather than to chiefs, district officers and the District Commissioner as in the past? Noting that the agriculture officer and agriculture instructors were also deeply involved in the same unsavory business of prosecution, TAA asked: 'What sort of work are they supposed to be doing here in Nassa?'[3]

Obviously, TAA here adopted for its own purposes a basic tenet of British conceptions of democracy and justice—the independence of the judiciary. The argument that an accused person should not be prosecuted and tried by the same man did not, however, impress the District Commissioner who was under no misapprehension about the variations from the classic British model which obtained under the colonial administration in Tanganyika. He wrote: 'The Chief has the power to prosecute wrong-doers, to deliberate the merits of the case and also to pass judgment, and this power he has exercised for quite some time.'[4]

---

[1] Shiza, interview. Membership reports at TAA meeting, Mwanza, Nov. 1952, Sagala papers.
[2] Shiza was first chairman of a local cooperative society in 1953, then chairman of the Buchililio Union in Geita, then vice-chairman of the Victoria Federation of Cooperative Unions in 1954 (Shiza, interview).
[3] Busega TAA to D.C., 5 Jan. 1953, MZDF. (Orig. Sw.)
[4] D.C. to Busega TAA, 9 May 1953, MZDF. (Orig. Sw.)

For that matter, TAA was probably not under any misapprehension either. It was neither the first nor the last time that politicians in Sukumaland and elsewhere in Tanganyika would appeal to British standards to buttress their arguments against the colonial administration and in favor of the sort of government the British themselves enjoyed at home.

The Busega branch also pushed with some vehemence an issue which still angered African traders: restrictions on the transportation of food crops across district lines when the government, Asian companies and Europeans in Mwanza imported food from outside without challenge. Did the prohibition apply only to Africans? The District Commissioner replied that the rules were made to protect the people of all districts against famine by requiring each district, including those in Sukumaland, to protect and reserve their own food produce. Beyond this, the government sometimes brought in food from outside as a service to the people.[1] Sensible as the rules may have seemed from the government's viewpoint, enterprising Africans felt not only the annoyance of restrictions, but the weight of *de facto* discrimination.

Before 1952, the Mwanza branch of TAA had selected its office-bearers locally, then more or less automatically served as provincial headquarters, too. Chombo, as provincial secretary, had tried to foster unity on a provincial basis, but he was only momentarily successful with the 1947 provincial conference. His successor, Chasma, seemed to have had little contact with TAA branches other than those within his own Mwanza District.

Bomani, Munanka and Kandoro, however, had larger designs; and the 'Lake Province' TAA of the period 1952–4 was largely their creation. They were elected to serve as provincial officers, a provincial TAA committee with representatives from TAA outposts throughout the province was selected,[2] and provincial conferences were held with some frequency. With strong TAA organizations in six districts—Mwanza, Shinyanga, Ukerewe, Geita, Bukoba and Musoma—and a collection of representatives and minor outposts elsewhere, Lake Province TAA discussed the possibility of asking that territorial TAA headquarters be switched to Mwanza in view of the fact that TAA activities at the headquarters in Dar es Salaam had become 'dormant'.[3]

[1] Busega TAA to D.C., 10 Feb.; D.C. to Busega TAA, 9 May 1953, MZDF.
[2] Kandoro, p. 20.
[3] Petro, interview.

4 THE SUKUMA UNION: FURTHER INTO THE
COUNTRYSIDE

As with TAA, the Sukuma Union flourished in 1953–4 because individual farmers in rural areas were angered by excessive government interference in agricultural and veterinary matters and because the Union came forward with full-time officers dedicated to the task of mobilizing support in something more than *laissez-faire* manner beyond the confines of the towns. Branches then proliferated, especially in Maswa District where the chiefs were most conservative and their rule weighed most heavily on their people. By early 1954 the Union listed a total of 3,221 members, more than half of whom were in Maswa District.[1] Branches sprang up also along the lake shore in Mwanza, Kwimba and Geita Districts where many Sukuma were immigrants, where communications were good and where the impetus for enterprise and for dissent gave strength to economic and political associations.

In early 1953 the Union decided that one full-time salaried officer was a necessity for the growth and expansion of the Union in rural Sukumaland. W. J. M. Ng'wanamashalla, a bright young Sukuma (who was to receive an Indian Government scholarship for study in Calcutta the following year) was selected to begin work in April 1953 at a salary of 120 shillings per month. The Union soon discovered, however, that there was not sufficient money in the treasury to pay Ng'wanamashalla's salary, and he was dismissed.

The Union did not succeed in solving the problem of lack of funds on the one hand and the need for a full-time worker to supervise branches on the other until the leader of the Nassa branch of the Union, Lameck Bogohe, volunteered his full-time services without salary.[2]

The New Leadership: Bogohe

More than any other single individual, Bogohe turned the Union into a potent political force in 1953 and 1954. He was for the Sukuma Union what Kandoro was for TAA—a tireless campaigner

---

[1] Register of SU branches with membership figures, in L. M. Bogohe, selected papers privately held (hereafter cited as Bogohe papers), Nassa, Tanzania. I am indebted to Mr Bogohe for making available to me papers of historical importance from his personal files. Fifteen per cent of the Union's membership was registered with branches outside Sukumaland.

[2] Minutes, 24, 26 Apr.; 7, 12 May; 11 July 1953, SUF.

devoted to the task of establishing a hitherto elitist association on a strong rural base, of making politics make sense to the people of the countryside. The son of a wealthy farmer–trader–fisherman, Bogohe went to an African Inland Mission primary school in his home town of Nassa, then on to middle school in Musoma. After entering the police force in 1946, he continued his education on a part-time basis while serving in Dar es Salaam and in the Tabora Province. While with the police, Bogohe established a branch of the Sukuma Union in Tabora. On returning to Nassa in 1953, he so revitalized the Nassa branch of the Union that Union leaders in Mwanza had nothing but praise for his work, suggesting even that the Nassa branch with some thirty-five members 'is stronger perhaps than headquarters.'[1]

Bogohe wasted no time in his new assignment. He wrote immediately to all branches urging them to work hard on behalf of the Union and informing them that he planned to visit all parts of Sukumaland to inspect existing branches and open new ones. He travelled then for weeks at a time—first in Maswa and then elsewhere—holding meetings, enrolling members, and establishing new branches. He worked vigorously to rouse the people's participation and to represent their various complaints to the district or provincial administration.[2] Wherever the Union made inroads, the inevitable conflict with native authorities, jealous of their prerogatives, developed. The chairman of one branch of the Union reported that he had been jailed two days without food by a local headman 'for being a member and spreading the association in the village.'[3] Rather naively, Bogohe at first seemed to believe that the laudable aims of the Union—progress, education and development for Sukumaland—would unite native authorities and Union organizers, despite the divergent interests of the two groups in relation to the elemental political considerations of authority, power and respect. Suffice it to say that Bogohe's presence in a chiefdom for two weeks of meetings—including the bringing of gifts of goats and chickens in the manner usually reserved for native authorities or European government officers—was not likely to endear him to local rulers.

Under Bogohe's leadership, the Union reached a high watermark

[1] Bogohe, interview, 11 Feb. 1965; Minutes, 19 June 1953, SUF.
[2] 'Visiting report: the tour of inspection and opening new branches of the Sukuma Union in Sukumaland and outside Sukumaland,' n.d. (August 1953), SUF.
[3] 'Visiting and inspection reports No. 2,' n.d. (Oct. 1953), SUF.

of its activities and influence during the final six months of 1953. In an October report Bogohe listed thirty-two Sukuma Union branches with local secretaries inside Sukumaland and beyond. However, he had membership lists and correspondence from a handful of branches only: his own Nassa area, the lively Geita branch, and the branches he himself had recently visited or established in Maswa. Some branches existed mostly on paper and others depended on visits from Mwanza-based officers as their only significant element of program. Nevertheless, and due almost entirely to the large numbers of new members recruited by Bogohe, the financial condition of the Union had improved markedly by October. Impressed with Bogohe's work, the committee of the Union—headed by the president, Tito Budodi—made Bogohe general secretary and agreed to pay him a monthly salary.

From his Mwanza headquarters, Bogohe pursued a number of imaginative tasks. To keep a more well-informed eye on legal developments in the territory, he ordered six volumes of Tanganyika Laws from the government printer in Dar es Salaam and requested that the Sukumaland Federal Council send the Union copies of all council minutes and extant native authority legislation. He proposed to inaugurate a Sukuma Union newspaper published in the Swahili language while continuing to publicize Sukuma Union affairs through the Sukuma language publication, *Lumuli*. He enlisted the interest of the Mwanza social development officer in making a film history of the Sukuma, including both traditional and modern activities. The Union decided to push ahead with plans for an independent secondary school and to re-investigate the possibility of official registration for the Union.[1] Bogohe wrote to the Nyasaland headquarters of the Nyasaland African Congress, to the Nairobi headquarters of the Kenya African Union and to the Bahaya Union in Bukoba asking for copies of their by-laws and for any advice they might have for the Sukuma Union.[2]

While Bogohe revitalized the Union's operations at headquarters, the Geita and Maswa branches of the Union remained focal points of local activity. At the Buchosa branch in Geita—which had some 160 members by the end of 1953—members were

---

[1] Registration proved to be unnecessary. The school and the film posed too many insurmountable financial difficulties.
[2] Bogohe letters of 28 Oct. 1953, SUF.

M

concerned primarily with the ineffectiveness of people's representatives (or councillors) at the Sukumaland Federal Council and with low market prices for cattle. The branch also demanded payment for government-sponsored communal labor projects, an accounting from the government as to the disposition of all taxes and fines, a determination by the government as to which parts of the district were for Africans and which for Asians and redress of specific complaints against native authorities and against the Veterinary, Forest and Fishery Departments.[1]

In Maswa where the branch expressed similar concerns but where the chiefs were stronger than in Geita, problems between Union members and native authorities took a more serious turn. Some members in Maswa were jailed, and certain chiefs prohibited the collection of membership dues or refused to publicize meetings of the Union. Bogohe undertook another three-week trip to the district in November, and tensions with native authorities were at least temporarily smoothed over.[2]

Peak and Decline

Until 1954 the Sukuma Union appeared to enjoy the approbation, even the helpful encouragement of the government. The Mwanza District Commissioner, T. M. Unwin, and Bogohe seemed to enjoy a relationship of mutual respect and friendship. Bogohe's letters to Provincial Commissioners in Tabora and Tanga (where the Union had branches), explaining the Union's purposes and enclosing by-laws, were courteously acknowledged, and the Tabora Provincial Commissioner wrote that he had read the material 'with interest and approval.'[3]

On 5 and 6 December 1953, seventy-five leaders gathered at the Welfare Center in Mwanza for the most important meeting in the Union's history. Representatives attended from branches in all the districts in Sukumaland and from Musoma, Kahama, Tabora and Zanzibar.[4] The meeting discussed at great length the problems of Sukumaland as the people and the Union perceived them. Following the December meeting, Bogohe—with the help of District Commissioner Unwin—sought to arrange a meeting

[1] Minutes of a meeting of the Buchosa branch of SU, 9 Oct. 1953, SUF.
[2] Safari Report No. 3, n.d. (Dec. 1953), SUF.
[3] P.C., Tabora to Bogohe, 28 Dec. 1953, SUF.
[4] Maswa District sent a large proportion of the Sukumaland delegates, reflecting the strength which resulted from Bogohe's tours and his personal concentration on the growth of the Union there.

with Provincial Commissioner Rowe 'at which various points which disquiet the people could be discussed and explained.'[1] Rowe agreed to the meeting, and Bogohe drew up the following agenda for discussion:

1. Necessity for destocking.
2. Destocking (procedures).
3. Prices paid by Tanganyika Packers.
4. Restriction on export of animals and animal products.
5. Restriction of movement of crops between districts.
6. Value of Fisheries Officers.
7. Fisheries Officers' powers of fining on the spot.
8. Double licensing fees paid on (firewood).
9. Yields of cotton and cattle cesses and use to which these have been put.[2]

The Union also requested that the administration consider a trial suspension of rinderpest inoculations; that it investigate corruption among clerks and headmen related to destocking; that arbitrary and punitive assignments to communal labor projects be eliminated and compulsory labor on the personal property of native authorities be abolished; that the people, not the government, select and dismiss native authorities; and that the Union be permitted to meet despite the opposition of particular chiefs.

The administration looked into a number of the Union's specific complaints and reported the varying results to Bogohe. With regard to the problem of holding meetings, the District Commissioner of Maswa wrote:

It has been explained thoroughly to all Native Authorities that *although they would like the Union banned in their areas, the policy of Government is to allow freedom of speech.* It has been agreed that the Sukuma Union should call on the Chief, Subchief, and Mwanangwa [headman] in any area in which it wishes to call a meeting, and that *the meeting must be allowed*[3].

He added that if speakers advised people not to obey the law, they could be prosecuted.

In early February 1954, Bogohe projected an extensive series of tours to all Union branches both inside and outside Sukumaland. He hoped to build up the strength of the Union in other areas as he had in Maswa. The tour never materialized, however. After a dispute with the Union about salary and finances, Bogohe

---

[1] Unwin to Bogohe, 30 Dec. 1953, SUF.
[2] Bogohe memorandum, 6 Jan. 1954, SUF.
[3] D.C. to P.C., 2 Feb. 1954, MADF. (Italics mine.)

was dismissed from his position as general secretary. No sooner had Bogohe—the only full-time employee of the Union—been relieved of his post than the government prohibited the participation of civil servants in the Union on the grounds that the Union was a 'political association.'[1] Four of the Union's leading officers then resigned rather than give up their civil service appointments.

At the same time, the Tanganyika African Association, which was rapidly increasing in strength, had begun to dominate political recruitment in the field. Its top leaders worked for TAA on a full-time basis and were therefore unaffected by the prohibition against the participation of civil servants. TAA added Bogohe to its leadership roster in April—a move which certainly assisted in mobilizing Sukuma Union strength, particularly in Maswa, beneath the TAA banner. TAA campaigners championed the grievances of Sukuma farmers and cattle-owners in the rural areas in more dramatic and uncompromising fashion than had the Union. With grave losses in both leadership and initiative, the Union discussed in May and June the need to 'distinguish the Sukuma Union from the Tanganyika African Association.'[2] Discussion remained largely academic, however, because the Union had no one to carry its work to the people. After the departure of Bogohe, the Union reverted to its pre-Bogohe ineffectuality.

The situation in Maswa, meanwhile, had become increasingly intractable. Francis Mgeja, a subchief who had been most uncompromising in his attitude toward the Union, wrote the District Commissioner in February 1954 reviewing the incidents of the previous six months from his point of view. He charged that some Union members who defied authority said that they were acting explicitly in line with advice from Bogohe. He alleged that Union members said they could not be held accountable to headmen, subchief or District Commissioner, but only to the Union headquarters in Mwanza. He concluded:

I have seen and I confirm the undesirable path being taken by the Sukuma Union and its members...It is the same path which was beginning to be taken by the Kenya African Union which was banned in June 1953...In sum, the words and actions...of the Union and its members [raises the question]...what is its purpose? To build the country or tear it down?

[1] UNVM, 1954, p. 75. Circular of 19 Mar. 1954.
[2] Minutes, 9 May and 6 June 1954, SUF.

The members of the Union oppose all sorts of programs without sufficient reason.

Noting that people would get the idea that they could chase out their native rulers altogether, he added: 'I feel sure that in the coming days the life of the people of Sukumaland will enter dangerous times unless the central government examines [this matter] with care and as quickly as possible.'[1]

Although Bogohe made every effort to put the Maswa branches of the Union under proper discipline and control in conformity with the rules and regulations of the Union and of the government,[2] the administration decided in mid-February to move decisively against 'irresponsible' political associations. The newly arrived Provincial Commissioner, S. A. Walden, supported by Governor Twining, viewed the political associations now as subversive of the entire native authority structure. There would be no more approbation of political activism; the increasingly explicit challenge to the administration's structures and programs could not be tolerated.

5 TAA: THE NEW POLITICS OF CONFRONTATION

In 1953 the government had made its first overt move to curb African political activity. In August a circular 'announced that the Governor had ordered, with the approval of the Secretary of State [for the Colonies]...that in future members of the senior and junior services of all races...might not be members of political associations.'[3] Civil servants were given three months to resign from the Tanganyika European Council, the Asian Association and TAA.[4] Though the ruling was explicitly applied to all races and their respective political associations, there can be no doubt that it was directed primarily at TAA. Based, of course, on the British principle of an impartial civil service, the ruling, nevertheless, made no sense in Tanganyika in 1953 unless it was designed to cripple what the government regarded as a developing opposition movement. African political activity, however, was going to develop regardless; the only question was whether

---

[1] Mgeja to D.C., 10 Feb. 1954, MADF.
[2] Bogohe to Maswa SU, 23 Feb. 1954, Bogohe papers.
[3] UNVM, 1954, p. 75.
[4] The regulation was not applied to the Sukuma Union until early 1954.

it would be more or less enlightened, more or less 'responsible.'[1]

Ironically, the leadership of Lake Province TAA—by far the strongest TAA branch in the territory—was not at all affected by the new ruling. All the top officers were either non-civil servants or ex-civil servants. The provincial by-laws framed in 1952 had even prohibited provincial officers from holding jobs with the government or with European or Asian concerns. The Mwanza District branch suffered the loss of two prominent leaders, but there was no dearth of others willing to carry on. The rural branches in Busega and Geita did not have civil servant leadership so they, too, remained unaffected.

The branch in Shinyanga, however, was all but decimated. It was a difficult choice for Petro, the district secretary, but ultimately he resigned from TAA to carry on with his salaried government job. A number of the other local leaders were civil servants in Shinyanga township who faced the same decision with the same result. Petro entrusted TAA's books to Saidi Ali Maswanya, a local trader and expoliceman. Maswanya did not become an active political force in Shinyanga until 1957, but from that date he embarked on what became a remarkable political career. Petro, still a lower echelon civil servant, today views Maswanya, now a minister in the Tanzania government, with a certain ironic perspective based on personal knowledge of accidents and turning-points in history.[2]

Tanganyika's First Nationalist
Political Tour

In mid-1953 the leaders of Lake Province TAA moved decisively into the countryside. In September Kandoro came from Tabora to join Japhet Kirilo, the Meru spokesman at the United Nations the previous year, and Abbas Sykes, territorial secretary of TAA,

[1] The Tanganyika Administration's explanations and the United Nations Visiting Mission's criticisms are summarized in UNVM, 1954, pp. 75–7, 123. Julius Nyerere, at that time territorial president of TAA, submitted a critical memorandum to the Governor in which he argued: 'The vast majority of the educated Africans in this Territory are in the Civil Service and banning them from membership of political organisations is equivalent to banning the Tanganyika African Association, the only political organisation in the Territory. This, Your Excellency, is a serious blow to our political development.' Nyerere to the Governor, 10 Aug. 1953, in M. I. Kitenge, selected papers, privately held (hereafter cited as Kitenge papers), Mwanza, Tanzania. I am indebted to Mr Kitenge for making available to me papers of historical importance from his personal files.

[2] Interviews: Petro; Maswanya, 18 Nov. 1964.

in a political tour of the Lake Province.[1] For almost a month they traveled from Bukoba to Musoma publicizing the specifics of the Meru Land Case and seeking support for TAA. An important moment for TAA, this was the first time in Tanganyikan history that top political leaders with a decidedly nationalist orientation systematically scoured town and countryside alike over a large geographical area. Kirilo had organized the Meru, and the Sukuma Union under Bogohe had launched its own brand of touring earlier in the year; but TAA was now breaking the ground for a national movement which would seek to unite tribe with tribe, to integrate town and countryside in the name of freedom from colonial controls for all Tanganyikan Africans.

None of the three principals in this epoch-making tour was himself from the Lake Province and not even Kandoro had yet moved to Mwanza permanently. Sykes came to represent TAA's territorial organizational headquarters in Dar es Salaam; Kirilo, to argue that the struggle of the Meru people was of more than parochial interest, that it symbolized and highlighted the struggle of Africans everywhere; Kandoro, as the prophet, apostle, and chief organizer of a new politics, revolutionary in every respect. Membership was for every African as membership in TAA had always been, but TAA's style was now new. As Bomani had with the cooperatives and Bogohe with the Sukuma Union, TAA's full-time politicians now went out to *get* members. They barnstormed on political tours intended to recruit mass support. They sought to establish a hierarchy of provincial, district, branch and sub-branch organizations.

Concerned as always with specific complaints and grievances, the ideology of the new politics offered something more: the crux was the unifying, simplifying, empowering desire for an end to alien control. Most particularly, in this instance, the spark was provided by Kirilo. Though addressing his audience now in Musoma, in Mwanza, in Ikizu or Biharamulo, he had spoken not long before at the United Nations. People in Sukumaland to this day remember Japhet Kirilo, and they knew of Kirilo and Kandoro (as of Bomani and Munanka) long before they had heard of Julius Nyerere.

TAA held provincial general meetings in October and November

---

[1] Interviews; a report by Kandoro entitled 'Report of TAA, Lake Province Branch, for 1953 and half of 1952,' (Orig. Sw.), n.d., Bogohe papers. See also Kandoro, pp. 25–6.

1953. The meetings were well attended by representatives from six or more districts and the typical grievances were aired. The agenda included selection of a delegate to attend a projected conference of African nationalists in Lusaka, Northern Rhodesia[1], and preparation of a memorandum to the East African Royal Commission on Land. The acting provincial secretary, Jeremiah Cleophas, travelled to Dar es Salaam in late October to represent the Lake Province group in a deputation to the Royal Commission led by TAA's territorial president, Julius Nyerere. The following month Munanka, president of Lake Province TAA after Bomani's departure, and Sylvester Herman, the Bukoba District TAA secretary, made further representations to the Royal Commission in Mwanza. Herman asked that land not be alienated to Europeans, that Africans be given more technical training in subjects related to land and agriculture, and that associations, like cooperatives, be permitted to guarantee security on African loan applications. Munanka pressed TAA's opposition to destocking before the Commission arguing that other methods could be employed to safeguard soil fertility, such as rotational grazing, farming and systems which he understood were employed in other cattle-rich countries such as Australia, Argentina and India.[2]

Violence in Bukoba

In December violence erupted in Bukoba. As in Sukumaland, opposition had grown to compulsory regulations and to Native Authority leadership so that the government banned meetings 'in the interests of law and order.'[3]

Nevertheless, TAA's president in Bukoba, Ali Migeyo, held a large public meeting at Kamachumu which police disbanded by force.[4] Bukoba TAA telegraphed the Lake Province headquarters that tear gas had been used, and Kandoro called an emergency session in Mwanza to discuss the matter. The meeting, which was also attended by leaders of the Sukuma Union and the Lake

---

[1] Munanka was selected as one of Tanganyika's delegates, but he was not permitted to leave the country as there was not sufficient time to obtain a passport and comply with international health regulations regarding yellow fever immunization. In any event, the Lusaka conference was not held. (I owe this point to Robert Rotberg.)

[2] Report by Cleophas on his trip to Dar es Salaam, 22–28 Oct. 1953, SUF; Minutes of a meeting of Lake Province TAA, 25 Nov. 1953, Bogohe papers.

[3] Lake Province annual report, 1954, LPF.

[4] Migeyo was imprisoned for one year after conviction for holding illegal meetings.

Province Growers Association, decided to send a delegation to complain to the Provincial Commissioner directly and to ask that tear gas never be used in Tanganyika in situations where there was no real disturbance. The Provincial Commissioner replied that the gas had been used to disperse an illegal meeting which refused to disperse when requested to do so. It was a critical enough situation to bring President Nyerere from Dar es Salaam to talk with the District Commissioner about the gassing. Nyerere received the same explanation. Mwanza leaders, however, were pleased that the matter received special attention from territorial headquarters and that Nyerere had 'seen with his own eyes' the state of things in the Lake Province.[1]

No sooner had the new year begun than Kandoro and a committee appointed at the November general meeting were off on another tour of the province. In twenty-five days they held public meetings in seventeen places in six districts, concluding at the end of January with another provincial general meeting in Mwanza. Emotions rose to such a pitch that Kandoro proclaimed 'to be governed by others...is shameful impotence.' Lazaro Bomani jumped up, tore his shirt and exlaimed in Sukuma; 'It is best that we control our own affairs with regard to land and livestock until we rule the country ourselves!' M. I. Kitenge followed, tearing off his tie and saying he would not wear it again until independence was achieved. The meeting decided to send a delegation to the Governor himself opposing destocking, cattle tax and cotton cess. A telegram to this effect was dispatched to Dar es Salaam. The Governor's secretary replied that the Governor would be arriving in Mwanza on a scheduled tour 12 February and that the representations of TAA should be submitted in writing to the Provincial Commissioner forthwith, together with a request for an audience with the Governor. Kandoro immediately copied the telegram to all TAA branches asking each to send its president and no less than six representatives to Mwanza by 10 February to prepare for the interview with the Governor.[2]

Hopes and Expectations

On 10 February TAA gave a farewell tea-party for the departing Provincial Commissioner, E. G. Rowe, and for the incoming

---

[1] Kandoro, pp. 29–31.
[2] Kandoro, p. 38; Kandoro to all presidents and members of TAA in the Lake Province, 3 Feb. 1954, SUF.

Provincial Commissioner, S. A. Walden. A large number of persons of all races, including European and Asian officials and unofficials, attended the unusual affair which was held in Mwanza's large Gandhi Hall. TAA was well represented with members from all branches. Its hopes and expectations were high in anticipation of an interview with the Governor two days later.

Aside from the words of farewell and welcome, TAA took the opportunity to express various of its views. Noting the formation of the Lake Province Council under Rowe's administration, TAA expressed its gratitude for the fact that five African representatives selected by the Provincial Commissioner had been seated on the council. Hopefully African representation would continue to increase and Africans themselves would elect their representatives in the future. TAA expressed the hope that African representatives would be elected to the forthcoming Mwanza Town Council and that the chairman would not be a government servant. TAA also expressed its confidence that undesirable legislation would soon be abolished and that the unfortunate use of tear gas in Bukoba would not be repeated.

TAA emphasized that its purpose was not to oppose the government, but to cooperate to attain the goal of self-government. Disagreements naturally arose because of the difference in point of view between the government and TAA. The major problem, though, was not that the government failed to help Africans sufficiently but rather that there was a fundamental lack of cooperation between the three major races in the territory. Noting that it would be difficult indeed to govern a country with people in it who maligned other groups as poor or of no consequence, TAA decried the European or the Asian who would associate with Africans only at tea-parties. TAA did not want a cooperation of words only, but of actions—a true cooperation.[1]

The outgoing Provincial Commissioner also addressed the gathering. A man who had dedicated more than five of the most creative and idealistic years of his professional life to the Lake Province, Rowe spoke with considerable feeling. He said frankly that if Europe had anything significant to give Africa, it was not Christianity or football ('many Africans I know can beat quite a

---

[1] Kandoro, pp. 34–7. The text of the speech checks with other copies the writer has seen. Curiously enough, Dr J. E. K. Aggrey's dictum about the white keys and black keys of a piano both being necessary for harmonious music, was quoted in the speech.

number of Europeans in both'), or even money, welfare, or technical knowledge, but rather the fruits of centuries of political and social experience. Rowe affirmed that there was nothing wrong in 'fair, knowledgeable and constructive' criticism. He had been inside the government for over twenty-five years and knew its weaknesses better than the public; but he also knew the strengths of its work. Touring the country asking people for their grievances against the government and the native authorities, as some African leaders who were present had recently done, would yield grievances to be sure, and produce some lies; but, he asked, were the people also asked what good things the government and the native authorities had done for them?

Turning to the specifics of some points TAA wished to discuss with the Governor, Rowe pointed out that the question of permission to export cattle for sale in Uganda depended on technical considerations of inter-territorial trade and precautions against livestock disease. Destocking and cotton cess were 'more serious and fundamental' issues, but money for development and protection of the land was necessary for progress. The remedies being applied in Sukumaland and the Lake Province had been tested and proved successful elsewhere. He challenged TAA:

> If you consider that they are not the best remedies, then it is up to you to produce better ones. But you will have to show that they *will* be successful, for it is dishonest to ignore the basic need. No-one likes being taxed and no-one likes being compelled to sell cattle. But a bankrupt treasury means a breakdown in all public life and a bankrupt and impoverished soil means the end of life altogether—so be sensible when you look at these things and not childish.

Discussion, thought, then sensible and helpful suggestions were the proper way to make 'genuine, sincere and honest criticism of things that are really wrong.' Rowe concluded his statement with the famous prayer of Reinhold Niebuhr:

> God grant us the courage to change the things
>   that ought to be changed
> The strength to endure the things
>   that cannot be changed
> And the wisdom to know the difference.[1]

But the interpretation of this 'difference' was precisely the point at issue. 'Constructive criticism' was difficult because, at least from the African side, the existence of a common interest was

[1] Draft of a speech by P.C. E. G. Rowe to TAA, 10 Feb. 1954, MZDF.

doubted; the whole establishment of colonial administration with its structured relationships between rulers and ruled was being called increasingly into question. It seemed to the African protagonist that the common interest was defined and imposed from above by alien rulers, that criticism could only be considered constructive if it did not fundamentally question already established government policy. Perhaps the forthcoming interview with the Governor himself would help to heal the widening gap.

Governor Twining: Dialogue Denied

The Governor arrived as scheduled but refused to grant an interview. Stunned, TAA sent representatives to the provincial office to make certain this was correct. It was. According to Kandoro's account, one TAA officer suggested that the delegation follow the Governor to the house of the Provincial Commissioner where he was staying, but Lazaro Bomani, who felt this would be a demeaning procedure, argued: 'We are not fools! We do not follow a ruler to his house but [see him] in his office only.'[1]

Munanka decided to contact TAA headquarters in Dar es Salaam for advice. The reply was for Lake Province TAA to take whatever peaceful steps it wished. TAA then held a meeting and decided to cable directly to the Secretary of State in London, with copies to the Governor, the Provincial Commissioner, the Legislative Council members from the Lake Province, and TAA headquarters. The telegram, originally in Swahili, read:

> Citizens of Her Majesty the Queen cry out before you their distress at destocking of cattle, cattle tax, and cotton cess; also their distress at being tear-gassed during a meeting in the Lake Province, Tanganyika. Representatives refused interview with Governor when he visiting Mwanza between 13th and 15th February...We plead these difficulties be removed from our country quickly. We do not want trouble, but peace.[2]

The telegram was signed 'Executive Committee, Tanganyika African Association, Lake Province.' Kandoro copied the telegram to all TAA members in the province in a letter sent out the same day. He asked all to remain calm, that 'we will get our rights and will pursue them by civilized means,' that members should await the reply to the telegram but be ready to come immediately to Mwanza when called. Kandoro concluded: 'God is with us.'[3]

[1] Kandoro, p. 38.   [2] Quoted in Kandoro, pp. 39–40.
[3] Kandoro to all TAA members, 15 Feb. 1954, Kandoro, pp. 39–40. A copy of Kandoro's letter, including the text of the telegram, was contained also in SUF.

The administration, meanwhile, made its position entirely clear. In a note to the Governor the Mwanza District Commissioner portrayed the politicians as 'discontented and self-seeking men who, by malicious propaganda [seek] to turn public opinion against [progressive] policies.'[1] Seeking to shore up native authorities against the attacks of 'irresponsible politicians,' the Governor addressed the Mwanza Federation of chiefs on 17 February. He emphasized the authority and power of chiefs and their role, together with the new councils, in implementing government policy. Speaking of the politicians, he said they were people:

who are trying to undermine the policy of the government and by trying to attract cheap-jack popularity they want to destroy the position of the chiefs and the native authorities...They represent nobody except themselves...I have read their papers about their complaints and they show that they are a lot of uneducated, ignorant people who either are unable to appreciate and comprehend what they are talking about, or they do not wish to hear the truth.

Indulging a note of rural romanticism which would seem remarkable had it not been common among colonial administrators at the time, the Governor commented that the politicians were 'people who feel that they no longer want to have the traditional work of Africans living in the country, developing their land, and tending their cattle, but who come to the towns to live lives of parasites.'[2]

---

[1] A brief note on suggested subject matter for H.E. the Governor's address to the chiefs of the Mwanza Federation, MZDF.

[2] Address by H.E. the Governor to the Chiefs of the Mwanza District at a Baraza Held on 17 Feb. 1954, MZDF. While this was the Governor's public posture and the basis for the repressive measures soon to be adopted in Sukumaland, he privately recognized shortcomings in both the conception and administration of specific government policies. Not long after his visit to Sukumaland, Twining reflected: 'For years I have been preaching to Provincial teams, to Provincial Commissioners' Conferences, to meetings of Members and to individuals that it is a great mistake to regard development as a thing which can be directed from Dar es Salaam and imposed upon an unwilling and ignorant population. The last thing they want is alien development imposed upon them with all its regimentation, extra taxation and things which are good for them without their ever being consulted. No doubt ...bureaucrats prefer to dictate policy from Dar es Salaam and the local ones prefer to impose their tyrannical will upon the people. The result is that a great deal of money is wasted on schemes which are unpopular, or at least not properly understood, and the benefits derived from development are only partial. The classic example of how *not* to do things is the Sukumaland Scheme. This was excellent, even brilliant, in conception and technically well executed. It has undoubtedly done a great deal of good, but it has never

In a note to the Provincial Commissioner after his return to
Dar es Salaam, the Governor emphasized the importance of 'the
fullest coordination and understanding' between district administrators and the native authorities and the necessity that the latter
*'through whom the work must necessarily be done—are themselves
as efficient as we can make them, have our full support and are
acceptable to the people.'* Noting the Lake Province's wealth and
'remarkable progress over the past few years,' Governor Twining

been properly put across to the people who, as far as I can make out, co-oper-
ate only to the minimum and then with reluctance, unless it is in respect of a
particular item which has some popular appeal.'
    Discussing specifically the questions of taxation and destocking, Twining
continued: 'There is no doubt that both the Cotton and the Cattle Cess form
unpopular ways of raising revenue and are being exploited against us by the
local political agitators. I do not suggest that we should make any revolutionary
changes, but perhaps the occasion when the new Graded Poll Tax is introduced
could provide an opportunity for re-considering the position...Another
unpopular thing is compulsory culling. This I think we will have to stick to,
but it is unfortunate that propaganda is telling the people that its only use is
to supply Meat Packers with their materials and thus pour large profits into
the pockets of some bloated Europeans in Dar es Salaam. Credence is given
to this idea by the fact that very often Meat Packers are the only buyer. The
fact that they have provided a market and kept prices up is overlooked. We
are already giving consideration to some African capital being put into Meat
Packers and given to the question of opening up other markets so that there
can be some competition with Meat Packers. There is demand for meat from
the Belgian Congo for instance, and when I was in Mwanza last the Lake
Cattle Owners Association were complaining that they were not allowed to
sell their cattle in Uganda. It so happened that there was no market at the
time, but if there is a market I think it would be foolish in an area where there
are two million cattle to try to prevent a few thousand going Uganda-wise and
Congo-wise. We should also have much more positive propaganda as to what
culling is all about and about Meat Packers. The Veterinary Department,
like all technical departments, are inclined to grumble louder and louder until
Government introduces a measure which we are assured will provide the
panacea, and then tyranically and without any regard for human rights, they
ruthlessly endeavor to administer the law. This is bad man management and
bad politics...There are many other things such as the establishment of a
new African-owned ginnery at Geita, and this and other projects for a "share
in the equity" must be cooked up...With regard to Social Services, I should
say that the Lake Province has been neglected to a large extent. It is true there
are two vastly expensive chromium-plated schools just outside Mwanza, but
we seem to have dissipated our resources on them and are a bit weak under-
neath.' But Twining's suggested remedies did not match his perceptions.
He proposed (1) the establishment of development committees chaired by
D.C.s and integrated with the hierarchy of local Native Authority councils,
and (2) 'a good deal more public relations'. (Twining to the Chief Secretary,
11 Sept. 1954, in S. A. Walden, selected papers, privately held (hereafter
cited as Walden papers), London. I am indebted to Mr Walden for permission to see this document, and others from the years of his tenure as
P.C., Lake Province.)

noted that the Lake Province 'is very much alive and it needs to be driven with a firm if light rein: but if we are not careful it may still get away from us, with unexpected and undesirable results.'[1] As events were to prove, he was correct.

[1] Minute to all Members and the P.C.L.P. (Provincial Commissioner, Lake Province), forwarded to the P.C. by the Member for Local Government, 31 Mar. 1954, Walden papers.

PART III

THE STRUGGLE FOR POWER

6

Administration Opposition, African Counter offensives and Proscription of TANU

The Governor's refusal to see the deputation of the Tanganyika African Association in February 1954 marked a turning point in the political history of Sukumaland and of the Lake Province. After the expectations which followed upon the February telegram from Dar es Salaam advising TAA to seek an interview with the Governor, and after Provincial Commissioner Rowe's speech about responsible criticism and discussion within the framework of common interests, the Governor's decision seemed an astonishing exercise of prerogative. Viewed in the light of later events, it was also a portentous beginning for Walden's administration in the province.

Clearly, Walden and Twining decided that strong measures against irresponsible politicians were necessary to the government's policies and programs and, in particular, to the continued functioning of native authorities on which the fulfillment of those policies and programs had been made to depend. Yet, it would be difficult to imagine any single act which would have more inflamed the opposition and consolidated discontent behind the various leaders whom the government was trying to discredit, been more conducive to continuing misunderstanding and the hardening of positions, and been more likely to produce the collision course in Sukumaland affairs which was, in fact, traced out over the next five years. The government's commitment to what Harvey Glickman has called 'Twining's Burkean notion of consultation with the African masses through their "natural" representatives' was not to die an easy death.[1]

In fact, 1954 was a year of veritable frenzy. TAA made itself *the* political force in Sukumaland while the Sukuma Union and the cooperatives, for different reasons, fell more into the political

[1] Harvey Glickman, 'Traditional pluralism and democratic processes in Tanganyika,' a paper delivered at the Annual Meeting of the American Political Science Association, Chicago, Illinois, Sept. 1964, p. 6.

background. The Tanganyika African National Union was born in Dar es Salaam in July. As territorial TANU's foremost early leaders, Julius Nyerere and Oscar Kambona, did not begin political tours of Tanganyika until 1955, the nationalist movement in the Lake Province—despite its assumption of the TANU name in mid-1954—continued to develop independently. For a while political activity mushroomed in reaction to the government's increasingly repressive offensive, but then provincial TANU headquarters and all branches in Sukumaland were proscribed in November 1954. By the end of the year the administration had disarmed the Lake Province activists of platform, office and organization. Discontent, however, could not be suppressed. It sought expression in various forms during the ban, culminating in the Geita demonstrations of 1958.

I   THE THREE ASSOCIATIONS

Interconnections and Differences

More than any others, Bomani and Bogohe personified the close organizational connections which had developed in the early 1950s between the cooperative movement, the Sukuma Union and TAA just as they illustrated the congruence of economic and political grievances and issues in the same period. Bomani was a leading officer of all three associations after 1951. Bogohe, too, was involved in all three from 1953. Second echelon leadership also tended toward multiple affiliations. Leaders of one of the associations often consulted with leaders of the others and attended their meetings.

At the beginning of 1954 Bogohe initiated an attempt to formalize the connections between the three principal Mwanza-based associations and others in the Lake Province.[1] A committee was formed and a meeting called for January 1954; but the attempt seems to have failed in the face of the overriding commitments of each of the organizations to its own affairs.

The interconnections of the three associations should not be overemphasized, however; there remained notable differences of thrust and emphasis. The cooperatives concerned themselves throughout—whether in their traders', producers' or consumers' variations—with breaking the economic domination and exploitation of Asians and establishing a base for further African economic

---

[1] Bogohe circular letter to all associations, n.d. (Dec. 1953), SUF.

aspirations in town and countryside. While TAA absorbed these concerns, its interests extended to larger social and political questions such as racial discrimination and the need for African advancement in all fields, the appropriateness of government and native authority schemes for economic and political development and requirements for progress toward the goal of self-government. The Sukuma Union, which began as a typical tribal association with rather parochial interests, became in the early 1950s a focus for discontent with traditional rulers who had become, as native authorities, functionaries of the colonial administration.

The cooperatives found, of course, that the furthering of their economic aims required political success in getting both governmental and indigenous support and produced political conflict where chiefs had vested interests with Asian ginners and traders or where chiefs and the government felt that Africans were not ready for undertaking certain types of economic enterprise. Sometimes the political implications of and requirements for economic change brought the cooperatives to the doorsteps of the manifestly political organizations for their assistance. Sometimes the cooperative movement itself undertook to represent its own interests in political as well as economic ways. TAA and the Sukuma Union, on the other hand, found that many political issues—both in town and especially in the rural areas—had an economic basis. Issues blended into one another and the numerical size of Mwanza's elite was still small; there was, essentially, one elite for a multiplicity of situations and a variety of organization.

Demise of the Sukuma Union

In the long run, the Sukuma Union was the first of the three associations to lag in terms of strength and influence, though the last to be barred by the government. No sooner had the Union lost Bogohe and a number of other leaders who could no longer participate in Union activities because of their civil service status, than it faced the prospect in April 1954 of registration under a new Registration of Societies Ordinance. A bothersome and time-consuming procedure at best and an implicitly threatening prospect at worst, negotiations for registration dragged out over a period of nearly two years. While applications were pending—and a separate application was required for each branch—Union leaders were enjoined from any activities in connection with the Union. While the administration maintained that the Union had 'not yet been banned' and that the government was 'still considering its application for registration,'[1] the Union's offices were closed and, prohibited de facto from functioning, it withered away. In March 1956 the administration made the demise of the Union official when it informed the president and vice-president, Budodi and Kilala, that the Union had been denied registration.[2]

Even without government harassment, the posture of the Sukuma Union would have been compromised in any case by its tribal definition at a time when tribal affiliation in Tanganyika seemed less important than the general economic and political division between the government and Asians on the one hand and Africans of whatever tribe on the other. TAA by 1954 had incorporated all of the Sukumaland-oriented issues which, though never the special preserve of the Union, had always been its main *raison d'être*. Albeit involuntary in the first instance, Bogohe's switch from the Union to TAA symbolized the increasing political hegemony of TAA. The banning of civil servants from the Sukuma Union reduced the Union to a mere remnant, whereas TAA already for two years had been independent of the leadership of civil servants. Finally, TAA developed in 1954 strong territorial links. With room, perhaps, for only one large political organization and strengthened even further with the advent of TANU in July, TAA easily pre-empted the political field.

TAA to the Forefront

Ironically, as has often been the case with nationalist movements in Africa and elsewhere, the emergence of an indigenous organization into the position of unquestioned political leadership followed hard upon, and was in part causally related to, the refusal of a colonial government to treat with it. Provincial Commissioner Walden wrote a lengthy letter to TAA in late February combining an explanation of the government's policies with severe and strongly worded criticism of TAA's ignorance, foolishness, and 'lying propaganda.' Echoing Governor Twining's own remarks before the Mwanza chiefs, Walden wrote:

Government will not tolerate agitation to nullify or damage its policies by people who are either only seeking to serve their own interests or have neither the knowledge or comprehension or the will to make any constructive contribution to the welfare of the people.

[1] D.C., Mwanza, to SU, Shinyanga, 5 May 1955, MZDF.
[2] D.C. to Budodi and Kilala, 13 Mar. 1956, MZDF.

He elaborated on the government's commitment to native authorities and then issued an explicit warning:

You have an excellent opportunity of helping your people by cooperating
with the lawful authorities...I would remind you that Native Authorities
are part and parcel of these. Before it is too late I would warn you to
consider seriously the error of your ways, as otherwise you are bound to
find yourselves in trouble.[1]

The leaders of Lake Province TAA were in no mood to listen to
such advice. Tear-gassed in Bukoba and snubbed by the Governor
in Mwanza, they were certain now that their protests and representations were receiving no consideration whatsoever from the
government. In early March Kandoro fashioned a series of impassioned and eloquent proclamations addressed to 'Members of
TAA and all Africans who have not yet become members of TAA.'
He trumpeted a call for all Africans to answer the call for freedom,
to seek together through TAA all the good things of life. He cited
the examples of Napoleon, Bismark, Gandhi, Nkrumah and
Aggrey as men of all races who had raised up their own people;
he lauded the British customs of freedom and democracy which
fostered free speech and the existence of political associations
such as TAA, assuring the members that an answer to TAA's
February telegram would be forthcoming 'according to the customs of the British Government.' Failing an answer, TAA would
be justified in sending another appeal, together with a delegation,
to England. He assured the presidents of TAA branches that TAA
was a legal organization and that they should pay no heed to
'childish and stupid threats.'[2]

TAA officials also wrote again to the Governor renewing their
case and objecting to their treatment at the hands of government
officials who reprimanded them in harsh language and scorned
them as 'ignorant' and 'useless.' If we were such, TAA leaders
argued, then there was no need for the British Government to
bring its people to Tanganyika in the first place. TAA emphasized
that it was not the aim of the organization to fight with the government, but to bring petitions before the government. Yet, when
petitions were brought, TAA was 'threatened and told if we
don't watch our actions we will be in danger.' Pointing out that
tear gas was only used by armies fighting their enemies, TAA

---

[1] Walden to the president of TAA, 22 Feb. 1954, reproduced in the original
English in Kandoro, pp. 46–50.
[2] Kandoro, pp. 41–4.

asked that 'if we Africans are enemies we should be told so.'
Concluding, the letter asked for the Governor's sympathy and the
abolition of the detested natural resources regulations.[1]

Meanwhile, other channels for registering TAA's complaints
were opening up through contacts with the Fabian Colonial
Bureau and certain members of the Labour Party. The secretary
of the Colonial Bureau, Marjorie Nicholson, had met with TAA
President Munanka in Mwanza on 1 February. Unable to lunch
in town because of discrimination at the Mwanza Hotel, they
nevertheless had an opportunity to discuss political matters at the
TAA office and they corresponded in subsequent months.[2]
Munanka wrote also to Fenner Brockway (a Labour Member of
Parliament), sending him information about Lake Province TAA's
activities together with a copy of the February telegram to the
Secretary of State.[3] In reply to inquiries then from Brockway,
the Secretary of State repeated the Tanganyikan government's
explanation that tear gas was used to disperse an illegal meeting
which had refused to comply with a police order to disperse and
the refusal to receive the TAA delegation was due to the Govern-
or's feeling that no good purpose would be served by discussing
once again matters which previously had been explained.[4]

[1] *Ibid.* pp. 45–6. The Governor's office replied on 2 May to TAA's letter of
10 March. Dar es Salaam asked that TAA 'consider and appreciate' that His
Excellency 'cannot meet all the demands that are made upon his time' and
'must necessarily decline to receive those petitioners the substance of whose
petitions would not warrant His Excellency in granting a personal interview,
particularly when repeated and full explanation of the subject matters of the
petition has already been given by the Provincial Commissioner.' The letter
pointed out that consultations with Native Authorities and District Councils
preceded any decisions on the matters raised and, while this was 'not to say
that political organizations have not their part to play in representing their
views when Government is formulating policy' they must do so as in other
countries through established authorities and must 'accept authoritative
answers as the voice of authority' if they wish to be effective. Finally, 'while
it is the firm wish of Government that political associations should have full
freedom to develop on constitutional lines' the letter pointed out that 'flouting
of Native Authorities,' 'incitement to disobedience of the laws,' or 'unconstitutional behaviour' would be 'dealt with according to the law.' (Dar es
Salaam to the chairman, Lake Province TAA, 2 May 1954, LPF.)
[2] Nicholson to I. C. Chopra, 19 Feb. 1954; Nicholson to Munanka, 4 May
1954, FCBF.
[3] Munanka to Nicholson, 10 May 1954, FCBF.
[4] Lyttelton to Brockway, 30 Mar. 1954. A Swahili translation of the letter
appears in Kandoro, pp. 58–9. Nicholson and Munanka discussed Brockway's representations in Nicholson to Munanka, 14 July 1954, and Munanka
to Nicholson, 27 July 1954, FCBF. Brockway sent Munanka a copy of the
Secretary of State's letter, but pressed the Secretary further on the floor of

While the conflict between TAA and the government was being acted out at higher levels, TAA continued its penetration of the rural areas. For weeks at a time, Kandoro and Bogohe, now assistant treasurer of TAA, toured every district in the province hearing the usual grievances, checking the finances of the branch organizations, and dramatizing the refusal of the government to receive representations and make the desired policy changes.[1]

With the unequivocal stands taken by the Governor and the Provincial Commissioner in February 1954 on the one hand, together with TAA's late 1953 and early 1954 push into the countryside on the other, conflict between chiefs and politicians spread and intensified. Both chiefs and government officers worked overtime to stem the rising political tide. As one Kwimba chief said in addressing the local chiefdom council:

There are some people these days trying to dirty and to confuse people's hearts and minds. The best policy is to steer clear of such persons and to quickly inform the authorities about them. Government and Native Authorities cannot tolerate such people and they will be severely punished. Health and peace consist in cooperation together in our work of caring for the land and the welfare of our people.[2]

For their part, District Commissioners and district officers made more frequent appearances at local council meetings. At one chiefdom council, a District Commissioner stated that TAA and the Sukuma Union were trying to compete with the government and that their leaders were out to mislead people on natural resources and tax matters, to take the people's money, and to build positions for themselves by discrediting native authorities. The Provincial

Parliament asking that he 'exert the greatest influence to see that representative bodies of Africans are received and that tear gas is not used for the dispersal of gatherings in the Protectorate.' Lyttelton replied that he could give 'no such assurance' (*Hansard*, House of Commons, 7 Apr. 1954). On 10 Apr., the P.C. wrote TAA that the Secretary of State had received TAA's February telegram and had informed the government of Tanganyika that he saw 'no reason to interfere' (Kandoro, p. 55). Kandoro immediately copied the P.C.'s letter to all members of TAA throughout the province. At a subsequent all-night meeting, TAA's executive committee decided that a TAA delegation should be sent to the Secretary of State in person and then to the United Nations (Kandoro, pp. 56, 69–70). The Brockway question and the Lyttelton reply were printed in *East Africa and Rhodesia*, 29 Apr. 1954, which is where Kandoro and other Tanganyikans found the text (Munanka to Nicholson, 27 July, 1954, FCBF; and Kandoro, p. 59).

[1] Mimeographed itineraries of TAA political tours, and Kandoro letter to all TAA officers, 20 Apr. 1954, SUF.

[2] Report of a meeting of the council of Magu chiefdom, 8 Feb. 1954 (orig. Sw.), Kwimba District files (hereafter cited as KWDF).

Commissioner distributed copies of the Governor's February speech to District Commissioners and all native authorities in all districts 'so that the chiefs are left in no doubt of the attitude of Government both towards them and toward people whose sole desire it is to stir up disaffection.'[1] The speech was read often at council meetings where only the most intrepid individuals raised questions or objections. The government also printed Swahili broadsheets bearing the title, 'Association of Truth,' in an attempt to counter with TAA's own methods the latter's propaganda.[2]

2 TAA BECOMES TANU[3]

The Struggle in Maswa

In 1954 the most intense conflict between politicians and native authorities occurred in Maswa District where the Sukuma Union and a new branch of TAA at Malampaka made inroads into the home areas of two of Sukumaland's strongest and longest reigning chiefs: Majebere of Mwagala and Ndaturu of Ntuzu.

At a March meeting of the Maswa Federation Council, the District Commissioner criticized the chiefs for slackness in the enforcement of destocking and soil erosion measures and ordered that prosecution of offenders should begin at once. More authoritarian even then many of his compatriots, District Commissioner A. N. Baillie may have aggravated the situation in Maswa in 1954 in much the same way that District Commissioner Neville French did in Geita in 1958. Like French and Provincial Commissioner Walden, Baillie preferred to deal in the most summary fashion with 'irresponsible political opposition.' Before the Maswa chiefs, Baillie said that the government in the past 'had shown great tolerance towards' such unions as the Sukuma Union and TAA, but that 'stronger action must be taken against their attempts to spread civil disobedience and discontent among the Sukuma.' At the meeting it was established that:

1. Chiefs, Sub-Chiefs and Headmen would make lists of all Members of such unions and forward copies to the Boma [District Office].
2. These listed persons to be among the first called out for communal labour after the rains.

[1] P.C. to all D.C.'s, 22 Apr. 1954, GTDF.
[2] Kandoro, pp. 53–4, and interview with J. W. T. Allen, Dec. 1963.
[3] See also my forthcoming essay, 'The Emergence of TANU in the Lake Province,' in Robert I. Rotberg and Ali A. Mazrui, eds., *Protest and Power in Black Africa* (New York: Oxford University Press, 1970.)

3. Their refusal to be followed by prosecution and if found guilty, such persons to be imprisoned *without option* of fine...
4. That their unanimous views on introducing corporal punishment for civil disobedience be forwarded to the Deputy Provincial Commissioner and Provincial Commissioner.[1]

The Maswa chiefs returned to their chiefdoms apparently strengthened in their determination to give no quarter to the political associations.

In April TAA's leader in Maswa, Stanley Kaseko, requested a series of meetings in Malampaka and neighboring areas, but the District Commissioner refused permission because Kaseko 'refused to promise to cease spreading lies about destocking, soil erosion, and tribal labor.' Kaseko denied that such lies were spread in TAA meetings and asked why the District Commissioner now prohibited free speech when he had welcomed TAA's opening in Maswa with an encouraging letter in February. He affirmed that it was not TAA's purpose to oppose the work of the native authorities or the government, but to receive the views and complaints of Africans and bring them before the government.[2] The District Commissioner subsequently permitted Kaseko to hold meetings, but only after securing permission from himself or the police and only as long as there was no troublemaking. Kaseko developed an appropriately innocuous agenda, obtained the appropriate permission and held his meetings.

In May the Provincial Commissioner took a similar position for the province as a whole. He informed all chiefs that political associations would be permitted to hold meetings if they first sought permission through the proper channels. He ordered the attendance of chiefs at all meetings in their chiefdom 'accompanied by as many people as possible who favour the chief'; chiefs were to counter all erroneous statements made by members of political associations at their meetings. He reminded the chiefs that under the Native Authority Ordinance they were empowered to refuse permission for meetings and could break up meetings which had already received government permission if they judged there was a danger to law and order. At his next TAA meeting in Mwagala, Kaseko invited Chief Majebere, his headmen, and his people to attend. He also invited the District Commissioner or district

---

[1] Minutes of a meeting of the Federation Council of Maswa District, 8 Mar. 1954, MADF.
[2] D.C. to Kaseko, 24 Apr; Kaseko to D.C., 26 Apr. 1954, MADF. (Orig. Sw.).

officer to be present, noting that they would be given an opportunity to reply with the government's views if they desired.[1] The uneasy *modus vivendi*, however, lasted only until August when open conflict erupted in Maswa, providing the occasion for even more stringent government action.

The Registration of Societies Ordinance

In April, meanwhile, the Legislative Council had passed a Registration of Societies Ordinance to permit closer government regulation of political associations. Chief Kidaha, as yet the Lake Province's only African representative on the Legislative Council, supported the bill as one which would free people from irresponsible organizers, but he warned that 'there should be proper and careful publicity...so that particularly the African population understand that there is no idea of trying to suppress lawful activities of societies.'[2] The ordinance, however, gave the government the power to define what was and what was not to be considered 'lawful'; and it was designed precisely for the suppression of political activities, such as those of TAA in the Lake Province, which the government was not willing to tolerate. Speaking to the Legislative Council in May, the Governor said:

My attention has been drawn to attempts which have been made in some parts of the territory by self-seeking individuals, usually men of straw, who, having appointed themselves as political leaders, have tried to stir up the people against their Native Authorities, and in some cases the Central Government, by exploiting local grievances real or imaginary. They do not hesitate to collect money; indeed, large sums of money, from many ignorant or unsuspecting people which they have little qualms in using, or rather misusing, for their own benefit and aggrandizement. This cannot be allowed to continue and Government will not tolerate such activities which are contrary to the best interests of the people and are designed to damage, if not destroy, good government. Respect for authority, which is an inherent trait in the African character, must be preserved.[3]

[1] D.C. to all chiefs, 1 May 1954, MADF. (Orig. Sw.) Kaseko to D.C., n.d. (May 1954), MADF.
[2] TLC, 14 Apr. 1954.
[3] *Ibid.* 12 May 1954. The Ordinance was No. 11 of 1954, signed into law by the Governor on 24 Apr. 1954. The Ordinance—especially after it had been used to close the Mwanza and Malampaka branches of TANU later in the year—appeared to many a repressive measure. In reply to a question from John Hynd, M.P., in the House of Commons on 2 Mar. 1955, the Secretary of State explained that the purpose of the Societies Ordinance was 'to protect Africans from exploitation by unscrupulous society organisers' and that it gave the government the power to 'declare illegal a society which is used for

Later in the month TAA's President Nyerere, a temporary member of the Legislative Council in place of Chief Kidaha, spoke to the issues raised by the Governor's speech. Nyerere

considered that all sensible Africans would support the Government in dealing with trouble makers; but he drew attention to the great difference between trouble-mongering and criticizing the Government justifiably... He hoped that people were not going to take the Governor's warning as meaning that from that time onwards no criticism of either local or central government was going to be tolerated. If that happened a large number of people were going to be without their only means either of making useful suggestions to the authorities or of merely expressing their views.[1]

In accord with the Societies Ordinance, the administration notified native authorities in Sukumaland and the Lake Province that registration requests were required before the end of June for all associations. At the same time the Provincial Commissioner reproduced Swahili copies of the section of the Governor's May speech quoted above, entitled the excerpt 'Governor Warns Political Troublemakers,' and forwarded copies to all District Commissioners and chiefs asking that the speech be given 'the widest— and most telling—publicity.'[2]

any purpose prejudicial to law and order or at variance with its declared objects' (Quoted in Selwyn-Clarke to Kambona and Munanka, 4 Mar. 1955, FCBF). In a draft memorandum to the Secretary of State for the Colonies the Fabian Colonial Bureau said the ordinance 'seems to be an unnecessary piece of legislation in a quiet territory, and it is difficult to believe that any genuinely subversive activity could not be dealt with by other methods.' The memorandum continued: 'Judging by the tone of references to the Tanganyika African National Union in the Observations of the United Kingdom Government on the United Nations Visiting Mission Report 1954, it is apparently believed that the leaders of this organisation are "self-appointed," irresponsible, and in some cases subversive. Moreover, three branches of the Union have been suppressed—according to replies given in the House of Commons, for subversive activities. Members of my Committee have met some of these leaders... We feel that the tone of the comments in the *Observations* is entirely at variance with our own impressions and bears a striking resemblance to earlier comments on other African politicians who are now Ministers in other territories.' Noting its view that Africans were inadequately represented in the governing bodies of the territory, the Fabian Colonial Bureau said that the 'Tanganyika Government at present appears to underestimate the importance of political activity and education' (Hilda Selwyn-Clarke to Lennox-Boyd, 4 Apr. 1955, mimeographed draft, FCBF).
[1] Summarized in UNVM, 1954, p. 77. Nyerere's speech in full appears in TLC, 25 May 1954. Writing to the Fabian Colonial Bureau in July 1955, Nyerere said: 'A few months ago the Governor toured part of the country making speeches which would make a man in Peru think that the Mau Mau is in Tanganyika and not in Kenya' (Nyerere to Lady Selwyn-Clarke, 4 July 1955, FCBF). [2] P.C. to all D.C.'s, 2 June 1954, MADF.

Provincial Conference: June 1954

TAA's third large provincial meeting of the year was held in Mwanza on 27 June. Under increasing pressure from native authorities, from district and provincial officers, and now from Dar es Salaam, TAA decried harassment of its members and of the organization itself. Munanka noted that the president and secretary of the Bukoba branch had been jailed 'for standing up for our rights' and that leaders in Nassa, Malampaka and Geita has also undergone harassment in previous weeks. Reaffirming that the purpose of TAA was not to oppose the government but only to seek the correction of errors where they existed, Munanka—following Nyerere's lead in the Legislative Council—regretted the equation which the government and others were making between criticism and troublemaking. He struck out at non-Africans who, he said, lobbied for the suspension of a sort of political troublemaking which did not exist. Munanka said he would not like to see anyone abandon the political fight because of harassment.[1]

Kandoro addressed himself to the usual issues regarding livestock and land, buttressing his arguments for man's freedom to use the land and to govern its animal and vegetable kingdoms with quotes from the Bible and the Koran. Complaining that Africans were being held back and discriminated against in relation to the other main races, he argued that Africans suffered from separate and unequal schools, poorer hospital facilities, bad roads, low wages, no loan provisions, less justice in courts and expulsion from their own lands. He maintained that the government's proposed policy of parity in the Legislative Council and non-racial graduated taxation must bring real equality to Africans in all the above areas. As Munanka summarized TAA's view in a later letter to the Fabian Colonial Bureau:

In a country like this when absolutely nothing of importance is being done by the Government, it is at our loss to find that we are being taxed heavily without getting increased facilities from the Government.[2]

Kandoro deplored the 1954 increase in cattle tax by 200 per cent (from half a shilling to a shilling and a half per head) and queried once again the purpose of the cotton cess. Finally, citing the United Nations Declaration on Human Rights, he spoke of freedom

[1] Speech quoted in Kandoro, pp. 63–5.
[2] Munanka to Nicholson, 27 July 1954, FCBF.

of speech and assembly and of equal representation for all individuals in the government of the country.[1]

The Birth of TANU

While Lake Province TAA had on its own initiative stepped up the pace of its activities in 1953 and early 1954, Julius Nyerere had been giving considerable thought to the necessity of transforming TAA territorially into a potent nationalist organization which would 'fight relentlessly until Tanganyika is self-governing and independent.'[2] With a Master of Arts degree from the University of Edinburgh, Nyerere had taken a teaching position at a Roman Catholic school at Pugu near Dar es Salaam. Elected territorial president of TAA in 1953, he set out to remodel TAA's constitution on more political lines. In 1954 he invited a group of TAA members to Dodoma to discuss his proposals and in July a four-day conference of TAA convened in Dar es Salaam to act on the proposals. A new constitution was adopted and TAA became the Tanganyika African National Union.[3] Of the seventeen men who gathered for this historic meeting, five were from Lake Province TAA, Kandoro and Bogohe among them.[4]

The agenda, as well as the attendance, reflected the importance of Lake Province TAA, but it also revealed that TAA's uncompromising militancy in the Lake Province may have posed problems for TAA's territorial president as well as for the government.

The first item on the agenda was a discussion of Lake Province TAA's by-passing of territorial headquarters by sending telegrams and letters outside the territory without first notifying or clearing with TAA in Dar es Salaam. According to Kandoro, Nyerere had sent a letter to Mwanza criticizing the Lake Province action as 'very bad politics.'[5] When the question was discussed by the full TAA meeting in July, it was decided that Lake Province TAA 'had the right to act in this manner because the

---

[1] Kandoro, pp. 60–3, 66–70.
[2] Quoted from the TANU constitution in Bennett, *Makerere Journal*, No. 7 (1963), p. 3.
[3] *Ibid.* p. 3, and Taylor, pp. 95–6.   [4] Kandoro, p. 74.
[5] Kandoro, p. 71. Kandoro noted that Nyerere warned, as had the Provincial Commissioner, that if Lake Province TAA was not careful it would get into trouble. Munanka is said to have replied to Nyerere that such ideas were those of people who were not confronted directly with the difficulties of the Lake Province, and that the Lake Province leaders had no alternative but to act as they did.

problems had not received attention from headquarters.'[1] The meeting decided, however, to dismiss the general secretary of territorial TAA, who had brought charges against the Bukoba president of TAA for a loss of 8,000 shillings in party funds, because *he* had failed to consult with territorial or provincial headquarters!

Despite Nyerere's apparent reservations about TAA's operations in the Lake Province, the Lake Province group seemed strong enough in this first meeting of TAA–TANU to assure that decisions and judgments relating to the Province went in their favor. The meeting requested the leaders of Lake Province TAA 'to continue with their good work as they had done in the past.' In the future, however, all representations to the United Nations were to pass through Dar es Salaam headquarters. On the Lake Province's favorite issues of destocking, cattle tax, cotton and coffee cesses, a committee headed by Nyerere was picked to make representations to the Ministry of Local Government.[2]

3   TOWARD PROSCRIPTION

Kaseko versus Ndaturu

Meanwhile, in the Lake Province, the relations between government authorities and politically active groups deteriorated, and mutual suspicion and distrust increased. In July open conflict broke out in Musoma when the District Commissioner attended a TAA meeting and berated the leaders for 'stupidity' and 'lies.'[3] The same month, attendance at the first all-Sukumaland Agricultural Show in Kwimba District was held far below expected levels because rumors spread that people who entered the fairgrounds would be conscripted for service in the military and sent to Kenya to fight the Mau Mau.[4] In August, Kaseko of Maswa TAA (now TANU) while expanding his efforts throughout the district, came into direct conflict with Chief Ndaturu, then with a virtual coalition of Maswa chiefs.

The trouble began when Kaseko wrote directly to Chief Ndaturu, informing him of the time, place and date of a projected

[1] Kandoro, p. 75.

[2] 'Minutes of First TANU Conference, Dar es Salaam, July 7, 1954' (orig. Sw.), Kitenge papers, and in Kandoro, pp. 73–82.

[3] Musoma TAA to P.C., 23 July 1954, and subsequent correspondence. Also a file note by the D.C. in question, LPF.

[4] Lake Province Annual Report, 1954, LPF; interview with A. G. Stephen, 20 Nov. 1964.

TANU meeting in Ntuzu chiefdom and virtually directing the chief and his headmen to assure that everything would be properly prepared.[1] Even if he had had no doubts whatsoever about TANU, it would have been all but impossible for a strong chief like Ndaturu to take such cavalier treatment. Ndaturu's response was swift: he wrote immediately to the District Commissioner refusing permission for the meeting. The District Commissioner wrote Kaseko countermanding the permission previously granted for the Ntuzu meeting. He warned Kaseko that under no circumstances could headmen be asked to notify people of meetings of non-governmental organizations; and that if anything of this sort ever arose again, the matter would be taken immediately before the Provincial Commissioner.[2]

Kaseko then wrote an indignant letter to Ndaturu asking whom he thought he was to oppose TANU when the Governor himself permitted TANU to organize in the territory and the District Commissioner had given permission for the specific meeting in question. Accusing Ndaturu of being anti-African, Kaseko asked whether he was on the side of the Europeans, or Asians or Arabs and whether the people of Ntuzu were Europeans or Asians that they had to be prevented from being informed about an association pledged to African unity. Suspicious of the fact that he had seen no signature of Ndaturu himself, but only that of the district officer who had signed the District Commissioner's letter, Kaseko asked Ndaturu to send him his own signature if he really opposed TANU in his chiefdom. Kaseko asked for a quick reply, as *he* intended to take these matters before the Provincial Commissioner. At the same time he wrote to the District Commissioner asking: 'Did you sign it for him? Was it in fact you who refused our meeting in Ntuzu?'[3]

Ndaturu replied immediately affirming his prerogatives in his own chiefdom and his right to prohibit any meeting he wished. According to the chief, even a citizen of Ntuzu 'could not question' such a decision as Kaseko had presumptuously taken upon himself to question. Ndaturu unequivocally reaffirmed that neither Kaseko nor any of his followers were permitted to hold any meeting in Ntuzu.[4]

[1] Kaseko to Ndaturu, n.d. (Aug. 1954), MADF. (Orig. Sw.) Kaseko had requested the meetings in a July 21 letter to the D.C. Permission was given by the D.C. in a letter to Kaseko, 27 July, MADF.
[2] D.C. to Kaseko, 19 Aug. 1954, MADF.
[3] Kaseko to Ndaturu, Kaseko to D.C., 20 Aug. 1954, MADF. (Orig. Sw.)
[4] Ndaturu to Kaseko, 27 Aug. 1954, MADF. (Orig. Sw.)

Kandoro came to Kaseko's assistance on the provincial level and the struggle continued. A delegation of twenty-two TANU leaders and members delivered a letter to the Provincial Commissioner who agreed to see a delegation of no more than six persons on 10 September. On that date the Deputy Provincial Commissioner met with the delegation which included Kandoro, Bogohe and Kaseko. They were informed that the initial permission given for meetings simply meant that the District Commissioner had no objection to the meeting. If either the native authority or the police objected for their own reasons, the District Commissioner would be inclined to follow their advice. In reply to a question, the Deputy Provincial Commissioner said it 'would serve no useful purpose' for him to attempt to 'reconcile' them with the chief since 'it was unlikely that the chief would be induced to welcome them unless he received an apology.'[1]

In September Kaseko went ahead with meetings without permission. He was reported to have harangued that hospitals did not have good medicine; that Europeans received high wages and automobiles whereas Africans got low wages; that chiefs were dismissed without consulting the people; that agriculture, forestry and veterinary officers wasted the money of the native treasuries; and, most alarming of all, that if Africans united they would be able to govern themselves. Two chiefs broke up illegal meetings. One told the people they would continue to destock, to pay tax and to be called out for tribal labor; if they refused, they would be taken to court.[2]

The Ban: November 1954

Eight years later, after Tanganyika's independence, Kaseko was to become the Area Commissioner in Maswa District. But now the evidence against him was collected by the Maswa Federation of Chiefs, he was tried for holding illegal meetings, and sentenced to jail. In late October, Kandoro again appealed to the Provincial Commissioner on behalf of the Malampaka branch of TANU, which was still hoping to hold meetings even without Kaseko.

But the government in Dar es Salaam and the provincial administration moved against TANU's entire Mwanza-based

---

[1] Quoted from a 'brief record' of the meeting prepared by the Deputy Provincial Commissioner and sent to Lake Province TANU, 14 Sept. 1954, LPF.

[2] Letters from various chiefs to D.C., Sept. 1954, MADF.

organization. Police confiscated all books and records from the TANU office and from the homes of Munanka and Kandoro. On 1 November the Provincial Commissioner informed the two leaders that the Registrar of Societies had refused to register the Lake Province branch of TANU on the grounds that it 'is being or is likely to be used for purposes prejudicial to or incompatible with the maintenance of peace, order and good government.'[1] The Mwanza District and Malampaka branches were also closed. Though the administration subsequently permitted registration of TANU branches at Bukoba, Musoma, and elsewhere in the Lake Province, no branches were permitted in Sukumaland until 1958.

The 1954 U.N. Visiting Mission

Two months before the ban, the 1954 United Nations Visiting Mission had begun its tour of Tanganyika in the Lake Province where, by its own account, the Mission received 'an intensive introduction to present-day African political thought and organization.' At various points in its tour the Mission found that TANU was described as 'the former African Association in a reorganized form.'[2]

Nowhere was this more true than in Mwanza where provincial TANU—in all but name—was a virtually undifferentiated continuation of the active, organized, intensely political TAA which had developed over several years. In July and August, existing TAA branches had simply notified the government of the change of name and carried on with their activities as they had in the past. In late August, Kandoro was still using provincial TAA stationery with 'Association' crossed out and 'National Union' added in ink. Provincial TANU's memorandum to the 1954 Visiting Mission was presented by the same people and elaborated many of the same arguments which previously had been TAA's: opposition to alienation of land, particularly in the Meru case; opposition to

[1] Registrar of Societies to Lake Province TAA, 27 Oct. 1954, FCBF. In a Minute to the Chief Secretary in September, Governor Twining had written: 'The Lake Province is our No. 1 security risk at the moment and has overtaken the honour of that place from the Northern Province. We must have a first class man in charge [of the police] with a first class Special Branch working with him. The establishment must be increased to meet all possible needs of the Province.' Noting that 'we cannot afford to have a discontented Police Force at Mwanza above all places,' Twining directed that adequate housing for the police be built at Mwanza 'without any further delay.'

[2] UNVM, 1954, pp. 10, 74.

destocking, cattle tax and cotton cess; protest against discrimination against Africans in education, health, hotels, loans, employment; desire for better education, hospitals and communications.

TAA had pushed explicitly for 'independence in the near future' in 1951 and for greater African representation as early as 1948. Now in 1954 TANU's memorandum 'pressed for a timetable of steps to be taken, in consultation with the people, towards the goal of self-government.' One member 'pointed attention to the fact that the United Nations had already given Somaliland a target-date for independence.' Insisting that Tanganyika was an African country and 'not a country of all races, as people of other races say,' TANU's memorandum stated:

We are the owners of this country; there are more of us than of any other race...therefore it is just and proper that there should be African majorities in such councils as the Legislative Council, county councils and town councils, and that the African representatives on these councils should be elected by the people.

TANU objected to 'loose references to Tanganyika as if it were a colonial possession of the United Kingdom,' asked that the flag of the United Nations be flown with the British flag, and that a United Nations office be established in Tanganyika with a branch in each of the eight provinces.[1] Unlike previous TAA petitions which had been presented in English, the 1954 TANU memorandum was presented in Swahili—symbolic, perhaps, of a more conscious insistence on the separateness, distinctiveness and rightness of being African.

An estimate of the membership of TANU at the time of its proscription is not easy to make. At the end of 1954, TANU claimed something less than 10,000 members in the province.[2] A more conservative estimate might have placed late 1954 membership in the province at 5,000 and, in Sukumaland, perhaps better than half that figure. As the United Nations Visiting Mission pointed out, however, 'the general following which the union's leaders may command now or in the future is a matter of greater importance than its numerical strength.' Certainly thousands of people who never paid membership fees heard TAA–TANU's message in the Lake Province sympathetically, and the total impact of TAA–TANU can hardly be assessed. It was the Mission's judgment that 'if put to a test, its following would prove

---

[1] *Ibid.* p. 13.   [2] Lake Province Annual Report, 1954, LPF.

to be large, and its emergence as an important political force must therefore be recognized.'[1]

The Lake Province leadership confidently held this view. On one occasion after the Provincial Commissioner fulminated against Munanka for opposing the British administration and making off with people's money via TAA, Munanka is reported to have challenged the Provincial Commissioner to allow the people of the province to choose which of the two of them they would prefer to govern them. Similarly, he proposed that the people of Tanganyika be allowed to choose between the Governor and the president of TAA.[2] The government's decision to proscribe TANU in late 1954 was, of course, a testament to the association's actual and potential strength. Though the government rationalized the ban as a measure for safeguarding the government's planned programs of local government and natural resources development, the wisdom of the ban was questionable. Given TANU's actual and potential strength, any policy of repression could not help but have a time limit—and a sequel.

4 DURING THE BAN

By the close of 1954 the government had accomplished, at least temporarily, the feat of squelching in Sukumaland the most obvious manifestations of what it regarded as irresponsible political activity. TANU was legally proscribed. The Sukuma Union lingered on the books until 1956, but to all intents and purposes it was defunct two years before that date. The cooperative movement continued to flourish but was to be successfully purged of overt political concerns.

Before discussion of the underground political activities of the 1955–8 period, the precise nature of the government's proscription should be clarified. The ban simply brought to an end the existence of TANU branches in Sukumaland. There was no provision against being a TANU member, against attending TANU meetings outside Sukumaland or even, at first, against gathering together in groups for purposes of discussion. The last-mentioned loophole was plugged when, at the instigation of Provincial Commissioner Walden, native authority orders were promulgated in early 1955 requiring written permission from the district

[1] UNVM, 1954, p. 13.   [2] Kandoro, p. 72.

office, the police and the local native authority before any public meetings could be held.

In 1957 an amendment to the Registration of Societies Ordinance made not only meetings, but any activity on behalf of a proscribed society, unlawful. This measure was specifically applied to the politically sensitive Geita District in May 1958 when the government moved to outlaw 'any activities of TANU' in the district, including the selling of newspapers and membership cards, in an unsuccessful effort to forestall opposition to the multiracial Geita District Council.[1]

What happened, however, to the political leaders? It is an important question because of the importance of individual leadership to the fledgling politics of the 1950s. Kandoro left Mwanza soon after TANU closed and returned to his home in Kigoma to farm. When he returned on a visit a year later, he was seized by the police and taken to the District Commissioner. The Commissioner declared his presence 'contrary to the public interest,' and gave Kandoro three days to leave under the terms of the Removal of Undesirable Persons Ordinance. Kandoro was directed to proceed to Kigoma and 'thereafter to remain outside the Township of Mwanza until further notice.'[2]

Munanka stayed in Mwanza. While employed by a local automobile dealer, he busied himself on the side with two economic associations—the African Cattle Trading Union (Lake Victoria) and the Lake Province Africans General Trading Company. In 1956 he served as chairman of the South and West Lake Trades Council, a coordinating body for trade unions throughout the province set up with Rashidi Kawawa's encouragement as an adjunct to the Tanganyika Federation of Labor. He remained in correspondence with the Fabian Colonial Bureau in England where sympathetic members of Parliament raised questions to the government concerning the ban on TANU in Sukumaland. He circulated printed handbills announcing Nyerere's arrivals in Mwanza in 1956 and 1957. Until he took up a national TANU post in Dar es Salaam in 1958, Munanka remained Mwanza's foremost politician. It was to Munanka that politically interested men from rural areas came when they wished to discuss TANU activities or the possibility of opening a TANU branch. In town, Munanka led discussions at the Welfare Center in the evenings

---

[1] Speech by P.C. to the Sukumaland Federal Council, 14 May 1958, LPF.
[2] D.C. to Kandoro, 15 June 1955, MZDF.

and gave out TANU cards to leaders from localities outside Mwanza.

Bomani, meanwhile, occupied himself with the cotton coopera-tives, which continued to expand rapidly during the middle 1950s. The number of registered societies grew from 65 in 1954 to 198 in 1956 to 275 in 1958. The percentage of the total cotton crop handled by the cooperatives grew from 32.5 per cent in 1954 to 85.4 per cent in 1958. In that year fourteen unions of societies were registered as compared to eight in 1955. In 1956 the Victoria Federation opened its first ginnery at Kasamwa as it moved to take a role in ginning as well as purchasing. Total grower mem-bership moved beyond the 100,000 mark as the cooperatives spread from their original strongholds along the lake in Geita, Ukerewe, Nassa, and in nearby Ntuzu, south into the heartland of the five Sukuma districts and northeast into Musoma District.[1]

The Cooperatives and Politics

Bomani travelled to Dar es Salaam for the December 1954 session of the Legislative Council a month after the institution of the ban on TANU in Sukumaland. At Pugu he met Nyerere, and the two discussed the political developments which had taken place in the Lake Province. Nyerere suggested that Bomani should concentrate his efforts exclusively on the cooperatives. They agreed that the cooperatives were crucial to the development of the country and that without proper leadership they would not survive. Given the government's attitude, any obvious involvement by Bomani in politics or mixing of politics with the cooperatives might be prejudicial to the economic task. Bomani might be jailed and the cooperatives might then collapse. The two agreed that Bomani should take no official political role though he could, as a mem-ber of the Legislative Council, represent African political views.[2]

In his first speech before the Legislative Council, Bomani identified himself as a representative of 'peasant farmers' who understood 'the sufferings of the poor people better than any other person who does not belong' to that class. He said he hoped to 'help Government to understand well the problems of this country and put right what is wrong.'[3] In this and subsequent

---

[1] 'Cooperative movement in the Lake Region, Tanganyika, East Africa' (Cooperative Department, Mwanza, 1962), Appendix A.
[2] Bomani, interview.
[3] TLC, 12 Feb. 1954.

sessions, Bomani took up a variety of matters relating to education, welfare and economic development. In Mwanza he concentrated on the economics and administration of the cooperatives.

As Bomani and other cooperative leaders became responsible for the year-round operations of an organization which required skill and hard work to handle financial and administrative tasks, they concentrated their attentions on these problems and had less time —with, of course, some exceptions—for more political preoccupations. In unions and primary societies, too, cooperative leaders and committees—beholden to their constituents in the villages as well as to the government—spent their time on economic rather than political affairs. In the increasingly differentiated social milieu of the middle 1950s, the distinction between economic and political became more valid than it had been in the late 1940s or early 1950s.

There can be no doubt that political discussions took place in Mwanza and in the countryside among cooperative personnel and between them and others during the years of the ban on TANU. But this was true of almost anyone either inside or outside the cooperatives who had more than parochial interests. Local primary societies were in no sense cells of TANU in disguise. Even to think of them as 'holding units' would be misleading.[1]

[1] George Bennett has suggested (on the basis of interviews with Nyerere and Bomani) that 'the branches of the Victoria Federation of Cooperative Unions ...were able to serve as holding units throughout the period of Tanu's proscription: political education could go on there unofficially, after the co-operative business had been dispatched and the Government's co-operative officers had departed.' Bennett suggested that the government's refusal to register TANU branches in Sukumaland 'did enable the Government to check Tanu's development' there, but he believed that 'this did not inhibit Tanu's effective progress in the area for in the Lake Province, as the Visiting Mission recorded, the co-operative and political movements were "intermixed"' (Bennett, *Makerere Journal*, No. 7 (1963), p. 5).

While in a general sense it is clear that the continued spread of the cooperative movement into the countryside in the middle-1950s was one factor which served to prepare the way for TANU's rapid extension into rural areas in late 1958 and 1959, the evidence gathered from a variety of sources by this writer suggests that the cooperatives did not play much of a political role during the ban. The intermixture of economic and political ideas and activities in the associations of the early 1950s has been documented in this thesis as well as by others. Liebenow and the United Nations Visiting Mission, however, both carried out their investigations *before* the ban on TANU. Their frame of reference was the previous few years when the generalization about 'intermixture' was quite true. Even before the ban, however, a 'division of labor' was developing between TANU and the cooperatives. After months of pressure from the government and painstaking effort by Green and the Cooperative Department, the cooperative movement limited itself more

Political matters constituted no part of the formal meetings or day-to-day business activities of the cooperatives. Nor is there evidence that political agenda were brought forward after formal meetings had concluded and government cooperative officers had departed. In any case, meetings took place for the members at large only once or twice a year. Also, in the atmosphere of repression then obtaining, leaders and members alike feared covert as well as overt politics at a time when the government's Special Branch of political investigators was becoming well known.

For strategic and practical reasons, then, leaders who were interested in both cooperatives and politics decided that the insulation of each from the other would be beneficial to both. TANU cards were sold secretly throughout the 1955–8 period, but only on an individual basis. Some individual cooperative society leaders were politically involved, but the network of political contacts reaching out from town centers like Mwanza and Shinyanga into the villages did not depend organizationally upon the cooperatives. Political education continued only in the indirect sense of interesting people in organizing, having them gather occasionally to discuss some of their problems and training a few men with secretarial and leadership skills who might later find their way into TANU in a political capacity. Even then, once inducted into the structure and ethos of the cooperative movement, most men tended to stay rather than enter the more risky and less remunerative posts TANU had to offer when it reopened in 1959.

Even when Bomani became an active liaison between national TANU headquarters and insurgent Geita politicians in late 1957 and early 1958, this direct political involvement did not go below the top leadership of the Victoria Federation based in Mwanza. Even then, Bomani's role as Legislative Council member (with frequent opportunity for contact with Nyerere in Dar es Salaam) was the more significant factor in his political involvement, not his leadership of the Victoria Federation as such. At village level, it appears that even in 1957–8 when politics moved from clandestine card selling to mass action, the politicians (again with some individual exceptions like Shiza, Sanja and Kaseko) were different

exclusively to the not inconsiderable problems of launching viable units of cooperation. After the ban—and after Nyerere and Bomani had agreed on the tactical value of distinguishing politics and the cooperatives—the cooperatives played no appreciable political role.

people from the local cooperative society leadership; and they depended upon their own quite distinct network of political contacts.[1]

Outside Contacts and Attempts to Secure Registration

The activities of the other prominent organizer of the 1953–4 period, Lameck Bogohe, illustrated the sort of political activity which continued despite the ban. Bogohe returned to his native Nassa where he had been known for his work with the local growers' cooperative as well as with the Sukuma Union, TAA and TANU. In Nassa where the independent political and economic farmer–trader group was very strong, Bogohe was elected in 1955 as a people's representative to the village, subchiefdom and chiefdom councils and ultimately to the Sukumaland Federal Council itself. He was one of half a dozen politically oriented persons who were able to infiltrate the council system by way of election in the mid-1950s. The group was able to express its views, but little was accomplished since the Council was dominated by the chiefs together with councillors who were little more than 'henchmen' of the chiefs.

At the same time, Bogohe remained in touch with TANU outside Sukumaland. Whenever Nyerere passed through Mwanza on his way home to Musoma District, Bogohe and other Sukumaland leaders met him at Bomani's home. Such an occasion was early July 1955. Nyerere had resigned his teaching position at Pugu and was to spend several months at home (teaching the Zanaki language to a Catholic father) before deciding finally to take up national TANU leadership on a full-time basis from Dar es Salaam.[2] Bogohe traveled with Nyerere and several others to Musoma and Tarime where TANU meetings could legally be held. Again in late September Bogohe traveled to Musoma for a series of meetings. In mid-October he attended the second annual TANU conference in Dar es Salaam as a delegate from Musoma.

After the Dar es Salaam meetings, Bogohe returned to Nassa. In December 1955 he spent two weeks in Maswa re-establishing his old political contacts. He held no meetings; it was his aim simply to lay

---

[1] The information in the preceding paragraphs was compiled from interviews conducted by the writer and by his research assistant, Pastor Balele.

[2] Rev. Arthur Wille, interview, 22 May 1964; Nyerere to Selwyn-Clarke, 4 July 1955, written from Musoma, FCBF. See also Bennett, *Makerere Journal*, No. 7 (1963), p. 6.

the groundwork so that the Provincial Commissioner could be told that people were prepared to open branches with responsible leaders, proper accounts and the like. Early in the new year he met with selected leaders in Mwanza and Nassa for similar discussions.[1]

A series of letters requesting permission to reopen TANU came forward in 1956 and 1957.[2] Bogohe, Kaseko and M. I. Kitenge of Mwanza wrote the Chief Secretary in February 1956 expressing regret that the government had not warned the political leaders of their mistakes before banning TANU; 'we were prepared to listen to the views of the government and follow them.' They asked for the reopening of TANU in Mwanza 'in accord with the developments in Tanganyika as a whole.' They affirmed that they were ready to follow Nyerere's leadership and the leadership of others who would be chosen 'according to arrangements as desired by the government.' They also wrote to TANU President Nyerere in Dar es Salaam to ask if he might approach the Chief Secretary in person for permission to reopen TANU in Mwanza. They concluded their letter: 'We are tired of waiting. We want to get to work. Time does not wait for us.'[3]

After the government acknowledged receipt of the February letter, but without comment on its substance, it remained for Bomani to pursue the question further in the Legislative Council. Already in November 1955 he had vigorously opposed the government's introduction of a Penal Code Amendment Bill which permitted the government to prosecute persons for making statements 'likely to raise discontent.' Pointing out that Britain had no equivalent legislation and that the wording of the bill was so loose as to make convictions dependent entirely upon the predilections of a judge, Bomani argued that the bill would all but abolish freedom of speech and would 'make the growth of political movements in this country an impossibility.'[4] In May 1956

[1] Bogohe, interview.
[2] Kambona had reported to the Fabian Colonial Bureau in October 1955 that 'protracted negotiations between TANU leaders and Government' had 'so far proved fruitless' with regard to reopening the Mwanza and Malampaka branches of TANU. He indicated there was some hope that they 'may be allowed to reopen next year' (Kambona to Fabian Colonial Bureau, Oct. 18 1955, FCBF).
[3] Bogohe, Kitenge, and Kaseko to the Chief Secretary; also Bogohe and Kitenge to Nyerere, 23 Feb. 1956, Bogohe papers. (Orig. Sw.).
[4] TLC, 3 Nov. 1955. The Ordinance was No. 49 of 1955, signed into law by the Governor on 10 Nov. 1955. Nyerere and TANU strongly opposed the bill and cabled objections to the Colonial Secretary and the Trusteeship Council (Nyerere to Fabian Col. Bureau, 13 Dec. 1955, FCBF).

after TANU branches in Morogoro and Tanga has been closed by the government, Bomani pressed for the reasons for the earlier refusal to register the Mwanza, Malampaka and Nassa branches. He asked if they might be registered after new applications, and, if not, 'will Government state conditions under which it could be prepared to review its decision?' In reply the Chief Secretary repeated the wording of the original order and added: 'Any application for the re-opening of these branches would doubtless be considered on its merits.'[1]

The activists in Mwanza and Nassa responded to this tantalizingly ambiguous statement by sending in new applications, but the government continued to refuse permission for TANU branches in Sukumaland and even for public observance of the anniversary of TANU's founding.

In late July in Nassa, Bogohe and two other local leaders who had been pressing for the reopening of TANU were arrested for meeting without a permit. The charge was true—Bogohe and fifteen or twenty others met frequently—but Chief Kapongo was unable to find witnesses and the charges were dropped. Those interested in politics, nevertheless, continued during the 1955–8 period to meet secretly in small groups and to travel outside Sukumaland to attend annual TANU conferences. TANU cards continued to be sold clandestinely. The cards were brought into

---

[1] *Ibid.* 11 May 1956. The proscription of TANU in Sukumaland produced some questions in the English Parliament. On 8 Dec. 1954, John Hynd, M.P., asked why the Mwanza branch had been refused registration. The Colonial Secretary replied that the branch was being used 'for purposes prejudicial to peace, order and good government.' Pressed further by Hynd for the specific reasons and for a statement of the unlawful or unconstitutional methods adopted by the Mwanza branch, the Colonial Secretary refused to elaborate ('TANU, Nyerere and government action', memorandum by John Hatch, typescript, in the Tanganyika file of the Labour Party, Transport House, London).

A year later, in March 1956, Arthur Skeffington, M.P., asked the Colonial Secretary for 'the reasons for the Tanganyika Government's refusal to allow the Tanganyika African National Union to reopen its branch in Sukumaland.' Notwithstanding the repeated efforts of previous months to obtain legal approval for TANU branches in Sukumaland, the Secretary replied: 'No recent application has been received by the Registrar of Societies for the registration of a branch of the Tanganyika African National Union in Sukumaland, although some time ago registration was refused to certain branches in the area because the registrar was satisfied that they were being used for purposes prejudicial to the maintenance of peace, order and good government. This decision was welcomed by the great majority of the African population in the area' (quoted from *Hansard* 7 Mar. 1956, in Fabian Colonial Bureau to Nyerere, 16 Apr. 1956, FCBF).

Sukumaland by Nyerere on his visits and by local leaders such as Munanka in Mwanza, Bogohe in Nassa, Kaseko in Maswa, P.C. Walwa and Sylvester Lubala in Kwimba, and Saidi Maswanya and Shabani Mohamed in Shinyanga, who travelled periodically to Musoma, Bukoba, Tabora and Dar es Salaam to obtain them.[1]

Again in August 1957 Nyerere came to Mwanza. His arrival was heralded by handbills bearing the Swahili title, 'We for Ourselves,' asking people to meet Nyerere at the railroad station and to welcome him along the route into central Mwanza. The day after his arrival another printed circular signed by Munanka, Kitenge and Ng'wanamashalla 'on behalf of all who love Democracy' appeared, outlining demands for elections throughout Tanganyika. The circular, benefiting from Ng'wanamashalla's knowledge of Latin and with overtones of the Communist Manifesto and the Declaration of Independence, began: 'Vox populi, vox Dei.' Certainly one of the more unusual if not one of the more important documents of the nationalist struggle in Tanganyika, it continued in Swahili with occasional parenthetical insertions in English (as noted in parentheses):

The voice of the people is the voice of God.
All who love democracy unite!
Every voter should have one vote.
To be forced to cast three votes for persons of different races is government of *servitude* (Imperialism) and it may go to hell!
'Multi-racial' government is racialist government—*Take care!*...
Selection of Ministers by the government itself is the kernel of the government of *servitude*—destroy it NOW for
We want *every man the right to vote.*
We don't want any Hitler-style government here!
We despise government of 'forcible seizure' (Colonialism) completely.
Soldiers of Freedom onward; do not fall behind.
We have lived by self-help, serving our Mother Tanganyika.

---

[1] In early 1957, Nyerere wrote in *Sauti ya TANU*: 'More than two years ago all our branches in Sukumaland were closed down. We have been waiting all this time for Government to prosecute TANU for the crime that TANU committed in Sukumaland. Encouraged by this silence I approached the Provincial Commissioner and asked him to allow us to reopen our branches. I discovered that our former leaders there had since committed a fresh crime; they had been invited to a Governor's party and had not attended the party! If this reason is embarrassing—I certainly cannot be blamed for it. (On making enquiries the persons concerned told me that they were never invited to attend the Governor's party in question)' (*Sauti ya TANU*, No. 1, Feb. 1957).

To refuse here is a great step toward complete destruction of *Government
of Servitude*—Unite NOW!
God, we fall at your feet that you may preserve our Freedom.[1]

Bogohe reports that Nyerere came loaded with TANU cards on
this trip. Hundreds of cards at 2 shillings each were sold at Bomani's
house on the day Nyerere was in Mwanza. Small printed booklets
outlining the purposes of TANU were also sold for 1 shilling each.

All over Sukumaland attempts were made to register TANU
branches in 1956 and 1957, but the government remained un-
yielding. In 1957 the Societies Ordinance was amended to make
'quite certain,' as Nyerere explained it, 'that when a branch had
been declared an unlawful society or refused registration (which
I believe amounts to the same thing) it meant that any activity by
any person on behalf of such a society in such an area was illegal.'[2]
The government crackdown on TANU activities—which John
Hatch, then Commonwealth Secretary of the Labour Party, said
strongly suggested a 'vendetta'—intensified in 1957 also in other
parts of the country.[3] Nyerere himself was prohibited from addressing public meetings, and additional branches of TANU were
closed at Pangani and Handeni. At the same time, the government
encouraged the development of the United Tanganyika Party—a
party conceived and sponsored by the colonial administration and
designed to fit the image of the multi-racial society which it
believed itself to be constructing.

Political Resurgence in Shinyanga:
Maswanya and Mohamed

In Shinyanga, too, politics began in 1956–7 to press against the
restrictions imposed by the administration. Two men who were to
become leading figures in the political and administrative life of
Tanganyika in the post-independence era took active leadership
roles. They were Saidi Ali Maswanya and Shabani Mohamed.

Maswanya was a Muslim Nyamwezi from Tabora. Educated
at Tabora Secondary School, he later joined the police force. Like
Bogohe, he learned a good deal about police methods, evidence,

---

[1] 'Madai ya Kutaka Uchaguzi wa Watu Wote Tanganyika' (Demands for a
General Election in Tanganyika), 16 Aug. 1957, a one-page circular signed by
Munanka, Ng'wanamashalla and Kitenge (printed by Lake Printing Works,
Mwanza), Kitenge papers.
[2] *Sauti ya TANU*, No. 14, 29 Oct. 1957. See also above, p. 182.
[3] Hatch in a letter to the *New Statesman and Nation*, May 18, 1957, reproduced
in *Sauti ya TANU*, No. 12(B), May 25, 1957.

law and government—knowledge which was to assist him in his later political activities. He recalls that Nyerere—whom he had known at Tabora—read a good deal and occasionally passed him an interesting book; he recalls reading about Dr J. E. K. Aggrey and about Booker T. Washington. At a special police training session in Uganda, Maswanya read a book on English politics which had a significant impact on his thinking; he recalls that it discussed *inter alia* 'how to operate as a politician' and 'how political propaganda helps establish governments.'

After ten years of police service, Maswanya resigned his position and set out independently in business and trade. He joined TAA in 1952 and moved to Shinyanga in 1953. The same year Joseph Petro, TAA's Shinyanga secretary, turned to Maswanya when Petro found that he had to resign from TAA to remain in his civil post. Well educated, experienced, politically minded and no longer a government servant, Maswanya was a natural choice as successor.

Deprived of its core of civil servants, TAA in Shinyanga had become totally inactive and Maswanya did not set about immediately to construct a new organizational base. Spurred on by friends, he took a more active role in 1956–7. He went to the nearest legal TANU office at Tabora for membership cards and advice, then sold TANU cards discreetly, enlisted some 100 members in the township and a few from outside and formed a local TANU committee. Capitalizing on his knowledge of law, he reasoned that there would be nothing illegal about his activities because TANU headquarters in Dar es Salaam was registered as a territorial organization. As such it was entitled to enlist members throughout the territory unless specifically proscribed in a given area. No branch in Shinyanga had ever been proscribed or denied registration. He calculated, too, that if one association were denied registration, he could immediately re-establish it under a different name, operating in the meantime until the new refusal of registration came through. He was prepared to do a bit of juggling with a TANU signboard and a Cattle Trading Association signboard—either or both of which he could hang on the outside of his house depending on the current status of the respective associations.[1]

In March 1957 Maswanya applied for registration but within three weeks he received the reply that registration 'has been

[1] Maswanya, interview, 18 Nov. 1964.

refused.'[1] There was no explanation, not even the standard formula
usually employed by the registrar to the effect that 'the Society is,
or is likely to be, used for purposes incompatible with law, order
and good government.'[2] Disappointed, he wrote to Nyerere:

We know that TANU branches at Mwanza and Malampaka were proscribed by the Government, but that should not contaminate our District
nor, for that matter, the whole of Sukumaland or Lake Province.

We, in Shinyanga District, feel that by being refused the registration of
our branch of TANU, a peaceful union, we have been refused one of the
fundaments of human rights as declared by U.N.O. General Assembly
on 10.12.48 for all peoples of the world to enjoy. (Article 20 of U.N.O.
Fundaments of Human Rights refers.) As we have not been informed by
Government the cause of its refusal to register our branch nor do we
know or see any such cause we feel to have been unfairly treated. We
therefore ask you to take up this matter with the Government so that this
is set right... TANU is very popular with the African public in this
District.[3]

He continued, nevertheless, to sell membership cards and take
up people's complaints. His main locus of operations was the
market place where he had numerous friends who sold tea in
small shops. He went from store to store talking politics with
whoever was interested. Not only townspeople but also cattle
traders and farmers in town for the market could be contacted this
way at a time when village touring by someone of Maswanya's
status could not have been done secretly. Maswanya did not
actually sell cards in the market place; he took interested card
purchasers to his home. Nor did Maswanya distribute cards to
others to sell. There was no system of representatives in villages
as was sometimes the case elsewhere. It was a small-scale operation
performed only on an individual basis. As TAA had never penetrated far beyond the borders of the township, so TANU during
the ban worked under the same limitations.

With the United Nations Visiting Mission scheduled to arrive
in Sukumaland in August 1957, Maswanya desired to prepare a
memorandum on behalf of TANU members in Shinyanga. The
District Commissioner granted permission for 'private' meetings
indoors for purposes of discussion prior to the arrival of the

[1] Maswanya to Nyerere, 1 Apr. 1957, LPF.
[2] This point regarding the refusal for registration of the Shinyanga branch was
   made in a letter from TANU to the Labour Party, 12 Apr. 1957, Labour
   Party files, London; also in *Sauti ya TANU*, No. 14, 29 Oct. 1957.
[3] Maswanya to Nyerere, 1 Apr. 1957, LPF.

Mission and a memorandum was prepared. The Mission did not stop in Shinyanga so Maswanya took the petition to Tabora TANU headquarters for presentation to the Mission. The memorandum asked for the opening of TANU branches in Sukumaland and for increased African representation on the Legislative Council in proportion to population rather than on the basis of multi-racial formulas. Maswanya also sent to the Provincial Commissioner a request to meet personally with the Mission in Mwanza, but it was received 'too late for arrangements to be made.'[1] Maswanya may not have taken 'no' for an answer; he is believed to have met the Mission's train at Luhombo Station on its departure from Sukumaland.

Maswanya left Shinyanga to become Provincial TANU Secretary at Tabora in November 1957. Shabani Mohamed, a Tabora-born Muslim who had earlier established himself in the taxi business in Shinyanga, immediately filled the leadership gap. Whereas Maswanya's favorite location for purposes of political propagandizing was the market, Mohamed's was the Welfare Center where dances were held in the evenings. 'I was a big dancer at that time,' he has recalled with a smile.

Mohamed became particularly involved in agitation against the establishment in Shinyanga of a statutory multi-racial district council. Like District Commissioner French in Geita, the District Commissioner in Shinyanga was anxious to make his district one of the early starters in the race to set up the new type of council. In contrast to Geita, however, the Shinyanga native authorities were strongly entrenched, indigenous rulers who were not amenable (as were their Geita counterparts) to the administration's arm-twisting techniques. The powerful chief of Usiha, Hussein Makwaia (the younger brother of Kidaha who took over when the latter resigned in 1955), was particularly opposed to the new council scheme and unusually sympathetic, for a chief, to TANU. With important traditional authorities and the new political organizers like Mohamed united in opposition to the council idea, and supported by the people, the District Commissioner found that a chorus of 'No's greeted him wherever he addressed the public on proposals for implementing the new council system. Operative now, as in Geita later, was a network of political contacts stretching from Mohamed and others in the townships into the countryside. What Mohamed has referred to as 'our nationalist

[1] P.C. to D.C. 20 Aug. 1957, SHDF.

P

in the village' was probably a clerk with primary school education, a medical dispenser, a local trader who travelled occasionally to the town, or a teacher or relative of the chief who had more than local exposure and interests. These were the intermediaries who kept political activity going at the grass roots once leaders like Mohamed had made the initial contacts in outlying areas.

Inside Shinyanga town, Mohamed's strength was especially strong and the District Commissioner had no more success than in the outlying chiefdoms in winning approval for the multi-racial council idea. Mohamed was arrested or briefly held in custody on a number of occasions—primarily for convening illegal meetings—and a propaganda war appears to have taken place between the District Commissioner and Mohamed, who were continually at cross purposes.[1]

By the time TANU opened legally in Sukumaland in October 1958, Mohamed's position was such that he became Organizing Secretary General E. A. Kisenge's chief assistant in setting up TANU organizations throughout the five districts.

Trade Unions

A few trade unions—for mine workers, drivers, tailors, domestic servants, hotel workers and government servants—existed in Mwanza and, to a lesser extent, in Shinyanga in the years following the Second World War. In the mid-1950s the trade unions pro-liferated and grew stronger. This was due partly to the stimulus of Rashidi Kawawa's leadership of the unifying Tanganyika Fed-eration of Labor. Kawawa made several visits to Mwanza which were instrumental in the development of trade union strength. It is also true that every year more African workers became aware of their grievances, and they were more desirous of and more knowledgeable about how to express them. In this context, political and would-be political leaders in Mwanza and Shinyanga townships, frustrated by the ban on TANU, found by 1957 that they could channel some of their enthusiasms into the labor movement.

Trade unions, however, were not ideal front organizations for direct political activity any more than were the cooperatives. The trade unions had their own rationale for existence and their own

---

[1] Mohamed, interview, 11 Sept. 1964. Almost any public place or occasion was suitable for making covert political contacts: the vegetable market, local *pombe* (beer) shops, sports events, cattle markets, etc.

organizational preoccupations which did not permit easy extension beyond African wage earners in towns or mine compounds to the politically more important populations of the rural areas. Nevertheless, in addition to fighting for higher wages and better working conditions, the unions did provide some degree of cover for political activity—particularly, as with the cooperatives, for the top leadership in Mwanza. Trade union leaders could sell TANU cards, get politically interested town leaders together in meetings where matters of general concern could be discussed and occasionally even develop contacts in rural reas.

Munanka in Mwanza and Mohamed in Shinyanga did, in 1957 and 1958, associate themselves closely with the activities of the Tanganyika Federation of Labor. Richard Wambura, another Mwanza-based leader who was to emerge into political prominence after 1958, received his baptism into politics through the South and West Lake Trades Council, which he served as secretary in 1957. Wambura, a Mwikoma from Musoma, recalls that he and other labor leaders felt rather strongly by 1957 that nothing significant could be done with trade unions unless political agitation could bring a more general change in the prevailing power structure. More than half of the Council's discussion, Wambura recalls, concerned political affairs. The Council, too, submitted memoranda to Alan Lennox-Boyd, Secretary of State for the Colonies, on his visit to Mwanza in 1957. In addition, Wambura himself occasionally travelled to rural centers to talk with individuals who could be relied upon to place into wider circulation news of the current political situation, or the ideas of politically inclined Mwanza leaders.[1]

[1] Wambura, interview, Nov. 1964.

7

The Crisis in Geita

A climatic moment in the history of postwar politics in Sukuma-land—and in Tanganyika—occurred in Geita District in 1958. In Geita in that year a strong administration met head-on with a citizenry aroused in opposition to the imposition of a multi-racial district council. The dissidents protested by the hundreds at illegal meetings. Ultimately thousands marched to Mwanza to lay their complaints before the Provincial Commissioner himself. The administration met the uprising with its usual show of force. It could not, however, halt the breakdown of local government in Geita nor prevent 'the Geita affair' from becoming a *cause celebre* for Nyerere and TANU. News of the events in Geita reached the attention of the British Parliament and of the United Nations. While the events in Geita did not of themselves explain subsequent changes in colonial policy—external political pressures from the United Nations, from London and from elsewhere in Africa were at least as important in producing a redirection of policy as factors internal to Tanganyika—the break-down of government in Geita was so sudden, so dramatic and so complete that developments there had considerable catalytic effect on the process of change territorially.

Geita was the final battleground for the ideas of the Twining administration at the grass roots. After Geita, the administration's policy of ignoring or sidetracking what it viewed as bothersome and, in its view, unrepresentative politicians collapsed. The com-mitment to 'multi-racial' or 'non-racial' territorial and local mod-ifications of the Legislative Council and the native authorities had to be unequivocably abandoned. In the Lake Province itself, TANU was permitted to reopen its branches in Sukumaland. An all-African council was established in Geita. After civil disobedience spread to other districts, the most bitterly resented natural resources legisla-tion of the previous ten years was revoked at the November 1958 meeting of the Sukumaland Federal Council.

The victories for dissidents in Geita and in Sukumaland had substantial impact not only on the administration, but also on TANU's image and effectiveness territorially. The Geita crisis dramatized the essence of the conflict between colonialists and nationalists. It underlined the differences between those who emphasized relationships of parity between the races and those who looked toward an independent African state, between those for whom self-government was only a distant goal of policy and those for whom it seemed an immediate and necessary possibility. It provided valuable propaganda for the nationalist movement through a juxtaposition of images: repressive administration versus popular protest. Nyerere publicized the Geita events in his broadsheet, *Sauti ya TANU*. Watched by Africans throughout the territory, the struggle in Geita became a symbol for the nationalist struggle everywhere in Tanganyika. Geita in 1957 and 1958 provides a most revealing case study of pre-independence nationalist politics at the most local level.

As the first phase of territorial elections in September 1958 approached, the principal question was whether TANU or the multi-racial United Tanganyika Party would emerge as the front runner. While TANU was thought to have considerable strength and the United Tanganyika Party was known to be relatively weak, few predicted the overwhelming victories which TANU achieved in all constituencies. While events and personalities throughout the territory contributed to TANU's impressive showing, it can be said that events in Geita crystallized nationalist feeling and acted as a catalyst at the polls—not only in Sukumaland, but beyond. With the electoral triumphs of TANU in 1958-9, combined with a redirection of colonial policy under a new Governor, the path to further constitutional advances became clear. TANU would lead the way to independence.

I   MULTI-RACIALISM FOR THE DISTRICTS

The Geita Setting

Geita had always been an atypical area. Not originally inhabited by the Sukuma, Geita was mostly virgin forest until Sukuma immigration changed the face of the land and made it, by the 1950s, an extension of Sukumaland proper. In the late 1940s, waves of Sukuma emigrated from the heavily populated districts east of Smith Sound into the new land. Then the government undertook a coordinated program of tsetse fly eradication and attempted controlled settlement on a large scale. By 1950 Geita's population had increased 50 per cent over the previous five years. There was an obvious need for closer administration than the distant Mwanza District headquarters could provide. Geita became a separate district with its own District Commissioner and headquarters offices in 1950.

The mixture of tribes resulting from the Sukuma immigration into Geita made for jealousy and tension. This was especially true in Karumo and Buchosa along the lake shore where Zinza and Sukuma populations were concentrated. Here, too, the chiefs installed by the government in the 1920s and 1930s were most clearly non-indigenous and, by the critical period of the mid-1950s, obviously effete and ineffective. Heavy Sukuma immigration weakened the native authority system even more. Whatever the reason for their abandonment of the old life in central Sukumaland, the immigrants were likely to be more vigorous, more independent and more impatient of established authority than their brethren who remained at home.

Looking back after the convulsions in Geita in 1958, a District Commissioner pinpointed the political potential which had always been latent in the district. Noting that in 1959 the position of the chiefs had been 'drastically changed,' he wrote:

but the effect of the change is only to bring theory into line with reality in a district where the Chiefs lack outstanding personality while the people have no emotional bond of tribal unity, and find a sense of common purpose only in common political action and activity.[1]

The Sukuma Union, the Tanganyika African Association, cotton cooperatives, trade unions and fledgling African-owned transportation companies surfaced in Geita before they appeared in most rural areas of Sukumaland. Karumo and Buchosa were invariably the centers for incipient political activity in the district; they played the same role in Geita that Nassa did in the rural portion of Mwanza District. With TANU banned in Geita as throughout Sukumaland, a great upsurge of secret, and then overt, illegal political activity—which was to trigger reaction far beyond the district itself—followed upon the attempt of the administration in 1957 and 1958 to install in Geita a statutory multi-racial district council.

[1] Mwanza District Annual Report, 1959, MZDF.

Policy from Dar es Salaam

As we know from Chapter 2, the Tanganyikan administration sought in the year following the Second World War to add representative elements to the existing native authority system and to stimulate economic development. By the early 1950s there were two additional principal concerns. The government desired a decentralization of responsibility from Dar es Salaam to provincial, county and district units. Concurrently, it wished 'to establish a working partnership of the three main races'[1] by instituting 'inter-racial,' 'multi-racial,' or 'non-racial' councils at county and district as well as provincial levels.

In addition to the problem of how much power to devolve to the lower tiers, there was perplexity as to how best to integrate African native authority structures with the proposed local multi-racial units. The government examined several possible models of integration. In 1957 it rejected proposals that would have established multi-racial structures parallel with, but separate from, native authorities in favor of transforming existing native authority advisory councils themselves into multi-racial district councils.[2]

The Member for Local Government explained that 'wherever Native Authorities are accustomed to the co-option of non-Africans there are possibilities that they may now be prepared to accept non-Africans in the more formal association of district councils.' He noted that this state of affairs obtained in thirty of the fifty-seven districts in Tanganyika; these included all five of the Sukumaland districts where non-Africans were added to district advisory councils between 1954 and 1956. The Member went on to say that 'Provincial Commissioners are thus being asked to set themselves the immediate task of investigating the possibility of setting up councils in these areas as a matter of priority.'[3]

Initial Reactions

Soundings of District Commissioners began in the Lake Province almost immediately after the Member for Local Government's report was published. The Provincial Commissioner

---

[1] *Local government memoranda*, No. 1, Part I (Dar es Salaam, 1954), p. 9.
[2] *The county council in Tanganyika: 1951–1956* (Dar es Salaam, 1956).
[3] *Second interim report on the county council in Tanganyika: 1956–1957* (Dar es Salaam, 1957), p. 8.

suggested the five Sukumaland districts as 'possible starters in the Rural Council race' as early as January 1958, but reactions from district officials were profoundly and unanimously negative. A letter from the Mwanza District Commissioner stated:

The initial reaction of the Council was one of intense suspicion and the great majority of members favoured outright rejection of the proposal. The reasons for this attitude can be summarized as follows:-
 i) the fear that the number of non-Africans on the Council would be greatly increased
 ii) the fear that the proposals were the 'thin end of the wedge' and were a manoeuvre by Government to give non-Africans an increasing and eventually a dominant say in local Government
 iii) the fear that the power and prestige of the Native Authorities would be reduced and eventually undermined
 iv) that the widely differing habits, customs and interests of the three races would be a serious obstacle to effective cooperation
 v) that Africans as a whole were not yet ready for non-racial local government councils.

The District Commissioner went on to explain that 'the Council agreed to defer making any decision pending the report of a special sub-committee which it requested should be given permission to visit one or other of the districts in which non-racial councils were already functioning.'[1]

Ultimately, the proposals were rejected by all the Sukumaland districts except Geita. In noting that Geita would be the only district in the province to make the experiment, Provincial Commissioner Walden pointed out that the new council would have the advantage of a wider revenue base, due to the inclusion of non-Africans, and that the positions of chiefs, chiefdom councils and the Sukumaland Federal Council would in no way be compromised. He concluded with the hopeful remark that 'Geita would no doubt provide the necessary encouragement [in other districts] by means of the example shown after it had been in operation for a short time.'[2] But Geita provided a different example and another sort of encouragement than those Walden had anticipated.

The Selection of Geita

Why was Geita—among all the districts of Sukumaland—chosen

[1] D.C. to P.C., 10 May 1957, LPF.
[2] Minutes of District Commissioners' Conference, Musoma, Nov. 1957, LPF.

for the experiment? With the legacy of alien chiefs, the mixture of tribes and the activist frontier psychology of Geita District, might it not have been expected that Geita would pose more, not fewer, problems than other districts?

Provincial Commissioner Walden maintained that the district was selected because 'the great majority of the inhabitants of Geita have themselves agreed that a local government body of this kind should be established, and secondly the district of Geita is flourishing and wealthy enough to justify this form of local government.'[1] Sukumaland's only European settler, the European-owned and -operated Geita Gold Mine, Roman Catholic and Protestant missions and an Asian-owned and -operated cotton ginnery were found in the district. This provided the sort of context in which it was expected that practical force could be given to the multi-racial concept. Geita looked good on paper, and the built-in tendencies for instability referred to above initially tended to disguise rather than to illuminate the potential dangers. Would not a new local government scheme work more readily where people were generally more independent and amenable to change? Would not a council with increased powers gained largely at the expense of the chiefs (in spite of what the government said to the chiefs) function effectively in an area where chiefs were weak and little loved? The Geita District Commissioner, in fact, maintains that he viewed the new council as a potential 'safety valve' for the energies of activists. He looked, too, for popular elections to replace government nominations in 'a year or so' after the inauguration of the council.[2]

District Commissioner Neville French—a young, hard-working, dynamic ex-naval officer—figures importantly, both in the initial selection of Geita as the experimental district and in the direction which events in Geita subsequently were to take. Like Walden, he was somewhat of an autocrat and had a penchant for strong and direct exercise of authority. He combined an unusual capacity for carrying out to the nth degree any policy with an impatience which meant that, once committed himself, he 'couldn't stand people

---

[1] Opening speech to the Geita District Council, Mar. 14, 1958, LPF. (Orig. Sw.)
[2] French, interview, 2 Dec. 1963. The composition of the Geita council was to be as follows: (Africans) 7 chiefs, the liwali of Geita Minor Settlement, 13 subchiefs, 9 headmen, 19 elected commoners, 4 nominated unofficials; (Europeans) D.C., D.O., medical officer, assistant conservator of forests, agricultural officer, veterinary officer, 4 nominated unofficials; (Asians) 2 nominated unofficials (Walden papers).

not seeing the point.'[1] There are indications that he was a difficult man with whom to work—at least for those under his jurisdiction. His superiors, on the other hand, judged him an extremely capable administrator and throughout the Geita crisis Walden gave French his complete support.

In January 1958 Walden described the steps which French had taken during the previous year to sound out the new council idea in Geita:

Enquiries in Geita about the possibility of establishing a District Council were initiated by the District Commissioner who discussed personally the proposal with each Chief. The Chiefs were requested to discuss the proposal with their advisers and Chiefdom Councils. The whole matter was then debated at a meeting of the District Advisory Council in April. A vote was taken at the end of the debate and, with Government officers abstaining, there were 29 votes in favour of the proposal with only 1 abstention. Of the 29, 14 were unofficial 'commoner' Africans who included 11 elected people's representatives. The proposal was subsequently raised at numerous barazas held by the District Commissioner and the District Officers where all persons were given an opportunity to air their views. Apart from the usual suspicions raised, viz. that the proposal was a cloak for Government's intention to seize the land and hand it over to Europeans and Asians, such suspicions being dealt with on the spot, there was no sign whatsoever of any mistrust of the Chiefs' or Government's motives. The District Commissioner is confident that those who are capable of understanding the position are in favour of the establishment of a District Council.[2]

However, French himself has explained that the native authorities were originally not in favor of the proposals. They saw, quite rightly, that their powers would ultimately be whittled down as a result of accepting the new scheme. In spite of what he has described as 'some misgivings' as to whether the multi-racial councils might be premature, French urged the chiefs to consider that change was inevitable. He pointed out that the best idea would be to anticipate change by accepting a voluntary diminution of powers then, rather than waiting for forced diminution of powers or outright deposition later.[3]

[1] Harold Platt, interview, 2 Feb. 1965. French's attitude toward Africans who criticized him was always caustic. After difficulties arose in Ukerewe when he was District Commissioner there in 1950–1, a group of 'Citizens' petitioned the Governor. After replying to certain allegations they had made against him, French wrote: 'Any DC who does his job faithfully will lay himself open to scurrility by stupid but sometimes vicious agitators who are too common in the District' (French to the P.C., 2 Feb. 1951, LPF).
[2] P.C. to the Ministry of Local Government and Administration, 7 Jan. 1958, Walden papers.   [3] French, interview.

What seems to have happened is that French, anxious to be an innovator, pushed the idea through in Geita where chiefs—unlike those elsewhere in Sukumaland who successfully opposed the multi-racial idea—were too weak to resist. Walden gladly accepted since it appeared the only district in his province where it seemed possible to try the experiment. The Member for Local Government, F. H. Page-Jones, meanwhile, was able to muster only a handful of 'guinea pigs' in the territory as a whole and, satisfied that the District Commissioner and the Provincial Commissioner were confident of the prospects in Geita, Page-Jones moved ahead. Because of the government's continuing addiction to the doctrine of working only through native authorities on matters pertaining to local government, all failed to assess correctly the implications of a most important fact: the weakness of the Geita chiefs and their isolation from the bulk of their people allowed them (regardless of—or indeed despite—the merits) to be more amenable to governmental persuasion than their compatriots in other districts. Unfortunately, the success of the operation in persuasion fostered for government officials—if for no others—an illusion of consent which had little basis in fact.

2 MOUNTING OPPOSITION

The administration might have proceeded more cautiously, given the fact that native authorities in the other Sukumaland districts were so resolutely opposed to the idea of statutory multi-racial councils. The advisory councils in Kwimba, Shinyanga and Maswa stated views similar to those of the Mwanza native authority already quoted. After Geita had opted in favor, the administration failed in another attempt to convince the other Sukumaland chiefs and the Geita chiefs, subjected to the hostility of their peers, seceded from the Federal Council. In addition to the very correct judgment that they would personally lose power and prestige under the new system, the Sukumaland chiefs felt so strongly because they feared the implications of the multi-racial concept itself. Especially the more sophisticated chiefs were knowledgeable about affairs in Kenya, South Africa and the Central African Federation of the Rhodesias and Nyasaland. They were suspicious of the administration's new emphasis on multi-racialism, its fostering of the United Tanganyika Party and now its attempted invasion of even the sphere of African local government. There was awareness, too, of the growing power of TANU in the territory and of its outspoken opposition to the multi-racial dogmas of the Twining regime. By 1957–8 some chiefs were more sympathetically inclined toward the nationalist movement than they had been even a year or two before.

In the final analysis, the administration could only argue that the proposed councils would have more power and more money, that non-African representation would constitute a very small minority of the total membership of the council, that non-Africans would never replace traditional African local authorities and that non-Africans would not be given more favorable opportunities to secure land. As Cranford Pratt has pointed out, the government was guilty of inconsistencies and vulnerable to criticism, even granting the initial premise of multi-racial development. The Sukumaland chiefs and people, however, would not grant that premise. No amount of argument could convince the skeptical that multi-racial councils would not inevitably increase the influence and power of non-Africans at the expense of Africans.

Bomani versus Walden

The issue of the multi-racial councils was such as to unite, however briefly, chiefs and nationalist politicians. When the government presented the enabling legislation for the councils to the Legislative Council for debate in September 1957, Paul Bomani rose to oppose the bill:

I fail to understand why the chiefs should be deprived of their powers now. I know a District Council which would not be supported by the traditional organization of the chiefs, will not be respected by the people . . . I think that this Bill is seeking to impose [something] upon the people . . . I fail to understand why the Governor cannot delegate powers to the local councils which are now in existence . . . I fail to understand why the central Government isn't prepared to give more powers to the native authorities which are established . . . I think our local government should be based on something solid. It should be built on the foundations of the existing local councils.

Bomani argued that the bill 'would cause chaos and trouble in this country; and that is why I would hate to see it go through.' Nyerere, who had temporarily replaced Chief Kidaha in the Legislative Council, supported Bomani's arguments. Nyerere insisted that councils should be built around chiefs and existing native authorities, that trials should be made in areas like Sukumaland before the new scheme was adopted wholesale and that, above all, any new scheme required the full support of the chiefs. He hastened to add that he had seen no indication that chiefs had given their support.[1]

Between the September and December meetings of the Legislative Council, a Select Committee looked further into the question of the new councils. It reported in December and gave assurances that the government could proceed without anxiety. Bomani rose to reject the report and to speak specifically of Geita:

> Now the Honourable the Mover said that the District Council cannot be implemented or started unless and until the people of that area wish to have it. Now I know for certain that the Geita District is going to have a District Council next year and the people have not been consulted, so I would request the Member concerned to look into this matter because we do not want to have a Council started and then after a few months people would come and say: 'This has been imposed on us. We did not expect this and we did not welcome this.'[2]

The Minister of Local Government and Administration, former Provincial Commissioner Rowe of the Lake Province, was concerned enough with Bomani's remarks to initiate new inquiries to Mwanza about the council. Walden replied that Geita still wished to become a district council and advised 'for political reasons, that the Council should be established at the earliest possible date, e.g. 1st March, 1958.' He reported that French had 'once again consulted with the Chiefs and people of his District in order to ascertain their present reactions to the proposal that a District Council should be established.' Acceptance of the proposal was unanimous in four chiefdoms; in several others there were a few dissidents. Walden argued it was 'quite clear that the Chiefs and people of Geita District, with very few exceptions, are still very much in favour of the establishment of the District Council.' He concluded his report with a statement epitomizing part of his philosophy of colonial administration and underlining

[1] TLC, 21 Sept. 1957.

[2] *Ibid.* 13 Dec. 1957. Nyerere proposed that further action on the enabling legislation for the multi-racial local councils be postponed until further discussions had been held with representative chiefs at a territorial conference of chiefs scheduled the following month in Mzumbe. His proposal was rejected by the government. Citing a series of compromises, and compromises on compromises, which he had proposed on a variety of issues during his four months' service on the Legislative Council—but all of which had been refused—Nyerere said he could not remain when the lack of any spirit of give and take prevented him from performing any useful function. He resigned from the Council immediately after the debate of 13 Dec. on multi-racial local councils (*Sauti ya TANU*, No. 18, 16 Dec. 1957).

a quality in his administration (shared, among others, by Twining, French, and earlier by Rounce) which led unquestionably in part to the final showdown:

In this connection may I draw attention to the inherent danger of referring back to the people as a result of statements by a gentleman like Paul Bomani which conflict with the views of the Administration on the spot? Once the decision has been made it is clearly desirable that Government should go ahead with all speed and implement the policy agreed upon. Further reference to the people must inevitably rouse in the minds of some of them the suspicion that Government is not anxious for District Councils to be formed. The fact that there is danger in this procedure is confirmed by the withdrawal of certain Districts which originally agreed to the proposal...The great majority of tribesmen are still incapable of understanding what is involved, and if Government allows itself to be swayed by the opinions of a vociferous minority who have only their own interests at heart, Government clearly puts itself in the position of ceasing to govern.[1]

Despite Bomani's continuing opposition, the Legislative Council approved the required enabling legislation and in March Walden addressed the first meeting of the Geita District Council.

[1] P.C. to the Ministry of Local Government and Administration, 7, 11 Jan. 1958, Walden papers. Walden tended to interpret events in the Lake Province and elsewhere in Africa in terms of what he apparently perceived to be the menacing spectre of an irresponsible black nationalism on the rise. As early as 1955, Walden wrote: 'One of the purposes, in fact the main purpose, of the meeting which His Excellency had with certain Provincial Commissioners in Dar es Salaam at the beginning of September 1955 was to consider whether, in view of happenings in neighbouring territories, it was possible for Tanganyika to continue to be unaffected by these. It was agreed that it was not possible and that repercussions were inevitable. A common pattern has emerged both in Kenya and Nyasaland, and ultra nationalism is all too evident. The Mau Mau rising in Kenya, Nyasaland troubles, and statements made by African leaders in Northern Rhodesia, all point to the same end—a black Africa with the speedy removal of all non-Africans, and the complete domination by Africans of the so called immigrant races...Both Kenya and Nyasaland are warnings to us, as in both cases considerable amount of blame is being laid at the foot of Government because the keystone of Government, the Administrative Officer, has lost touch with the Africans and has therefore lost their confidence...In this Territory we are at present fortunate inasmuch as we have not yet reached the stage which has been reached in Kenya and Nyasaland, and in many districts the Administrative Officer is still regarded as the adviser of the people...It is therefore a matter of vital importance that Government should recognise the special position which the Administrative Officer has in this sphere of African relations and ensure that everything is done to see that this position is not lost' (Memorandum, by Walden, n.d., Walden papers). Unfortunately Walden's formula—good relations between administrative officers and Africans based on a paternalistic definition of the administration's role—was no more likely to avoid expressions of African discontent in the Lake Province than elsewhere.

He congratulated the people of Geita on the progress they had made and promised that after two years the District Commissioner would be replaced as chairman by someone elected from the council itself. He also issued his typical warnings against trouble-makers:

> There are always a few who...like to oppose any new form of development. The Government...can get plenty tired, even violently angry, with people who mouth ignorant slogans and try to hinder the proper development and better methods of local government and central government...I wish to warn them most strongly that they should stop their smear campaign.[1]

The multi-racial council experiment was launched—but only temporarily. Within a few months the council would be defunct because more people were more willing actively to oppose it than French, Walden, or officials in Dar es Salaam had anticipated.

Opposition at the Grass Roots

As early as the initial set of public barazas in April and May 1957, District Commissioner French had met with 'the usual suspicions ...that the proposal [for a multi-racial district council] was a cloak for Government's intention to seize the land and hand it over to Europeans and Asians.'[2] Such an argument appeared ridiculous to the administration, and officials too easily assumed that arguments could the more easily be disposed of in proportion to their degree of apparent absurdity. Insufficient consideration was given to the possibility that ridiculous arguments might be widely believed; and that they might express, in however awkward a fashion, fundamental dissatisfactions.

Geita's withdrawal from the Sukumaland Federation in 1957 over the multi-racial council issue enhanced anxiety in Geita. The Sukuma chiefs had urged the Geita chiefs to reject the council. At a meeting in Malya in May 1957 some even 'shouted to the [Geita] chiefs to act with the people.'[3] Thus, the isolation of the Geita chiefs from the rest of Sukumaland became necessary to the establishment of the new council in Geita; and French found it

---

[1] Opening speech to the Geita District Council, 14 Mar. 1958, LPF. (Orig. Sw.)

[2] P.C. to the Ministry of Local Government and Administration, 7 Jan. 1958, Walden papers.

[3] Chief Charles Masanja, interview, 12 Nov. 1964.

no more difficult to pry the abused Geita chiefs loose from the undesirable influences of the Federation than he had in convincing them in the first place to accept the council.[1]

The isolation of the Geita chiefs, however, was not tantamount to the isolation of Geita. 'Word went around Geita that the chiefs had sold the people, [that they had] acted against a Sukumaland Federal Council resolution.'[2] Though the people and the incipient politicians of Geita had little love for the native authority system, the large and active Sukuma population in the north and east of the district suddenly identified with the Sukuma chiefs and people on the other side of Smith Sound who also were fighting against the multi-racial council idea. However uninterested they may previously have been in the affairs of the Federal Council, the sudden hiving-off of Geita from an established Sukuma institution appeared threatening to Geita Sukuma; they seemed to be faced with a perpetuation in the District Council of alien chiefs compounded by a strengthened position for Europeans and Asians.

On his January 1958 tour of the district to bring the new council scheme once again before the people, French had encountered some vocal opposition and some negative votes in Karumo, Buchosa, and Msalala. It was in Msalala, where the chief later reversed himself to oppose the council, that French seemed to encounter the most outspoken expressions of dissent.

This opposition is confined to a few Councillors...who...have clearly been briefed and primed on the manner in which objections should be raised by their relatives on the other side of Smith Sound. The objectors are nearly all petty traders and owners of tea shops who have occasion to visit Mwanza, and may well be connected with Mr. Paul Bomani. One of them in fact said 'Anyhow, our Paul Bomani...will ensure that we get justice.'[3]

In fact, French had faced a question team of four men who had arranged in advance to ask penetrating and embarrassing questions from various locations in the crowd. The leader of the group was Ernest Kizimba, an uncle of the chief of Msalala, a headman for ten years and a sometime participant in TAA activities. The questioners needled the District Commissioner with the usual questions

---

[1]   Geita District Annual Report, 1957, GTDF.
[2]   Charles Masanja, interview.
[3]   P.C. to the Ministry of Local Government and Administration, 11 Jan. 1958, Walden papers.

about loss of land to non-Africans, inequality in the courts and how the chiefs had been browbeaten into accepting the council scheme. When the crowd was not satisfied with his answers, French is reported to have become angry and to have left the baraza after declaring to the crowd: 'You will agree in the end!' No vote, apparently, was taken.[1]

The small number of negative votes in Karumo and Buchosa (five and ten respectively out of several hundred) represented only the visible part of the proverbial iceberg. One man who emerged as a leader of the Geita uprising a scant few months later has admitted that when French came to Buchosa in January 1958, he did not dare to speak up in the meeting. He relates that a district officer had visited the chiefdom the previous month saying that anyone who made trouble when French arrived for the public baraza would be jailed. The same district officer is remembered as having said at one meeting: 'You talk of self-government, but can you manufacture even this match-stick?' On another occasion he reportedly held a baraza to ascertain people's views on the council, but permitted no questions.[2]

In January 1958 few people yet knew the evils of the proposed multi-racial council and French was more or less correct when he reported that there was apparently little opposition then to the proposals. But it is worth noting that only a few hundred people registered their views either way. A public baraza was in itself a questionable method for ascertaining the wishes of the people. Most of the people didn't appear on such occasions, and those who did were likely to be friends and supporters—rather than critics—of the native authorities under whose auspices the barazas were held. This was a flaw characteristic of administrative structures and procedures which utterly failed to bridge the gap between rulers and ruled. It was a flaw which both symbolized and obscured a fact which was becoming increasingly obvious to greater numbers of people who were becoming more inclined to register their views: that political legitimacy and popular consent were lacking for the colonial regime and its programs.

3 THE UPRISING

It was and is the view of Walden, French and the administration

[1] Ernest Kizimba, interview, Feb. 1965.
[2] Interviews with various Geita leaders, Aug. 1964.

Q

that the Geita uprising was the work of a few agitators inspired and directed from outside Geita and liberal in their use inside Geita of techniques of intimidation. It was and is the view of African nationalists that the Geita uprising was a virtually spontaneous reaction of the people against an alien system which pleased itself to impose on the unwilling inhabitants of Geita a multi-racialism that had been decisively rejected in other districts wherever people were given a real opportunity to express their views.

There were facts which make it easy to understand how the administration arrived at its view. The power of the pen was wielded from Dar es Salaam and Mwanza. Bomani's and subsequently Nyerere's involvement clearly had a catalytic effect. When Geita leaders came to feel they had the sympathy and support of the rest of Sukumaland and of the territory's foremost African nationalist leaders, they proceeded with greater confidence. On the other hand, what eventually occurred in Geita—whatever its connections with outside catalysts—can be interpreted finally as nothing less than a popular uprising. Leaders and catalysts, whether from inside the district or from without, could never have moved thousands of people to action unless those people wanted to be moved. The truth usually partakes of more than one perspective, but often unequally. It is the nationalist view of the Geita events which, though oversimplified in some respects, is finally the more persuasive of the two interpretations.

Complaints Proliferate

After French's January tour, the Provincial Commissioner received an anonymous letter from 'the people of Geita' entitled: 'Report of the people of the District concerning the District Council.' The letter rehearsed the usual complaints and suspicions about the Council and stated that the opinion of the people was that more time should be allowed for further discussion of the matter: 'we had only one day and have had it sprung upon us.' It asked that representatives from the district be allowed to observe the scheme in operation elsewhere before making any final decisions and that the 'representatives should not be Government servants but people chosen by ourselves.' The letter concluded:

We have often told our Chiefs that we do not agree to this Council being set up in Geita. Why do they not forward our wishes to Government? It is regrettable if the Chiefs will not listen to our needs when we put them forward and send them to Government. Do we not know what they are saying?[1]

Except for an occasional lack of clarity the letter was well written, logically organized, and very well typed. Perhaps this was even more reason to dismiss it as the work of a semi-educated local agitator with no real claim to the views of more than a handful of discontents, or inspired from outside the district by Bomani or his Mwanza cohorts. The letter was so interpreted by the administration. Letters of this sort—especially anonymous letters—usually received some attention from the Special Branch but, in general, were not taken very seriously.[2]

Whether the administration's interpretation of the letter's origins was or was not correct is less important than the fact that French and Walden were willing to regard as somehow irrelevant to the central issues any expressions of dissent from persons who had, or were thought to have had, contacts with anyone outside Geita District. In their view, anyone who questioned or opposed the council was infected with nonsensical ideas from *ipso facto* disreputable elements elsewhere who, it was assumed, had contact with Bomani in town and came, hence, under the influence of irresponsible nationalist political groups. This was a reductionist 'devil' theory which encouraged consideration not of the issues but of the background and experience of the people who brought their views to bear upon the issues. Given its policies and program, the administration had every reason to be wary of the new elite groups which were emerging as the necessary corollary to educational and economic advance. It was they who challenged most strongly the administration's commitment to the outworn credos of indirect rule and its Sukumaland variations. Ironically, the inability of the administration to deal rationally and responsibly both with the fact of new leadership and with the new questions raised, preluded the consolidation of a substantial portion of public opinion behind the very groups which the administration continued to label 'irrational' and 'irresponsible'.

In any case it was quite impossible to insulate Geita from the outside world. Every attempt to do so stirred more suspicion; every effort to move ahead on the assumption that Geita could be made an artificial vacuum encountered more resistance. While

[1] 'The People of Geita' to the P.C., 15 Jan. 1958, Walden papers. (Orig. Sw. with an English translation by the government.)
[2] A. W. J. Eyers, interview, 6 April 1965.

French stumped Geita in support of the council proposal in January 1958, the widely circulated, Sukuma-language, Catholic mission publication, *Lumuli*, reported the protests of Sukuma and Ukerewe chiefs against multi-racial councils. The chiefs were quoted to the effect that Africans would have less voice under the new system and that acceptance of the councils would mean 'that we are politically doomed.'[1] Is it surprising that feeling grew among some in Geita that their chiefs had betrayed them? By 1957 the previous physical isolation of Geita District from the rest of Sukumaland had been largely overcome through improved transportation and communications. Goods, men and ideas moved freely across Smith Sound. Kin relationships tied Sukuma in Buchosa, Karumo and Usambiro to their fellows in Mwanza, Kwimba or Maswa. Many of Geita's more enterprising citizens travelled frequently to Mwanza and some of Mwanza's entrepreneurs had interests in Geita. Where physical isolation had broken down, it was not possible to enforce psychological isolation.

From February on, events moved rapidly indeed. Having failed to find satisfaction in the public barazas held by French in January, dissidents gathered together in meetings of their own. Kizimba and Wilson Bunuma, a Sukuma trader in Usambiro, attended the annual TANU conference at Tabora. A small number of politically concerned farmers, traders, teachers and clerks met secretly at Kasamwa in Usambiro, and deputized one of their number, Wilson Mwihende, a teacher, to go with a letter to the Governor in Dar es Salaam saying that Geita did not want the new council. The Governor reportedly refused to see Mwihende, but the Chief Secretary is said to have received the letter on his behalf.[2]

Meanwhile, Augustine Madaha, a Zinza subchief in Karumo who was known to be secretly active in TANU and opposed to the council, was dismissed by French.[3] The Assistant Minister for Labour, Derek Bryceson, reported that three or four court clerks from Geita and Sukumaland wished

that their opinion should be recorded somehow, that they thought that the majority of inhabitants of Geita District were neither consulted nor in favour of the formation of the District Council. They put forward the

[1] *Lumuli*, No. 112, Jan. 1958.
[2] Hezeroni Mpandachalo, interview, Aug. 1964.
[3] Interviews: French; Madaha, 17 Feb. 1965. Madaha was later to become a leading political figure not only in Geita but in the Lake Province and nationally as a member of TANU's National Executive Committee and as an Area Commissioner.

view that it was only the *Wazee* [elders or old men] who had been consulted and they (the *wazee*) were too well-disciplined to demur.[1]

Under pressure in his own chiefdom, Chief Abdullah Chasama
of Msalala also backtracked on the council issue. He is reported to
have been the only chief who refused to sign the instrument
transferring powers from individual native authorities to the new
council before its inauguration in March. Madaha, the clerks and
Chasama could not be labelled as outside agitators nor easily
discounted as local discontents. Dissent on the council issue was
finding support inside as well as outside the Geita governing
establishment.

Nyerere's Involvement

Nyerere, too, became actively concerned with developments in
Geita. A year previously he had begun publication of a cyclostyled
news-sheet, *Sauti ya TANU* (The Voice of TANU). He wrote
sometimes in English, sometimes in Swahili. His aim was to
provide Europeans and Asians as well as Africans with TANU's
views on government policy and on the nationalist struggle.
In March 1958 and subsequent months, he wrote frequently and
pointedly on the evolving crisis in Geita. After the new Geita
District Council had met for the first time in March, Nyerere
strongly criticized Walden's opening speech, then expanded on
certain acts of intimidation alleged to have been committed by
District Commissioner French.

The multi-racial District Council which was recently imposed on the
people of Geita district is obviously unacceptable to the people. But the
good Provincial Commissioner has a convenient theory to offer. He says,
'Although the establishment of a District Council has been approved by
the great majority of the people in Geita, there are always a few people
who, because of their stupidity, like to oppose any new form of development.' Very strong words indeed. But the good Provincial Commissioner
does not tell the public how and when he ascertained that 'the great
majority of the people of Geita' approved his multi-racial baby; or indeed
what proof he has that those who criticize Government 'always' do so
'because of their stupidity.'

Nyerere went on to charge, using as a basis a previous complaint
by Bomani in the Legislative Council, that the Geita District
Commissioner 'carried a pistol to a public meeting and waved it in
the air threatening to shoot any one who claimed to be a member

[1] Quoted in Stubbings to French, 20 Mar. 1958, LPF.

of TANU.' Nyerere claimed that French 'ordered a sub-chief [Madaha] to take an oath denying membership of TANU,' dismissed him for questioning the legality of the oath, then tried 'to cover up this dismissal so that it might appear to be resignation.' Finally, Nyerere said the Geita District Commissioner had 'prohibited the selling or reading of the Swahili newspaper *Mwafrika* in Geita district, because he believes it, wrongly incidentally, to be a TANU newspaper.' Nyerere concluded:

Instead of investigating these complaints the good P.C. threatens that Government would 'rapidly become tired and even angry' with these 'stupid' and 'loudmouthed' people who smear the good name of the good D.C. Is anger the prerogative only of our rulers?[1]

Of course, the question of whether or not the people of Geita agreed to the council could not be settled by the claims—verbal or in print—of either side. And the details of charges and rebuttals and the degree of their truth or falsity was less important than that the charges were being leveled. To such a point had relations between the government and the governed deteriorated. The situation was ripe for explosion.

In late January Bomani had written French informing him that he proposed to visit Geita in his capacity as a member of the Legislative Council. French reminded him that permits to hold public meetings required advance naming of speakers and topics. Bomani then requested permission for Nyerere, who had attended independence celebrations in Ghana the previous year, to speak on 'Impressions of Ghana.'[2] This topic would have given Nyerere every opportunity to discuss the principles of multi-racialism versus those of advancement toward democracy within a primarily African state, and French refused permission. Bomani also recalls having received a letter from the Deputy Provincial Commissioner indicating that if Bomani went to Geita, he would 'bear the consequences.'

As visiting *per se* was not prohibited, Nyerere and Bomani went to Geita anyway. Bomani says he had never before seen such crowds as those which greeted Nyerere in Karumo, Buchosa, Busambiro and Msalala. He recalls that thousands of TANU cards were sold on the trip, that everywhere people flocked with spirit and enthusiasm to catch a glimpse of Nyerere.[3] Nyerere, of course, had no

[1] *Sauti ya TANU*, No. 26, 27 Mar. 1958.
[2] D.C. to Bomani, 28 Mar.; Bomani to D.C., 29 Mar. 1958, GTDF.
[3] Bomani, interview.

permission to speak. He greeted the crowds silently. Though no speech was given and no public meeting held, the tour was a major political event. Nyerere's visit acted as a catalyst to the pattern of discontent which was rapidly developing in Geita. Nyerere himself became so convinced of the seriousness of the Geita situation that before he left the area he sent a telegram to friends in the British Labour Party asking them to take up the matter with the Colonial Secretary. He is said also to have cabled the United Nations.

The First Arrests

Later in April, French held a baraza at the chiefdom headquarters at Nyakaliro in Buchosa, at which he talked of the benefits of the new council, but emphasized that stern measures would be taken against fomenters of illegal political activity. People rose to object that the chief had not consulted them. Someone asked if, with multi-racialism, friendly and neighborly relations would be developed between non-Africans and Africans, whether they would eat together, whether non-Africans also would participate in communal labor projects, whether intermarriage would be allowed. French told him that if he had nothing worthwhile to say, he should sit down. Members of the audience then became angry and others stood up. French told them to sit down. They refused. One young Sukuma trader and political activist, Albert Muhaya, said French was threatening them. French asked him to repeat what he had said, and with the stick he sometimes carried he motioned for Muhaya to come forward. Thirty or forty more people then stood up with Muhaya and the meeting noisily broke up. Muhaya subsequently collected signatures in support of a charge that French had threatened himself and others with a gun, but the charge was false and Muhaya was jailed.[1]

Early in May, in what by now was a familiar pattern, a group of individuals led by a local trader, Issa Kaburi, posed hostile questions at a government baraza in Usambiro. The next day the questioners were arrested. One of those taken into custody was Kizimba. Another of the questioners offered himself for arrest when he heard that the police were looking for him. On behalf of the accused, Bomani contacted an Asian lawyer, N. K. Laxman, who agreed to take the case. French, in his capacity as magistrate,

---

[1] *Lumuli*, No. 135, Jan. 1959; interviews with French, Mpandachalo and Simon Ngusa, Aug. 1964.

heard the case in Geita, but the prosecution failed for lack of evidence since no one would testify.[1]

The next step toward open defiance came as the government moved to tighten its control on Geita. Hurt by Nyerere's April tour, alarmed at the spread of overt opposition to the already functioning multi-racial council together with increasing support for TANU, and annoyed at card-selling to individuals who were then registered with TANU branches outside Sukumaland, the government promulgated an order in May which specifically prohibited TANU activities of any sort in Geita District. At the same time, the administration refused to permit a delegation of Legislative Council members (including Bomani and Captain J. Bennett of Bukoba, a European inclined to be critical of the government) to tour the district. But news had already spread that the Bomani delegation was on its way and a particularly large crowd had gathered at Bukokwa in Buchosa. A local leader, Hezeroni Mpandachalo, was selected to talk with Bomani and Bennett on their arrival. About noon a message came from Mwanza that the visitors had not been permitted to come as planned. Mpandachalo then, not unnaturally, got up himself to speak.[2]

Mpandachalo's speech marked an end to the period of covert activity and hostile objections raised at the barazas of chiefs and district government officers. It marked the beginning of a new phase of civil disobedience initiated by the dissidents. Without a permit Mpandachalo took the platform at this Bukokwa meeting in May and went to jail as a result. On his release six weeks later, he openly defied the government by holding another large-scale illegal public meeting. After his second arrest hundreds of people flocked to the district office in Geita and thousands went subsequently to Mwanza. Until today Mpandachalo is remembered by many in Geita as having been the first fearless and uncompromising leader directly and overtly to challenge the government.

A Militant Leader: Mpandachalo

Mpandachalo was born in Seke chiefdom, Shinyanga, about 1907.[3] He attended an Africa Inland Mission school through Standard IV, was subsequently a tax clerk, a farmer, a laborer and

---

[1] Kizimba, interview.
[2] Interviews: Mpandachalo, Bomani.
[3] Except where otherwise noted, material in this section is drawn from interviews with Mpandachalo and Simon Ngusa, August 1964.

clerk with the Sukumaland Development Scheme and a shop-owner. Curiously for a revolutionary, Mpandachalo identifies Dr J. E. K. Aggrey and George Washington Carver as early inspirations. He read about the two men in Swahili booklets which were available through the Africa Inland Mission bookstore, and Aggrey particularly seemed a great leader who 'cries out for the rights of Africans.' Mpandachalo became acquainted with Nyerere's speeches at the United Nations and in Tanganyika and by 1957 he had become concerned with the multi-racial question. Fearing that Europeans and Asians would take over the country behind the cloak of multi-racialism, he argued that it would be the same as in Kenya where Kenyatta had been seized for fighting for African rights.

In early 1958 Mpandachalo became prominent among the growing group of dissidents in Buchosa. Together with Mwihende, Muhaya, the former Sukuma Union leader, James Bubele and others, he talked with Paul Bomani in Mwanza about the multi-racial problem. Trends in Kenya and South Africa, as well as in Tanganyika, were discussed. After Muhaya's arrest in April, Buchosa leaders gathered more frequently for covert discussions. Mpandachalo travelled to Karumo, Usambiro and Msalala for talks with dissidents there.

As more persons became alarmed with trends in the district, more were interested in talking over what to do about it. In this context threats by French and the arrest of certain leaders served only to intensify discontent. With French's support of Chief Paulo and vice versa, hostility focused also on the chief. At one point, Mpandachalo recalls, there was discussion of a plan to seize the chief, take him to the Provincial Commissioner and declare that he was not wanted by the people of Buchosa. Dissident leaders invited French to illegal meetings and mailed him complimentary copies of *Sauti ya TANU*.[1]

Gradually, the dissidents could count on a naturally evolved network of communications and contacts. Those most likely to be involved in the developing opposition movement were traders, teachers, mission employees or catechists;[2] former government clerks, police officers or medical aides—men who had broken the bonds of rural life through education, experience, travel, study

[1] French, interview.
[2] This does not assume any role on the part of European missionaries who adopted for the most part a 'hands off' attitude toward politics.

and employment. Through petty traders who were also farmers there was a link to other men who were simply farmers. When the farmers came to the trading centers to get supplies, they fraternized with the traders. When the traders tilled their own fields, they were neighbors of the farmers. While trading centers and mission stations were the initial focal points for leadership, the network of contacts spread easily from there into the countryside where grievances were sufficient in themselves to support dissent. An elder out of sympathy with the local headman or alien chief, an ambitious young committee member of a primary cotton cooperative society, a farmer tired of rules and regulations—any of these men might become the representative, the messenger, the intermediate link from dissident leaders to followers. Small meetings could be held with selected persons from several villages; then news of the discussions spread by word of mouth over wide areas.

A trader–farmer as well as an ex-government servant with a mission education, Mpandachalo found himself in a potentially strategic position: he could combine political ideas with a capacity to enlist support for those ideas in rural areas. At home in both worlds, he could talk the language of politics and protest in the trading centers and the language of the farmer on his homestead. And in Geita where a high percentage of the total population approximated the farmer–trader prototype, the two languages and the two worlds were less disparate than elsewhere in Sukumaland, except Nassa. It was Mpandachalo's genius that he made use of the materials available to him to weld, in the face of opposition from the entire administrative structure in Geita and Buchosa, a political force which ultimately was to prevail.

After it became clear at the May gathering in Bukokwa that Bomani had not been permitted by the government to appear, Mpandachalo rose to ask the crowd of several thousand if they knew what 'Mseto' was. He answered '*Mseto ni utumwa*': multi-racialism is slavery. The people became very angry and Mpandachalo said that their land would be taken by force. He then asked the crowd rhetorically: 'Where did the Chief get permission to sign [approval of the District Council] for the people?' The crowd got very excited and responded that they had not been asked by the chief. 'We don't want the Chief,' the people agreed. Mpandachalo says they asked that they choose whom they wanted to be chief, affirming that the present chief would 'lose the country.'

Mpandachalo then asked the people to contribute money to 'get rid of Mseto.' He collected 380 shillings, and another local leader, Ernest Wabanhu, subsequently went to Mwanza to use the funds to telegraph the United Nations and the Colonial Secretary.

That night Mpandachalo was arrested by French for holding an illegal meeting and collecting funds without permission. He was taken to Geita together with a number of others who were accused of having aided him. At the trial, Mpandachalo remembers the judge asking him: 'Have you refused to accept the authority of the chiefs?' Mpandachalo replied: 'We all refused, not me alone.' The judge continued: 'Did you collect money?' Mpandachalo replied: 'Yes, but we all collected money.' The judge concluded: 'Where did the money go?' Mpandachalo replied that it was used to send a telegram to the United Nations. He was sentenced to one month in jail and a 100 shilling fine.

With Mpandachalo in jail, others openly expressed their indignation at the state of affairs in Geita. M. I. Kitenge, the Mwanza-based trader–politician who was active in Geita affairs and something of a pamphleteer, wrote a bruising tract the very day of Mpandachalo's arrest, describing the series of arrests in Geita during April and May. Entitled 'For an Omen of Multi-racial Government in Tanganyika Look at Geita,' Kitenge's tract argued:

Africans are being denied the right to question and to speak in government meetings. I remind the government that it should honor its obligations with regard to the rights of man which are fundamental to freedom and security and the birthright of all men. Tanganyika is not a country of troublemaking; if trouble comes it is doubtless brought on by the government. Citizens are being harassed without reason...

Where do these difficulties originate if not in the imposition by the government of multi-racialism? Why are not the other two races reviled by this government of multi-racialism? Why are not they treated contemptuously by the servants of the government? Doubtless because, after securing all his limbs and throwing him down violently, they cooperate to trample their African brother underfoot until he is dead.[1]

In an impassioned letter to the Lake Province members of the Legislative Council, following Mpandachalo's conviction, Kitenge decried the refusal of permission to the Bomani delegation and the arrest of Mpandachalo and others in Buchosa. He deplored the methods of force, threat, search and seizure employed by the

---

[1] M. I. Kitenge, 'For an omen of multi-racial government in Tanganyika look at Geita,' 20 May 1958, Kitenge papers. (Orig. Sw.)

Geita authorities and argued that another parliamentary delegation
should be dispatched to ascertain the real views of all the people.
He charged that multiracialism was being brought into the district
by force and that people were being 'treated like animals' in an
effort to compel them to accept it. He said that Geita people
rejected their chiefs because the chiefs had misrepresented and
not properly consulted their people. He called for the abolition
of the multi-racial council and for popular elections for a new
council or the re-establishment of the previous native authority
advisory council. He countered the familiar government charge
that the entire Geita problem was inspired from outside by TANU
with the assertion that it was not TANU activities which were in
question but the rights of the people of Geita who wished to see
multi-racialism abolished from their district. He concluded with a
prophetic warning: 'Finally we citizens of Geita say without
hesitation that we will boycott the government of Geita if it will
not listen to our complaints.'[1]

At the same time, Nyerere again ventilated the situation in
Geita in *Sauti ya TANU*:

The Lake Province has two very bad districts. One is Geita, the other
Musoma. Public discontent in those two districts has reached a dangerous
point. Government must know this but prefers to fool the public. Are
we to believe that the people of those districts are particularly evil
minded? There are coincidences in these matters which suggest the very
contrary...How does it come about that trouble seems to coincide with
the presence of certain officials in certain areas?...If the Police could
keep out of politics and act as impartial referees between law abiding
citizens and the rest, including bush governors who think they are above
the law, then the Law would be our greatest friend. The reasons why
lunatics have been trying to provoke the people into violence is the fact
that they know we are virtually invincible if we remain a law-abiding
organization.

Under the title 'A Lesson from History?' Nyerere concluded with
a quote from Thomas Paine:

When I consider the natural dignity of man...I become irritated at the
attempt to govern mankind by force and fraud, as if they were all knaves
and fools...When [the government]... assumes to exist for itself and
acts by partialities of favour and oppression, it becomes the cause of the
mischiefs it ought to prevent.[2]

[1] Kitenge to Lake Province Members of the Legislative Council, 28 May
1958, Kitenge papers.
[2] *Sauti ya TANU*, No. 29, 27 May 1958. It was for statements concerning
certain D.C.s in this issue that Nyerere was later convicted of libel. According

The 'Kenyatta' of Geita[1]

After serving his one-month prison term, Mpandachalo returned to Geita and paid his 100 shilling fine early in July.[2] He wasted no time, however, in reimmersing himself in the political struggle: he went immediately back to Buchosa to start again. On the night of 8 July he chaired a secret meeting of twelve at Wabanhu's home in Bukokwa. The meeting decided: (1) that a full boycott of the multi-racial government would be staged; (2) that representatives would be sent to see Nyerere; and (3) that a telegram would be sent informing the government that on 11 July the boycott would begin with a public meeting at Nyakaliro at which Mpandachalo would speak.

On the eleventh the meeting was held as scheduled. Mpandachalo has estimated that about 2,000 persons were there. His speech called on the government to abolish *Mseto* (multi-racialism) and to get rid of the 'United Tanganyika Party chiefs.' If these demands were not met forthwith, he called on the people to stop paying taxes, to stop destocking, to stop turning out for communal labor on government work projects and to stop respecting the government and Europeans generally. The following day the police attempted to arrest Mpandachalo, but they were prevented from doing so by a group of his supporters who feared for his safety after the police had refused their request that some of their number accompany him to Geita. Mpandachalo held another illegal meeting on 13 July and collected additional contributions. He had decided that defiance was the only recourse against the

to *Mwongozi*, Nyerere 'took full responsibility for the article. He said that it was written to draw the Government's attention to "serious discontent" in the Geita and Musoma areas.' In court Nyerere said that he 'wrote nothing until I was provoked by the Government action which purported to close down my branch in Geita' (*Mwongozi*, No. 2, 14 July 1958, extract in FCBF).
[1] Mpandachalo has compared his early leadership role and subsequent imprisonment with that of Kenyatta in Kenya. Though the comparison is not really apt, there were some grounds for Mpandachalo's feeling for the importance of his own role. Geita was one of the few places in Tanganyika where the fight for independence took on some of the characteristics of the more desperate Kenya struggle. It was Mpandachalo who led the most critical phase of the Geita struggle; it was he who developed a charismatic quality which motivated people to protect him from arrest and to march by the thousands when he was finally taken by the police; it was he who organized a protest political movement in defiance of restrictions and went to jail. Yet, he says, on his return the Mboyas and Odingas of Geita forgot their "Kenyatta."
[2] Except where otherwise noted, material in this section is drawn from an interview with Mpandachalo.

Geita administration and he knew that it would be only a matter
of time before the police would return to get him.

While the meeting was still in progress, a contingent of well-
armed police arrived in seven Landrovers with three European
officers. This was the special motorized division called by French
to Geita some weeks before to deal with illegal meetings. The
police disembarked from their vehicles and paraded with their
rifles. Although the police asked for Mpandachalo, he remembers
that 'one old man rose, happy to be seized, because this is our
country.' The man was handcuffed along with Mpandachalo.
An officer read the law on refusal of arrest. Mpandachalo replied
that he had not refused arrest; the people had prevented him from
going because they did not want him to go alone. Mpandachalo
was placed in one of the Landrovers, and again several persons
tried to accompany him. These were then arrested. When others
moved toward the Landrovers, they were dispersed with tear
gas. Mpandachalo relates that on the trip he was struck twice by
a policeman with the butt of a gun. In Geita he was put in isolation
and denied food for refusing to name accomplices.

The following day about 1,000 people, mostly from Mpandachalo's village in Buchosa, arrived to demonstrate. Others followed
and French himself estimates that some 2,000 people converged
on the district office in Geita the week that Mpandachalo was held
there. French felt they were a demonstrative mob and had to be
kept away from the office. The District Commissioner refused to
talk with the crowd until they had selected twelve leaders. After
they did so, French says that for the entire week of 14–19 July
he talked with them four or five hours a day.[1] Mpandachalo
relates that one sympathetic African subinspector of police reported
that the Governor phoned and that 'not since the British came
has anything like this been seen.'

The crowd's demands were three: to dismiss the chiefs, to
abolish the multi-racial council and to release political prisoners
jailed as a result of the illegal meetings over previous months.
With French himself unwilling to satisfy these demands, the
dissatisfied leaders announced that they would go to Mwanza
that weekend to see the Provincial Commissioner. Meanwhile,
elsewhere in the district, people were refusing to sell their cotton
or cooperate otherwise with government officials. They sang a

---

[1] French, interview.

traditional song of boycott and defiance known throughout Suku-maland, but invested now with new political meaning.

> Who has burned my house to the ground?
> What evil wizard has burned it down?
> Oh come let's go and spear him twice.
> Let's go and spear him twice.[1]

It became the theme song of political protest and boycott in defiance of the Geita administration.

It was the end of the road, however, for Mpandachalo. He was convicted for convening illegal meetings and for resisting arrest. When he was released in May 1959 after nine months in jail, he was received with honor at the legally reopened TANU headquarters in Mwanza and feted in Buchosa. He was elected to the Geita African Council in 1960–1 and became the headman of his home village in 1962. But these were more modest roles than he had hoped to assume on his return. With a tinge of resentment, he explains that while he was in jail, others came to the fore to take the places of himself and others who had broken the ground for politics in Geita.

The March on Mwanza

With Mpandachalo in jail, Augustine Madaha of Karumo, Wilson Bunuma of Usambiro, and Simon Ngusa of Buchosa emerged as the principal leaders of the protest movement. They participated in discussions with French at the Geita District office and subsequently led the trek to Mwanza. Madaha was the Zinza subchief who had been dismissed by French earlier in the year for TANU activities. Bunuma was a prosperous trader. Ngusa was a cooperative society organizer and trader in Masanza I and in Geita. It was these three who, when they found themselves thwarted in Geita, decided to take their case directly to the Provincial Commissioner.

Word of the march to Mwanza spread quickly and the protesters went by the thousands. It was one of the most remarkable political events in Tanganyikan history. The Provincial Commissioner's annual report for 1958 quoted the number officially at 1,500 persons, but the total in fact was considerably greater. Erwin Gaetje, a European dairyman who ran the only ferry from Geita to Mwanza at that time, carried most of the people who went over.

[1] Translated from the Sukuma by Henry K. Madoshi.

He has estimated the total at between 4,000 and 5,000 persons. The then provincial security officer confirms the Gaetje estimate.[1] The trekkers came from all of the chiefdoms of northern and eastern Geita and beyond. Each area had its own meetings, and people were encouraged to drop what they were doing and go to Mwanza. Most travelled by bicycle. The cotton cooperatives closed their stores and, though it was the height of the buying season, no cotton was bought for a week.

The leaders, as Ngusa explains, used every available means of propaganda. They did not work through traditional community leaders except for the unusual few who had taken an interest in politics. The messengers who took the news into every village were those who had been part of the semiorganized but highly effective network of contacts developed over the preceding months —an old man who had once served with the police, an African tribal dresser, a young man with Standard IV or VI education. No longer was it necessary to communicate through secret meetings or via messages left in a banana tree. By this time the power of the existing native authorities was so weakened that Ngusa has claimed with justification that in July 1958 he was more powerful in Buchosa than the chief or subchiefs. The same was true for Madaha in Karumo and Bunuma in Usambiro. In Msalala, of course, the chief had finally opposed the council and was therefore legitimate not only traditionally but politically. Everywhere the people followed the new leaders or the few traditional figures whom they trusted.[2]

French, Walden and A. W. J. Eyers, the provincial security officer, feel that people were intimidated by their leaders into attending the illegal meetings of the previous months and into participating in the Mwanza trek. French says non-cooperators would have been prohibited from grazing or obtaining water supplies and even from using the shops. While it is quite true that ostracism of this sort was a traditional form of community punishment in Sukumaland, it is also clear that it was the sort of

[1] Lake Province Annual Report, 1958, LPF; Erwin Gaetje, interview, 20 Feb. 1965; Eyers, interview. See George Bennett, 'The development of political organisations in Kenya,' *Political Studies*, v, No. 2 (June 1957), 125, for an interesting example of an early protest march in Kenya.

[2] Ngusa, interview. Compare the account of TANU activity and neighborhood organizations in northern Unyamwezi in R. G. Abrahams, *The political organization of Unyamwezi* (London: Cambridge University Press, 1967), pp. 167–71.

technique which by its very nature could only work successfully on the few. Ngusa admits that for propaganda purposes a milder form of persuasion—the imposition of a traditional fine of a chicken or a goat—was mooted for the Mwanza trek, but that no one was actually fined. With such numbers involved, it is impossible to believe that most came primarily because of intimidation, whether of one form or of another. Gaetje observed that the people were very cheerful, that they ungrudgingly paid the 1 shilling fare, that they were singing when they crossed to Mwanza—hardly attitudes one would expect of the intimidated. Gaetje also has correctly observed that if many of these people had not really wanted to go, they could easily have slipped away en route without anyone knowing the difference.[1]

On Monday 21 July the crowd gathered on a sports field in Mwanza about one block from the provincial government offices. Eyers is undoubtedly correct in suggesting that the trek stimulated its own feelings of elation, expectation, even celebration among those assembled. But there were also the three previously enunciated concrete political aims: abolition of the multi-racial council, dismissal of the chiefs and release of political prisoners. The demonstrators camped on the field, and ultimately the Provincial Commissioner treated with their spokesmen. Walden told them he would forward their complaints to Dar es Salaam but that the crowd must disperse and the people return to their homes. The demonstrators, however, refused to move. They decided to send their own delegation to see the Governor and 6,000 shillings were collected from the crowd. Bunuma, Ngusa and Madaha were selected to leave on the next plane for Dar es Salaam. A new set of leaders, among whom were Wilson Mwihende, Ntobi Mussa and Bernard Tigaliwa, then took over at the sports field to wait for results. They continued to resist all efforts of the administration to convince them to return to Geita.

Meanwhile Nyerere had written to the Fabian Colonial Bureau in London:

Geita District in the Lake Province is virtually in a state of emergency. Government has increased the Police force in the District. Thousands of people held a meeting recently to which they had invited the Provincial Commissioner. Naturally, he did not attend. The people 'dismissed' their chiefs and have informed Government that unless those four chiefs are dismissed and the imposed District Council abolished they will not

---

[1] Interviews: Eyers, French, Gaetje, Ngusa, Walden.

R

cooperate with the Government. Government's answer was to increase the Police force in the District and at the same time to hide the facts from the public.

Geita is now virtually a Police State, and however much one likes to give the new Governor a chance one cannot connive at obvious oppression. . . Please, shake up the Colonial Secretary over Geita. I dislike hysterics. But I do not like Geita District. It is dangerous. Government is saving the face of a couple of individuals by driving a whole, otherwise peaceful, district to a point of dangerous discontent.

In a postscript, E. A. Kisenge, TANU's organizing secretary-general, added: 'A telegram has just been received that more than 10,000 people are gathering at Mwanza.' Nyerere then penned a further note indicating that on the previous day he had received information that 'there were thousands of people in Mwanza from Geita to see the Provincial Commissioner' but that when Rashidi Kawawa 'saw the Minister about this [the Minister] pretended that he had no such information.' Nyerere concluded:

If all is well in Geita as the good Government has repeatedly been telling the people what makes so many people trek from Geita to Mwanza to see a Provincial Commissioner they would otherwise avoid? Jimmy [Betts], you must demand an explanation on the dangerous situation in Geita. In fact an explanation is not enough. There must be an enquiry into the situation in Geita.[1]

Meanwhile, the Bunuma–Madaha–Ngusa delegation had arrived in Dar es Salaam. They were met by TANU leaders Nyerere, Kawawa, and Munanka. On Friday 25 July, Kawawa took the delegation to see the Chief Secretary and the Minister of Local Government and Administration. The delegates were told that

---

[1] Nyerere to T. F. Betts, 29 July 1958, FCBF. Upon receiving the Nyerere letter, Betts called Member of Parliament Arthur Skeffington who 'agreed to find some way of raising the matter with Lennox-Boyd before the recess and is very anxious to prosecute it.' John Hatch, Commonwealth Secretary of the Labour Party, was also notified (Betts to Nyerere, 29 July 1958, FCBF).

A few days later in *Sauti ya TANU* Nyerere reviewed the history of the Geita story from April 1957. Commenting again on the crowd which had gathered in Mwanza, he wrote: 'This crowd, now reported by the press to be about 2,000, and its own delegates to be nearly 6,000, must be a fairly big crowd. We know that at the ground they made a collection of nearly Shs 6,000/– to fly a delegation of three to Dar es Salaam. In all our experience we have never known any crowd to collect so much money on the spot. This crowd must be either very big indeed, or very discontented, or both. Is it not incredible that the Government of Tanganyika could for so long have remained unaware of or insensitive to discontent so serious as to make so many people trek from Geita to Mwanza?' (*Sauti ya TANU*, No. 37, 28 July 1958).

their representations would not be received until the crowd in Mwanza had dispersed. Back in Mwanza, however, the crowd was insisting that it would not disperse until the delegation had presented their demands in Dar es Salaam. Bomani spoke to the gathering to advise a return home now that it was assured that the protests would receive attention in Dar es Salaam. Lacking concrete evidence that their demands had been complied with, the demonstrators refused. An impasse had been reached. Now again—after five days on the sports field—the people were given orders to leave. After a final warning, tear gas was thrown and they were dispersed by force.[1]

Later the same day the delegation was permitted to put before the government their three demands. Ngusa recalls that Minister Rowe volunteered the delegates some information on the philosophy of multi-racialism and on the strength of the United Tanganyika Party. The delegates returned to Mwanza after being told that the Governor himself would come to Geita shortly.

Accounts differ, as so often they do in cases like this, on how much warning the Mwanza crowd received before the forceful dispersal and what consequences were incurred. Nyerere decried the lack of warning:

One would have expected such a big crowd to be given time to disperse. These people had come from Geita and were on the Sports ground where they were cooking and sleeping. They could not 'disperse' and 'go home' in a matter of minutes. But this apparently is what some brilliant Government official expected a huge crowd to do. Mr. Bomani had hardly left the crowd when the Police was ordered to disperse it with tear gas, truncheons, and all that. Many people are known to be lying in hospital with broken limbs (although this too is denied by Government!).[2]

Eyres, however, points out that the crowd has been repeatedly warned to leave over a three-day period; that they were given 'probably an hour' to vacate the area after the final warning; that the police commander acted with great restraint; and that the people, as much as possible, were shepherded to the boats which were waiting to take them to Geita. He admits that there was some panic and a stampede but that all injuries sustained were minor and that no deaths whatsoever occurred as a result of the police action. On the other hand, a middle school teacher in Mwanza insists that a relative of his *was* trampled to death at

[1] Interviews: Bomani, Madaha, Ngusa, Walden.
[2] *Sauti ya TANU*, No. 37, 28 July 1958.

the time.[1] Whatever the facts, the legend that has grown up around the events of 1958 is that one or more persons died.

4   AFTERMATH AND INVESTIGATION

Geita remained unsettled and local government continued in disarray for several more months. As for the discussions in Dar es Salaam between the three Geita spokesmen and government officials, Provincial Commissioner Walden informed the citizens of Geita that he would let them know the outcome of those discussions 'in due course through the usual channels.' In the meantime, he warned that initimidation of the sort which he said characterized the recruitment of participants for the Geita demonstrations would be 'dealt with' and that the government would not 'be brow-beaten by threats of violence.'[2] Writing again to T. F. Betts at the Fabian Colonial Bureau, Nyerere said:

I know privately that one Assistant Minister who happened to visit Mwanza a day after the Geita crowd had been tear-gassed by the Police was so convinced that Government was provoking trouble that he was on the verge of tendering his resignation... I know the Empire is shrinking but if there is some room somewhere...then I would seriously recommend the kicking upstairs somewhere of...the Provincial Commissioner, Lake Province...[He] cannot do this country much good.[3]

At the end of the year, the administration itself admitted:

There has been a strong reaction against the paternalism and tight control on the lives of Geita's population, which [has been] a very marked feature of the District's life...Perhaps more than most Districts, Geita has been the scene of major, even dedicated, effort by Government Officers in the field of development...It is a discouraging reflection on our methods that we have not carried the people with us in these schemes and plans, so full of hope for the future. By the middle of 1958 in the minds of men in Geita District, confidence and trust in Government stood at its lowest ...The basis of Government, that is to say, the consent of the people had in large measure dissolved.[4]

The Governor Visits

Within this context of continuing dissatisfaction and unrest, the new Governor, Sir Richard Turnbull, arrived in Geita at the end of the first week of August to get a first-hand impression of the

[1] Eyers, interview; Phileimon James Hezronie, interview, Feb. 1965.
[2] A Statement by the Provincial Commissioner, 28 July 1959, GTDF.
[3] Nyerere to Betts, 16 Aug. 1958, FCBF.
[4] Geita District Annual Report, 1958, GTDF.

situation. He conferred with Walden, French and Eyers and talked with African leaders of the protest movement. Bunuma, Madaha and Ngusa presented to the Governor a written memorandum restating the substance of their oral representations in Dar es Salaam two weeks before. As Nyerere later wrote to Betts: 'I am somehow convinced that the new Governor means well... He has, fortunately, already visited Geita and spoken to the representatives of the people there whom the Old Guard regard as trouble-mongering agitators.'[1]

In one respect, however, the Governor's visit did not go smoothly. At the Geita sports field a large crowd had gathered in anticipation of his arrival. Though he had not intended to hold any public meetings, Turnbull indicated that under the circumstances he was inclined personally to address the crowd. Eyers, French and Walden advised him strongly against doing so, but the Governor decided to go. He asked that no police and no uniforms of any description accompany him. When, together with Eyers and French, the Governor arrived at the field, someone who had been making a speech told the crowd to take no notice of 'our visitors.' When some, nevertheless, tried to get on their feet in deference to the Governor, the speaker asked them to sit down. The crowd remained seated, and after a moment the Governor and his party left the ground.[2] It was probably another moment without precedent in the colonial period of Tanganyikan history.

Illegal meetings continued to be held in Geita during August and September. On 11 August, a few days after the Governor's visit, 'the most spectacular' of all convened in Karumo. The government estimated that 'some 3000 persons were present.' They were forcefully dispersed, and the government noted subsequently that 'their dispersal has had much to do with the fear in which the motorized platoons are now held.'[3] Two representatives 'on behalf of Geita Africans' sent a telegram to the United Nations detailing that '120 policemen together with 14 Landrovers arrived. We were teargas bombed again and some of us sustained injuries.' They concluded, 'For God's sake please save Geita from tyranny.'[4] In July and August and subsequent months, scores of

[1] Nyerere to Betts, 16 Aug. 1958, FCBF.   [2] Eyers, interview.
[3] Geita District Annual Report, 1958, GTDF.
[4] United Nations: T/Pet.2/226, 6 Oct. 1958. The petition was by Mzee Sefu and Adam Omari. Again in September, after a meeting of the Pan-African Freedom Movement of East and Central Africa in Mwanza, a serious incident occurred in Geita. Nyerere described it this way: 'After the Conference

persons in Geita were brought to trial and sentenced to jail on
charges which included addressing a meeting without permission,
provoking a disturbance during a baraza, preventing the arrest of
an accused person, inciting people not to pay taxes, fining people
illegally and maligning and threatening a headman.[1] Madaha
was among those who ultimately joined Mpandachalo, Muhaya
and other earlier offenders in prison.

A Confidential Report

After French's departure on leave in late August, a new District
Commissioner, J. T. A. Pearce, took over the administration.
He was charged with the dual task of writing a confidential report
on the origin and nature of the disturbances and of returning
local government to a sound footing.

Pearce's report[2] first reviewed the early stage of obtaining
consent for the proposed council. He noted that the district
advisory council had voted 29 to 1 in favor of the proposal in
April 1957. He found that between April 1957 and January 1958
some thirty-seven public barazas were held, together with many
informal meetings called by the chiefs and subchiefs, on the
subject of the proposed council. He estimated that 2,000 people,
or 3.5 per cent of the taxpayers, attended the barazas and that
another 2,000 heard explanations of the proposals.

Though the disturbances 'arose apparently as a result' of the
establishment of the district council in March 1958, Pearce felt
that the existence of the council itself was 'irrelevant to the problems of the Geita District.' He pointed out that the areas of
unrest were Buchosa, Karumo, Usambiro and northern Bukoli
where 'substantial Sukuma immigration' had taken place. He
elaborated:

No troubles occurred elsewhere and the inference must be that without
Sukuma immigration, the breakdown in traditional local government
would not have taken place...The people of Geita are relatively unsophisticated, and the immigrant Sukuma population owes no traditional

Kawawa went to Geita, the forbidden land of the Tanganyika Administration.
At the market place in Geita a crowd gathered around his car. That gave
Police a magnificent opportunity to demonstrate to both Kawawa and the
naughty people of Geita just how powerful the Government of Tanganyika is.
Without warning the crowd was tear gassed' (Nyerere to Betts, 26 Sept. 1958,
FCBF).

[1] D.C. to P.C., 30 Aug. 1958, GTDF.
[2] Pearce to the P.C., 15 Dec. 1958, source wishes to remain anonymous. Except
where otherwise noted, material in this section is drawn from the report.

loyalty, and gives none, to the chiefs of the areas into which they have been accepted as settlers.[1]

He pointed out that good local government had to have either strong native authorities or properly functioning councils—neither of which Geita enjoyed.

Pearce identified three types of persons who objected to the district council. The first group, the well-educated, numbered perhaps 100 to 200. They objected in principle to multi-racial representation. The second group, with some education, objected that non-African council members might manipulate business and finance to the detriment of Africans. They objected to non-Africans paying local rate because they feared non-Africans would thereby gain rights to the land. The third group comprised most of the population. For them the slogan 'hatutaki mseto' (we don't want multi-racialism) stood for the rejection of 'everything evil or disliked.' Specifically, the people feared they would lose land to Indians and Arabs, that 300 Europeans were waiting in Mwanza to establish estates in Geita, that Africans would become slaves and be branded on the forehead, that Indians would be appointed subchiefs and headmen. In the popular mind all native authorities from the chiefs on down were regarded as 'watu wa mseto' (people of multi-racialism) who had sold the people to the hated new system.

Finally, like Walden, Pearce decided that fanaticism, rumor-mongering and intimidation had been widespread, that many feared social ostracism and had gone along with the protests without knowing to what they were objecting. It was his view also that the change from indifference to opposition was 'stimulated by forces from outside the district.'

Pearce was right about some things but wrong about the most important ones. While he made a genuine attempt to understand what had happened in Geita, he was unable to abstract himself sufficiently from the presuppositions of the administration to evaluate the facts with adequate objectivity and perspective. He seems to have been quite accurate in his correlations of education and sophistication with the types of objections raised against the council. On the other hand, he did not sufficiently appreciate the implications of the fact that the three disparate groups he identified *agreed* that the council was undesirable and should be opposed.

[1] Pearce to P.C., 15 Dec. 1958.

One implication certainly should have been that the council issue was something more than irrelevant to the problems of Geita. Further, there is nothing quite as unconvincing as identifying 'forces from outside the district' to imply that things would have been different 'inside' if only isolation from the 'outside' could have been achieved. Multi-racial councils had been decisively rejected by native authorities and people in the neighboring districts of Sukumaland, and to consider that Geita might blissfully have ignored this fact was unrealistic.

Further, while there was much point to emphasizing the background and contributory factors of Sukuma immigration and the resulting lack of identification between chiefs and settlers, these could only with difficulty be proffered as sufficient conditions for the breakdown of local government in Geita. Indeed, they might not even have been necessary conditions. Experiments with multiracial councils broke down in three other districts in Tanganyika at about the same time. And might not breakdown have occurred in Kwimba or Mwanza, Maswa or Shinyanga if the chiefs had accepted the councils against the objections of people and politicians?

In Geita itself, as Pearce admits, the earliest currents of opposition to the council appeared in Msalala chiefdom. But this was precisely where a traditional chief, ruling his own (Nyamwezi) people without the disrupting factor of immigration, was most quickly susceptible to the same considerations that motivated his colleagues across Smith Sound. After he became aware of the dangers to his own position—both from the diminished powers for individual chiefs which the new council implied and from rising currents of political feeling in his own chiefdom and elsewhere—Chief Chasama opposed the council, as did all other strongly based indigenous leaders in the province. May it not then follow that strong opposition appeared in Karumo, Buchosa and Usambiro later rather than earlier precisely because the chiefs were weak in relation to their people and did not at the outset express the dissatisfactions actually felt by their constituents?

While the initial acceptance of the council by the chiefs delayed the crisis, it also made a more serious crisis all but unavoidable. The chiefs identified with the District Commissioner in a scheme they felt might give them some needed outside support, but the tactic didn't work. In the final analysis, the disturbances in Geita did not occur because of a weak native authority structure. They occurred because a weak native authority structure allowed the administration to press forward with a scheme which would have been blocked even earlier by a strong native authority structure. It could only have been wishful thinking to believe, as Pearce and the administration seemed to believe, that strong native authorities in Geita, or anywhere, could have instituted the council scheme without difficulties.

Pearce, like Walden and French, was unable to see that multi-racialism was an anomaly in Tanganyika in 1958. Especially was this true at the district level where the administration itself had eschewed multi-racial innovations until the middle 1950s. Forcing the councils, then, produced an issue capable of motivating almost any African to oppose the government. Certainly this was true in Geita where Africans of all degrees of education and occupational experience formed a united front. Nor were the protestants all immigrant Sukuma. There were Zinza, Nyamwezi, Manyema and Sumbwa as well, both among leaders and followers. To be sure, opposition to multi-racialism focused a host of resentments and dissatisfactions from the most sophisticated to the most unsophisticated kind. What was notable was that these centered on the main issue in Tanganyika at the time: whether Tanganyika was going to evolve into a primarily African state as Ghana had, or whether it was to adopt some variant of the ill-fated multi-racial partnership experiment being attempted in the Rhodesias and Nyasaland. It is to the credit of the people of Geita that they grasped the essence of the issue and that they acted decisively to help influence the course of Tanganyikan history.

Nyerere's Perspective

After TANU's success in the September elections, Nyerere wrote to Betts that 'the atmosphere has been suddenly revolutionized.' He indicated that he and the new Governor had succeeded 'in a remarkably short time in establishing [a] fairly good working relationship.' He described events in Geita and how the provocative stance of certain officials complicated both the Governor's tasks and his own. He mentioned the tear-gassing of a crowd which gathered to receive Rashidi Kawawa on his visit to the district in September. He noted that the 'Governor' of the Lake Province (meaning Provincial Commissioner Walden), after consultation with the Chief Secretary, refused to entertain the

possibility of a trades union meeting to be held in Mwanza.
Wrote Nyerere:

Imperialists never learn. . . I am sure the Governor, if he knew the facts,
would deplore these actions. But these very people are his main advisors
and however well intentioned he may be I cannot see how he can always
overrule them without fear of taking heavy risks. . . He is not the President
of TANU and I am not Her Majesty's Representative in Tanganyika. . .
But I am convinced that we both want an atmosphere in Tanganyika in
which political controversy, however hot, can take place in peace and
dignity. My lieutenants can embarrass me if they were to do things which
I would have to back up but which were in direct opposition to my express desire to maintain an atmosphere of peace in the country. In the
same way I feel that these actions of the Administration cannot but
embarrass the Governor by being contrary to what I am convinced is
his own desire to remove this unnecessary and artificial tension.

Elaborating on the danger which he felt Walden and other senior
officials in Dar es Salaam posed to the country, Nyerere explained:

They know that TANU is invincible as long as there is no violence in
the country. They have all the machinery of publicity at their disposal.
They know that violence can easily be blamed on a nationalist movement.
A violent atmosphere, therefore, would be the best for them. One of
them mentioned to me, perhaps inadvertently, that TANU could not
struggle for more than two weeks if there were violence.

Don't misunderstand me. There is no likelihood of a break of violence
in this country. . . The people of Tanganyika have no faith in violence.

In this regard, Nyerere interpreted the peaceful protests in Geita
as of significance even beyond TANU's first overwhelming
electoral victory: 'What happened in Geita and is still happening
there has assured me of a greater achievement for TANU than
the last elections.' Nyerere concluded:

The future of 9 million people is involved here. It is possible that what
happens in Tanganyika can affect the history of people far beyond our
own borders. There is now more than a chance that we may work our
democratic revolution here in a manner that might revolutionize the
whole trend of events in East and Central Africa[1].

[1] Nyerere to Betts, 26 Sept. 1958.

8

Repercussions and the Reopening of TANU

With the events of mid-1958 in Geita dissatisfactions elsewhere in Sukumaland could no longer be contained. Pressures which had been building since the administration's stepped-up programs of the early 1950s, and especially since the ban on TANU in late 1954, became volatile. Pent-up grievances found popular expression. The Provincial Commissioner still regarded these evidences of disaffection as the work of 'the unscrupulous agitator ...rousing an unsophisticated, simple, and credulous peasantry.' He admitted, however, that 'in some cases docile and easily-led' Sukuma had proved themselves not only 'an easy prey' but also the 'willing victim.'[1] He also recognized that agitators could be local as well as extra-local in origin. But the founding conference of the Pan-African Freedom Movement of East and Central Africa (PAFMECA) held in Mwanza in September 1958 allowed him once again to assign some measure of responsibility for the difficulties in his province to outside influences.

I DISTURBANCES SPREAD

The PAFMECA Conference

Of the PAFMECA Conference, Walden wrote:

Extremism received fresh impetus from the meeting of African leaders in Mwanza in September, whereafter a policy of black nationalism, 'virile and unrelenting,' was broadcast. The fresh disorders which broke out in the Mwanza and Kwimba districts immediately afterwards could not but have owed something to the atmosphere so engendered.[2]

The PAFMECA Conference may, in fact, have had some impact. Certainly, the reception of African leaders contrasted markedly with that afforded Governor Turnbull in Geita the month before. Nyerere, Kawawa and Munanka attended the conference on

---

[1] Lake Province Annual Report, 1958, LPF.   [2] Ibid.

behalf of TANU and Tanganyika. The conference elected Munanka, who had joined TANU's Dar es Salaam staff as national treasurer earlier in the year, secretary–treasurer of the first PAFMECA caretaker committee.

In addition to discussion of larger issues of Pan-Africanism, democracy and the rights of non-Africans, cooperatives, labor unions, the press and preparation for the forthcoming conference of African states in Accra, the conference expressed the hope that 'the administering authority shall find it possible to allow the people of Sukumaland to participate freely in the political activity of the country.' Though many of those in Mwanza who, the conference recorded, produced 'untiring crowding round the conference chamber' probably learned little, even a fragmentary exposure to the fact of the conference and its general range of concerns must have impressed a few.[1] Some may well have been inspired to reflect on the common interests and problems which united Africans within and across territorial boundaries; others to believe that repression as in Sukumaland need not necessarily be the lot of African political leaders.

On the other hand, the PAFMECA Conference seems not to have been widely known outside Mwanza town. Events in Geita, however, had been carefully watched from the outset by leaders and people alike in the neighboring districts across Smith Sound.[2] Even without PAFMECA the moment of expression of pent-up grievances had arrived for the rest of Sukumaland. Geita, more than PAFMECA, provided the catalyst to further disturbances.

Illegal Meetings and Popular Resistance

In Mwanza, for example, the District Commissioner reported that 'political disturbances in the district increased rapidly after Geita dissidents had visited Mwanza in July' and resistance to natural resources legislation, 'starting in the chiefdoms near Mwanza, spread rapidly to the whole district.' Illegal meetings 'provided a popular alternative forum' to village and chiefdom native authority councils. At chiefdom level native authorities 'frequently found their actions challenged...because discussion and consultation was not taken to the lowest level.' Even the

---

[1] A report on the first meeting of PAFMECA held in Mwanza, Tanganyika, 16–18 Sept. 1958 (PAFMECA headquarters, c/o TANU, Dar es Salaam, 23 Sept. 1958), FCBF.

[2] Interviews by research assistant Pastor Balele.

government was forced to admit that village councils, which were 'dormant at best and moribund in some cases, provided no forum for public debate among the citizens.'[1]

With crisis at hand it was time to lament the shortcomings of the past. In Kwimba: 'Too frequently the Parish councillors have merely agreed to the suggestions of the Chiefs, and have not put forward the view of the ordinary cultivator.' In Mwanza native authorities 'awoke to find they no longer had any control over their people...The cause may be largely ascribed to the steadily diminishing contact of Native Authorities with the people, neglect of Parish Councils, particularly, and a revulsion against traditional levies of beer, livestock, etc. for services rendered.'[2]

With councils so artificial and ineffectual, Africans met elsewhere to discuss their grievances. Though 'no pugnacious intent was evident' in these meetings, the administration's legalistic attitude labelled the meetings as 'defiance of territorial legislation and Native Authority orders.' What were people to do, however, if the councils offered no hope of open discussion, not to mention redress of grievances, and any other meetings required advance government permission which was most unlikely to be granted? TANU, after all, was still banned. With nowhere else to turn leaders and people alike decided to meet as they wished in spite of the government and the chiefs. Stupidly but predictably, the government interpreted this as 'an attempt to achieve a breakdown of law and order' which, therefore, could only be dealt with by the police and, where the crowds were large, by motorized units.[3]

Certainly the dissidents did not at first regard law and order *per se* as the critical issue. They were concerned rather with a set of specific grievances. Yet, when the government itself defined the issue as one of law and order and made it in practical terms impossible for grievances to be aired in any way which was not illegal and disorderly, this precipitated a transformation in the very nature of the protest. The dissidents adopted the tactic of civil disobedience in rejection of the colonial system itself—its order and its laws. When this happened, opposition became, in the words of Walden, 'unreasoned';[4] and an attack was launched

[1] Mwanza District Annual Report, 1958, MZDF.
[2] Kwimba District Annual Report, 1958, KWDF; Mwanza District Annual Report, 1958, MZDF.
[3] *Ibid.*   [4] Lake Province Annual Report, 1958, LPF.

on *all* government programs including those which may have been of value.

Thus, in addition to the attack on the native authority system itself, civil disobedience in Mwanza and Kwimba soon focused on natural resources legislation, veterinary centers, taxation and land issues. The advent of the defiant attitudes was dramatically recounted by the Kwimba District Commissioner:

Until October, 1958 was a most satisfactory year. Tie-ridging and manuring had gone well. There had been the second highest cotton crop and a very large paddy crop...There was an average of 7000 dippings monthly...Veterinary centers worked well...East Coast fever research received great cooperation...

In October the District Commissioner visited one of the proposed dipping sites...to find that a complete reversal of opinion had taken place... There was also opposition to manuring and tie-ridging, the presence of African Veterinary Assistants and Natural Resources Centres. This feeling, which was largely stirred up by people from outside the District, spread rapidly through Usmao, Sima, Magu, and Ndagalu Chiefdoms. So swift was its effect that the Bungulwa dip ceased to function almost overnight.

Opposition to cattle tax and destocking led to 'a mass refusal' to have cattle counted in the census. The government's response was the usual:

The refusal was followed by several unlawful assemblies...Arrests were made, and some of those arrested were released by the crowds. Two platoons of Motorized Police were brought in and on Saturday October 25th unlawful assemblies were twice dispersed by tear gas and baton charges.[1]

A rinderpest inoculation campaign encountered strong local opposition and 'had to be painstakingly carried out with three times the normal Veterinary Staff, taking ten times the period normal for inoculations, and with close support from District Police and motorized company.'[2]

[1] Kwimba District Annual Report, 1958, KWDF.
[2] Lake Province Annual Report, 1958, LPF. Like cattle dipping, rinderpest inoculations had not always been clearly salutary and, in a few instances, cattle had died from bad injections. More frequently, of course, cattle died of other causes and were simply erroneously thought by the people to have died because of injections. In any event, the result was the same: discontent. There was also a belief that the administration intentionally killed cattle with the needle to obtain more quickly its destocking objectives. Such an interpretation certainly seemed to make sense from the cattle owner's viewpoint. He was periodically forced to have his cattle counted and to dispose of a certain percentage through sale or slaughter. Weren't dipping and inoculation just

In the politically charged atmosphere, land became a critical issue also. 'Vocal and heavily-attended gatherings...protested about continued use by non-Africans of certain alienated estates, both freehold and leasehold.' At Ukiriguru traditional *basumba batale* leaders took the initiative in gathering people to prevent Europeans from the Agriculture Research Station from digging sand in an area which had been closed to Africans by native authority legislation designed to prevent soil erosion. Some non-African prospectors were even prevented from operating legitimate claims by 'crowds of local Africans.'[1] These popular expressions of disapproval achieved unusually quick results in some cases, indicating that at least some of the complaints were sound or that the government was worried about the general situation, or both.[2]

In other incidents in the Mwanza District, dam building suffered because of poor local (paid) turnout; pasture improvement work 'had to be abandoned in the face of large scale demonstrations'; 'antagonism to forestry activity was expressed by a large number of the population... as a plank in the anti-Natural Resources platform'; the Game Department's base in Busega was transferred to Mwanza after a game scout was assaulted by 'violent' locals near the Simiyu ferry; the proposed extension of the boundary of the Serengeti National Park inside the Masanza II chiefdom 'met with considerable, organized opposition'; a 'public outcry against cattle tax' forced the district advisory council to meet an extra time in December to 'reframe part of the estimates'; and the arrest of some leaders for illegal meetings in Bulima resulted in a trek to Mwanza and a tear gas dispersal on the edge of town.[3]

other ways of accomplishing this objective? Nevertheless, civil disobedience took stronger hold in some areas than in others. Some natural resources centers remained popular and were not boycotted. In some parts of Nera chiefdom even new dips were requested.

[1] Mwanza District Annual Report, 1958, MZDF; *Lumuli*, No. 135, 15 Sept. 1958.

[2] The government took under consideration the revocation of two alienated estates for 'non-fulfillment of covenant'; some illegal mining was uncovered; because of African protests against digging in areas closed to Africans, the area in which prospecting required prior approval of the D.C. was 'increased from a radius of six miles round Mwanza to the whole district' and 'new sand claims were located on the Lake shore to avoid erosion in riverbeds and gullies' (*Ibid.*).

[3] Mwanza District Annual Report, 1958, MZDF; Charles Mponeja, interview, August, 1964.

In his annual report for 1958, Provincial Commissioner Walden made clear his attitude toward what was happening in Sukumaland as he neatly summarized the civil disobedience which had occurred also in a third district—Maswa:

The lengths to which such wrong-headedness can go, especially when allied with the utterance of that magic word 'uhuru,' was well illustrated in Maswa District, which reported the deliberate contamination and damaging of dams built at the request of the people themselves to provide a sorely needed source of water supply to humans and animals; the destruction of cassava crops planted as a famine measure; the boycotting of certain Government services for which the people themselves have clamoured and paid; and finally,...the culminating folly of all, the removal back to the cattle bomas of manure already carted to the fields.[1]

Evaluation

The widespread civil disobedience in the three districts was understandable after the repression of the previous years and the more immediate catalyst of the Geita uprising. But to what extent could such crowd behavior be properly described as 'spontaneous,' to what extent 'fostered,' and if fostered, by whom or what?

The Mwanza District Commissioner wrote that the difficulties 'apparently resulted from internal stresses between Native Authorities and the general populace, led by the Basumba Batale in most cases.' He added that ' "politicians" utilized the ensuing friction to attempt to achieve a breakdown in law and order.' The Provincial Commissioner, too, reported that the 'deliberately fostered campaign of civil disobedience [operated] through traditional community societies.' But rather at variance with this, he also said that 'agitation was started up by local politicians'; and in the same paragraph, 'many of the agitators were not local people, but bands of hooligans mounted on bicycles who could move rapidly from area to area and stir up the unsophisticated peasant'.[2] So, though they were not sure of the precise 'mix' and sometimes appeared to contradict themselves, administration authorities reported that traditional community leaders, local politicians and outside hooligans were all involved—not to mention masses of the people themselves.

It is notable that the names of a few outstanding individual leaders did not emerge from the disturbances in Mwanza, Kwimba and Maswa as they had from the earlier events in Geita. Senior

[1] Lake Province Annual Report, 1958, LPF.
[2] *Ibid.*; Mwanza District Annual Report, 1958, MZDF.

political leaders like Bomani, Bogohe and Kaseko, more recent arrivals like Wambura, and even second echelon leaders like Kitenge and Stephano Sanja seemed not, in any sense, to have led the demonstrations. Though the political campaigns of previous years provided a backdrop to the sudden overt expressions of disaffection, leadership seemed in this particular context more local and more ephemeral.

Developments in Geita, on the other hand, tended to inscribe names along with events. The 'Geita affair' was the first major breakthrough for nationalists in Sukumaland, and the struggle in Geita lasted over a longer period of time. The charismatic Mpandachalo early became a focus of attention, and he went to jail as one of Sukumaland's first political martyrs. Understandably, the names of the three delegates who went to Dar es Salaam, and of the individuals designated to parley with the administration in Mwanza at the time of the sit-down demonstration there, survived. Finally, the Geita leaders, thrown suddenly to the fore in 1958, moved quickly into positions on the reconstituted African district council in 1959. There was no equivalent vacuum in the other districts where older forms and personnel were replaced more gradually.

In the parlance of social science, the disturbances on the Mwanza side of Smith Sound were more anomic than their predecessors on the Geita side. They arose suddenly and subsided as suddenly. There was less need to develop structured leadership. There was less opportunity, for what leaders there were, to move into institutionalized positions of status and from thence to the threshold of historical recollection. From official reports and the comments of participants, it seems clear that where disturbances occurred in Mwanza, Kwimba and Maswa, almost anyone was likely to be involved—traditional and non-traditional, old and young, educated and uneducated. This was true whether or not particular individuals rode bicycles 'from area to area' to 'stir up' others, whether or not they appreciated on its merits a particular natural resources measure, whether or not they interested themselves personally and actively in politics. There seems little point, too, in discussing gradations of 'spontaneity' or 'fostering,' of 'encouragement' or 'coercion.' Despite the administration's resort to the use of the word, 'coercion' as the term is generally understood does not really arise in this context. As for 'encouragement' or 'fostering,' people respond neither to a demagogue nor to an enlightened and far-sighted prophet unless they are angry enough to listen and desperate enough to act.

In Shinyanga District, on the other hand, no large-scale civil disturbance took place. A more conservative, less politicized part of Sukumaland, Shinyanga had not been as exposed to modernizing economic and political movements as Mwanza and Geita, or even Kwimba and Maswa. The Sukuma Union and TAA never achieved the strength in Shinyanga that they achieved elsewhere. No TANU branch existed there before the ban was imposed in 1954. The cooperative movement, too, did not penetrate the district significantly until the late 1950s. At the same time, the native authority system was probably more effective than in many parts of Sukumaland. As a result there was less open conflict between chiefs and people. While the citizens of Shinyanga were probably as quietly disobedient of unpopular regulations as were Sukuma elsewhere, and while one Shinyanga personality, Ali Makani, launched a sustained individual protest against compulsory destocking which did tap deep sources of resentment in the district, circumstances apparently did not prompt people in that district generally to the massive, direct action, protest campaigns adopted by their brothers to the north.

Feelings of discontent were nevertheless widely shared in Sukumaland in 1958. Many were tired of the entire system of authority in all its manifestations—chiefs, headmen, European administrators, technical officers and impersonal regulations. All these pressed upon them annoyingly and heavily from above. Suddenly, people found themselves strong enough to do something about their problems—if not through the accepted channels which were blocked, then outside them. They discovered that the colonial mystique was more fragile than many had thought, that it was vulnerable to assault, that the final common denominator for the Europeans, too, could only be force. For both the administrators and the administered, the lesson of civil disobedience in Sukumaland in 1958 was that the colonial system no longer enjoyed the minimal assent of the public which was a requisite condition for its continued effectiveness.

2   REPEAL OF UNPOPULAR LEGISLATION

The Lower Councils: A Kwimba Example

In October and November 1958 dissatisfaction was expressed not only by crowds and individuals but also through the regular channels of the native authority councils. In the latter months of the year the councils received considerable attention from chiefs who were making an effort to re-establish their authority and from the administration which was trying to stem the tide of the disintegrating native authority structure. In Kwimba the administration enlarged the village councils from ten to twenty members and encouraged the public to attend. Members of the public could listen and express their views but not vote. Beginning in August council meetings in Mwanza were regularly attended by an administrative officer and there was 'lively debate...when discussing controversial topics such as rinderpest, cattle rate, agricultural rules,' and the like.[1]

In early November the chief of Magu in northern Kwimba wrote to the District Commissioner that village meetings indicated that people were anxious to stop paying taxes and to abolish certain detested rules. The chief upbraided them for 'progress in loud-mouthed noise-making' but noted that few understood, for example, what the native treasury actually was. No one was willing to pay any taxes, many believing all the taxes went directly to the central government and had nothing to do with native administration in their home area. The chief explained that all taxes were used by the native treasury itself, and that without money coming into the treasury, no schools or hospitals could be built, and progress generally would cease. He reminded his listeners that years before when taxes had been low, there had been only one school and no real hospital in the entire Kwimba District.

In two of the meetings people still insisted on the abolition of cattle tax but volunteered to pay a substitute flat local rate of ten shillings with promise to reconsider if this proved insufficient to assure their educational progress. In other meetings the people first 'refused completely' to pay anything and adamantly renewed their opposition to the long-held usual list of grievances. The chief then blamed 'bad lazy people' who understood nothing of central government or native administration for planting the 'bad seed' of misunderstanding between people and their native authorities. He asked that people consult with him about anything which they felt needed attention. According to him, the people agreed that the best policy was first to discuss and evaluate matters

[1] Kwimba District Annual Report, 1958, KWDF.

among themselves, then to take them to the people's representatives and to the chiefdom council for further action.[1]

Walden's Dilemma

On 8 October, 1958, the Provincial Commissioner wrote to all District Commissioners announcing a meeting of the Sukumaland Federal Council 'during November to revise existing Sukumaland legislation.' He asked for 'proposals you and your Native Authorities may have as soon as possible.'[2]

The Mwanza Commissioner's reply clearly underlined the inadequacies of previous natural resources policies:

i) Greater individual productivity should be encouraged by instruction, demonstration and participation rather than by edict and prosecution...

ii) There should be no legislation to force a man to have enough food or to enrich himself, only to protect his neighbors and the community from the results of his neglect.

iii) Even rules of communal benefit, e.g. soil conservation, must be better designed to enable supervision and enforcement...

iv) Rules should be adaptable, positive action taken to rehabilitate closed areas, to popularize soil conservation and to give people some positive visible benefits to aim at...

v) There is a nucleus of progressive farmers. They should be given the utmost help, so as to point the lesson of progress and its real benefits in cash.

vi) Unenforceable legislation, or unpopular measures relying on Native Authorities for enforcement, are worthless and serve only to undermine the efficacy—and possible probity—of Native Authorities.[3]

In Kwimba, meanwhile, the district advisory council 'decided to abolish cattle tax and to reduce the cotton cess in the event of price falling.'[4]

Walden, however, was soul-searching until the very eve of the Malya meeting. Called to Dar es Salaam for consultations, he prepared a memorandum entitled 'P.C.L.P.'s [Provincial Commissioner Lake Province] Notes on Suggested Course of Action' in which he asked, 'What does Government consider the essentials on which a stand *must* be made?' He outlined the campaign of previous months against native authority rules and orders, particularly natural resources legislation. He reiterated the formulae

[1] Report by the Chief of Magu to the D.C., 3 Nov. 1958, KWDF. (Orig. Sw.)
[2] P.C. to all D.C.'s, 8 Oct. 1958, LPF.   [3] D.C. to P.C., 15 Oct. 1958, LPF.
[4] Kwimba District Annual Report, 1958, KWDF.

that the campaign was 'in general against law and order,' that 'intimidation plays a large part,' and that 'the troubles we are experiencing in the Lake Province are directed from outside, and I think from TANU headquarters or leaders.' The critical question, of course, was not where to place the blame, but what to do: 'How far does Government go in assisting local authorities in the enforcement of their Rules and Orders?' Noting that the unpopular legislation 'is more often than not at the instance of officers of Central Government [and that] it may well be that Native Authorities themselves will wish to get rid of most, if not all, of this unpopular legislation,' Walden queried 'Should we stop them from doing so? Alternatively, they may refuse to get rid of legislation which we ourselves feel has now become vexatious. Should we make them?'[1]

The real locus of power could not have been more unequivocally identified nor the sham of representative local government in Sukumaland more clearly exposed. Yet, there was pathos in Walden's final questions. The Walden era in the Lake Province was ending. Obviously, Walden's queries revealed his continuing preoccupation with authority as the substance of administration and with the decisive exercise of power (albeit 'in the interests of the people') as effective technique. This attitude toward colonial governing had characterized the Walden administration since the day of its inception in February 1954. No more than before could Walden see that other more creative paths might have been open to him, that more far-sighted policies and a less heavy-handed style might have forestalled the crises of 1958, that strong administration could not of itself solve all problems. Consistently and persistently, he had accused African leadership of 'unreasoned' arguments and 'wrong-headedness.' It did, after all, depend to some extent on one's point of view. Would it not have been noteworthy if in mid-November 1958 Walden had apprehended even in retrospect that some of the administration's ideas and approaches might have been 'unreasoned,' that he himself might occasionally have been guilty of 'wrong-headedness.'?

Looking to the future, the Provincial Commissioner argued that if priorities could be laid down 'at the highest level and a

---

[1] 'P.C.L.P.'s notes on suggested course of action,' 11 Nov. 1958, Walden papers. I am indebted to S. A. Walden for making this document available to me.

decision reached as to what is and what is not important...the position of the provincial administration will become more and more important and officers in the field will be called upon to shoulder more and more work and more and more responsibility.' He argued that 'to cut down essential staff required to assist them in this is quite ridiculous,' maintaining to the end that the troubles in Sukumaland were coming from the 'outside.' Walden concluded his memorandum with the plea: 'It appears essential J.K.N. [Julius K. Nyerere]...should be seen by the Governor and informed of the position which will arise if he continues, or his followers continue, in this line of policy.'[1]

Again Walden failed to identify the direction in which events were moving. Field staff were to be drastically reduced in number in 1959 after the repeal of much natural resources legislation. A period of dyarchy leading toward independence would also significantly circumscribe the importance of the provincial administration. Finally, Nyerere and TANU had won decisively a first round of Legislative Council elections in September. They were to win decisively again in February's remaining contests. In July 1959 Nyerere and four other Africans would take their places as Ministers in the first step toward responsible government. The Walden administration in the Lake Province—indeed the Twining administration in Tanganyika—was passing rapidly into history.

The Sukumaland Federal Council: November 1958

On November 11 at Malya the twenty-second meeting of the Sukumaland Federal Council convened. Chief Majebere opened the meeting and welcomed the Deputy Provincial Commissioner in lieu of Walden who was still in Dar es Salaam. A large number of observers were in attendance. They wanted the rules changed and wanted to make their presence felt. This was unusual for Malya meetings, which were ordinarily so routine. Majebere welcomed the observers but pointed out that they had no permission to speak during debate; if they had objections, he said, they were to be raised at home in their own villages to their chosen representatives.

The Deputy Provincial Commissioner read the opening speech Walden had prepared. Walden noted the importance of the occasion, then differentiated several categories of legislation then on the books. First were rules originally designed to teach better

[1] *Ibid.*

techniques of agriculture to improve the general welfare and to raise the monetary income of the Sukuma. These he judged had outlived their necessity because, with the lessons learned, people themselves would be inclined to follow the rules voluntarily. Second were laws, such as compulsory measures for famine prevention, which had no further meaning or applicability due to changed conditions. Finally, there were regulations which he judged were still of great value, but which needed to be sorted out from among no longer useful laws of the first two categories. In the third category Walden placed local rate. If local rate revenues were curtailed, no progress would be possible with schools, hospitals and other social services.

Walden stressed that no government could govern without laws. Laws had to be made to safeguard the rights and augment the general welfare of individuals, the community and coming generations. Turning to specifics, however, he persisted in entertaining the fiction that the council system from village upward enabled the Federal Council to hear the views of all in Sukumaland. He announced that the times required the assumption of more power by the council. Chiefs, now, rather than District Commissioners would chair the Federal Council's committees. Walden closed, nevertheless, with an allusion to the still implicit and overriding authority of the administration: 'The central government will enforce all just and proper decisions of the Sukumaland Federal Council.'[1]

The Council then divided into committees to consider in detail the entire range of Sukumaland legislation. Some of the more progressive chiefs had been arguing for years for changes in the rules. They had not necessarily argued that what was advocated by the administration was technically bad, but that it could not successfully be forced. Chief Charles Masanja of Nera, for example, had asked in 1956 that destocking be abolished and had proposed that the dangers of soil depletion and erosion be attacked through alternative means. Reportedly, the Kwimba District advisory council agreed, but the proposal was vetoed by the administration. When the destocking issue came to the fore again in 1958, the provincial administration asked the chiefs to ascertain the people's views. Chief Charles's reply was: 'You are forgetting we raised this question years ago. We *know* the position. We want

---

[1] Minutes of a meeting of the Sukumaland Federal Council, 11–15 Nov. 1958, LPF. (Orig. Sw.)

to inform the people that destocking is revoked. They are fed up. We know their answer.'[1]

The councillors, too, played an unusually active role at the November Malya meeting. Spurred from without by the recent civil disturbances and permitted now to air their true views within the chamber, councillors in combination with chiefs had no difficulty ridding themselves of most of the unpalatable legislation. Compulsory destocking, manuring and tie-ridging were abolished. Cattle tax—in principle a graduated tax which the administration regarded as progressive—was rescinded in favor of flat local rating. It was admitted that the change might result in a loss of revenue; if so, the chiefs and the people together would consider alternative sources to make up the difference.

The cotton cess was kept, but with a sliding scale adjusted to market prices. On cattle and rinderpest inoculations, the Council had no power to abolish the relevant legislation since it was an interterritorial rather than simply a local question, and referred the matter to the Legislative Council for decision.

A host of minor rules and regulations pertaining to land, water, forests and stock were also debated. Specific measures were either rescinded or endorsed, but the emphasis throughout was consistent. Where rules relied on persuasion and seemed generally to respond to a felt need, they remained. Where forceful implementation on pain of penalty was required, measures were modified or abolished altogether. As Provincial Commissioner Walden wrote: '[The year] 1958...must be termed as the end of the era of paternalism, particularly in Sukumaland.'[2]

3   AGAIN TANU

By the fall of 1958 the government had no choice but to reconsider the registration of TANU branches in Sukumaland. Even the chiefs saw the handwriting on the wall and urged the administration to revise its policy. In addition to the state of unrest in Geita and other Sukuma districts, they noted that TANU had triumphed in September elections in other parts of Tanganyika— including some areas where TANU branches had also for a time been banned. The second phase of the 1958–9 elections, set for February, was to include Sukumaland.

[1] Chief Charles Masanja, interview.
[2] Lake Province Annual Report, 1958, LPF.

In a memorandum to the Provincial Commissioner in late September, government sociologist Hans Cory took account of the various pressures—local and international—militating toward change:

The moment has come to revise Government's policy towards T.A.N.U. because of:

- i) the result of elections;
- ii) the subjects discussed at the Mwanza (P.A.F.M.E.C.A.) convention;
- iii) the examples of policy in Ghana and Nigeria;
- iv) the irresistible strength of T.A.N.U.'s aims, which cannot be expected to slacken or to be replaced.

A party which will occupy nearly all unofficial seats in the Legislative Council cannot be considered just subversive and treated with suspicion and a show of force...Refusal of registration of the party has to be reconsidered...If Government now misses the right moment for a change, it must consider its reaction to an increasing pressure of the people fairly unanimous in its subversive actions. Will we find an effective answer to a policy of civil disobedience? (Kawawa's studies in India.) If we have no answer today, we will not find any if the situation demands one. Concessions made under compulsion never bring opponents together.

Cory elaborated on the dilemma posed by elections:

It is an anomaly that a party is prohibited, but that its members must be allowed to organize election campaigns in the areas where they otherwise are not allowed to speak in public. It is especially irksome that even under these circumstances they win the election.

He pointed out that the PAFMECA Conference 'has shown that the African leaders begin to shape in their minds the future of East Africa.' He recommended that the government 'consider this as an important move on their side and begin to work on the same issue.'

Proffering the debatable hypothesis that between the government and TANU 'there exists no disagreement in principles,' Cory advocated a compromise which would permit 're-examination of registration' if there were 'an equivalent promise by T.A.N.U. to avoid deceitful demagogy.' He looked for moves to improve 'the general atmosphere and alleviate the exaggerated pressure.' Noting that 'T.A.N.U. leaders think they must fight in order to remain popular,' he suggested that 'perhaps they could be shown that it will be much safer for them to be the future masters if they negotiate step by step political achievements of the Africans'. Finally:

We cannot demand that T.A.N.U. abandons its prestige-winning actions but we can insist on good behaviour and on avoidance of criminal libel. I repeat that all this should never have the appearance of concessions but that of proof of our good intentions if the opposition behaves states-man-like. This attitude is especially opportune if we have to expect finally to have to grant demands.[1]

There was really no alternative. The government permitted TANU to open in October. Of course, the same case might well have been argued some years earlier to the advantage of both sides, but the aphorism 'better late than never' afforded some solace. Even with the change in 1958 there could still have been a problem as to who was to define and what were to be the definitions of good behaviour and deceitful demagogy. Fortunately, TANU took upon itself much of the responsibility of internal discipline after its Sukumaland branches were allowed to open. The government, for its part, shifted the presumed burden of deceitful demagogy and criminal libel from the party as a whole to the errant individual. These postures permitted for the first time a dialogue between TANU and the government. Though there was disagreement and conflict in the 1959–61 period of dyarchy, surprisingly good working relationships developed. Once the government's policy became permissive rather than repressive, once it became creatively inclined toward an African-led future rather than stagnantly preoccupied with the schemes and tasks of a European-dominated past, progress became possible.

An Organizer: Kisenge

A Mwanza TANU headquarters opened on 12 October 1958, almost exactly four years after the original ban on the party had been imposed. With word from the Governor that TANU could be reopened in Sukumaland, Nyerere sent E. A. Kisenge, TANU's organizing secretary-general, to Mwanza. Kisenge recalls that he 'found nothing except excitement' when he arrived. His Land-rover was met by throngs of people some twenty miles south of the town. Once in Mwanza, vehicles and people formed processions through the streets. With Bomani at his side, Kisenge spoke to the crowd at the centrally located Victoria Federation building and announced that TANU headquarters would be open the following morning.

Kisenge then called on Provincial Commissioner Walden.

---

[1] Cory to P.C., 20 Sept. 1958, Walden papers.

Reportedly, Walden surveyed Kisenge, pronounced him a 'reasonable man,' then issued the usual warnings about penalties for misbehavior, indicating that it might be well for Kisenge to rid himself of a few of the more unsuitable local politicians. Kisenge expressed surprise that there were such persons but said he was prepared to do so if Walden would dismiss some unsuitable government officials—in particular, one District Commissioner whom he mentioned. Such a confrontation would have been impossible even a few short months before. Walden and Kisenge were presiding over the end of an era. It is likely that both men understood this as they spoke.

Kisenge, using a house in Mwanza for bedroom and office, started straight away with long days and long evenings of TANU organizational work. In November he sent Shabani Mohamed, who served as Kisenge's principal lieutenant, into Kwimba, Maswa and Shinyanga Districts to hold meetings, set up branches and collect funds. Collection of funds proceeded at a pace such that within a month it became financially possible to purchase TANU Landrovers for each district. Kisenge has spoken of collecting 20,000 shillings in a single day in Mwanza; Mohamed, of gathering 50,000 shillings in a one week trip into the districts. Kisenge himself travelled to Geita to deliver the new vehicle bought with the funds which had poured in from across Smith Sound.

His trip to Geita was a repeat of his triumphant entry into Sukumaland some weeks before. He was greeted at the edge of the district by a crowd which then formed a procession for the trip to Geita town. He spoke to a large gathering of enthusiastic supporters, called on District Commissioner Pearce, then repaired to the new TANU office for two days of organizing and fund-collecting. In public meetings in Geita—and later in Mwanza—he urged that there be no violence, stressed that TANU wanted peaceful progress and asked that criticisms of the government be brought first to TANU for channeling to the proper authorities for consideration.[1]

Enforcing Discipline

The government still had rules about advance permission for public meetings and approval for collection of funds. Kisenge made every effort to follow correct procedures. His correspondence with District Commissioners and other government officials

[1] Interviews: Kisenge, 28 Nov. 1964; Mohamed, 11 Sept. 1964.

was courteous. On one occasion, too, he addressed a meeting of Sukumaland chiefs in Mwanza and told them he needed their cooperation. He asked them to report to him immediately if they found any TANU leader or member abusing his position or creating particular difficulties for local authorities. He said that TANU did not oppose destocking, cattle tax or any other measures advocated by the agricultural and veterinary departments. He told the chiefs that TANU did not oppose native authorities and that any TANU member who disregarded policy directives would be expelled from the party. Though people had become angry with the chiefs because the government had forced them to become tools of the administration, Kisenge pointed out that the chiefs were still 'our chiefs,' deserved respect and should not be regarded as the enemies of TANU.

Problems arose of course. The lifting of the ban released energies and emotions which naturally took the form of action rather than waiting. Furthermore, the propensity for spontaneous demonstration which had developed over the previous six months was not to be immediately curbed just at the moment when people's demands were beginning to be met and when opportunities for personal advancement seemed to many to depend on seizing the initiative. Self-styled leaders developed a penchant for calling meetings of their own in the name of TANU; but activity of this sort was, in the view of Nyerere and Kisenge, likely to prejudice once again the entire TANU operation in Sukumaland.

In November, therefore, Kisenge issued printed circulars detailing 'Some Instructions for TANU in Sukumaland.' After pointing out that only district TANU offices were to be registered and that all chiefdom TANU offices would be under the control of the respective district offices, he emphasized that 'no branch whatsoever' would be registered other than through the provincial TANU headquarters. Similarly, no meetings were to be held without first requesting permission from both the relevant chief and the District Commissioner himself. No representations were to be made to the government by any chiefdom branch except through the district TANU office. All problems and requests for advice should be channeled in the first instance to the district offices. Furthermore, the instructions continued, 'it is absolutely forbidden' to collect money without proper TANU receipts and prior permission of the provincial TANU headquarters, to spend TANU funds without provincial headquarters' approval, or to use the name of TANU, photographs of the president, badges, banners or the like without the permission of TANU headquarters in Dar es Salaam. Finally, members of TANU were to seek the advice of TANU officers before 'joining any other association whatsoever, political or otherwise.'[1]

A few days later Richard Wambura, now serving as provincial TANU secretary under Kisenge, issued a further appeal underlining TANU's intention to conduct its affairs in a legal, cooperative, and aboveboard fashion:

Beloved countrymen...WE WILL GET...OUR FREEDOM BY PASSING THROUGH THE FRONT DOOR...THOSE WHO INTEND TO USE THE BACK DOOR BY HOLDING SECRET MEETINGS AFTER TANU HAS OPENED IN SUKUMALAND CERTAINLY ARE ENEMIES OF THE FREEDOM OF TANGANYIKA.

Come, my countrymen, the ball is on the field and wise competitors always recognize that they achieve victory without fouls or disturbances.[2]

It took some time, however, for Mwanza leaders to bring local enthusiasms under control. There were isolated infractions of policy and disciplinary responses from authorities. A Kwimba subchief, for example, found in late November that 'TANU' meetings were still being held in his area without permission. He wrote to the local TANU branch chairman reminding him of the regulations on advance permission for meetings. He argued that obeying the law would strengthen TANU and progressive politics now that the government had registered TANU. He warned, however, that some TANU leaders disregarded the purposes and by-laws of TANU itself by misleading people into disrespect for central government and native authority legislation; such leaders were a danger to the party and were not wanted by the party. He suggested to his local TANU leaders that they 'read carefully' the by-laws of TANU.[3]

'Battle of the Simiyu'

Despite the opening of TANU in October and the repeal of much detested legislation at the Sukumaland Federal Council in mid-November, a final major instance of civil disaffection and disobedience occurred late in the year. Dubbed 'The Battle of the

---

[1] Kisenge circular, 12 Nov. 1958, MZDF.
[2] Wambura circular, n.d. (Nov. 1958), KWDF.
[3] Subchief of Inonelwa to the chairman of TANU, Misasi, 27 Nov. 1958, KWDF.

Simiyu River' by a European agricultural officer, and as 'the most dangerous situation' he had 'ever faced' by Richard Wambura, the incident illustrated that suspicion of the government among the general populace was not yet overcome.[1] It dramatized, too, not only the continuing tendency of the government to resort to force, but also the new inclination of TANU leaders to try to channel protest activity into legal paths.

The incident arose out of dissatisfaction with a particularly wide-ranging rinderpest inoculation campaign in Busega. As the campaign proceeded against considerable resistance, the administration decided it was necessary to arrest offenders. But—as had happened with the first attempt to arrest Mpandachalo in Geita— a large crowd gathered in sympathy with those arrested. The crowd converged at the Simiyu River ferry, leading the police to assume that the crowd intended to prevent them from transporting the arrested men. The crowd refused to disperse even with the use of tear gas. Wambura, having arrived by coincidence some minutes earlier, urged the motorized police contingent not to use tear gas against the even larger crowd on the other side of the river 'without first warning the people.' He asked if he could 'intervene instead...to talk to the *Wananchi* [countrymen] and see if he could settle the trouble.'

Wambura did succeed in dispersing the crowd without further violence, though he had to appeal to the police a second time to forestall direct action against the crowd. His account, written the following day for *Mwafrika*, is of considerable interest:

I told the Wananchi that, although I did not know whether their friends had committed offences or not, the law should prevail as this was not the first time they had seen people arrested by the Police, and been acquitted. I went on to tell the Wananchi that they would be of no assistance to their friends who had been arrested by gathering together there and making a lot of noise, and that this would only serve to increase the disturbance, and perhaps instead of only six people being arrested, fifty or one hundred might be arrested if they persisted in gathering there, and furthermore many of them might well be hurt. I told them that the business of following the Police after they had arrested an offender is bad, and a breach of the law, and that they should stop doing this from today.

I told them to send two or three people to Mwanza to find out the offences of their friends, and that they should assist them by employing an advocate and that this was the only peaceful way. I explained to them also that we, the African people, are not the humblest of all races, but we are also the most peaceful of all races, as we have no guns or cannon or

[1] Interviews, Charles Allen, 4 Mar. 1964; Wambura, 11 Nov. 1964.

pistols. I told them that TANU believes that our guns are our mouths, and our pistols paper. The Wananchi were overcome with joy at my words. Finally I asked them if they accepted my statements, and whether they would follow this example, and they agreed to do so with great joy. At this point two sections of Police started coming after us, one trying to surround us, and immediately I ran to find the Police Officer and to beg him not to start using tear gas, as the people had agreed to go away. Then all the people who had at first been sitting down quietly were standing, and started running away. I thanked the Police Officer for having listened to me a second time, and he agreed to do so. When the Wananchi saw that the police sections had withdrawn, they started collecting together again, and sitting down as they had done at the beginning, and I told them that we only had thirty minutes left to disperse from this place, and that they should not return and gather together anywhere again without Government permission, and that if they wanted to follow up their complaints with Government in the correct way, they should attend the meeting of the Chiefdom Council which was to take place in their Chief's court on the following day, at which the district commissioner Mwanza would be present also.

I asked two people to remain behind there to explain to me the cause of this trouble, and I said goodbye to the Wananchi. In the space of half an hour no one was left there, except the two people whom I had asked to remain.

In his letter to *Mwafrika*, Wambura was caustic in his criticism of the handling of the incident by the authorities:

I myself had never before been to Masanza I, nor did I know a single person in the crowd there, but in spite of this I was able to disperse this crowd without trouble, but, mark you, the district commissioner and the Chief, who spend the whole time amongst the Wananchi, who are their servants, could not do so!!!! Then the Police say 'Have no doubts that we have tear gas.' Really, will peace between the people and Government be brought about by tear gas, truncheons and the Police Force. Perhaps!!!!!!!!![1]

In a crisis situation of this sort, people were certainly more inclined to follow the advice of TANU leaders than to listen to the government, the police, or the chiefs. This was the central significance of events throughout Sukumaland in 1958 and the reason why TANU had to be recognized and legalized. The recourse only of a bankrupt administration, police action could never in itself have established or preserved the basis of consent necessary for the implementation of policy. If, however, TANU could be encouraged to be a responsible body along the lines clearly desired

[1] Wambura to *Mwafrika*, 27 Nov. 1958, Walden papers.

by Nyerere, Kisenge and Wambura, then ordered progress could be made toward new goals.

In any case, the government could no longer prevent the emergence in Sukumaland of a political force which, within three years, was to govern the country. In the interim provincial TANU officers like Wambura, and more local leaders like those in Geita, enjoyed a *de facto* authority which at times surpassed that of European administrators or native authorities. The administration, to be sure, still held the reins of power; but under Turnbull's governorship the constitutional transition to self-government had clearly begun. After the departure of Provincial Commissioner Walden in March 1959 and the arrival of his more forward-looking successor, G. T. Bell, the gradual devolution of power to Africans at the territorial level was mirrored in Sukumaland at provincial and district levels. Consultative relationships developed between senior governmental officials and their counterpart TANU secretaries. Independence was no longer indeterminately distant.

Nyerere in Sukumaland

In late November Nyerere made his first visit to Sukumaland since the reopening of TANU. In Mwanza he addressed a huge crowd of some 10,000 persons at the old airport ground outside the township. It is said today that when he asked the crowd how many TANU members were present, so many people held up their green membership cards that the whole assemblage looked 'like grass.' Nyerere talked at length of the forthcoming elections to the Legislative Council and of TANU's drive toward the goal of self-government. But he stressed, too, that TANU intended to follow rules laid down by the government for public meetings and that native authority legislation and native authorities themselves were to be respected.[1]

Accompanied by Bomani, Kisenge, John Rupia (TANU's Shinyanga-born vice-president) and Bibi Titi Mohamed (the territorial leader of TANU's women's section), Nyerere toured Sukumaland. He gave a major address and spent a day in each of the five districts. Everywhere he was greeted with processions, songs, dances and gifts. People flocked by the thousands to hear him. Uniformed contingents of the TANU Youth League kept

[1] The Mwanza District Annual Report, 1958, estimated the crowd at 8,000. But see Taylor, p. 177. Bennett, *Makerere Journal*, No. 7 (1963), p. 12, gives additional details on the content of Nyerere's speech.

order at meetings. Nyerere was so impressed that in a later written message of thanks he praised the youth for achieving in just a month what it had taken TANU four years in other areas to accomplish. No sooner had Nyerere departed than arrangements began to be made for his next visit some time early in the new year.[1]

By January 1959 TANU had an established organization in every Sukumaland district. Some 140 branches and sub-branches had been opened. Thousands of membership cards continued to be sold—so quickly, in fact, that demand persistently exceeded available supply.[2] In January and February district TANU leaders and committeemen toured extensively to alert people to the importance of the forthcoming elections. In February three TANU supported candidates for the Legislative Council, including Paul Bomani for the African seat, were returned unopposed. TANU's party organization continued to spread into every corner of the land. By March 1959 TANU's triumph—or at least the first phase of its triumph—was complete. Sukumaland—which for years had been politically in advance of most of the territory, then was subjected for four years to a repressive ban—had rejoined the rest of Tanganyika.

[1] Kisenge to 'My brothers and all leaders and members of TANU,' 12 Dec. 1958, Kitenge papers.
[2] Kisenge, interview.

PART IV

THE NEW REGIME

9

Toward Independence

Once the critical decisions had been made in London and Dar es Salaam, the transition to independence came rapidly. In March 1959 the Legislative Council met for the first time with the thirty members elected the previous September and February. Governor Turnbull announced that a Council of Ministers would be set up in July in which five unofficials, including three Africans, would serve. In October the Governor informed the Legislative Council that the next general election would be brought forward from 1962 to September 1960 and in December that responsible government would be granted following the elections. TANU won seventy of seventy-one seats on the Legislative Council in an election in which only thirteen seats were contested. When the new Legislative Council met in October 1960, it was announced that a constitutional conference would be held in March to consider the final plans for independence. Internal self-government— a *de facto* reality since the appointment of Ministers following the September elections—became official in May 1961. On 9 December 1961, Tanganyika became an independent nation.

In Sukumaland events followed a parallel course. In 1959 and 1960 TANU successfully contested elections to councils at local and district levels. Provincial and district TANU leaders and government officials debated constitutional proposals for African district councils with elected majorities, wound up the affairs of the South East Lake County Council and the Sukumaland Federal Council and dealt in tandem with problems which arose during the dyarchial transitional period. The power of chiefs declined, though many began to cooperate wlth TANU. TANU reached its height of activity and popular support in the twelve to eighteen months before independence. It had become a national movement with whose aims nearly every African could agree. Nevertheless, by 1960 there were murmurings of opposition sentiment in some areas. No more than any other government or party—colonial or otherwise—would TANU find itself free of imperfections, or escape the human propensity for disagreement and discontent.

I   TANU ASCENDANT

Organization and Leadership

At the time TANU reopened in Sukumaland, the party territorially had achieved the organizational structure characteristic of its mature phase before and after independence. The TANU Youth League and the women's and elders' sections were already in existence, and the hierarchical party structure from sub-branch and branch to territorial annual conference and National Executive had been systematically articulated throughout the country.[1] Given the physical characteristics of the country and the nature of the new nation's political problems, local units were the most vital for the proper functioning of the party. As Bates has explained:

> The crucial point in TANU organization has been the district. The branches have been too small and widely scattered to employ professional workers; the provinces are too large and spread out to be cohesive units. At the district level, the secretary is a paid official, generally appointed from Dar es Salaam though occasionally a strong district Committee appears to have some part in the matter. His rival for local power and also for control of finance is the district president [or chairman], who is usually a parttime official; he was originally not paid but now receives a *posho* allowance. These two party officials are usually young and of varying educational level; many of them do not speak English. They have in the past provided the chief links between the central headquarters of TANU and the grass roots, and their role in interpreting policy has been vital.[2]

When Kisenge came to reopen TANU in Sukumaland in October 1958, he worked from the pattern previously established elsewhere. Within a matter of weeks district TANU offices were in operation, branches and sub-branches had sprung up in virtually every corner of the land, and units of the Youth League, the women's section and the elders' section began to function at district headquarters and in other major centers.

In the individual Sukumaland districts, leadership sometimes was assumed by the TANU secretary appointed by the Dar es Salaam headquarters and sometimes by the locally elected chairman. In either case, forceful personalities, both Sukuma and

[1] For details on the organization of the party, see Bates, pp. 451–7.
[2] *Ibid.* p. 456.

non-Sukuma, had opportunities to move rapidly upward in the party hierarchy and, after independence, into the new government. Men who made good records as regional or district TANU officials in 1958 and 1959 were likely to be appointed Area Commissioners (which replaced the colonial District Commissioners in 1962) under the independent government in the early 1960s.

In Shinyanga and Geita, for example, Shabani Mohamed and Augustine Madaha respectively held the post of TANU secretary. Owing their positions to appointment rather than to election and both being non-Sukuma, they nevertheless had already established strong roots in their adopted districts. The locally elected TANU chairman of Shinyanga, Hamisi Abdulfatahi, an artisan and trader who had previously played no major political role, proved decidedly subsidiary to the driving force of Mohamed's leadership. In Geita, Wilson Bunuma, a more prominent personality who had been a leader of the Geita demonstrations in 1958, was elected chairman, but was jailed for illegally forcing someone to leave the district. Meanwhile, both Mohamed and Madaha moved on to higher posts. In 1960 Mohamed followed Wambura as provincial TANU secretary and in 1962 Nyerere appointed him to North Mara as Tanganyika's first Area Commissioner. Madaha was elected Member of the TANU National Executive in 1959 and appointed Area Commissioner of Shinyanga in 1964.

In Maswa and Kwimba Districts, appointed TANU secretaries came and went in more ephemeral fashion, and elected TANU chairmen assumed the primary leadership roles locally. In Maswa Stanley Kaseko—the vigorous leader of TAA and TANU in Malampaka in 1954—became chairman. Elected chairman also of the Maswa District Council, Kaseko was appointed as Area Commissioner of Maswa in 1962. In Kwimba, too, the elected TANU chairman, Peter C. Walwa, emerged as the driving force of the party. A Sukuma with a secondary school education, Walwa had served for ten years as a railway stationmaster. Subsequently, he became a trader and shopowner in Kwimba. A disappointed applicant for treasurer of the Kwimba Native Treasury in 1957, he emerged in 1959 as a new and most ambitious and hardworking TANU leader. In 1960 he was appointed TANU secretary in Morogoro and subsequently provincial secretary in Tanga. Since Independence he has served as a Regional Commissioner and as a Junior Minister in the Ministry of External Affairs. Another local Sukuma who had played a role in the Sukuma Union and in political affairs in Sukumaland—Sylvester Lubala—emerged as TANU chairman after Walwa's departure from Kwimba in 1960. Like Kaseko in Maswa, Lubala moved into a position of prominence in the District Council and ultimately became Area Commissioner of Kwimba in 1962.

Although district level leadership was of the utmost importance for the tasks of party construction locally, the most powerful and influential political figures in Sukumaland in 1959 and 1960 were Richard Wambura, the provincial TANU secretary, and Paul Bomani, still the only African member of the Legislative Council from Sukumaland and, until September 1960, general manager of the Victoria Federation of Cooperative Unions. Wambura held the reins as TANU's top provincial officer until he was elected to the Legislative Council from Maswa in 1960, at which time Shabani Mohamed replaced him in Mwanza as provincial TANU secretary. Wambura later became the first Regional Commissioner in the Lake Province in March 1962, then Regional Commissioner of Tabora (1963–4), then Junior Minister in a series of important ministries. Bomani, who was actually more concerned with national than with Sukumaland affairs, served as Minister for Agriculture and Cooperative Development (1960), Minister for Agriculture (1961), Minister for Finance (1962–5) and Minister for Economic Development (1965).

Recruitment and Program

During 1959 and 1960 TANU conducted a ceaseless campaign for membership and funds, and the party attempted to spread its political message into every corner of Sukumaland. Permission from the government was still required for all political meetings and for the collection of funds, and at times even political uniforms were not permitted. Though provincial and district TANU leaders fostered compliance with the legalities, reminders from government officials and from party leaders were frequently necessary to restrain local organizers.

The rules made matters difficult also for the chiefs. Native authorities were not allowed to advertize TANU meetings; they were to concern themselves only with the legitimate business of the central and local governments, not with the affairs of non-governmental associations. Later, apparently recognizing the impossible position which would develop if an attempt were made to isolate TANU activities from the life of the community and from existing local government units, the administration relented to the extent of allowing TANU to designate two persons from each subchiefdom to serve in a quasi-official capacity to spread news about TANU meetings.[1] Though some native authorities were able unofficially and informally to align themselves with TANU (and thereby to survive the change-over to a new administration), these were relatively few. Most proved unable to convince TANU leaders of their nationalist credentials. It is a moot question the extent to which a higher percentage of native authorities might have survived the transition had they been permitted to advertize TANU meetings and to play a more active political role in 1959–60.

After Nyerere's visit to Sukumaland in January 1959 and the departure of Kisenge, the district party organizations took the tasks of campaigning for TANU into their own hands. Quickly they became quite professional. Customarily, a half dozen district leaders—the secretary, chairman, leader of the women's section, an elder or two, and various members of the district committee—plus perhaps a provincial officer or a visiting dignitary from Dar es Salaam, toured a series of villages. Public meetings featured local TANU choirs lauding TANU leaders and policies in song, remarks by local party personnel and usually several major speeches by the visitors. In early 1959, topics inevitably included the 'Aims and Objects of TANU' and information on the forthcoming Legislative Council elections and TANU's candidates. As people became familiar with 'aims and objects,' 'activities and policies' were stressed.

Nor did the campaigns in the countryside subside after the elections. District TANU leaders continued a program of regular safaris which took them to every chiefdom and major center in the district monthly and to virtually every village once every two or three months. Leaders spoke of the meaning of the Legislative Council results, stressed the importance of local council elections, announced the phases of constitutional advance, and passed on to the populace statements made by Governor Turnbull and by TANU President Nyerere. At major turning points—the appointment of five elected ministers on 1 July 1959, the anniversary of the formation of TANU on 7 July and the attainment of responsible government in October 1960—processions

[1] D.C. circulars to all native authorities, 18 Feb. and 2 Apr. 1959, KWDF.

and dances embellished large public meetings. TANU leaders spoke, too, of the Pan-African Freedom Movement for East and Central Africa, and in November 1959 persons of all races were asked by TANU to cooperate in the implementation of a PAF-MECA boycott resolution to forgo the purchase or handling of South African goods.[1] By September 1959 topics for speeches had become more various: 'TANU Policy and Activities,' 'Democracy', 'Constitutional Changes,' 'Citizenship,' and 'Local Government.' By late 1959 the emphasis had shifted from large public meetings to membership drives carried out on a village basis by clerks or secretaries of local sub-branches.[2]

In addition to speech-making, recruitment of members and collection of funds, TANU's activity in the countryside included response to the complaints of individual citizens. Though direct conflict between TANU and the government had been muted after TANU's electoral triumphs and the colonial administration's decision to proceed with deliberate speed toward responsible government and independence, there was still substantial disagreement between them—particularly on the role of native authorities and the evolution of local government institutions. Like TAA, the Sukuma Union, and TANU before 1959, the TANU of the period of transition still functioned as a mouthpiece for protest and an endless list of local grievances were brought to TANU for redress. Relations with the Asian and Arab communities in the major trading centers also became more tense as African leaders found themselves on the threshhold of greater political power *vis-à-vis* the immigrant groups which Africans had always resented.[3]

Whatever the issue, TANU leaders were on hand to represent African interests as they understood them. But often guidelines of general policy available from Dar es Salaam proved irrelevant or inapplicable to specific problems. At the local level, the period of transition was a time not only of organizing and building support for

[1] *Sauti ya TANU*, No. 57, 22 Sept. 1959.
[2] Walwa to D.C., 15 Oct. 1959, KWDF.
[3] Two examples are typical. At Malampaka in Maswa District, the local Indian Association complained to the D.C. that African trade union organizers 'enter anybody's premises at any time and take away the employees they like for meeting or any other purposes and thus, hinders our trade and house work' (Indian Association to D.C., 20 Oct. 1959, MADF). At Malya a TANU-inspired boycott against a local Asian-owned general store for alleged inefficiency and arbitrary refusals of service was 'fully supported by all Malya inhabitants' (Chief Charles to D.C., 28 Oct. 1959, KWDF).

the party, but also of exploiting whatever weaknesses the administration and native authorities permitted themselves and whatever
grievances individuals might wish passed on to higher levels of
the as-yet colonial government. The rhetoric of public meetings,
too, sometimes drew TANU leaders—like political leaders anywhere—into a realm of hyperbole. Starting from a clear and legitimate grievance, or expanding on a progressive theme, speakers
sometimes launched into questionable statements of fact and
interpretation. It was a time of improvisation, of groping and of
ad hoc responses to specific difficulties and opportunities. Not yet
a governing power, TANU could still afford some of the luxuries
of the opposition critic.

Elections 1959

TANU's first major electoral test in Sukumaland came with the
February installment of the Legislative Council elections of
1958–9. It turned out to be no contest, however, as TANU sponsored candidates ran unopposed; no opposition groups among any
of the three major races crystallized to the extent of fielding a
candidate.

The Sukumaland districts plus Ukerewe, Musoma and North
Mara formed one constituency for South East Lake. At stake were
three seats in the Legislative Council—one for each of the three
races. Voting was on a common role, but every voter had to vote
for a candidate of each race in order to make his ballot valid.[1]
Despite a restricted franchise, Africans still constituted more than
two-thirds of the total electorate. 'It was clear that TANU's
ability to influence African voters might determine the results in
a European or Asian political contest, since Africans were expected
to be a majority of the voters in most constituencies.'[2] Though
TANU was reluctant to participate in an election based on the
principle of racial parity which it strenuously opposed, it decided
to contest the election in hopes of strengthening its hand. By endor-
sing particular European and Asian candidates

TANU realized that...it could probably elect a coalition of members
who either had been TANU candidates or had enjoyed TANU support.
If this move proved successful, the Party would then be in a better
position to bargain with the government and to press for rapid advance
toward self-government.[3]

[1] For details on franchise qualifications and election procedures see Chidzero,
pp. 146, 269–70.   [2] Taylor, p. 171.   [3] *Ibid.*

After TANU's September victories it was clear that the government-encouraged United Tanganyika Party was moribund and that a candidate with TANU's stamp of approval was sure to win against any candidate of whatever race which TANU opposed. Within this context, Africans and non-Africans sought to find candidates for the European and Asian seats who would be acceptable to TANU and to all three communities. A European lawyer, J. S. Mann, and an Asian businessman, C. K. Patel, were selected. The Provincial TANU secretary, Richard Wambura, and the candidate for the African seat, Paul Bomani, signed Patel's and Mann's nomination papers. In turn, Mann and Patel signed for Bomani's candidacy!

Patel had long been a prominent figure in Mwanza and one of the leading Asian businessmen in the Lake Province. A manager for Asian- and later African-owned cotton gins, he became thoroughly and sympathetically involved with African initiatives in the cotton business. Respected also by Europeans and Asians for his business acumen and seemingly inexhaustible energy, Patel was the logical candidate for the Asian seat.[1]

Mann, an English solicitor, joined the colonial service in 1951 and served as a resident magistrate in Tanganyika for three years before establishing a law practice in Mwanza in 1954. The only European advocate in Mwanza in private practice and one of the few Europeans of any description outside the administration, he served as an unofficial European member of various local government bodies and seemed to Europeans an obvious choice for the Legislative Council seat. He was well known to Asians because his legal practice kept him in close touch with Mwanza's Asian businessmen. Finally, he was more acceptable to Africans and to TANU than many another European because during the turbulent

---

[1] Born in India in 1903, Patel had emigrated to East Africa in 1924. After three years in Kenya and Uganda he moved to Mwanza where he opened a retail trading shop. In the early 1930s he entered the cotton business as a ginnery agent. After the Second World War he became manager for three (eventually six) Asian ginneries and in 1956 was appointed managing agent of the first African-owned ginnery of the Victoria Federation of Cooperative Unions at Kasamwa (Geita District), and later of the Federation's second ginnery at Ushashi (Musoma District). At various times Patel was secretary or President of the Lake Province Ginners Association, the Hindu Union, the Mwanza Education Board, the Red Cross and the United European and Asian Mwanza Chamber of Commerce. He also served as a member of Tanganyika's Lint and Seed Marketing Board and as a representative on the South East Lake County Council (*Who's who in East Africa*, Part II, p. 30; biographical file, Regional Office of Information, Mwanza; Patel, interview, 26 Jan. 1965).

mid-1950s he had defended Africans charged by the government with political crimes.[1]

Paul Bomani, of course, was the candidate for the African seat. Perhaps the most widely known African in the South East Lake constituency, he had been identified for nearly ten years with local economic and political associations striving for African advancement. A leader of the Tanganyika African Association and of the Sukuma Union in the early 1950s, he became the master-builder of the cooperative movement in the South East Lake area and the principal architect of the massive Victoria Federation of Cooperative Unions. He had considerable experience with local government—including the Mwanza Township Authority and the Lake Province Council—and had served as a nominated member of the Legislative Council since 1954. Already a national figure by 1959, he was one of Nyerere's chief lieutenants and a leading contender for a ministerial post in any TANU government. Because of his study in England, his fluent command of English, his shrewd business sense and his previous experience with government bodies including the Legislative Council and the respect for him by Europeans and Asians as well as by Africans, he was on any reckoning the most suitable candidate for the African seat. Bomani, Patel and Mann were returned unopposed in the February voting.

TANU in Sukumaland then busied itself with local elections. In 1959 in Geita and in 1960 in the other Sukumaland districts, TANU candidates successfully contested elections to newly constituted African District Councils. The new local councils replaced the ill-fated multi-racial district council in Geita and the native authority advisory councils in the other districts. They superseded the chiefs as the constituted native authorities. New local government constitutions retained chiefs and selected lower level native authorities as *ex officio* members of the new councils; but a two-thirds majority were to be popularly elected representatives and the chairman of the council was to be elected by the councillors. Following what was becoming a well-established pattern customary to Tanganyika 'exceptionally few non-TANU candidates were successful and few constituencies were contested.'[2]

[1] Appointed to the Mwanza Town Council in 1955, Mann became vice-chairman and in 1958 chairman. He was elected vice-chairman of the South East Lake County Council in 1955. Before entering the colonial service, Mann had served with the Royal Air Force and lectured on Air Force law in Amman and Cairo. [2] Lake Province Annual Report, 1960, LPF.

In Shinyanga, for example, all forty candidates in the first elections to the new African District Council in August 1960 were TANU supporters and all were returned unopposed.[1] A similar mono-lithic trend obtained in Geita. In Kwimba on the other hand, five of fourteen constituencies were contested with as many as six candidates standing for one-, two- and three-member constituen-cies. However, only one of the Kwimba seats went to an indepen-dent; the others were won by TANU candidates. In Maswa eight seats were contested but TANU candidates were returned in each. In Mwanza all four contested constituencies were won by TANU. However, an independent candidate, Fabian Ngalaiswa, a leader of the Sukuma Union in earlier years and later identified with the African National Congress, was returned when TANU failed to find a candidate to oppose him.

The 1960 district elections, however, sparked the first signs of local discontent with TANU's methods. In general each TANU district organization sponsored one candidate for each seat. Sometimes other would-be candidates were actively discouraged from standing, and reports indicated that in Maswa and Kwimba some who had originally put their names forward withdrew after receiving 'threatening' letters from local TANU officials.[2]

Elections 1960

Further problems arose with nominations for the Legislative Council elections of September 1960. Territorially TANU hoped for another sweeping victory which would give it a clear mandate during the period of responsible government. At the local level, provincial and district TANU leaders were eager to impress their party superiors in Dar es Salaam with reports of dynamic and unified support for TANU from the people of their respective areas. At the same time, some dissatisfaction with the men and with the methods of local TANU organizations was beginning to be felt. In some parts of Sukumaland the splinter opposition African National Congress (ANC), formed by Zuberi Mtemvu after his defection from TANU in 1958, established outposts. Those skeptical of TANU's assertive thrust toward monolithic control at the local level, and others excluded by chance or circumstance from the inner councils of provincial, district and branch TANU organizations, struck independent postures.

---

[1] Thirty-three of the forty candidates had never served previously on the District Advisory Council.   [2] Maswa District Annual Report, 1960, MADF.

Chief Charles Kaphipa of Bukumbi, for example, decided to stand for the Legislative Council from Mwanza District.[1] Young and well-educated, he felt he had a role to play in Tanganyika's future as well as her past. He had joined TANU in 1958 (secretly, since native authorities were not permitted membership in political associations) and, when he read the announcements inviting nomination papers from those wishing to stand for the 1960 elections, he applied to the TANU office in Mwanza. The difficulty was that Bomani was the incumbent from Mwanza. In order to activate his own candidacy, Kaphipa had to put himself in a competitive position *vis-à-vis* Bomani. Bomani, of course, was selected by the district TANU committee as the TANU candidate while Kaphipa's application was regarded as tantamount to opposition to Bomani personally and, by extension, to TANU itself. In his home area of Bukumbi, where he was still chief, local TANU personnel even attempted to enforce community sanctions of boycott and ostracism against him. Kaphipa has said that he did not interpret his own candidacy as opposition either to Bomani or to TANU. He believed that people should have a choice between good TANU candidates and that the party should accept the choice of the people rather than vice-versa. Though this was to be the philosophy adopted in practice by TANU in the National Assembly elections of 1965, Kaphipa was ahead of his time in 1960.[2]

In 1960 Mann and Patel were not renominated by TANU for the European and Asian seats from the Mwanza constituency. Apparently, they had, in separate ways, run afoul of TANU in the eighteen months since their initial nomination and election.[3]

[1] The three-member South East Lake constituency of 1959 was divided into eight constituencies (corresponding to the eight districts in the Province) for the elections of 1960. Seven were single-member constituencies. Mwanza retained—in addition to the 'open' (i.e. African) seat—reserved seats for a European and an Asian, but elected as before on a common roll (see Chidzero, pp. 271–2).

[2] Mwanza District Annual Report, 1960, MZDF. Kaphipa, interview, 3 Sept. 1964.

[3] It is difficult, if not impossible, to know exactly what considerations were involved. One authoritative source has related that Mann incurred the wrath of provincial TANU secretary Wambura when the latter helped Mann extricate his automobile from a muddy ditch. Mann is said to have failed to thank Wambura and to have inadvertently splashed mud on him as he drove away. Wambura is said not to have forgotten the incident and to have opposed Mann's renomination in 1960. Apocryphal or not, the story doubtless symbolizes the mutual disenchantment which developed between TANU and Mann.

They were replaced by Barbara Johansson and N. K. Laxman, both of whom had been elected with TANU support to the Legislative Council in 1959 from Bukoba in the West Lake constituency. Johansson, a Swedish missionary and teacher, had served as headmistress of a girls' school in Bukoba since 1948. She had intended to return to educational and social work in 1960 but President Nyerere proposed her name to the TANU National Executive to heal the split on Mwanza nominations 'between extremists and moderates who couldn't agree' on a candidate.[1]

Like Johansson, Laxman had not sought nomination from Mwanza but was shifted there at the behest of the National Executive. Born in Mwanza and educated in Indian schools in the town, Laxman earned a law degree in London before returning to Mwanza in 1956 to establish himself in private practice. Like Patel, he took a prominent role in community affairs and earned the respect of Europeans and Africans as well as Asians. Like Mann, he put his professional knowledge at the disposal of African clients accused of political crimes. This gave him standing with TANU.[2]

Maswa, Kwimba, Geita and Shinyanga had single-member constituencies of their own in the 1960 elections. In all four cases TANU-sponsored candidates were returned unopposed. Richard S. Wambura received endorsement for the Maswa constituency, Chief Francis C. Masanja for Kwimba, Bartholomew D. Mwiza for Geita and John G. Rupia for Shinyanga. Wambura was a native of Musoma, but in the East Lake constituencies TANU leaders of national prominence—Isaac Bhoke Munanka and Nyerere's younger brother, Joseph K. Nyerere—were standing for election. Of course, Wambura had worked for years in Mwanza and served in 1959–60 as provincial secretary of TANU with geographical responsibilities which included Maswa. British parliamentary and electoral tradition permitted finding

It is widely believed that Patel, despite his intimate connections with the VFCU, had helped secretly to foster an African-led opposition movement to the VFCU. The would-be competitor, the Saidia Waafrika Company, gained support in some areas but was quashed through a combination of strenuous TANU opposition and of government support for a continuing monopoly for the VFCU. Patel has denied ever having had any connection with Saidia Waafrika, and has continued to hold high positions with the VFCU. Whatever the facts, Patel submitted his application papers but was rejected as a candidate.

[1] Johansson, interview, July 1964.
[2] Biographical file, Regional Office of Information, Mwanza; Laxman, interview, April 1964.

constituencies for the candidates rather than candidates from the constituencies and, where it seemed appropriate, TANU followed this practice. Shinyanga provided another such instance. Rupia, a past vice-president of territorial TANU, had been born in Shinyanga but had for many years lived in Dar es Salaam where he was a prosperous businessman.

Geita and Kwimba, on the other hand, fielded candidates with stronger local roots. Mwiza was born and educated in Geita and served as treasurer and assistant secretary of the Geita District native authority from 1950 to 1958. Masanja was the youthful chief of Usmao in Kwimba District. It is difficult to ascertain the precise reasons why these men were picked by TANU for the 1960 contests. Aside from superior qualifications—which objectively, each may have had relative to others who may have sought TANU's support—some have expressed the view that Mwiza was picked by the National Executive because he was a Zinza in a district where Zinza were worried about a preponderance of Sukuma in positions of power. Others have said that Masanja was picked in Kwimba to soften the conflict which had been developing there and in other districts between TANU and Sukuma chiefs and other traditional elements. Politically, the young chief seemed an appropriate choice because he had sided with dissidents against the colonial government during the disturbances in Kwimba in late 1958. He was especially popular with the people because of his overt opposition to destocking.

As in 1959 the Sukumaland candidates—five Africans, one European and one Asian—were all elected unopposed. They took their seats in the new Legislative Council in October 1960. Seventy of seventy-one seats were won by TANU-supported candidates and, under TANU leadership, Tanganyika took the next critical step toward independence—responsible government. Bomani held the portfolio of Minister for Agriculture and Cooperative Development in the new Council of Ministers headed by Chief Minister Nyerere. In March 1961 Bomani, Johansson and Laxman jointly opened an office in Mwanza which they equipped and paid for themselves. Laxman became also a representative to the East African Legislative Assembly and continued to practice law. Johansson cultivated special interests in community development problems, organizing programs of instruction for women in cooking, sewing, health and citizenship in outlying parts of the district.

U

Wambura worked outside the province for a time, but returned in March 1963 as the first Regional Commissioner of the Lake Province. Rupia, Mwiza and Masanja opened offices in their constituencies. Rupia, however, spent most of his time in Dar es Salaam, Mwiza soon came to be regarded as ineffectual even by his own constituents, and Masanja eventually courted political disaster through association with opposition political movements. All seven, however, were to serve as Members of the Legislative Council and (after 1 May 1961) as members of the National Assembly until independent Tanzania's first national elections in 1965.

2 COUNCILS IN TRANSITION

The triumph of TANU—and with it the triumph of the democratic idea of popular representation—forced the transformation by 1960 of all institutions of local government. During the 1950s the administration had fostered the modification of earlier patterns of native authority administration with the formation of a hierarchy of local councils. Ostensibly elected by the people, councillors sat with the executive native authorities to deliberate matters of policy. The councils, however, were only advisory; the councillors were most frequently *protégés* of the chiefs rather than popularly designated representatives; and the councils served more as propaganda arms and enforcement agencies for the administration's already established policies than as sounding boards for public opinion. Increasingly discredited in the late 1950s as local politicians, and then TANU itself, assessed their workings and found them wanting, the councils changed in complexion and then in constitution after 1959. Ultimately, the district and subdistrict councils which emerged after independence were more English than those that the British had instituted in Sukumaland in the 1950s. Native authorities, *ex officio* chairmen, official voting majorities and the illusory powers conferred by the colonial regime were abandoned in favor of popularly elected majorities, officers elected by the council itself, and statutory executive, legislative and financial powers of the sort actually enjoyed by local governing bodies in England.

Cory: Theories and Realities

Of course, self government had always been the aim of the

colonial administration. Writing on the proposed Sukumaland Federation in 1945, Hans Cory, the principal architect of Sukumaland's pyramid of local government councils in the 1950s, wrote that 'if we open the avenues of economic progress we must expect political aspirations on the part of the people.' He quoted the Colonial Secretary to the effect that government policy was to advance the territories not only socially and economically, but also toward the 'ultimate goal of Self-Government.'[1] Ironically, Cory himself was to see the attainment of that 'ultimate goal' and to serve, a scant fifteen years later in 1960, as the government's principal adviser in discussions with TANU on the formation of the new councils.

Like Governor Twining and most other Tanganyika administrators, Cory had always regarded the chiefs as the natural leaders of any future African political institutions, however distant. Even with modern political changes, the chiefs 'were and shall remain the leaders.'[2] Though he sensed from an early date the development of a political consciousness and a yen for leadership independent of the chiefs, he apparently never perceived the inherent contradiction between his twin goals of perpetuated chiefly leadership and a democratic constitution. Throughout the 1950s he pressed the increasingly dubious proposition that if chiefs and people, with government leadership and support, could combine their efforts in local councils, the chiefs would have 'a method of preparing their survival,' the people would enjoy the rudiments of democracy, and the colonial government would forestall the 'premature demands of radical politicians.'[3]

In fact, the course of future events became clear to the chiefs more quickly than to Cory. In June 1958—even before disturbances had erupted in Geita—Cory reported to the government that 'a number of chiefs of the Sukuma Federation showed... a marked move to the Tanu camp.'[4] Soon they were asking the government to permit the opening of TANU branches 'wherever they are desired by the people.'[5] In order for the chiefs to preserve leadership when it was increasingly difficult for them to see 'another way than to follow their people who go step by step and

---

[1] Cory, 'Tentative working plan for the Sukuma Federation,' 1945, Cory papers.
[2] Cory, 'Memorandum to the chiefs of Tanganyika Territory,' n.d., Cory papers.
[3] Cory, 'The councils and the native authority,' n.d., p. 8, Cory papers.
[4] Cory, draft memorandum, untitled, 19 June 1958, p. 1, Cory papers.
[5] Minutes of a meeting of Sukumaland chiefs, Mwanza, 31 June 1958, SHDF.

day by day into the TANU camp,' Cory argued that the chiefs 'must develop and even if we have to help them a strong policy of nationalism and of demands on Government...They must become a Tanganyika Union with the chiefs as the natural leaders and their people the great mass of members.[1]

TANU, however, was already an established national movement; it was too late for nationalist-minded chiefs to move in any direction other than toward TANU. Three months later—after the Geita disturbances and TANU's victory in the first territorial elections—Cory himself acknowledged the 'irresistible strength' of TANU and recommended that the government completely reverse its attitudes and policies toward the party.[2]

The Formation of African District Councils

Since TANU's advance had not been forestalled by the expedients Cory had proposed between 1953 and 1958, it became necessary for the government to deal directly with TANU on the composition and constitutions of local government councils in 1959 and 1960. No longer would the councils be the creations alone of the administration and the chiefs. No longer would indirect election on the pyramid system foreshorten the possibility of the direct expression of public opinion. A letter from the TANU district secretary in Kwimba to the District Commissioner typified TANU's criticism of the councils:

Writing on behalf of the District Committee of this Union, I have the honor to express the deep sentiments and great dissatisfaction we feel with the present formation of the District Advisory Council of our District.

Up to the present day, the council consists of Chiefs and a group of a few headmen who are nominated by the Chiefs at their own pleasure!... in former days a chief...enjoyed an unlimited power of jurisdiction which he up to date maintains to some extent...the nominated headmen in the council...are no less than...echoes of the words and concepts of the chiefs whose nominees they are...

One sees clearly that the council is definitely onesided and as such it

[1] Cory, draft memorandum, untitled, 19 June 1958, p. 2, Cory papers.
[2] Cory to P.C., 20 Sept. 1958, Walden papers. See also above, pp. 249–50. A year later Cory reported: 'Both the politically active and passive parts of the people are led by TANU. The chiefs are members of TANU...Many of the chiefs consider this membership a good security of their position. Probably that is true...' (Cory, 'Position of chiefs in rural N.A.'s,' n.d. (1959), pp. 1–2, Cory papers).

cannot be properly effective on the side of the unrepresented viz: the subjects. As the political conditions are there is really a need of having a fully elected body of representatives chosen or voted for by the people themselves.[1]

Thus, a trial of strength between the districts and the central government developed.[2] Impressed by the announcements of constitutional advance at territorial level, each district sought for itself popularly elected councils and 'full responsibility' in local government affairs. For its part, the administration emphasized that 'local government bodies can only operate to the extent to which they are authorized to do so by law, which can only proceed from the Central Government through the Legislature.'[3] The crux of the problem centered on the position of the chiefs. Some politicians were eager to shunt native authorities aside as quickly as possible; the administration wanted them to continue in positions of executive responsibility under the new representative councils.

With divergent inclinations and general confusion at a premium, the administration established an *ad hoc* committee of government and TANU leaders and district representatives to hammer out a draft model constitution which might then be applied with variations to each of the five districts. This committee met early in 1960—Cory for the government; Bomani, Member of the Legislative Council, and Wambura, TANU provincial secretary, for the TANU leadership; and delegates from each district who were acceptable both locally and to TANU. Chiefs and native authorities were not themselves represented on the *ad hoc* committee: it was their positions which were principally at issue.

As Provincial Commissioner Harris said later, the 'trick' was to 'marry' certain basic principles which the government held essential with 'the ideas of local leaders.'[4] Cory wrote:

The basic idea of the [draft] constitution as far as the Central Government was concerned, was a way to keep the peace in the districts. No doubt the public opinion six or seven months ago had transferred its target of dissatisfaction from Central Government to Local Government. Radical demands for changes such as deposing the existing chiefs, for responsibilities of councils without control by Central Government, and for executive powers of councils were brought forward and the District

[1] TANU Secretary to D.C., n.d. (1959), KWDF.
[2] Lake Province Annual Report, 1960, LPF.
[3] Lake Province Annual Report, 1959, LPF.
[4] Harris, interview, 4 Apr. 1965.

Commissioners in accordance with the existing structure of administration became involved in the struggle.

In this situation it was decided...to contact unofficially the local office bearers of TANU and negotiate with them a constitution acceptable to both the Central Government and the people, by which step the nefarious and self-seeking agitators would be eliminated.[1]

Through the process of negotiation, Cory was able to firm up a number of aspects of the constitution which had dissatisfied him and to preserve some status for the chiefs: 'the continuation of the present dynasties was guaranteed and also the election of the chiefs for lifetime...The responsibility of chiefs for Law and Order is emphasized and a very modest share of the chiefs in the appointment of subordinate officers is acknowledged.' Nevertheless, Cory found the new constitution

not in the parts concerned with the position of chiefs, absolutely satisfactory, but I think it is the best which could be achieved in their interest ...It may not be realised everywhere that these provisions were only achieved after considerable controversy...It is necessary at this turning point of history to count with the forces as they are and not as they should be in accordance with tradition and wishful thinking.[2]

The time has passed in which the political development of the Africans could be determined by the issues of ordinances by the Central Government. Ordinances are necessary but they are only of practical value... if they have been accepted by the people before they can be formulated by Government.[3]

The draft constitution was submitted in May 1960 to the Minister of Provincial Affairs and, through Wambura, to TANU headquarters in Dar es Salaam. 'Agreement in principle was received from both. When submitted to the Native Authority Councils in each District it was readily accepted, subject to various detailed amendments suited to local circumstances.'[4] In each district chiefs were retained as executive officers in their respective areas, but the balance of power had shifted irretrievably to TANU. Elected majorities controlled the new district councils, and the councils themselves elected their own officers. Chiefdom, subchiefdom and village councils were similarly transformed to allow for elected majorities. As TANU was 'the only organised political

[1] Cory to P.C., 16 May 1960, Cory papers.
[2] *Ibid.*
[3] Cory, 'Position of chiefs in rural N.A.'s,' n.d. (1959), p. 2, Cory papers.
[4] Lake Province Annual Report, 1960, LPF.

party of great influence', it found itself, after local elections in 1960, in control of all the councils in Sukumaland.[1]

Attempts to Revivify the Sukumaland Federal Council

The Sukumaland Federal Council, however, remained in an anomalous position. Deliberately de-emphasized by Twining and Walden and crippled by the phasing out of the Sukumaland Development Scheme and the closing of the Malya headquarters after 1954, it played a less and less significant role in Sukumaland affairs in the later 1950s. Upstaged after 1955 by the South East Lake County Council,[2] the Federal Council met perfunctorily once a year instead of the two or three times per annum it had averaged under Provincial Commissioners Hall and Rowe. Meetings required permission of the Provincial Commissioner and usually were allowed only when Walden had something which he wished to discuss. Walden downgraded the council apparently because he did not want to continue a trend toward increased power and responsibility for the chiefs if this meant—as it seemed to—more difficulties for the administration in getting across its own ideas. In the early years it was easy to use the Council as 'a sort of weapon...to implement government policy,' but as the years went by, the council began to feel that it could 'do or reject' what it liked[3]—a situation which could not easily have been countenanced by the government, least of all by Walden.

During 1958, 1959 and 1960 there were attempts to reinvigorate the Council from within. Majebere of Mwagala, Ndatura of Ntuzu, Salamba of Usule, Charles Masanja of Nera, Hussein Makwaia of Usiha and Charles Kaphipa of Bukumbi were among those appointed to a committee to study the aims of the Federation. The committee emphasized the importance of the Council for the unity and progress of Sukumaland as a whole and advanced a series of proposals to strengthen the Council.[4] These were rejected by Walden who perceived an 'inner cabinet of chiefs' taking over the function of the Council and 'aiming at being

[1] Cory to P.C., 16 May 1960, Cory papers. According to the P.C., G. T. Bell, the Cory draft constitution was distributed by the government throughout the territory. Apparently, it also became the model for African District Councils outside Sukumaland (Bell, interview, 8 Apr. 1965).

[2] For a discussion of the South East Lake County Council, see above, pp. 35–6.

[3] Chief Charles Masanja of Nera, interview, 12 Nov. 1964.

[4] Minutes of a meeting of the committee to look into the aims of the Federal Council, 3 Oct. 1958, LPF; interviews: Chiefs Charles Kaphipa, Charles Masanja, Hussein Makwaia, 6 Oct. 1964.

entirely independent of Central Government.'[1] Chief Charles of Nera indicates that the people favored the strengthening of the Council and that TANU was not necessarily opposed to the Council at that time. But it was impossible to 'get government assistance for the furtherance of any of the proposals.'[2]

By late 1959 it was clear that a more thoroughgoing examination of the future role of the Federal Council—and in particular its relationship to new African District Councils with elected majorities bent on autonomy—would be necessary. The November meeting appointed a Select Committee to draft a new constitution for the Federal Council. Unlike the 'aims' committee of the previous year, the Select Committee had a majority of councillors over chiefs. Charles Kaphipa was made chairman and, with Charles of Nera and Hussein Makwaia, the younger educated chiefs constituted a majority of the chiefly minority. The younger chiefs, plus Ndaturu of Maswa, were the principal proponents of a strengthened and up-dated council, but there was 'strong emotional feeling' among others that Sukumaland should continue to have a governing council of its own.[3] A draft constitution requesting delegation of more power to the Federal Council as opposed to separate district councils was devised.[4]

Though constitutions were being simultaneously drafted for the districts and for the Federal Council, the government made clear its intention to give precedence to the former. Districts were not advised to consider their relationships to a federal council, but the Federal Council was advised to consider its relationship to the district councils and to await the outcome of district constitutional negotiations before making final its own proposals. This determination of priorities was not at all surprising. The colonial administration had for some time considered the Council an anachronism and even Cory's proposed extension of a pyramid of councils from villages to the Legislative Council by-passed the Federal Council entirely. Furthermore, it was thought that TANU might be skeptical of the continuation of an intermediate level, tribal-based Council and, from 1959 on, TANU exercised substantial influence with regard to the structure, composition and functions of local government bodies. Though

---

[1] Walden to Chief Majebere, *et al.*, June 6, 1959, LPF.
[2] Charles Masanja, interview.   [3] *Ibid.*
[4] 'Proposed constitution of the Sukumaland Federal Council,' 7 May 1960, KWDF.

the Select Committee continued its work in the hope that a re-structured Federal Council might yet prove acceptable, the new TANU government to be formed in September 1960 as a responsible government would have to make the final decisions. Nothing fruitful could be accomplished before that time.

TANU and the Federation

In December 1960 a conference convened at Malya to discuss again the prospects for a superior council for the Sukumaland districts, but this time it was a conference not of chiefs but of representatives of TANU-dominated district councils.

All the more amazing, therefore, that the conference should recommend, as it eventually did, a new federal council! The meeting was called at the request of the Kwimba African District Council and its chairman, Sylvester Lubala. He urged the other delegations to join him in supporting the formation of a federation of districts, which would provide a way for the large Sukuma tribe 'to catch up with other tribes which have made great progress such as the Chagga.'[1] The Shinyanga delegation, led by vice-chairman of the African District Council, Shabani Mohamed, and the Mwanza delegation, led by the chairman of its Council, Stephano Sanja, supported Lubala and the Kwimba delegation on the desirability of a superior council for purposes of unity and progress. The Maswa delegation, led by J. B. Ngogeja, balked at first but eventually agreed when assured that Maswa would not be asked to contribute more than it would receive. It was decided that Geita would be invited also to join the new federation.

Provincial Commissioner Bell pointed out, however, that no guidelines had as yet been set down by the new government in Dar es Salaam. He promised to take up the matter personally with the Minister for Local Government and Housing, Rashidi Kawawa. He cautioned that the establishment of the proposed superior council would depend on the new government's views and that the earliest any new federation council could be convened would be 1962. It was agreed that a federation council would have financial and administrative powers delegated to it by the District Councils, but no other power over them.

A tentative agreement was reached that the future Federal Council should consist of delegates from the District Councils and that it should be a

[1] Minutes of a meeting to consider formation of a federation of Sukumaland districts, Malya, 5 Dec. 1960, LPF. (Orig. Sw.)

coordinating organization to advise on staff conditions and salaries, reforms of customary law, and to administer any joint services which the four Sukuma District authorities might wish to initiate.[1]

Demise of the Federal Council

By early 1961 the new government had begun to clarify its views and found that it was opposed to the continuation of any tribally based regional council. Bell has recalled that Nyerere told him late in 1960 or early 1961: 'You must break the Sukumaland Federal Council. We can't have another Katanga here.' According to Bell, Nyerere realized that the principle of 'divide and rule' would help TANU's cause in Sukumaland, but events in the Congo were even more decisive in producing his explicit directive to scuttle the Federal Council.[2] Before Katanga broke away from the rest of the Congo, the assumption in Mwanza had been that the Federal Council would continue though its projected relations to district councils were far from clear. On the other hand, the colonial administration 'always felt the Sukuma were so strong that, should they band together, and should their leaders be anti-TANU, they would have all of western Tanganyika.' Bell's view is that, Katanga aside, Nyerere would have recognized Sukuma solidarity as a potential problem for the new goverment.[3]

Though objective assessment suggests the inappropriateness of comparison between Sukumaland and Katanga, or even between Sukumaland and Buganda, it may be that such a presumed comparison was one of the factors operating in the minds of administrators and party leaders when the council proposals were finally disapproved in 1961. It seems most likely, however, that an old and somewhat anomalous regional council simply did not fit sensibly into a uniform national system of local governing bodies. The new government had decided that the best pattern of local government would be one based on district councils. After internal self-government was proclaimed in May, Bell discussed with the government the possibility of the federation continuing simply as a 'supplementary service body' and coordinator of training school programs, but the Minister for Local Government, Job Lusinde, expressed 'no enthusiasm at all.' When Bell talked with Turnbull, the Governor said simply, 'I suppose that is it.'[4]

[1] Lake Province Annual Report, 1960, LPF.
[2] Bell, interview. Bell says that the directive was oral, never written, because the government was apparently reluctant to commit the order to paper.
[3] *Ibid.*   [4] *Ibid.*

In Sukumaland no more meetings with regard to the formation of a superior council were held either by chiefs or by TANU-led district council committees. The fifteen-year history of the Sukumaland Federal Council had come to an end.

3 DYARCHY: COOPERATION AND CONFLICT

During the transition to independence, the relationships between TANU provincial and district leaders on the one hand and colonial administrative officers on the other proved markedly cooperative. The same, however, was not generally true of the relationships between TANU personnel and native authorities, especially on the more local levels. Chiefs, subchiefs and headmen, quite understandably, were unsure of their position and feared for the future. TANU stalwarts, anxious to rid themselves of the colonial era in all its manifestations, pushed early and hard for maximum reduction or elimination of the power and influence of native authorities. Then when persons with an independent bent also began to challenge TANU's local hegemony in certain areas, the strain on the body politic intensified. Some decried TANU's undemocratic tendencies; and TANU—not yet sure enough of itself to be flexible internally or tolerant of criticism from without —became increasingly authoritarian.

TANU and the Administration

Once Tanganyika's pattern of constitutional advance had been clarified, paternalism with a strong admixture of authoritarianism was no longer a tenable posture for administrators. G. T. Bell, who took over from Walden as Provincial Commissioner in July 1959, played the same role in the Lake Province during Tanganyika's rapid transition from colonial dependency to independent state that Governor Turnbull did territorially.[1] Personally, Bell had no taste for the exercise of power for its own sake and, from the point of view of policy, he believed that popularly elected majorities might have been introduced into Sukumaland a decade earlier than they were. He was, therefore, a congenial man for provincial TANU leaders to work with. He had the wit and tact

[1] Ironically, Turnbull, as Governor of Aden a few years later, played a role analogous to that of his predecessor, Governor Twining, in Tanganyika. Sir Humphrey Trevelyan replaced Turnbull as Governor to preside over Southern Yemen's accession to independence—thus becoming the 'Turnbull' of the transition there when Turnbull himself no longer could perform that function.

to understand the difficult role that enlightened TANU leaders had to play during a transition period in which they needed both to consolidate the sentiments of their constituents behind the anti-colonial independence movement and to work with the colonial administration through a final phase before 'uhuru' could be complete.

Bell abjured policy *pronunciamentos* and made every attempt to avoid the sort of public debates which might prove embarrassing either to the government or to TANU. At times of difficulty or disagreement, he found discussions in a committee or a quiet chat around a table with selected leaders an 'infinitely better' technique. On certain critical issues—as with the question of a reconstituted Sukumaland Federal Council—he delayed decisions locally until the emerging TANU government in Dar es Salaam was sure of the direction it wished to take. And he was flexible rather than rigid with regard to the time-hallowed procedures of British colonial administration. For example, when local politicians wished to by-pass a hostile District Commissioner on a particular issue, Bell did not order them to take the matter first to the District Commissioner as another administrator might have done. He told them they could bring their case directly to him if they wished but that he would then send it to the District Commissioner first anyway. Whether or not this produced substantively different results in particular instances is less important than that Bell's administrative style was such as to allow the administration and TANU to work together.

C. C. Harris, who took over the province during Bell's leave in early 1960, adopted a somewhat more flippant but equally flexible attitude. He has recalled that in his first conversation with provincial TANU secretary Wambura—when they discovered that they disagreed over some particular—Wambura said, 'But then you won't be here much longer.' Harris replied with matter-of-fact wit, 'I suppose you know more about that than I.' He pointed out that he, Harris, was a civil servant, whereas Wambura was a politician. Harris noted he had been in Tanganyika twenty-three years without ever having had to face an election whereas Wambura presumably would—at which Wambura laughed.[1] In any case, Harris was able to enlist Wambura's assistance on the *ad hoc* committee for drafting a new constitution for the Sukumaland districts and his constructive intervention in a highly

[1] Harris, interview.

explosive situation resulting from a Sukuma raid of Masai cattle in April.

Wambura and the Sukuma-Masai 'War'

For decades the Sukuma of eastern Maswa had suffered periodic raids of their cattle by Masai. Suddenly on 3 April 1960, a group of Sukuma from Kanadi chiefdom turned the tables and raided the Masai. Some 750 cattle were taken by a raiding party of about sixty persons and one Masai was killed. Five hundred Masai set out in pursuit of the raiders and the stolen cattle. Units of the Northern Province and Lake Province Field Forces were rushed to Musoma and Maswa to prevent further violence. Harris flew to meet Chief Edward of the Masai and the two, together with the District Commissioners of Monduli (Masailand) and Maswa converged on Kanadi chiefdom to which the cattle had been traced. Both the Masai and the Sukuma were present in strength but Field Force units kept them separated. A difficult period of negotiations then began.

The Sukuma eventually agreed to equitable terms for compensation of the Masai, but the details of the settlement are less important here than the way in which the settlement was reached, including TANU's role in achieving it. Apparently, Chief Mgema of Kanadi was fearful of consenting to compensation because of opposition and criticism from his own people (some of whom had conducted the raid) and especially from local political personalities who were looking for any opportunity to discredit him. Harris discussed the difficulties with Wambura and Bomani in Mwanza. He pointed out that eruption of a 'tribal war' just before independence would be very bad publicity internationally: but that if the Sukuma did not agree to the Masai's just claims for compensation, there would be no way of preventing stern Masai reprisals in the near future. Wambura and Bomani agreed that something needed to be done. As Harris reported later:

Wambura agreed to go to Maswa and make certain that local politicians did not impede negotiations. He was flown into Maswa on the afternoon of April 17th. I flew to Maswa on the morning of April 18th and held a meeting with the Chiefs that afternoon. It was immediately apparent that Wambura had succeeded in protecting their flank against petty local politicians and that they were now prepared, with some optimism, to put over proposals for compensation to the Masai along the lines suggested by me.

On the following morning I held a baraza at Maswa attended by D.C.s

Monduli and Maswa, Chief Edward and three Masai, and the Native
Authorities and District Council of Maswa. Provincial and Maswa
District T.A.N.U. representatives were present. The arguments both of
the danger of inter-tribal war and of the established custom of compensation being payable by the people of an area into which stolen stock
had been traced, were accepted. Both Masai and Sukuma spokesmen
expressed the desire for better relations between the tribes and a more
modern approach in recognition of the fact that both Masai and Sukuma
are citizens of Tanganyika...

Credit must be given to the T.A.N.U. Provincial Secretary (Mr. Wambura) for his immediate and responsible appreciation of the situation and
his intelligent and unobtrusive work at Maswa which undoubtedly was
largely responsible both for the greatly improved atmosphere at the
baraza on April 19th and for the restoration of self-confidence in the
Chiefs.[1]

Harris also praised the Sukuma Chiefs Majebere, Ndaturu and
Mgwesa of Kimali for the skilful and responsible role they played
in restoring order and in assisting the negotiations toward an
equitable settlement. It was one of the few times and one of the
last times in Tanganyikan history that colonial administrators,
chiefs and TANU leaders worked together in the solution of a
major crisis.

On other occasions, too, Wambura intervened on the side of
moderation and sensible government. In one of its first sessions in
the later months of 1960, the newly elected Maswa African District
Council decided to amend its constitution (based on the draft
prepared by the *ad hoc* committee and approved by the government and TANU headquarters in Dar es Salaam) by abolishing
subchiefs. The councillors also dismissed all agricultural instructors and veterinary guards, doubled the local rate without
first consulting the people, voted themselves 25-shilling overnight
allowances and advances from treasury funds, and ordered building
materials for ten new primary schools without ascertaining the
probable availability of teachers to run them. Bell asked Wambura
(who was also then the Member of the Legislative Council from
Maswa), to talk with the councillors. Wambura did, but he was
not able to convince the council that its unilateral actions were
unacceptable. The Maswa Council continued to be difficult
throughout the year and only strong directives from African
Ministers in Dar es Salaam eventually succeeded in curbing
some of its more excessive inclinations. In another instance the

[1] Harris, 'The raid and the search,' pp. 3–5, a paper kindly shown me by the
author.

Mwanza District Commissioner reported that a local council in the district had come very close to voting itself out of existence 'largely due to some highly impassioned but generally very reasonable criticism of its effectiveness by Mr Wambura.'[1]

In general, Wambura maneuvered effectively in his difficult 'in-between' position *vis-à-vis* rearguard colonial administrators and impatient nationalists. In the Tanganyika of the transition he was known on both sides as a skilful and tactful operator. While he undoubtedly had to be responsive to the attitudes struck by local TANU personnel, he minimized unnecessary conflict with the administration. While he fully shared the passionate striving for dignity, self-expression and independence which inspired his contemporaries, he regretted at times the behavior of local TANU organizers and district councillors and took a strong line with them when he felt it to be necessary. Unlike some of his less far-sighted colleagues, Wambura understood the need for maintaining the authority of the central government at a time when power was being devolved into African hands in Dar es Salaam.

In fact, in less than two years much had already changed. At the end of 1959, Harris had written:

The year commenced with a fairly high degree of local political tension throughout most of the Province, and incidents of the 1958 pattern continued on a less frequent and more localized scale until mid-March. . .

Politically, the Tanganyika African National Union found it difficult to ensure conformity with the party line except in the general demand for responsible government. Local officials not infrequently embarrassed the organization by fire-eating speeches as well as by low standards of financial integrity. . .

[With the acceptance] of constitutional reforms whereby the Chiefs would be ex officio members of councils consisting of a majority of representative councillors. . . coupled with the general satisfaction with Territorial Constitutional progress, the Province witnessed a progressive relaxation of local tension and the year closed in a period of comparative calm and cooperation.[2]

A year later Bell was able to report:

The general outcome of [the year's] important developments, enabling the people to manage their own affairs, together with the general satisfaction with territorial constitutional progress and the forceful line adopted by local T.A.N.U. leaders in conformity with the party line, has led to even greater political calm and greater cooperation between the

[1] D.C. to P.C., 25 Feb. 1960, MZDF.
[2] Lake Province Annual Report, 1959, LPF.

public and Government representatives than at the end of the previous
year.[1]

National and provincial leaders urged their constituents to
obey their chiefs because chiefs had now accepted TANU policies
and to cooperate with non-Africans who were prepared to assist
TANU attain its object of self-government. They urged the people
to work harder, pay their taxes, and interest themselves in the
economic development of their country. At times even TANU
organizations below the provincial level earned the admiration of
their latter-day colonial administrators who expressed appreciation
for TANU's 'sane counsels,' 'good race relationships' and generally 'cooperative attitude' in every district.[2]

Elected Councillors versus Chiefs

Because everyone knew by late 1959 that colonial administrative
staff would not long remain in the territory, conflict between
European administrators and African nationalists moderated.
Among Africans, however, conflict sometimes intensified. With
the principal pre-independence battle against the British all but
won, intramural rivalries began to surface. Especially where it was
easy to label individuals in terms of a presumed identification
with the old order or with the new, and where there were those
who were anxious to apply the labels and mete out recriminations
or perquisites accordingly, conflict appeared. While the transition
to independence went relatively smoothly at the provincial level
because the administrators were bowing out and knew it and
because TANU leaders at this level were relatively secure personally in their own positions, within the districts a very different
sort of struggle was taking place.

TANU, of course, carried the message of freedom to the people
in the villages and often this task was performed with responsibility
as well as with passion. District councils, too, though they made
many errors of commission and omission, groped their way toward
standards of efficiency and public service. On the other hand,
TANU officers and TANU-sponsored district councillors were
sometimes men of dubious personal qualifications. Some fought

---

[1] Lake Province Annual Report, 1960, LPF.
[2] Kwimba District Annual Report, 1959, KWDF; Annual Report Madja
Planned Settlement Area, Geita, 1959, GTDF; Agriculture Department
Annual Report, Geita, 1960, GTDF; Shinyanga District Annual Report,
1959, SHDF; Mwanza District Annual Report, 1960, MZDF.

among themselves for leadership, influence, money and power; some sought to prevail against the District Commissioner and his 'stooges,' the chiefs, in every conceivable legal and illegal way.

In the two years before independence, relations especially between TANU partisans and native authorities at district level and below were touchy and difficult. One group was in ascendance, the other in decline. As the District Commissioner of Kwimba reported at the end of 1959:

The influence of TANU has spread steadily throughout the District and although the paid membership is still comparatively small compared to the number of taxpayers, there is little doubt that it exercises greater influence than the traditional Native Authorities.[1]

The District Commissioner of Maswa reported in 1960:

prior to the first meeting of the new Council, most of the Chiefs and Native Authorities deliberately withdrew from the political arena and resolutely refused to enforce any measure likely to prove unpopular. This attitude was revealed in many forms including desultory revenue collection, failure to assist in the recruitment of paid labour for road work, delays in the building of cattle crushes for the rinderpest campaign and a tendency to refer 'difficult' cases...to the Subordinate Court...At this time there was no doubt that the influence of the Chiefs and Native Authorities over their people declined, and the structure of local administration was proportionately weakened.[2]

The same was true to a greater or lesser degree in all the districts. It became increasingly clear to all that the future lay entirely with TANU. In the meantime, however, opportunities both for constructive progress and for damaging detours presented themselves to TANU enthusiasts.

Some of the excesses of the first sessions of the Maswa African District Council—including the premature attempt to eliminate all subchieftaincies—have been mentioned. From the beginning, the Maswa council was the most extreme of all the councils on the question of native authorities.[3] One may surmise that Maswa's volatility in 1960 arose from pent-up grievances against some of the most conservative and formidable of Sukumaland's chiefs. The situation was aggravated, too, by the character of Maswa's District Commissioner, A. N. Baillie. Baillie served in Maswa

[1] Kwimba District Annual Report, 1959, KWDF.
[2] Maswa District Annual Report, 1960, MADF.
[3] Though in Geita, of course, native authorities had lost any effective power in 1958–9.

X

an unusually long time—from early 1954 to mid-1960—and, according to Bell, Maswa endured under his leadership the most authoritarian rule of all the Sukumaland districts. When a popularly elected majority took control of the African District Council in 1960, its exuberance, therefore, was difficult to suppress.

In February 1961 the Maswa council passed a resolution suspending Chief Ndaturu of Ntuzu and sent a letter to Chief Minister Nyerere informing him of the action. Why Ndaturu was selected for special attention is not entirely clear. For years he had shared with Majebere the leadership of the Maswa chiefs; probably by 1961 he was more active and more powerful than Majebere himself. If so, he was the chief most likely to be resented. It should also be recalled that it was Ndaturu who had tangled most openly with TANU leader Kaseko in mid-1954, and that that encounter had led to Kaseko's conviction and imprisonment.[1] Kaseko was now vice-chairman of the African District Council and, since late 1959, re-installed as chairman of Maswa TANU. One may surmise that the settling of old accounts, together with contemporary irritations, figured in the attempt to suspend Ndaturu. The attempt failed, however, because the council had no power to order such a suspension. The District Commissioner informed the council that only the Governor had such power, that the council's resolution was therefore 'illegal' and 'invalid,' and that 'Chief Ndaturu should be informed by you in writing at once that he should resume his seat in the Council.'[2]

In Shinyanga District—which avoided the overt disturbances of 1958 and, like Nera chiefdom in Kwimba, combined strong traditional native authority structures with well-educated and forward-looking chiefs—the chiefs had great difficulty adjusting to the new distribution of power. In January 1960 the District Commissioner warned chiefs that dismissal by them of headmen without consulting the African District Council 'is not appreciated.'[3] He suggested that it would be better for the appropriate committee of the council to make dismissals on the recommendation of the chief. During the first session of the new Shinyanga African District Council later in 1960, 'the twenty ex officio members (i.e., chiefs and subordinate native authorities) staged a walkout of the Council.' The District Commissioner reported:

---

[1] See above, pp. 176–8.
[2] D.C. to Chairman of Maswa African Council, 23 Feb. and 2 Mar., 1961, MZDF.   [3] D.C. to all Chiefs, 9 Jan. 1960, SHDF. (Orig. Sw.)

Ex officio members complained of steamroller tactics by the elected members, the putting of questions to the vote without adequate discussion, that all real debate was taking place beforehand in the TANU office and that attendance at the Council, being purely a formality, was a waste of time. The Chiefs had also been put out of their 'dignified' chairs and made to sit at the back of the chamber like 'message boys.'[1]

The District Commissioner tried to mediate but the breach was not healed. As in other districts, matters remained for some time in a state of suspension because plans for the future of local government administration had not yet been formulated in detail by the TANU leadership in Dar es Salaam. At the end of 1961, 'one Chief was still suspended, one Subchief was awaiting the Minister's decision on his appeal against dismissal, and two Chiefdoms were controlled by Regents, the Minister's approval for elections to choose new Chiefs not having been obtained.' The Shinyanga council provisionally appointed two of its own members as regents in Kizumbi and Uchunga, but 'the people refused to accept them and they withdrew themselves.' Some chiefs, however, continued to play 'a useful part in Council business and the important post of Chairman of the Finance and General Purposes Committee was held by a Chief.'[2]

Elections for Subchiefs

In Mwanza, meanwhile, an attempt was made to avert an open struggle between chiefs and council over who was to control the appointment and dismissal of subchiefs by consulting the people directly. In 1961 elections were held for subchief in all but two of the district's chiefdoms. Leading members of the Council supervised the proceedings and from two to four candidates stood in each contest. Winners were then appointed by the Council, subject to approval by the Provincial Commissioner.

This election may well have been unique in Tanganyika: it was subsequently decided in Dar es Salaam that election of administrators—as distinct from councillors—was not appropriate to the evolving pattern of local government. It is of considerable interest, therefore, to note the results of these unique elections in which people at the grass roots—in the very midst of the transition to independence—directly expressed their views as to who should administer their local affairs. And the people had a real choice

[1] D.C. to P.C., 24 Sept. 1960, SHDF.
[2] Shinyanga District Annual Report on Rural Local Government, 1961, SHDF.

(of the sort which they did not exercise again until 1965) because a variety of candidates stood for election to each of the available subchief positions. The successful candidates ranged in age from twenty-six to fifty-two, in education from Standard IV to Standard IX. Most had had experience as agricultural instructors, tax clerks or teachers. Some had previously served as headmen, and one as a Deputy Chief. Some were related to the traditional ruling families in their areas, others were not. Only one of the successful candidates had previously served as a TANU official.

Thus, no pattern can be deduced from the results except that persons primarily identified professionally with TANU did not figure as prominently as might have been expected on the basis of their omnipresence at higher levels of the evolving body politic. In spite of the fact that enthusiasm for independence and commitment to TANU was very high in early 1961, local people expressed a preference in these elections for men known to them and of proven experience—even if this included some taint of service under the colonial regime. In part, this preference reflected the incompleteness even then of TANU's penetration and control at the most local level; in part, it indicated that the people recognized, despite their commitment to TANU, that the ablest candidates were not likely to be those who possessed TANU credentials alone. That TANU itself recognized this became apparent when, in 1962 and 1963, TANU-controlled district councils made appointments of divisional executive officers (who then replaced chiefs and subchiefs) along lines remarkably similar to the preferences expressed by the people of Mwanza in the anomalous elections for subchiefs in March 1961.

The Geita 'Parliament'

The internal struggle between councils and native authorities which dominated the affairs of the other Sukumaland districts during 1960–1 did not occur in Geita where it had, in effect, already taken place two years earlier. Most of the chiefs had resigned following the uprising of 1958, and those that had been permitted to remain in office were reduced in status and powers to executive officers in their chiefdoms. Where there had been resignations, new chiefs were eventually elected, but only as figureheads devoid of any real power under the local government constitution. Geita had an African Council with an elected majority in 1959—a year before the other districts—after the dissolution of the ill-fated multi-racial council of 1958. The new council 'conducted its affairs conscientiously and with dignity,' though the council frequently did 'revert back to its old recriminations against the Chiefs and others' who had supported the multi-racial council the previous year.[1]

The year 1960, however, was 'a year of improved cooperation' between the government, the council and the people;[2] and as the Geita council gained experience, it became an exemplar to the other districts. Geita was fortunate, too, to have during this period of transition a most tactful and farsighted District Commissioner, R. S. King. Like Turnbull and Bell at territorial and provincial levels, he brought to Geita a much-needed ingredient of flexibility, patience and genuine interest in and understanding of the hopes and aspirations as well as the strengths and weaknesses of Geita's leaders and citizens.

King had his problems with the constituent assembly in 1959 when there were some very 'stormy'[3] sessions. A year later, however, on the basis of his own very effective work in Geita, King was able to advise other District Commissioners about how to overcome strained relationships between the newly elected councils and the administration:

1. He had found it effective to appeal to the pride, individual and collective, of the councillors.
2. It had become important to form the personal acquaintance of the councillors and to resort to lobbying on important issues.
3. It was effective to express confidence in the good faith of councillors when they expressed their intention of working for the public good.
4. If possible, any common religious interests should be exploited and every effort should be made to solemnize the meetings.[4]

Perhaps these are common and obvious principles for building and maintaining effective human relationships. But, in the context of past practice and psychology in colonial administration—where crisp, direct, authoritarian officials like Walden, French and Baillie were more the rule than the exception, and where as Gavin Green has put it, 'the prefect type of administration that

---

[1] Lake Province Annual Report, 1959, LPF. The *liwali* of Geita, Petro Nyanga, provoked displeasure when he was found to have written a letter to the colonial government denouncing Nyerere, Bomani and TANU and asking that the British Government retain control of the country indefinitely.
[2] Lake Province Annual Report, 1960. LPF.
[3] King, interview, Nov. 1963 and Apr. 1965.
[4] Notes on a Provincial Conference of District Commissioners, Sept. 1960, GTDF.

you get in [English] public schools: law and order, rough justice, day to day administration'[1] tended to carry the day—King's recommendations were little short of revolutionary. They marked him a wise man among his peers.

King exercised leadership by advising, rather than by directing. He was willing to talk at any length with anyone and he worked quietly behind the scenes to accomplish his objectives. The initiative in Geita had, since 1958, been in the hands of the politicians, but King found this desirable as a training ground for the future rather than an intolerable break with the past. He worked effectively within this context and apparently enjoyed the confidence of the African leadership in Geita.[2] African leaders, while indicating with a smile that King was 'very clever,' have expressed genuine appreciation for his work in the district and especially with the Council in its earliest phase.

The Geita Council, in any case, was the first of the new African District Councils in Sukumaland to mature. It had the vitality of leaders fresh from a successful assault on the administration over the question of 'Mseto.' It had a one-year head start on the other councils. It benefited from King's farsighted and unostentatious assistance. By 1961 it had become a 'little Parliament' in the best sense. With native authorities no longer a political force and with the District Commissioner more concerned about the training of responsible leaders for the new Tanganyika than with working his own will on the inhabitants, the District Council in Geita was more fully *the* government than was true in any of the other districts. Within the Council a nucleus of top leaders became more or less a cabinet. This group made the major decisions on matters of policy, then sought support from the council as a whole, negotiating with the District Commissioner where necessary.[3]

Dar es Salaam: Guidelines before Policy

Even in Geita, however, the early phase of the development of the District Councils was marred by an inability of councillors

[1] Gavin Green, interview.
[2] Simon Hardwick, interview, 3 Dec. 1964. Hardwick served as an administrative officer with King in Geita.
[3] Hardwick, interview. As chairman and secretary of TANU respectively, Wilson Bunuma and Augustine Madaha had influence in the district, but they did not dominate the affairs of the council as did, for example, TANU chairman Kaseko in Maswa or TANU secretary Mohamed in Shinyanga.

to define the limits of their proper powers in relation to the central government and to the still extant native authorities. This was a disease from which all the councils suffered. Chief Minister Nyerere found it necessary to remind the five Sukumaland councils that a distinction was necessary between elected policy-makers in the councils and the civil servants who were not elected but who served as executors of policy. He told the councils that chiefs in local councils were the district's and the council's executive officers and 'must be given powers to enable them to perform their duties efficiently.'[1] At about the same time, however, a local newspaper reported that councillors 'are going about in the villages telling people that they are more important than the local authorities... They are already presuming to solicit people's goats, chickens, and beer and to take bribes.'[2] Government reports from the same period indicate that elected councillors had a tendency illegally to appropriate judicial functions in their home areas.

After internal self-government in May, the new Minister for Local Government, Job Lusinde, told representatives in Mwanza that while it was the Ministry's policy that Local Councils should be given more powers, a council would first have to demonstrate it was efficient and that it had responsible councillors. He stressed that councillors' duties were not executive and warned that they should not usurp the duties of, nor misguidedly compete for authority with, chiefs and other executive officials. He noted that some councillors demanded unreasonably large allowances and sometimes allocated themselves offices and living quarters at the council headquarters rather than living at home where they might better be in touch with the people in their own constituencies. He criticized careless budgeting and expenditures and the propensity of some to prolong meetings unnecessarily in order to draw big allowances. Lusinde, who had himself served as Executive Officer to the Ugogo Council in 1959–61, emphasized that administrative officers were not assigned to councils 'to interfere but to advise them in administrative and financial matters and to see that they spent their funds properly' and to provide a 'link between the Central and Local Government.'[3]

While District Councils pressed ahead as quickly as possible

[1] Nyerere statement to representatives of the Sukumaland district councils, 16 Mar. 1961. LPF.
[2] *Lumuli*, No. 189, Apr. 1961. (Original Sukuma)
[3] Ministry of Local Government to all Rural Local Authorities, 8 May 1961, SHDF; D.C. to P.C., 24 Aug. 1961, LPF.

with the curtailment of the powers of headmen, subchiefs and chiefs, the new government in Dar es Salaam remained un-committed on the future status of native authorities. In May 1961 the Minister for Local Government announced that it was 'Government's policy to establish as soon as possible efficient rural Local Authorities...of the type and standard which modern conditions require.'[1] Specifically, the councils would have authority over all persons regardless of race rather than over Africans alone. They would have more statutory powers than District Councils under the old Native Authority Ordinance had enjoyed. But would the entire membership of the new Councils be elected? And what of the chiefs? As late as October 1961, Prime Minister Nyerere said to the territorial chiefs' convention that he felt 'it would be very unwise to make any policy statement at present' on the position of chief.[2] Even on the eve of independence, the Minister for Local Government noted that 'several Councils continue to assume to themselves the power to dismiss Chiefs and Sub-chiefs who are Court holders.' In a circular he said he wished it to be understood

that Chiefs are not ordinary employees of Councils who may be dismissed like other employees according to the terms of Staff Regulations. The reason for their special position is that they exercise responsibility for the maintenance of law and order and are answerable in this respect to Central Government. The Minister, therefore, wishes Councils to be reminded that they do not have the power either to suspend or to dismiss Chiefs...It must now be made absolutely clear that no Subchief, who is also a Court holder, may be dismissed unless and until the prior approval of the Provincial Commissioner has been obtained.[3]

Thus, during 1961, while local councillors fought for greater power, Provincial and District Commissioners, in cooperation with TANU's African Ministers, insisted on restraining the councils and on preserving the authority of central government. However, while TANU leadership in Dar es Salaam strove to clarify the future direction of local government institutions before pronoun-cing on matters of overall policy, tensions and ambiguities abounded in the districts. Though certain guidelines were established, within

[1] P.C. to D.C.'s, 2 June 1961, SHDF.
[2] Report on Tanganyika Chiefs' Convention, 2 Oct. 1961, KWDF.
[3] Ministry of Local Government circular, LG/01, 24 Nov. 1961. I am indebted to A. J. Dixon, then of the Local Government Training Centre, Mzumbe, for providing me access to relevant circulars from the Ministry of Local Government for the immediate pre- and post-independence years.

the confines of these structures a council could do much. If it could not dismiss someone outright, it could—and often did—render that person completely ineffective. The Maswa Council, for example, tried to dismiss its secretary and was told it could not. It then tried to suspend him pending a decision from the Minister for Local Government and was told it could not. It then refused to cooperate with its secretary for the last six months of 1961 and eventually the Minister agreed to his dismissal. Also in 1961 the Maswa Council amalgamated village units and reduced the number of headmen from 283 to 153. While most of the changes were approved by the District Commissioner, he questioned a few with the result that he was told somewhat brusquely: 'Remember that the headmen who will be appointed are only those who were approved by the Council...This is a decision of the Finance Committee and must be followed.'[1] In Maswa and Kwimba deputy chiefs were replaced with court holders (hakimu) appointed by the Council. The Provincial Commissioner asked why only three of eight selected in Maswa were former deputy chiefs when Minister Kawawa had told the Council in March that existing deputies should be given first consideration for the new posts. The reply was that the others were illiterate or too elderly.

Restrained only in part and only for the moment, District Councils would achieve their aims more fully after independence. In 1962 all chiefs would be asked by the government to resign and District Councils would take over primary responsibility for the appointment and dismissal of executive officials in their districts.

Rivalry in Kwimba

In Kwimba the official relationship between Chief Charles Masanja of Nera and Peter C. Walwa, the district chairman of TANU, gave illustration of the tensions and differences which the time of transition inevitably produced—even among exceptional and sophisticated men who were personally on friendly terms.

The large chiefdom of Nera, located in the heart of Sukumaland, had been ably administered for many years. It was conservative in the sense that the native authorities were traditionally based and enjoyed strong support from the people. It was progressive in that its chiefs were well-educated, non-authoritarian, interested in development and capable of looking toward the future. This combination of factors contributed to delay in the emergence of

[1] Secretary of Maswa African District Council to D.C., 3 Aug. 1961, MADF.

protest politics in Nera during the 1950s. TAA and TANU activity, for example, were virtually non-existent—even in Ngudu —before the ban in 1954. In 1958 when other chiefdoms in the district—Usmao, Sima, Magu and Ndagalu—joined much of the rest of Sukumaland in campaigns of civil disobedience, Nera, like most of Shinyanga, remained quiescent. While cattle dips were being boycotted in Usmao in late 1968, more dips were being constructed in Nera. While Geita chiefs found they could no longer control subjects who were alien to them, while some Maswa chiefs reaped in sudden protest the rewards of years of authoritarian rigidity, and while weak and inefficient chiefs in rivalry ridden chiefdoms in Mwanza and northern Kwimba discovered that political ferment was the easy by-product of internal disintegration and modern influences from nearby Mwanza town, Masanja's position in Nera remained secure. His political genius, his rare human qualities, his unusual capacity as an administrator, and his willingness (while critical of TANU in some respects) to identify with the national surge for freedom and progress, were even more clearly demonstrated in the years after 1958 when he succeeded personally in bridging the change-over from colonial to independent government.[1]

In the 1950s in Nera as elsewhere, criticism was leveled against the traditional system of cultivation requirements. In late 1958 complaints (about unpaid labor and other matters) multiplied as political tensions grew and native authorities came under increasing criticism. For example, Chief Charles reported 'an expressed opinion' to do away with the citizens' yearly donation of food to the chief (*sikule*) so that he might 'fulfil his traditional functions.' Charles's handling of this matter was typical of his rational and pragmatic approach to the sorts of problems which became political dynamite elsewhere. Charles wrote to the District Commissioner:

I have no strong opinion on this. The matter is wholly in the hands of the people to decide which traditions they would wish me to keep... The matter was reported to me by the TANU Chairman (Walwa) and I have instructed Subchiefs to check on it and report to me in detail. I would not like to see such a thing turn into a political situation. What I want is a

[1] Chief Charles Masanja received a diploma in engineering from Makerere College and while still a young man assumed the chiefship of Nera in 1950 after the premature death of his elder brother, Balele. For a discussion of Chief Charles' administration in the 1950s, see Liebenow, *Journal of African Administration*, XI, No. 2 (Apr. 1959), 84–92.

sincere expressed opinion of the people so that I am not liable to blame whichever conclusion I decide to take.[1]

Late in 1959, Walwa vigorously protested Charles's selection of a new subchief by personal appointment rather than by popular election. The District Commissioner supported Charles on the basis of government policy as it existed at the time. He told Walwa that if he considered the method of choosing subchiefs out of date, he should bring the matter before a committee which was soon to discuss constitutional changes. On the other hand, subchiefs reported to Charles that certain TANU officials mishandled the affairs of the party in their areas. In such instances Charles sought to talk personally with all concerned and to discuss the matter as well with TANU chairman Walwa. In November 1959, however, he found it necessary to report to the District Commissioner that he and his subchiefs were often not informed in advance of TANU meetings as the law required and that 'much of the discussion in these meetings appears to foster ill-feeling between the citizens and native authorities.' He asked that no public meetings be permitted in Nera until some better understanding had been reached between native authorities, the government and TANU. Proposing a meeting with the District Commissioner on the question, Charles emphasized that he desired a 'good relationship' between the political party and the native authorities and that a peaceful atmosphere of both thoughts and words should be preserved.[2]

In 1960 and 1961 Charles himself undertook extended safaris in an active attempt to mitigate political tensions and misunderstandings, to publicize local and national developments, and to involve ordinary citizens therein. Indeed, the daily meetings in successive villages over weeks at a time approximated in style and thoroughness the safari technique inaugurated earlier by TANU leaders.

Thus Walwa and Charles often disagreed or were at cross-purposes institutionally during the sensitive transitional period, but both were able to carve out for themselves a continuing role in post-independence Tanzania. Walwa's course, as a militant TANU leader, was less replete with possible stumbling blocks than Charles's, the prominent chief. But with intelligence, flexibility and a sense of the future, Charles continued to serve his nation

[1] Chief Charles to D.C., Oct. 1959, KWDF.
[2] Chief Charles to D.C., 14 July and 9 Nov. 1959, KWDF. (Orig. Sw.)

after independence in a variety of important government posts. Few other chiefs have done so.

4   INCIPIENT OPPOSITION

TANU had not been in operation in Sukumaland a year before the first signs of organized dissent appeared. It is difficult to know in given instances what factors prompted opposition to TANU by a particular individual or group in a particular area at a particular time. The African National Congress, of course, had been formed in 1958 under Mtemvu's leadership, but no signs of the Congress appeared in Sukumaland until 1960. The year 1959 was a honeymoon year for TANU in Sukumaland: banned for four years, it attracted virtually everyone to its banner when it was finally permitted to open. The disenchantment of some, however, was the inevitable by-product of the struggles which took place locally both among TANU personnel and between TANU on the one hand and native authorities and other independent-minded persons on the other.

The Saidia Waafrika Company

The first major disaffection began as an economic rather than a political movement. In fact, the leader of the new movement, Samson Masalu, served as a member of the TANU District Committee in Kwimba during 1959. Masalu was a trader who had worked for some years as a clerk at Indian-owned and -operated cotton-buying posts. Some have said he nursed a grudge against the highly successful Victoria Federation of Cooperative Unions for putting him out of a job when the Indian buyers were displaced. He himself maintains that his sole concern was to provide improved marketing arrangements for cotton growers. In any case, he found himself opposed to the monopoly on cotton buying which the VFCU, with government approval, began to operate in 1959. He held a few meetings in Kwimba to protest the monopoly during the 1959 buying season and, as a result, apparently experienced difficulty in marketing his own cotton at VFCU buying posts that year.

In April 1960, on the eve of the new cotton-buying season, Masalu held a new series of meetings in his home chiefdom of Usmao to discuss the problem of the VFCU's cotton monopoly.

In the following months he extended the scope of his operations. By June he had procured incorporation of his company, which he called Saidia Waafrika (Assist Africans). He then applied to the Agriculture Department in Dar es Salaam for registration as a cotton buyer. He claimed the support of 4,500 persons in the Usmao and Ndagalu chiefdoms alone and scattered support in seven other districts. He applied to officials for permission 'to start at once either building new stores or renting disused stores from ginners at a number of named places in the Kwimba, Maswa, Geita, Ukerewe and Musoma Districts, in order that his Company might start buying cotton...by the 4th July 1960.' His request was denied because 'all primary buying should be done by Co-operative Societies,' and his organization did not meet the requirements of the Cooperative Societies Ordinance.[1]

Masalu's principal argument, and the touchstone of his appeal, was his criticism of the VFCU as being top-heavy with internal expenses which made it impossible to give growers a fair price for their cotton. Though no specific price was yet determined, Masalu indicated he would pay significantly higher prices than the VFCU's price for 1960 of $-/50$ per pound. No one was more aware than the growers that the price for cotton had declined from a high of $-/62$ per pound in 1955, to $-/52$ in 1959, to $-/50$ in 1960. This was less the responsibility of the VFCU (which had, incidentally, profited in popularity when a steep rise brought the price from $-/50$ to $-/62$ in 1954) than a reflection of the world market and, specifically, of price determinations by the Tanganyika Lint and Seed Marketing Board. Yet sophisticated reasoning by growers was not to be expected—especially when it could be observed that officials of the VFCU profited personally from the cooperative movement which they administered. Further, the difference between the price paid to the VFCU by the ginners and the price paid by the VFCU to the growers was $-/11$—an amount which seemed reasonable to the VFCU and unreasonable to its critics.[2]

Whatever the merits of the arguments on either side, D. H. Drennan, Assistant Director of Agriculture for the Lake Province, reported at the end of June:

[1] Assistant Director of Agriculture, Lake Province, to Director of Agriculture, Dar es Salaam, 29 June 1960, LPF.

[2] The $-/11$ was divided as follows: $-/02$ to the Native Authorities in the form of a cotton cess; $-/01$ to the Federation; $-/03$ to the Union; $-/05$ to the local society.

The sudden appearance of this Company, just at the beginning of the cotton buying season, had led to a complete break-down of existing arrangements for marketing and ginning; practically no cotton has been bought to date and no ginnery has yet obtained sufficient supplies of cotton to start work...It has become increasingly obvious...that growers were unwilling to start selling their cotton until they had first seen for themselves whether they would be able to obtain higher prices from the Saidia Waafrika Company and that even members [of the VFCU] would not willingly start deliveries to the Cooperative Societies until an authoritative statement could be made that Saidia Waafrika Company was not going to be able to buy during the 1960 season.[1]

In these circumstances, Emmanuel Bomani, who took over from his older brother Paul as General Manager of the VFCU in early 1960, requested—after consultations with the Minister for Social and Cooperative Development, George Kahama—that the government promulgate an order specifying that 'no cotton buying license be issued to any applicant other than a member Society of the Victoria Federation in all Districts of the Lake Province.'[2] Drennan, together with the Provincial Commissioner, decided to support this request and issued a statement to the effect that Saidia Waafrika 'will not be in a position to purchase any cotton legally during the present 1960 season.'[3] Saidia Waafrika was permitted to hold meetings but enjoined from stating that the company was in a position to purchase cotton that year. Masalu and his lieutenants held meetings in Kwimba and elsewhere at which they encouraged members to sell through the existing cooperative societies in 1960 but to anticipate the registration of the company as a cotton buyer in 1961. But later in the buying season he complained that some of his members were again being turned away from VFCU buying posts, and that his company was 'fighting for economic freedom—suppression of monopoly and nothing else.'[4]

Indeed, Drennan requested favorable consideration by the administration for Saidia Waafrika for subsequent years:

We have a certain amount of sympathy with the avowed aim of the Company, which is to give the cotton growing public of the Province a better reward for their efforts than they seem to be getting at the moment from the Victoria Federation. All reports received indicate that there is considerable public support for the Company, as well as considerable

[1] *Ibid.*   [2] *Ibid.*
[3] Drennan to all Agriculture Department officers and D.C.s, 29 June 1960, LPF.
[4] Masalu to Drennan, 25 July 1960, LPF.

dissatisfaction with the amounts being deducted by the Federation from the 'delivered to ginnery' price...We would be grateful if...you could give consideration to the possibility of the Saidia Waafrika movement being registered as a Cooperative Society, to participate in the primary buying of Lake Region cotton, in addition to the Victoria Federation, in future years. This would provide an outlet for the legitimate aspirations of dissatisfied members of the Victoria Federation and also for the considerable proportion of cotton growers who were not members of the Federation at the time agreement was reached with the Lake Province Ginners' Association to the effect that the Federation would carry out all primary marketing of cotton in the Province from 1959 onwards. Even last year non-members complained 'loud and long' about having to sell to the Federation and the opposition TANU seems to make it apparent that they are not taking sides in this purely internal dispute among the African cotton growers.[1]

A Consolidated Response: the VFCU and TANU

Impressed, apparently, by the potency of the threat from Saidia Waafrika, the VFCU issued a lengthy Swahili broadsheet entitled 'Ukweli Uko Wapi?' (Where is the Truth?). The circular described the process by which cotton prices were determined and ridiculed Saidia Waafrika for promising to buy cotton at 1 shilling per pound (a price which 'cannot be found anywhere in the world ...') and for making false promises. The principal burden of the circular, however, was to suggest that the Saidia Waafrika had really been founded and operated by non-Africans and that its African mouthpieces, including the president, were untrustworthy individuals who had been previously dismissed from other jobs. The circular explained that 'it is clear that this Company is being run by non-Africans...who contribute funds and teach their employees to stir up difficulties between the Unions and the growers.' In a transparent attempt to capitalize on anti-Asian sentiment, which had been such an important springboard of the cooperative movement in the early 1950s, the VFCU circular continued:

Why are...non-Africans helping this Company?

Because these non-Africans are not pleased to see Africans progressing in trade. Their aim is to further the commercial ambitions of their own race by trampling down African initiatives in commerce.

Saidia Waafrika replied with its own circular entitled 'Kweli ikisimama uongo hujitenga' (When truth stands falsehood runs

[1] Assistant Director of Agriculture, Lake Province, to Director of Agriculture, Dar es Salaam, 29 June 1960, LPF.

away). Having suffered from arguments *ad hominem* in the VFCU
circular, Saidia Waafrika responded in kind. It suggested that the
VFCU was a union 'for non-Africans mainly Englishmen'—the
same Englishmen whom Tanganyika Africans were now trying to
chase from the country. It denied that Saidia Waafrika had anything to do with non-Africans, arguing that if non-Africans were
behind it, Saidia Waafrika would not be in such an 'impoverished
state' and 'should not have failed to get an office and office equipment and other things such as motor vehicles and funds for our
employees' salaries.' Acknowledging that the president of Saidia
Waafrika (Masalu) was not a well-educated man, it proceeded to
make some comments intended to capitalize on resentment against
Paul Bomani's personal success. In an obvious reference to
Bomani's studies in England which were partly supported by
donations from cooperative societies, the circular said:

Others got their education from contributions of different sources...
and this can be termed farmers' sweat.

The circular continued:

We are fighting for the benefit of our poor farmers so that they may get
their rights instead of feeding the big stomachs of others...Our need is
to seek freedom for the farmer with his crops, not to live in a comfortable
house, to dress as Europeans, to eat rich foods, to have a fine car, and to
boast. These things bring pride to those debased persons.

The circular emphasized that Saidia Waafrika was proceeding
in line with legal requirements, which was the reason it had been
unable to purchase cotton as promised during 1960. Though the
company did not know what its status would be six months hence,
it had no intention of abandoning its fight for 'public justice
since we know where the truth is.' Claiming no dispute with
either TANU or the Central government but only with the
VFCU, Saidia Waafrika concluded:

It is not right to rule a person with his own sweat. Such things caused all
political leaders in African to cry out against governments which were not
fulfilling the desires of the people. Although the Saidia Waafrika Company
is being frightened with boycott, we are quite sure we have no enemies...
We are much obliged to all members wherever they are who cooperate
and cry out for freedom in selling their crops. And without intimidation,
after a short time, we shall succeed. Intimidation and discrimination are
the things which are contrary to civilization.[1]

[1] Both circulars were in the form of printed handbills, n.d., LPF. (Orig. Sw.)

Here, indeed, was the language of protest being applied for the first time in Sukumaland by Africans of the new political generation against other Africans of the new political generation. Carried to such a point, and given the historically based and continuing affinities between the cooperative movement, now institutionalized in the VFCU, and the nationalist political movement, now institutionalized in TANU, what had begun as an economically inspired movement could hardly help but eventually become political. Just as Bomani had had to deal politically with the central government to get the cooperative movement organized in the early 1950s, so Masalu would now have to deal with the central government—which was passing in 1960-1 from the hands of the colonial administration to TANU—to accomplish anything with Saidia Waafrika. As early as June, Drennan had anticipated some of the possible political ramifications of the Saidia Waafrika protest:

It is felt that public dissatisfaction with the existing cotton marketing arrangements may well be sufficiently strong for it to become an important issue in the forthcoming elections, should any African candidates in opposition to the TANU list which, for the Lake Province, includes prominent members of the Victoria Federation, make their appearance before the closing date for nominations.[1]

As the potential political, as well as economic, implications of the VFCU–Saidia Waafrika conflict became apparent, it did not take long for the TANU leadership to make up its mind. On the radio and in the press, Nyerere made strong public statements labeling the Saidia Waafrika initiative 'ignorant nonsense' and warning that a TANU government would do everything in its power to thwart those who were intent upon 'breaking' the cooperative movement. Apparently convinced that Asians who were discontented with the success of the African cooperative movements were behind Saidia Waafrika, Nyerere argued:

Who are these Saidia people?...

Not long ago they asked very high prices for processing cotton in their ginneries. When the Federation asked them to pay a little more to the grower so that he might receive a better price they said they could not afford it. Now today where did they get these millions to assist the Africans?

If it hadn't been for the strength of the Federation they would have robbed the farmer of -/07 extra and claimed it was justice... They know that in

[1] Assistant Director of Agriculture, Lake Province, to Director of Agriculture, Dar es Salaam, 29 June 1960, LPF.

Y

order to obtain once again an opportunity to suck the African dry, they
must destroy the growers cooperatives. They know that they can't destroy
them now with the help of government of the people. Therefore they want
to destroy them through bribery.

These better prices which you have been told you will receive are a sort
of bribery. Agree to take this bribe and your cooperatives will die and
you will be milked dry now more than ever you were in years gone by...

This is the most astonishing sort of stupidity.

Nyerere remonstrated that it was 'childish' to hold back harvested
cotton in the hope of getting better prices from Saidia Waafrika
and that 'people who delay will not get a good price because the
cotton buyers of the world can not wait until people who are
deceived by the Saidia people harvest and sell their cotton.'[1]

A Delegation to Dar es Salaam

Leaders of Saidia Waafrika drafted a memorandum in reply to
Nyerere, and Masalu and two others departed by train for Dar es
Salaam to press their case personally with TANU leaders. The
delegation first saw TANU's Organizing Secretary General,
Oscar Kambona and gave him a prepared memorandum which
elaborated the company's criticisms of the VFCU monopoly. It
explained that the organization had been formed by Africans in
Kwimba District, but that support from other districts quickly
developed—both among the more than half of the growers who
were not VFCU members and among some VFCU members who
were dissatisfied with the operations of the VFCU—which led in
turn to the rapid expansion of the company. Most importantly,
the memorandum sought to counter the impression that Saidia
Waafrika was an instrument of Asian interests and to establish that
it was loyal to TANU.

We are not intending to delay the progress of our Tanganyika and we are
not at all against TANU...Our aim is to correct some of the undesirable
aspects of the Victoria Federation and to help those growers who do not
agree with the Federation. The name of our organization...does not
mean that there are foreigners or Asians behind it who intend or pretend
to 'assist' Africans through us with the sole aim of exploiting them. But
it is we the indigenous Africans that are helping ourselves and our country
through this organization.

The memorandum appealed to TANU and to the Tanganyika
Elected Members Organization (TEMO) for their 'careful consideration.' It said that it believed Nyerere had condemned the

[1] *Ngurumo*, 25 July 1960; *Sauti ya TANU*, 28 July 1960; *Ilaka*, Aug. 1960.

organization because he 'was not well informed,' and that Nyerere's strong statements had created difficulties for the company since 'some of the leaders of TANU are now beginning to turn against us and are even saying that we are followers of the African National Congress.'[1]

The delegation then reportedly spent more than two hours with Nyerere and, in answer to Nyerere's questions, explained that they had no connection at all with Asians and that their intent had been to pay –/55 per pound, not the 1 shilling figure which they maintained had been broadcast by their detractors. Elaborating on the disenchantment of their supporters with the VFCU, the delegation cited unnecessary expenditures for office and staff, division of end-of-year balances among officers and committeemen rather than higher payments to the growers, exorbitant overnight allowances of 25 shillings for Federation committeemen, padded payrolls with two persons doing the work for which only one person was necessary and an unjustified sharp rise in the costs calculated for the ginning process from –/14 to –/28 per pound. According to Masalu's report of the conversation, Nyerere was surprised to hear of the increase in ginning costs even at the VFCU-owned ginneries, which he had apparently understood were not to increase their costs. Nyerere indicated that he would talk with Paul Bomani about the charges and he suggested that Saidia Waafrika change its registration from that of a company to that of a cooperative.

Reporting back to his Saidia Waafrika supporters, Masalu urged them to sell their cotton through the VFCU during 1960. Meanwhile, he submitted a formal request to the Cooperative Department to be registered as a probationary cooperative society for 1961 as Nyerere had suggested and encouraged the organization's leaders to use nothing but proper legal channels to establish its just claims. He criticized the VFCU for presuming to establish an identity between itself and TANU which excluded other groups, such as Saidia Waafrika, which were equally loyal to TANU. He deplored the fact that criticism of the VFCU was being represented as anti-TANU and even as pro-African National Congress sentiment and that the company's leaders could not but with difficulty receive a public hearing nor stand successfully in local council elections.[2]

[1] Saidia Waafrika to 'Honourables,' n.d. (July 1959), LPF.
[2] Minutes of Central Committee of Saidia Waafrika, Meeting No. 5, 25 Aug. 1960, Sukuma Union files.

Economics is Politics

Though Nyerere and others in Dar es Salaam may have accepted
Masalu's disclaimer with regard to Asian backing for Saidia
Waafrika and though Masalu may have taken comfort from the
courtesy of his reception by the territory's political leaders,
there were larger issues involved. Once one penetrated behind the
verbal screen of Saidia's appeals for freedom and rights, its con-
demnation of monopoly and its charges of mismanagement against
the VFCU, was Masalu's concept of a competitive cooperative
movement sound and practical? Any established and successful
organization is open to criticism. The real question was: Could
Masalu have run an efficient organization on a smaller scale than
the VFCU while giving the growers a higher price for their
cotton? The economic logistics of cotton marketing suggest that
he could not have done so.[1] And even had he been able, what
would then have been the fate of the VFCU which had taken
years to build and which was still one of the most remarkable
economic achievements in all sub-Saharan Africa?

If Masalu had offered higher prices, he might have crippled the
VFCU without thereby necessarily establishing a solid infrastructure for his own rival organization. He might soon have been
forced himself to lower prices. If he offered prices which were the
same or nearly the same as the VFCU, he would have been
redundant, though one might argue that competitive organizations,
each securely founded, would be forced to work toward eliminating
waste and maximizing the return to the grower.[2] But Masalu's
organization was not securely founded and government permission
to allow it to attempt to become so was an obvious risk. Protest
in Sukumaland had already proven on other occasions that it
could be instrumental in helping to bring down 'the establishment.'
But was it in this case capable of a subsequent positive contribution?

By September 1960 Drennan had decided in the negative and

---

[1] But see the discussion of the problems of monopoly in the Sukumaland cotton
cooperatives in de Wilde, vol. II, pp. 446–8.

[2] Aside from whether the 1 shilling price per pound was first bruited by an
ignorant but eager Saidia Waafrika partisan, as seems likely, or by VFCU
detractors of Saidia, a pertinent question was whether growers responded in
great numbers to the Saidia call because they expected to get the rumored
1 shilling or because they expected to get the considerably more modest –/55
quoted by Masalu. (Masalu to Senior Cooperative Officer, Mwanza, 22 July
1960, LPF.)

he refused to recommend the company's registration as a cooperative society. He pointed out to the Commissioner for Agriculture in Dar es Salaam that the regulations of the Cotton Ordinance would automatically entitle Saidia Waafrika to buy cotton if it became a registered cooperative and, cautious now about TANU's attitude, he suggested that he and the Commissioner for Cooperative Development 'put the matter up to the Council of Ministers for a ruling on what line is to be taken with Saidia Waafrika.'

At the same time, Drennan reported that an independent candidate supported by Saidia Waafrika had run strongly against a VFCU cooperative union manager sponsored by TANU in the August 1960 Legislative Council elections in Ukerewe, thus demonstrating the relative ease with which expressions of economically based frustration could be transformed into political dissent. Noting that a Saidia Waafrika meeting held in Mwanza in late August had been 'attended by large numbers of delegates from every cotton growing district in the Province,' he added:

There seems to be very little doubt that the movement continues to gain support and that it will need to be dealt with very tactfully if it is decided not to allow it to participate in cotton buying next year.[1]

The new TANU-dominated Council of Ministers, with Nyerere as Chief Minister, was sworn into office on 3 September. Paul Bomani became Minister for Agriculture and Cooperative Development and Gavin Green, who had worked with Bomani to establish the VFCU in the middle 1950s, remained as Assistant Commissioner for Cooperative Development, a post he had assumed in 1959. Saidia Waafrika was informed in late September that decisions on its status would eventually be taken. In the following months Masalu attempted to qualify Saidia Waafrika as a cooperative, as a company, as a ginners' buying agent— anything to permit his organization to purchase cotton from growers who wished to sell it to them. His demand seemed a simple one, but its implications and potential complications, both economic and political, proved unacceptable to the new TANU government. Masalu, therefore, after a year of representations to various levels and agencies of government, found that no legal alternatives were open to him. At year's end, the Ministry for Agriculture and Cooperative Development informed Saidia

---

[1] Drennan to Commissioner for Agriculture, 9 Sept. 1960, LPF.

Waafrika that the government had 'neither the right nor the duty to interfere' with the agreement negotiated between the VFCU and the Lake Province Ginners Association whereby all primary buying of African-grown cotton was to be done by cooperatives and all cotton stores previously owned by the ginners were sold to the VFCU.

Moreover, it is Government's considered view that a single organization, namely that of the Cooperatives, to deliver raw cotton to ginners will, with intelligent and helpful support from its members, ensure the best prospects for producers in an increasingly difficult and competitive market.

It is not, therefore, Government's intention to amend the existing provisions of the Cotton Ordinance... relating to the regulation of cotton buyers, and I am directed in conclusion to make it quite clear that Government will take all necessary steps to safeguard the marketing system which it considers to be in the best interests of the industry.[1]

As late as December 1960, Masalu had declined to join forces with the African National Congress in line with his oft-repeated contention that he was not interested in politics, but only in cotton, and that he was not opposed to TANU.[2] But frustrated in all his efforts to enter the cotton-buying business, Masalu openly began to identify himself with political opposition to TANU. Originally elected to the Kwimba African District Council as a member of TANU, he had by April 1962 become a member of the ANC. He held that TANU had contrived to ban Saidia Waafrika. He was quoted in *Lumuli* to the effect that 'It seems that the Victoria Federation is friendly with TANU so my Saidia Waafrika will be a friend of the Congress.'[3] The ANC, which had been active in parts of Shinyanga from early in 1960, thus developed a bridgehead in Kwimba. The ANC's activities were not to achieve much significance, however, until after independence.

---

[1] Permanent Secretary for Agriculture and Cooperative Development to Saidia Waafrika, 31 Dec. 1960, LPF.
[2] Drennan to Commissioner for Agriculture, 22 Dec. 1960, LPF.
[3] *Lumuli*, No. 212, 4 Apr. 1962. (Orig. Sw.)

10

Post-Independence Politics and Administration

Tanganyika became an independent state on 9 December 1961. Seventy-five thousand people gathered in Dar es Salaam to watch the midnight ceremony. A torch was lit and the green, black and gold flag of the new nation was raised on a summit of Mount Kilimanjaro. As throughout Tanganyika, crowds gathered in Mwanza, Shinyanga and other major centers of Sukumaland to hear Prime Minister Nyerere's independence address and to celebrate the momentous event.

With independence TANU's first aim was realized; but, as its leaders clearly understood, new and even more difficult tasks lay ahead. Instead of a party in opposition (or, more properly, a national movement bent on freedom from colonial rule), TANU was now both party and government. While 85 per cent of British civil servants decided to remain for a while after independence to ease the transition,[1] TANU alone defined policy. Within a year TANU reorganized local government and administration. Within two years non-technical administrative cadres at regional and district levels were almost entirely Africanized. Regional and Area Commissioners replaced their British predecessors and assumed as well the role of party leader in their respective areas. Divisional Executive Officers replaced chiefs who were asked by the new government to resign. Elected District Councils with substantial statutory powers came into existence. A hierarchy of regional, district and village committees charged with the formulation and implementation of development plans began to function.

The party, too, entered a new phase. Prime Minister Nyerere was so concerned with the task of revamping TANU for the crucial tasks of the post-independence era that he resigned as Prime Minister to free himself for the creation of a new TANU. The party would need to be both democratic in its linking of the government with the people and an instrument for development

[1] Taylor, p. 219.

to mobilize the people against 'poverty, ignorance and disease.'[1]
It promised to be no easy task to sustain the enthusiasm which
TANU had sparked for the fight to terminate colonialism. A new
fight had now to be waged against the more stubborn and fundamental conditions of Tanganyikan life itself.

For a variety of reasons local TANU leaders had caused resentment among some before independence; they continued to do so
after independence. A loss of mature leadership in party echelons,
as TANU leaders moved into government administrative posts
during the transition to independence, exacerbated difficulties
locally. Though Regional Commissioners were able to curb some
of the more questionable enthusiasms and abuses of power by
local TANU officers and TANU-controlled District Councils—
abuses which continued, unhappily, from the pre-independence
into the post-independence era—the opposition African National
Congress, and later the People's Democratic Party, made some
inroads in areas where disenchantment with TANU was marked.

After Nyerere's overwhelming victory in elections for President
of the new Republic in 1962, opposition withered or was suppressed. Under Nyerere's leadership Tanganyika (called Tanzania
after the union with Zanzibar in 1964) proceeded toward the
establishment of a democratic one-party state. Its one-party
characteristic achieved early fruition. The democratic aspect
began to assume reality when, in the National Assembly elections
of 1965, voters were given a choice of TANU candidates in each
constituency. A striking innovation in the theory and practice of
government, this experiment provided a hopeful augury for the
future.

I   TANU GOVERNMENT

TANU in Control: New Tasks, New Difficulties

With independence in the near future assured after the elections
of late 1960, TANU's principal goal, as stated at the time of its
formation in 1954, was all but realized. TANU leaders faced,
therefore, the necessity of re-defining the purposes of their

[1] Excerpts from Nyerere's announcement of resignation are quoted in Taylor,
p. 225; see also Bates, 'Tanganyika', pp. 431, 470; and Joseph S. Nye, Jr.,
'TANU and UPC: the impact of independence on two African nationalist
parties,' in Jeffrey Butler and A. A. Castagno, eds., *Boston University papers
on Africa: transition in African politics* (New York: Praeger, 1967), p. 237.

organization. Obviously, the post-independence task would be to govern the new nation and govern it effectively. TANU, the national movement for independence from colonial rule, would have to become government as well as party. As the government, TANU would have to plan, administer and rule. As the party, TANU would have to galvanize the support of its members, and of the population as a whole, toward the post-independence requirements of nation-building and economic development.

After the repression of the mid-1950s, the people of Sukumaland had flocked to the TANU banner in 1958 and 1959. TANU meant release from what seemed to most the arbitrary character of agricultural rules and regulations and freedom to organize politically in the struggle for independence. But in his November 1958 appearance in Mwanza after the ban on TANU in Sukumaland was lifted, Nyerere made a point of emphasizing that freedom could not be meaningful apart from responsibilities and obligations. Taxes, and probably higher taxes, would have to be paid. Officers of central and local government would need to be respected and obeyed even as provision was being made for greater popular participation in the political process. The need for material progress would require even greater attention to improved agricultural methods. In Mwanza a year later he said that independence would 'mean nothing to the African without work.' Insisting that 'uhuru ni kazi' (freedom is work), Nyerere sounded the note which was to become the basis for TANU's later emphasis on voluntary self-help schemes. Already he was attempting to prepare Tanganyikans for the psychological transition from a posture of embattled colonialism to one of embracing the rigors as well as the promises of self-government. With the departure of the colonial power, TANU would seek to redefine the enemy as 'poverty, ignorance and disease.' Having promised that an independent Tanganyika would be able to do as much in ten years as the British had done in forty, Nyerere stressed in Mwanza in early 1961 that independence would be 'our start for real work.'[1]

Re-educating the People

The new message was less simple and less compelling than the earlier call to *Uhuru*. People who were anxious to emancipate

[1] *Lake Province News*, No. 12, Nov. 1959; *Ilaka*, No. 32, 16 July 1960; *Lumuli*, No. 189, 17 Mar. 1961.

themselves from colonial rule were not equally anxious to embark on an 'operation bootstrap' phase of positive construction. Tanganyika's general economic backwardness dictated both the necessity for such a phase and the inherent difficulty of making any substantial progress. Moreover, the conservative Sukuma, with an economy already partly based on cash crops, were among the least likely candidates to feel the need for major changes in their way of life once the irritants of colonial administration had been removed. With independence in the offing and TANU shifting gears toward the same social and economic methods and goals earlier espoused by the British, people became less interested in TANU.

Quite clearly, there were false expectations among the less sophisticated about what independence would bring. Many apparently believed that taxes would be abolished, that government loans would be available to any and all persons for the asking, that Asians and Europeans would be forced to leave the country and would abandon property and businesses to Africans, that all government posts would be quickly Africanized, that rules and regulations which seemed annoying or restrictive would be rescinded, that much-needed medical, educational and social services would suddenly materialize. Many of those who had identified themselves closely with the struggle for independence felt that they should receive appointments to important government posts and were not easily persuaded that work with cooperatives, with labor unions or with the party was as important in the service of the country as employment in an important government post.

Immediately after his appointment as Regional Commissioner of the Lake Region in March 1962, Richard Wambura made a long safari throughout the eight districts under his jurisdiction. His purpose was to correct the mistaken impressions of many, to dispel what he called their 'despair and confusion.' His theme was the reorganization of TANU and the advancement of the country. He urged young people to work on the land rather than migrate to the towns. He said that unemployed persons would be asked to participate in some form of national service. He asked all to take part, as he himself would, in voluntary self-help projects to improve home construction and roads. He asked for patience on the question of Africanization: many technical posts could not be Africanized before Africans had received the necessary training. Further, as a member of the United Nations and a believer in human rights, the government could not chase out non-Africans from the country nor could Tanganyika rely always on loans from overseas. Hard work would be required during the struggle for advancement. In particular, non-paid voluntary labor on community self-help schemes was critical to nation-building in a country with human, but few capital resources.[1]

A Regional Conference: Internal Problems

TANU held its first post-independence Regional Annual Conference in late March 1962 with Wambura and Shabani Mohamed, the Deputy Provincial Secretary of TANU, presiding. That TANU felt somewhat sensitive and insecure at the very moment that it was ostensibly tasting the realities of power became clear as the conference progressed. With the struggle for independence won, TANU activity had fallen off in 1961. No annual conference, for example, had been held in that year. Recognizing that interest in TANU was flagging in the population at large, the conference decided that the party should undertake a census of members in every district and a campaign to enroll new members, collecting party dues across the board. It called for the strengthening of the TANU elders' sections and roundly criticized the Youth League for 'do-nothingism.' Strong complaints were voiced that African government leaders and members of Parliament were being treated with contempt, especially by non-Africans. The conference asked the National Assembly to take disciplinary action against any person guilty of disrespect toward the nation's new leaders. In forthcoming elections TANU members should not contest TANU-held seats and all TANU candidates would have to be certified by the party organization as outstanding and worthy TANU members. TANU leaders were urged to improve their knowledge of technical subjects through instruction from agricultural, veterinary, and other departmental officers, then to take this knowledge into the countryside.[2]

At each level—regional, district, branch, and sub-branch—the basic elements of TANU organization remained as before independence: an elected chairman, an appointed secretary, a committee composed of these and other officers plus representatives from subordinate TANU units and ancillary sections of elders, women and youth. Annual conferences were held at district and

[1] Press release, Provincial Information Office, Mar. 1962, LPF.
[2] Minutes of Provincial TANU Conference, 24–26 Mar. 1962, LPF. (Orig. Sw.)

regional level in preparation for the national TANU conference held each year in Dar es Salaam, and regional annual conferences picked representatives to sit on TANU's National Executive Committee. When Regional and Area Commissioners were appointed in 1962, they served as TANU secretary for their respective regions and districts—with the result that the positions of Deputy Regional and Deputy District Secretary of TANU were upgraded to become operational posts of some importance.[1]

At sub-district level—the most crucial level for successful or unsuccessful grass-roots political involvement after independence —TANU branches and sub-branches generally grouped themselves according to chiefdom and subchiefdom and, after the administrative units of local government were re-delineated in 1963, according to division and subdivision. Before independence the operating nerves of these local units, branch and sub-branch secretaries, were not paid salaries; only district and provincial secretaries were employed by TANU headquarters in Dar es Salaam on a professional basis. By 1964, however, divisional TANU secretaries were hired by the District TANU office and paid a modest fixed wage. Just as regional and district TANU secretaries and deputy secretaries are transferred anywhere in the nation, divisional secretaries are transferred anywhere within the district, or outside the district if appropriate. Subdivisional secretaries are also hired by the district TANU office and are transferable, though they generally are recruited in and remain to work in their own localities. Village secretaries are selected locally and receive a small percentage of fees and dues collected, but never any wage.[2]

Of course, it is not the village (or *gunguli*) but the *kibanda* which constitutes the crucial traditional unit of neighborhood organization in Sukumaland.[3] That TANU failed effectively to penetrate organizationally to the *kibanda* level may have been part of the reason for TANU's tendency to atrophy after independence.

The 'village', an artificial administrative unit created by the colonial government, usually combined three to six *vibanda*

---

[1] For a fuller description of TANU organization after independence, see Henry Bienen, *Tanzania: party transformation and economic development* (Princeton, New Jersey: Princeton University Press, 1967); also Nye, 'TANU and UPC,' pp. 225–9; 237–41. Bienen's excellent study provides a comprehensive and informed view, and a probing analysis, of politics, administration, economic development and ideology in post-independence Tanzania.

[2] Interviews with local TANU personnel.   [3] See note 1, Chapter 1, above.

under a headman paid by the government. 'Village' units continued in existence under the new TANU government, but they were reduced in number and enlarged to include up to a dozen *vibanda* or more. These amalgamated villages—presided over by a former headman if he proved acceptable to TANU or by a new appointee if he were not—provided the most local units of TANU organization, and it was at this level that TANU came closest to the grass roots through combined TANU–Village Development Committees. While the enlarged 'village' may seem a rational unit administratively, it apparently did not commend itself to people who were accustomed to organizing their community affairs even more locally among homestead groupings, or *vibanda*. While other factors such as shortage of trained personnel and poorly conceived and executed program figured heavily in the equation, deficiencies of structural adaptation may also have been important. In any case, TANU has experienced difficulty in maintaining wide popular support for and participation in village level organizations.

Elders, Women and Youth

Theoretically, semi-autonomous sections of elders, women, and youth should also have been organized down to the amalgamated village level though not, of course, any more than TANU itself, formally to the *kibanda* level. In fact, they seldom have operated effectively even at the sub-chiefdom or subdivisional level. There may be an officer or two for some or all of the sections at subdivisional or village levels, but rarely an active and functioning membership. Sometimes even officers have been non-existent at the lower levels, in which case the chiefdom or divisional TANU secretary might serve also as secretary for the elders or for the youth league or for both for an entire division. Before independence, when enthusiasm was high and nearly everyone moved with the TANU banner, many were at least nominally associated with one of the three sections and each section had, even locally, its own activities. After independence, a certain atrophy afflicted each of the three sections, as indeed it did the entire party.

Of the three, the Youth League has had the largest and most active membership. At least initially in some rural localities, the Youth League was able to capitalize not only on the general wave of enthusiasm for TANU, but also on the specific tendency of the Sukuma to form strong traditional social groupings of *basumba*, or young men, who were responsible at village and *vibanda* levels for discharging whatever tasks the neighborhood or community unit might require. The *basumba batale*, the leaders of the *basumba*, organized this work and also assisted local headmen in informing the people about any meetings or about visiting government officials—tasks quite similar to those which Youth League leaders were called upon to perform *vis-à-vis* TANU self-help schemes and political meetings. In a few instances, *basumba batale* themselves became leaders of local Youth League units. More frequently the creation of a local unit brought some other member of the *basumba* to the forefront though the *basumba batale* themselves might still become members.[1] Thus, Youth League strength varied a good deal from one locality to another: in some communities where TANU was especially strong, as in Nassa, most *basumba* were TANU Youth League members and there was an ongoing local program. In other areas fewer *basumba* joined and the Youth League was non-permanent or casual with periodic meetings to prepare for special occasions only. In still other areas it was inactive or defunct.[2]

Before independence, Youth League work was important to TANU's smooth functioning. Members were busy and earned prestige by having their work for independence so visible to their peers. There were opportunities, too, to move from leadership in the Youth League into regular party posts. After independence, however, interest in the League declined. With established party leaders suddenly enjoying the fruits of a dramatic rise to positions of power and influence, some Youth Leaguers were less enthusiastic about the modest functions they continued to perform. Others, particularly those *basumba* closest to traditional life in the villages, were not drawn to the new programs of economic advancement and nation-building for which the Youth League was now asked to set an example. Thus, the Youth League, which in Sukumaland had always been strongest among young men in the towns and trading centers rather than in the more

[1] With the deposition of the chiefs after independence, *basumba batale* had fewer functions to perform since local government and party activities were handled by TANU officials with the help of the Youth League. Dance societies, too, have assumed in recent years a larger share of communal labor tasks. The result of this dual encroachment on the traditional preserve of the *basumba batale* has been that *basumba batale* have for the most part simply ceased to perform their traditional functions.

[2] Conclusions on the TYL, the women's section and the TANU elders are drawn from interviews with party leaders and villagers, and from documentary sources. Quoted material is from interviews.

strictly rural areas, became after independence more limited to these. Small Youth League contingents have functioned sporadically at the behest of regional and district TANU leaders on this or that self-help project, membership recruitment or tax collection campaign; but they have not mobilized, nor have they had much continuing impact on the youth or the population at large in the countryside. In fact, the Youth League has been popularly known more than anything else for its interference in people's ordinary lives; and the government has on more than one occasion had to remind Youth League units in Sukumaland and elsewhere that they are not to assume the functions of policeman, special investigator or judge,[1] but to work under the leadership and direction of qualified party personnel on approved projects and in a manner consistent with national principles and policy.

The women's section has posed a problem of a different sort. In Sukumaland, while women traditionally play a co-equal role with men in the cultivation and harvesting of crops, they have not functioned in positions of authority in the traditional social and political structures. They also have not been as well educated as the men and are less prepared, generally, to adapt to more modern social and political organizations. Self-effacing and reticent, they sit together at the back of TANU rallies and meetings, nursing their children, talking among themselves, but never participating (except for traditional ululations of approval) in the public discussion.

It has been difficult to develop effective local units of the women's sections of TANU—or, after its formation as a separate organization, of the Umoja wa Wanawake of Tanganyika. The only really active women have been the handful of leaders who, through educational or vocational experience, or peculiarities of personal and family life, have forged for themselves a new and entirely untraditional type of role. Such leaders live, usually, in the major towns and trading centers where they have had some success with activities which include (in addition to political education) domestic science, health, child-care and literacy.[2]

---

[1] One man interviewed in an outlying area remarked: 'If one joined TYL he would surely be against his people!'

[2] In Mwanza town, for example, the women's section of some thirty active members sponsored a number of program activities. The chairman in 1964 was the wife of a bar owner and the secretary the wife of a medical officer. The group received special attention from the wife of the Regional Commissioner, the wives of visiting ministers and, especially, from the one female

While they do try to create membership units in outlying areas, they have had little success in developing ongoing branches or programs in these areas, though an occasional meeting is held when a women's section leader or community development officer visits an outlying district. The opinion generally held within and without TANU is that the women's units have never been very strong or active but have followed along. The women's section had basically been a few leaders without an organization, sitting with district and regional TANU committees or touring with groups of senior party officials.

At the local level, the elders have never been a separate section of TANU except in name. Chairmen of the elders are elected at regular party conferences at regional and district levels and sometimes also by more local TANU units. A small group of men known as 'TANU elders' are present at regional, district and sometimes subdistrict levels in the TANU hierarchy. Ordinarily, they are men who have over the years played a role in the development of nationalist politics in their localities but who are not interested in or qualified for the more demanding jobs in the regular TANU organization. Like the early supporters of the Tanganyika African Association and of TANU—and many of today's TANU elders were themselves in this category—they are often artisans or traders in the towns and major trading centers who have accumulated enough wealth and prestige both to be able to afford and to enjoy giving time to TANU, and to have their words weighed by those who hear them speak in public meetings. Essentially, the elders' section provided a means of expanding TANU membership since, as one Sukuma explained, 'It is easier for an old man to convince an old man than for a young man to convince an old man.'[1]

The existence of a special designation 'TANU elder' follows, of

Minister in the national government—Lucy Lameck. For the most part, the activity of the Mwanza women's section was not duplicated in other communities in the area.

[1] Nor has there been any discernible effort with TANU elders, as there was for a while with the Youth League, to encourage leading traditional figures at village level to assume analogous roles within TANU. 'TANU elders,' where they exist at the most local levels, are generally men over forty years of age who have emerged in the non-traditional economic and political sectors. One group of elders in a Kwimba locality, for example, included: a shopkeeper, a school teacher in a TANU-supported school, a district councillor, a chairman and a committee member of a local cotton cooperative, former and current local TANU officials and local headmen appointed by the new TANU District Council after independence.

course, from the status and functional importance of elders in most African societies, including those of Tanzania; but in the context of government and politics in Tanzania today it is primarily symbol without substance. While as members of TANU committees TANU elders may occasionally advise party officials on tactics, they have, unlike traditional tribal elders, no influence as a group on government or party policy which is formulated and handed down from above. While TANU elders usually accompany branch TANU chairmen and secretaries to annual party conferences, and while elders at district and regional levels may accompany Area and Regional Commissioners when the latter go on speaking tours among their constituents, the elders are not, as a rule, very much consulted on matters of import. Even in localities where TANU is strong, elders' sections are often described as 'doing nothing' or 'no longer in existence.'

Local Leadership

While TANU's ideals have remained high, TANU's post-independence difficulty with preserving and expanding its units on the ground has been related in part to problems of leadership. In addition to strengthening the independence of the nation and overcoming poverty, ignorance and disease, the outline of the new TANU's purposes included freedom and equal rights for every individual within a democratic socialist state. TANU members promised personally to embrace the following nine principles—principles which were stressed by TANU leaders at the first post-independence Regional Annual Conference:

1. All men are my brothers and Africa is one.
2. I will serve my country and all its people.
3. I will take every opportunity to help myself overcome poverty, ignorance, disease, and injustice.
4. Bribery is the enemy of justice; I will never receive or offer a bribe.
5. Leadership is a trust; I will not exploit my position or the position of another for personal advantage.
6. I will educate myself to the extent that I am able and use my knowledge for the benefit of all.
7. I will cooperate with all my fellows to build our country.
8. I will always be truthful and abstain from promoting discord.
9. I will be a trustworthy member of TANU and a loyal citizen of Tanganyika and Africa.[1]

[1] From 'Appendix,' *TANU: Sheria na Madhumuni ya Chama* (Dar es Salaam: Mwananchi Publishing Co., Ltd., n.d.).

z

There is no question but that Nyerere had made every effort to live by these principles and that men like Wambura at the regional level and others in the districts took them very seriously indeed. But while TANU's top leadership was as enlightened if not more enlightened than that of many or most governments, TANU personnel and operations at local levels often were less exemplary.

One of the difficulties was enlisting the most qualified people for responsible positions. The refusal of the colonial government to permit civil servants to participate in political organizations had isolated a high percentage of the middle ranks of Tanganyika's best-educated younger men from the mainstream of nationalist political development. Though top leaders like Nyerere, Bomani, Maswanya and Munanka had been able to leave government service or teaching to lead TANU nationally, the struggle for independence locally often was led by men who, for lack of further educational or other professional opportunities, found a post in TANU a natural vehicle for their somewhat less impressive talents and less well-directed energies. A disproportionate number of local TANU leaders were—and still are today—those who did not have the opportunity to continue from primary to secondary levels of education in the predominantly Christian mission schools, either because they were Muslims or because they had not the economic means or the ability to continue to the higher levels where so few places were available. Given a limited educational background and the citcumscription of alternative career possibilities which followed therefrom, such men were willing to tolerate the financial insecurity and irregular hours which party work always entailed in exchange for close identification with the nationalist movement and possibilities for personal advancement into positions of authority and power.

That these men were devoted nationalists is not in doubt. That they played an indispensable role in the struggle for independence cannot be questioned. Yet it is clear that many local TANU leaders have lacked the sort of qualifications which would have enabled them to work constructively with their fellows, as well as the less easily defined breadth of view which often distinguishes a good leader from a poor one. When leadership required more than making speeches and enlisting members—required in fact an ability to organize people and commit them to the tasks of self-improvement and nation-building—then the paucity of talent at the lower levels of TANU became manifest. It was a problem aggravated by the transfer in 1960 and 1961 of the most capable party personnel to government posts and of the promotion of qualified second-echelon party leaders from regional or district levels to national or regional party headquarters.

Reorganization of the Administration

While the party labored under conditions of declining popular interest and participation and some of the weaknesses of local TANU leadership and organization became apparent, the spotlight shifted in 1962 to the new government's plans for changes in national and local administration. While TANU Ministers and senior civil servants took over the reins of government in Dar es Salaam, profound changes were also effected in local government. William Tordoff summarized the changes in regional administration by mid-1964:

> Since Independence in December 1961 the former nine provinces and the Dar es Salaam 'extra-provincial district' have been replaced by seventeen regions; the all-purpose, civil servant, provincial and district commissioners have given way to political regional and area commissioners: the Chiefs have lost all their official powers; the former native authority councils have everywhere been replaced by TANU-dominated, predominantly elected councils; and a new courts system has been introduced, whereby courts at all levels form an integral part of an independent judiciary. Taken together, these changes constitute a revolution in provincial administration.[1]

In February and March 1962 African political appointees, called Regional Commissioners, replaced the senior colonial civil servants, the Provincial Commissioners. A similar shift was made at district level from District Commissioners, whether European or African, to politically appointed Area Commissioners. The new regional appointees were 'distinguished by their strong party connection and their local acceptability,' while for the new area officials, 'loyalty and service to the party were more obvious criteria than administrative ability or educational

[1] William Tordoff, *Government and politics in Tanzania* (Nairobi: East African Publishing House, 1967), pp. 96–7. Tordoff's chapter on 'Regional Administration' is an invaluable study of administrative reorganization locally. He describes structural changes and analyzes problems common throughout post-independence Tanzania in more systematic fashion than our focus on Sukumaland allows. His study is useful background for the present chapter. It was first published as 'Regional Administration in Tanzania,' *The Journal of Modern African Studies*, III, No. 1 (1965).

attainment.'[1] Many had served as provincial and district TANU secretaries before their designation to the newly created government posts. The new Regional and Area Commissioners served simultaneously as Regional and Area TANU secretaries, thus linking the party directly with the administration.

Regional and Area Commissioners were assisted in their administrative duties by senior civil servants known as regional administrative and area secretaries. On the party side, they were assisted by deputy regional and deputy area TANU secretaries. Depending on his own talents and interests, a Regional or Area Commissioner could spend more or less time on administration, more or less time on party organization, devolving accordingly greater or lesser amounts of responsibility on either his administrative or his party aide. Because of their past experience as TANU organizers and their generally less solid grasp of administrative matters, most of the new commissioners, at least at the outset, tended to devote considerably more than 50 per cent of their time to party affairs. Day-to-day tasks of administration were left to the administrative or area secretaries, except where particularly difficult or controversial problems or policy matters required the personal attention of the commissioner.[2]

While Tanganyika 'probably derived from Ghana the idea of having political regional and area commissioners,' the new system seemed especially appropriate to Tanganyika's needs. With independence, the few most experienced African administrative officers were needed in 'politically sensitive and policy-making posts' in the central government in Dar es Salaam. Yet, 'if the people were to be convinced that the government now in power was indeed their own government,' the highest posts at regional and district levels should be held by Africans. This would be possible if the posts were defined in relation to political as well as strictly civil service criteria and qualifications. At the same time, it was thought that the sometimes errant local party apparatus could be more closely controlled and made more cooperative and responsible by politicians. Finally, a government and a party united formally in the person of a political commissioner who spoke the people's language could move as one in every locality to

---

[1] This quotation, and those in the immediately following paragraphs, are taken from an early mimeographed draft of the Tordoff article cited above.
[2] The conclusions in this paragraph are drawn from observations by, and interviews conducted by, the author and his research assistants.

accomplish the psychological, political and economic tasks of nation-building.

The new TANU government defined the major political task of the post-independence era as economic development and it asked Regional Commissioners to take the lead. Prime Minister Kawawa stated that the entire emphasis under the new administrative scheme would be on development.

The success of a village, district, or region, and the value of those in charge of running these areas, will be judged in terms of what they achieve in development over a given period... [1] Within the limits of his Region, the Regional Commissioner is the principal representative of Government. He is responsible for the planned development of his Region in accordance with the three-year plan.[2]

All Area or District Commissioners and all administrative and technical staff were under the 'general supervision and control' of the Regional Commissioner.[3]

In the regions a hierarchy of development committees provided the organizational structure for the new government's attack on poverty, ignorance and disease. Regional and District Development Committees composed of senior administrative, departmental and technical officers and chaired respectively by the Regional and Area Commissioners—with membership expanded to include senior TANU party personnel—replaced the old Provincial and District Teams. Similarly, when subdistrict administrative reorganization was effected in 1963, development committees at divisional, subdivisional and village levels replaced the pyramid of Cory councils.

First Assignments in Sukumaland

In March 1962 President Nyerere appointed Richard Wambura the first Regional Commissioner of the Lake Region. Wambura, of course, had directed TANU's operations in the Lake Province in 1959–60. An elected representative to the Legislative Council from Maswa after 1960, he enhanced his reputation as a dedicated and responsible politician and consolidated his position in what Bates described in 1962 as a third echelon of younger men in TANU's national leadership.[4] Bomani, Maswanya and Munanka,

[1] Press release, Provincial Information Office, 2 Feb. 1962, LPF.
[2] Staff Circular No. 14, Establishment Division, Prime Minister's Office, 31 July 1962.
[3] *Ibid.*   [4] Bates, 'Tanganyika,' p. 457.

the Lake Province's senior political leaders, were then serving as Ministers or parliamentary secretaries in Dar es Salaam. For the post as Regional Commissioner Wambura was the next logical choice in terms of education and experience, including knowledge of the locality.

Shabani Mohamed, who had taken over from Wambura as provincial TANU secretary in 1961, was posted to North Mara as Nyerere's first Area Commissioner appointment in all of Tanganyika. Two other political leaders who were earlier prominent in Sukumaland—P. C. Walwa and A. S. Kandoro—received appointments elsewhere. Walwa, who had served as a provincial TANU secretary in Morogoro and Tanga after leaving Kwimba in 1959, was made Regional Commissioner of the Northern Region. Kandoro, who, after his expulsion from Mwanza in 1954, had served as a provincial TANU secretary in Dodoma and Tabora and subsequently as territorial administrative secretary of the TANU Elders' Section, became Area Commissioner of Mafia.

Sukumaland received its first African Area Commissioners in May 1962 when Mohamed was transferred from North Mara to Kwimba and when Changasi Nyakasagani, an Ikizu from Musoma, became Area Commissioner of Maswa. In Mwanza, Shinyanga, and Geita expatriate District Commissioners continued to serve, albeit under the supervision of Regional Commissioner Wambura.

Later in 1962 Nyerere assigned the first Sukuma political leaders to important posts in Sukumaland. Mbuta Milando became Area Commissioner of Geita. A fiery young ex-agricultural instructor who had made outspoken statements to the United Nations Visiting Mission in 1954, Milando had worked for TANU during the ban in Sukumaland and early became Nyerere's private secretary. In appointing Milando to the Geita post, Nyerere probably reasoned that Milando's youth and vigor—he was twenty-eight years old at the time—would be appreciated and effective in the district where 'young Turks' had played a critical role in the independence struggle.

Jacob S. Kaswende, a son of the important Shinyanga chief, Kaswende Shikila, became Area Commissioner of Shinyanga. Like the Makwaia family in Usiha, the Kaswendes were active, well-educated, and ubiquitous. Jacob made his peace with TANU and, during the transition, served in a number of posts with the Shinyanga African District Council and, after independence, as Executive Officer of the new District Council. In Kwimba

Sylvester Lubala duplicated Kaswende's move from Executive Officer of a District Council to Area Commissioner. Elected with TANU support to the Kwimba African District Council in 1960, he soon became Chairman of the Council, Chairman of TANU in the district and Executive Officer of the Council before receiving his appointment as Area Commissioner.

The political war-horse of TAA and TANU in Maswa, Stanley Kaseko, was appointed Area Commissioner of Maswa. Sukumaland's first political P.G. (Prison Graduate), Kaseko again became politically active in 1958 when TANU reopened in Maswa. He was elected district TANU chairman from 1959 to 1962 and chairman of the Maswa District Council from 1960 to 1962. With Kaseko's appointment Shabani Mohamed was transferred from Maswa to Mwanza, replacing the last British District Commissioner in Sukumaland.[1]

At the beginning of 1963, therefore, all of the Sukumaland districts had African Area Commissioners—and four of the five were themselves Sukuma. The fifth, Shabani Mohamed, had, of course, lived for many years in Sukumaland and a major portion of his responsibilities involved the town of Mwanza which was populated by Africans of a variety of tribal origins as well as by several thousand non-Africans. With Mohamed in Mwanza and Tanganyika's only four Sukuma Area Commissioners in the other four Sukumaland Districts, it would be difficult to argue that tribal compatibility and familiarity with the locality did not play an important role—at least in the first year—in Area Commissioner appointments in Sukumaland. Perhaps Nyerere calculated that new Area Commissioners would learn their new jobs best and most quickly on familiar ground and that the people, likewise, would be more accepting of a familiar face. Perhaps he felt that Sukuma officials could best counter the incipient and sometimes overt opposition to TANU among some Sukuma in the early months after independence. In any case, the desirability or necessity of such matching apparently receded in importance as the party in Sukumaland, as elsewhere, consolidated its position and as a cadre of experienced Area Commissioners evolved. By 1964 the number of Sukuma Area Commissioners had been reduced from four to two, and the two that remained—Kaseko

[1] Postings and biographical information from press releases and biographical file, Provincial Information Office, LPF. For further biographical data on individuals, see *Who's who in East Africa*, 1964 and subsequent editions.

and Lubala—had switched districts so that each was working outside his home area. Though appointments continued to be made on the basis of who could best handle the problems in a given district, henceforth tribal identification and experience locally counted for less—and experience and qualifications counted for more—in the total mix of factors considered.

New Regional Boundaries

In May 1963 five new regions were created in Tanganyika (with two more additions in October) because some 'were too large for effective administration.'[1] At first the Lake Region was to be split into three new regions: a Mwanza Region composed of Mwanza and Geita districts with headquarters in Mwanza; a Malya Region composed of Kwimba, Maswa and Shinyanga districts with headquarters at Malya; and a Mara Region of North Mara, Musoma and Ukerewe districts with headquarters at Musoma. By the time of reorganization in May, however, there were some changes. Ukerewe and Kwimba were added to Mwanza and Geita to form the new Mwanza Region. The Kahama district in the old Western Region was combined with Shinyanga and Maswa in a new Shinyanga Region with headquarters at Shinyanga.

John Malecela, a former district officer and foreign service officer who had replaced Wambura as Regional Commissioner of the Lake Region in March 1963, remained in Mwanza as Regional Commissioner for the truncated Mwanza Region. Malecela's appointment was of particular interest at the time as it was the first indication in post-independence Tanganyika that political and administrative posts at the higher levels of the party and the government were to be regarded as 'to some extent, interchangeable.'[2]

There were probably both practical and political reasons for the changes from the original plan. Ukerewe was more accessible,

[1] Tordoff draft (see note 1, p. 324, above).
[2] *Ibid.* Malecela, a Gogo, received his secondary education in Dodoma and at St Andrew's College, Minaki. He spent four years in India where he earned a Bachelor of Commerce degree from Bombay University. Returning to Tanganyika in 1959, he entered the administrative service as an assistant district officer. After a year at Cambridge University, he was appointed following independence as Third Secretary with the Tanganyika Mission to the United Nations and Consul to the United States. As Regional Commissioner, he became known as a tough and capable administrator, though inclined at times to be volatile and arbitrary. In late 1964, he returned to New York as Tanzania's Permanent Representative to the U.N. In 1968 he was appointed Tanzania's representative to the Organization of African Unity in Addis Ababa.

even by water, from Mwanza than it was over the very rough roads and unpredictable ferry which linked it to Musoma. With the need for economy an important factor, Mwanza was best equipped to handle extra districts. Finally, there may well have been some anxiety about lumping together into one region the three most conservative Sukuma districts—Kwimba, Maswa and Shinyanga—where strong chiefs like Makwaia, Salamba, Shoka, Charles and Francis Masanja, Ndaturu and Majebere were still influential and where opposition movements like the ANC and the PDP had during 1962 developed significant footholds. With Kwimba administered from Mwanza together with the three progressive lake front districts and the other two Sukuma districts joined with the non-Sukuma Kahama district in a long arc which geographically moved the center of gravity of the new region out of the Sukuma heartland (at Malya) to Sukumaland's southernmost border (Shinyanga), Nyerere and other TANU leaders may have felt that any possible further threat of consolidated Sukuma dissent might be minimized.

To the new Shinyanga Region, Nyerere appointed C. M. Kapilima, who had served briefly as provincial TANU secretary in the Lake Province in early 1959. A difficulty of time and geography, however, soon became apparent. Kapilima was posted as Regional Commissioner 700 miles away from his home constituency and equally far from Dar es Salaam where, as a member of the National Assembly, he would have meetings to attend. Thus, Kapilima was transferred in mid-1964 to Morogoro in exchange for the Morogoro Regional Commissioner, Chief Humbi Ziota, whose home constituency as a Member of the National Assembly, Nzega, bordered on Shinyanga. Chief Humbi was unusual as one of the few important traditional chiefs in Tanganyika to make a thoroughly successful entrance into the post-independence political arena.[1]

---

[1] Educated at Tabora secondary school, Chief Humbi Ziota was a clerk for the railways and for the government before becoming chief of Ussongo in Nzega District in 1943. He studied agriculture at Cambridge University and in Cyprus. In 1954 he was elected chairman of the Unyamwezi Federal Council and appointed a director of the Tanganyika Agricultural Corporation. He was nominated by the Governor as an unofficial member of the Legislative Council in 1957 and, like Chief David Kidaha Makwaia, was among the first Africans appointed to the rank of assistant minister. Awarded the M.B.E. for exemplary service during the colonial regime, he nevertheless—unlike Kidaha—aligned himself with TANU toward the end of the 1950's and was elected to the National Assembly from Nzega in 1958–59 and again in 1960.

Executive Officers Replace Chiefs

Most chiefs, however, did not fare as well. During 1960 and 1961 new TANU ministers had defended traditional chiefs and sub-chiefs against illegal dismissal from their positions by overzealous local TANU politicians acting through district councils. It was clear by 1961, however, that the entire native authority system would be revamped by the new TANU government. Already in early 1961 chairmen elected by the councils themselves had replaced *ex-officio* chairmen in District Councils. In April the Ministry for Local Government and Administration announced its intention to 'improve and strengthen the administrative machinery' of local authorities by moving away from any element of popular election in the selection of chiefs, subchiefs and headmen toward the appointment by district councils of 'permanent employees' who would 'progressively assume the duties of executive officers of councils at varying levels.'[1]

In late September and early October 1961, Nyerere personally met with representatives of the Tanganyika Chiefs' Convention to discuss the future role of traditional chiefs.[2] He told the chiefs that their identification with the colonial government during the time that politicians fought for independence had resulted in 'popular opposition to Chiefs in certain parts of Tanganyika at present.' Further, 'democracy demanded that the Chairman of Local Councils should be elected but this would clearly place the Chief, who in the past had been the sole ruler in his Chiefdom, in an anomalous position.' While the government 'fully realised the very grave dangers involved in breaking down this traditional set-up in Tanganyika:'

Against this the people's demands must, of necessity, be taken into account as otherwise Government would be accused of failing in its duty. People could not afford to be ostriches with their heads in the sand. No one could disregard the course of events which would surge on relentlessly.

Nyerere, who was himself the son of a chief, was telling the chiefs as gently as possible that there was no role for them *as chiefs* in modern local government. Nevertheless, a number of the chiefs pressed the Prime Minister for a policy statement to forestall concern about a too hasty removal of traditional chiefs so that, rather than dispensing with chiefs altogether, it should

---

[1] LG. 12/023 to all P.C.s, 20 Apr. 1961.   [2] See Listowel, pp. 320–1.

be made legally possible for particular chiefs to be removed from office where the people 'considered it desirable and in the interests of progress.'[1]

Nyerere, however, felt that the government could make no statement suggesting longevity of tenure for chiefs, but he was also unwilling to say unequivocally that chieftainship would be abruptly terminated. As Nyerere later explained to the Provincial Commissioner and the Lake Province Team in Mwanza:

The problem was whether to allow the post of Chief to die a natural death or to plan their transition to area executive officers. The problem was likely to be a temporary one as the educated sons of Chiefs would not wish to inherit so insecure a post and would prefer to serve the country in other ways. Government hoped that Chiefs would be replaced on their voluntary resignation when local conditions were suitable.[2]

While it was increasingly clear to all that the abolition of chieftaincy was only a matter of time, the government made no general policy statement and ambiguities regarding the status of chiefs persisted. Change came, then, in piecemeal fashion during 1962. While, as Nyerere had told the chiefs, 'each problem as it arose would be settled individually,' a planned transition to area executive officers was already under way. Locally, chiefs were encouraged to resign of their own initiative, and various chiefs did so during the course of the year. Chief Majebere Masanja of Mwagala, a chief for forty-five years, became the first important Sukuma to acknowledge the signs of the times when he resigned with effect from June 1962. Other chiefs followed. Chiefs who by late in the year had not announced their intention to resign were quietly informed by Regional and Area Commissioners that resignations would be required by 31 December.

As vacancies occurred, District Councils appointed acting executive officers to fill the posts until a complete reorganization of subdistrict administration could be effected and permanent appointments made. Surprisingly, acting executive officers were sometimes chosen from native authority cadres as when Mwanga Kulwa, formerly a subchief in Ntuzu, was selected to administer Mwagala after Chief Majebere's resignation. Political acceptability to TANU was a prerequisite to appointment, but TANU-

[1] This and previous quotations from 'Notes on a meeting between the Prime Minister, the Minister for Local Government and the Chiefs' Convention,' 2 Oct. 1961, LPF.
[2] Minutes of a meeting of the Prime Minister with Members of the Lake Province Provincial Team, 1 Nov. 1961, LPF.

dominated councils were not entirely unmindful of the need for administrative skill and experience. The choice was easiest in the rare instances where political acceptability and administrative experience appeared to coincide, as it did with Kulwa, or with Boniface Hima who was elected with TANU support to fill a vacant subchiefdom in Buhungukira in late 1961 and was appointed acting executive officer of Usmao after the rustication of Chief Francis Masanja in October 1962.

In August 1962 the Ministry for Local Government and Administration announced that the 'widely varying pattern' in rural local councils under the old native authority constitutions would be replaced with a pattern common to all districts. The Minister called for District Councils to submit proposals for the division of their districts into 'convenient' and 'natural' administrative units.[1] Previously existing chiefdoms or subchiefdoms could be fragmented or amalgamated as efficiency and suitability dictated. Predominantly elected divisional and village development committees would take over the functions of the former chiefdom and subordinate councils. On the administrative side, chiefs and subchiefs with suitable qualifications were to receive first consideration for appointment as Divisional Executive Officers. After the formation of the new divisions, a suitable number of subdivisions would be created and Assistant Divisional Executive Officers selected by the council to administer them. At village level, the number of headmen might be increased or decreased, but they were to be selected 'from among current village headmen who have demonstrated their capabilities.'[2]

While District Councils deliberated on their proposals, the Ministry for Local Government in late November issued a memorandum on the 'Position of Chiefs' which clarified once and for all the implications of subdistrict administrative reorganization and established a deadline for the changes. After 1 January 1963 chiefdoms would no longer exist as units of local government, and chiefs would no longer exercise legal or administrative powers or duties, though 'they would not be prevented from continuing their traditional functions.'[3] Chiefs would be replaced by Divisional Executive Officers appointed by District Councils and by Local Court Magistrates appointed by Regional Local Courts Officers

[1] LG. 51/04, 1 Aug. 1962.
[2] LG. 51/04 to all District Councils, 20 Sept. 1961. (Orig. Sw.)
[3] LGC. 11/04 to Executive Officers of all District Councils, 28 Nov. 1962.

responsible independently to the Minister. Provisions were laid down for the payment of gratuities to retiring chiefs. An era in Tanganyikan history was at an end.

Thus, District Councils were finally empowered, a year after independence, to proceed with the changes in administration and personnel which they had long desired. New divisions and sub-divisions were delineated so as to split up the larger chiefdoms and amalgamate the smaller ones. For the sake of convenience the boundaries of subchiefdoms were consistently followed, but these and the smaller chiefdoms were generally combined into entirely new units.[1]

The New Appointees

In spite of the government's announced intention to consider as many chiefs and subchiefs as possible for positions as executive officers, few chiefs in Sukumaland applied for the posts. Some were too old to make a new beginning; others knew that they did not have the educational qualifications necessary; most realized that their estrangement from the new elites which controlled TANU's local branches and the District Councils all but excluded them from serious consideration. A few chiefs were appointed executive officers or magistrates but, for the most part, such appointments were temporary expedients grudgingly acquiesced in by local political leaders in view of the demonstrable lack of other qualified personnel.

Chief Charles Kaphipa, for example, had provoked the wrath of Mwanza District TANU leaders when he indicated his desire to stand against Paul Bomani for the Legislative Council in the elections of 1960;[2] yet, at the age of thirty-two, with a Standard XII education, subsequent study in England, and five years of administrative experience as a chief, Charles was one of the most

---

[1] Nera's five subchiefdoms, for example, were parcelled out among three of Kwimba's seven new divisions. On the other hand, Mwagalla with its several subchiefdoms remained intact as one of Maswa's new divisions. In Mwanza the district's nine relatively small chiefdoms were combined into three divisions. To take maximum advantage of existing facilities, a divisional headquarters was usually selected from one of the former chiefdom head-quarters, though in cases where geography dictated otherwise it might be a centrally located subchiefdom headquarters. Subdivisional headquarters ordinarily corresponded to former subchiefdom headquarters. After re-organization, Mwanza went from nine chiefdoms to three divisions (changed later to five); Maswa went from eleven to seven; Shinyanga, from fourteen to seven; Kwimba, from six to seven; and Geita, from seven to six (changed later to seven). [2] See above, p. 271.

qualified and promising candidates in all of Sukumaland for a post as Divisional Executive Officer.

Charles's name did not appear on the list of recommendations originally sent by the Mwanza District Council to the Regional Commissioner, but Wambura asked the council to appoint Charles in light of the government directive stating that highly qualified chiefs should receive first consideration for the new posts. When the council refused, Wambura directed that Charles be appointed. The council insisted on its prerogative to choose its own staff; the Regional Commissioner invoked his power to enforce a rational and sensible choice in the face of parochial animosities and short-sighted local political attitudes. Charles was therefore appointed, but the council then refused to pay his salary. Strong measures by the Regional Commissioner were again required to bring the council into line. Ultimately, Charles served as Divisional Executive Officer of Mwanza's Busega Division until 1965 when he was appointed Executive Officer of an entire District Council in southern Tanganyika. Thus, Wambura's action in early 1963 prevented the premature throttling of a promising career in government service[1]

Subchiefs and native authority clerks fared far better than chiefs in garnering from one-half to two-thirds of the Divisional and Assistant Divisional Executive Officer appointments under the new administrative scheme. The number of purely political appointments was remarkably few. While scores of hopefuls applied for the new positions, those men most likely to be finally appointed were those who had prior experience with the operations of local government, yet were either young enough or had been sufficiently behind the scenes never to have earned the enmity of TANU leadership during the struggle for independence. Though this standard was not rigidly adhered to, Divisional Executive Officers and their assistants were theoretically supposed to have a minimum of eight years of schooling. This tended to exclude not only many of the older native authorities but also most district councillors (only three of the Mwanza District Council, for example, had more than Standard IV education) and most TANU branch secretaries and chairmen. It tended to favor

---

[1] In Geita the well-qualified Augustine Madaha—ex-subchief, political leader, TANU District Secretary, and member of the TANU National Executive— also was made a D.E.O. by Wambura against the wishes of the District Council. Madaha became an A.C. in 1964.

younger men, including a number who were relatives of traditional ruling families, who had received enough education for white collar positions but not enough to take them into the higher echelons of the civil service or to non-governmental positions in the larger towns.

In spite of the over-all supervision of the Regional Commissioner and his occasionally strong stand in specific instances, the occupation of executive officer proved a difficult one during 1963 and 1964. Salaries were modest and security of tenure was virtually nil. Executive officers were hired and transferred and dismissed with considerable frequency by the district councils. The appointments were political as well as administrative because the new officers had to be approved by the district TANU committee and by TANU-dominated district council committees, as well as by the Local Government Officer and the Regional Commissioner who were responsible to the Ministry for Local Government and Administration. The presence or absence of personal animosities and the results of political in-fighting were as likely to determine the future of an executive officer as his performance on the job. Under these conditions, the best candidates often were not attracted as applicants—especially as they were often the most likely to incur the disfavor of local politicians. Some councillors, too, coveted the positions for themselves and councils had to be continually reminded that, according to government regulations, councillors had to resign six months in advance of submitting any application for employment by the council.[1]

As of 1 January 1965, however, the Local Government Service Commission withdrew from the district councils its delegation of powers of appointment and dismissal of local executive officers. From that date, the Commission itself became fully responsible for local appointments. The prospect was for the building of a nationwide civil service of local executive officers which would establish higher standards, set and standardize better conditions of service and tenure and therefore attract more suitable candidates than those who had come forward during the rough-and-tumble first two years of appointment and dismissal under the aegis of district councils.

[1] As late as November 1964, the Geita District Council tried to appoint three A.D.E.Os from among its own members. R. C. Malecela wrote abruptly to the E.O. of the Council: 'You should bring to the notice of the Council that the commission of similar incidents, in future, will be dealt with very severely' (R.C. to E.O., 13 Nov. 1964, LPF).

336   The New Regime

The Deposed Chiefs

In the meantime, traditional chiefs went into eclipse. The few (like Hussein Makwaia, Charles Masanja and Charles Kaphipa) who received government appointments and obviously had careers of service ahead of them, were posted outside Sukumaland, or at least somewhere outside their own chiefdoms. Though some other member of the traditional ruling line then took over the chief's local responsibilities as head of the family, the geographical separation of the actual chief from his homeland reduced the importance of chiefdom-wide traditional ties and functions. The elder and less well-educated chiefs retired to their homes to cultivate the land. Those who had sufficient financial and material resources operated produce mills and contracted out tractors for plowing and trucks for transportation. But even where the chiefs remained within their home areas, they seldom continued —after the loss of their official administrative and judicial functions —to perform traditional ceremonies at the beginning of the agricultural year or otherwise functionally to sustain the traditional chiefly role. Before independence the more educated chiefs had come to regard traditional functions as primarily symbolic and, once they were relieved of political power, these symbols ceased to be important. Furthermore, many chiefs feared that anything they might undertake in the way of traditional functions—especially where large public gatherings were customary—might be misinterpreted by TANU and the government. Most, therefore, kept quietly to themselves.[1]

It is difficult to gauge the reaction in Sukumaland to the deposition of the chiefs from their positions as administrative and judicial arms of government. For the most part the changes were accepted quietly—a result which was aided by the government's tactic of abjuring dramatic statements on the issues while gradually eroding the position of the chiefs and extending over some months the replacement of the old system with the new. One seasoned observer, commenting on the lack of opposition to the displacement of chiefs, concluded that as an institution chieftainship was less important to the Sukuma than cattle—an insight supported by anthropologists who have noted the Sukuma capacity for adaptation to change except where, as with customs relating to cattle and certain agricultural methods, change appeared to threaten

[1] Interviews: Chiefs Charles Masanja, Charles Kaphipa and others.

fundamentally the socio-religious and material bases of their daily lives.[1]

The Chiefs of the Sukuma had been an import from the country to the west and north of Lake Victoria a century or two earlier and, during the years of British occupation, they had often become, in the eyes of their people, representatives of an alien colonial power. To the extent that chieftainship retained a traditional importance, it could, theoretically, continue since traditional chieftainship itself was not abolished. In practice, however, chiefship in Sukumaland had over the years become a composite of mutually interdependent traditional and colonially inspired elements—apparently not the least of which was the power conferred upon the chief as an agent of local government. So important, in fact, had this element become by 1963 that much of the form and function of traditional chiefship—the institution which provided the basis originally for the native authority system itself—all but collapsed as soon as the latter system, which had been constructed in part upon it, was dismantled.[2]

[1] The perceptive comment was from an American priest of the Maryknoll order who had spent many years in the Shinyanga area, the Reverend Alan Smidlein. I am indebted to anthropologists Gottfried O. Lang, Charles O. Noble and Warren J. Roth—all formerly attached to the Nyegezi Social Research Institute, Mwanza—for sharing their own supporting observations on this point with me.

[2] Rival traditional claims, however, continued to be put forward in some areas even after the independent government's new administrative structure had gone into operation. At first the government attempted to keep a careful watch on such matters; eventually it decided the more effective course was to ignore them as much as possible.

After the sudden death in November 1963 of Chief Edward Kamata of Sukuma chiefdom in Mwanza District, rival factions contested the succession. Kamata's son was selected by the electors and elders of the chiefly line to succeed his father, but the E.O. of the Mwanza District Council held that the election was void because it had taken place without the permission or knowledge of the government. Claimants for the chiefship were then referred to the District Council, but eventually the A.C. decided all claims should be submitted to him. With the government giving so much attention to the question, people apparently decided that the succession was a matter of importance after all and more hopefuls submitted their claims. A new election was held under government auspices, but rival claims continued to be advanced, much to the annoyance of officials who decided this was a way of 'bringing chiefly rule into the country of moving backward and inhibiting progress' (E.O. to A.C. to A.D.E.O., 4 Dec. 1963; A.D.E.O. to A.C., with note by A.S., 8 Oct. 1964, MZDF).

When conflicting claims were later advanced to the chiefship of Bulima, the A.C. wrote: 'We do not have the time to listen to claims which deprive us of time for building the nation. If this claimant desires to demonstrate [his interest in] building the country he should not be wasting time with

2　OPPOSITION POLITICS

Some African opposition to TANU had been voiced before
independence, but it crystallized in the immediate post-independence years of 1962 and 1963. The unsettling aspects of TANU
party activity at local levels and the obvious imperfections of the
neophyte TANU-controlled administration alienated some. Others
resisted the financial and political obligations which they saw
pressed upon them by the new regime—just as they had rebelled
against the taxation and legislation of the colonial administration.
The personal resentments and frustrations of those who found
themselves unwillingly by-passed in the earliest phase of consolidation of the newly evolving regime provided the grist for
another sort of discontent. Finally, there were some—particularly
a handful of better-educated chiefs, teachers and civil servants—
who believed (Nyerere's theories to the contrary) that democracy
required two or more political parties to provide for the sort of
organized competition which would encourage forthright expression of criticism or dissent and permit the fostering of possible
alternative policies and leadership. TANU could boast of one of
the most efficient, effective and united popularly based, nationalist
party organizations on the African continent. It could rightly
emphasize its important role in shaping a Tanganyika nearly
devoid of debilitating inter-tribal rivalries and divisive internecine
power struggles. Nevertheless, TANU had to deal with organized
political opposition as it moved toward the goal of African socialism
and the achievement of a one-party democratic republic.

The African National Congress

The Tanganyika African National Congress (ANC) was formed by
a dissident TANU leader, Zuberi Mtemvu, in 1958. In the belief
that Nyerere's leadership of TANU was too moderate, Mtemvu
defined the policy of his organization as 'Africa for the Africans

claims relating to chieftainship' (A.C. to E.O., Mwanza District Council,
14 Apr. 1964, MZDF). The E.O. agreed that the entire affair was 'nonsense'
because no complaints had been made against the chief, who was still alive,
and the chief had served faithfully during the years before his resignation.
He refused to allow the matter to be placed on the agenda of the District
Council (E.O. to A.C., 11 May 1964, MZDF). When Lupembe Masota of
Masanza I claimed the chieftainship of Masanza II after the death of the
latter's Chief Bahebe, the A.C. wrote in similar vein: 'The present task of the
government is to bring progress for the people which the English Colonialist
was unable to bring; it is not to sit around busying itself with little nuisances
or meaningless claims' (A.C. to Chief Lupembe, 13 Dec. 1963, MZDF).

only.' Yet he never posed an effective challenge to TANU. He was the only candidate of his party to contest the Legislative Council elections of 1958 and he and one other were the only ANC candidates in the 1960 elections. At the end of 1960 the ANC had nine organized branches as opposed to TANU's 498. Whenever Mtemvu stood for election, he was 'decisively, and derisively, defeated'—a performance which was repeated in his very weak showing against Nyerere in the presidential election of October 1962.[1] During 1961 and 1962, however, Mtemvu succeeded in forming provincial headquarters and branches in five new areas and the ANC probably reached the apex of its strength in mid-1962. As Taylor has pointed out, 'Although it still had little support from the general public, the fact that officials and money were found to open new branches indicated that the ANC was by no means dormant.'[2] Following his defeat in the presidential election, Mtemvu and other ANC partisans were re-absorbed into TANU— but not before the ANC had posed a challenge in several areas, among them Sukumaland.

In Mwanza, leadership of the ANC was assumed by Mzee Mkama, an elderly trader–politician, and Fabian Ngalaiswa, the young teacher who had earlier been instrumental in the formation of the Sukuma Union. In Kwimba the disappointed organizers of the Saidia Waafrika Company, led by Samson Masalu, gravitated toward the ANC. In Shinyanga relatives of the great chiefs of Usiha used the Makwaia name to rally support to the ANC banner in an area where the traditional ruling family still had strong popular support and where, as in Kwimba, the new TANU leadership sparked resentment. In Maswa where the political vulnerability of old-line Chiefs Majebere and Ndaturu occasioned their rapid decline and replacement by local TANU stalwarts—and where Majebere apparently attempted covertly to foster the ANC in his own chiefdom—the story was much the same. In Geita, however, ANC initiatives were less successful. The people of Geita had made TANU their own after the uprising of 1958, and more than any other district in Sukumaland Geita enjoyed popular control of local government and of the party organization.

Activities in Mwanza

Ngalaiswa joined the ANC in 1960—apparently the first important

[1] Bennett, *Makerere Journal*, No. 7 (1963), p. 11.   [2] Taylor, p. 199.

Mwanza personality to do so.[1] Perhaps another hundred persons joined when, in early 1961, F. E. Omido, the ANC's publicity secretary, came up-country to establish branches in the Mwanza, Bukoba and Tabora areas. After Omido left, Ngalaiswa and others set up an organization and applied for registration with the government. Michael Mashamba, a Sukuma with experience as a clerk and film projectionist, became provincial secretary; Ngalaiswa, treasurer; and Mkama, chairman. Mkama, a Kerewe, one of the original independent weighers of cotton in the late 1940's and active in TAA and TANU during the 1950s, had somehow fallen out with TANU leaders. From early 1961 he took a leading role in the ANC.

That the ANC appealed to a diversity of sentiments was clearly illustrated at a public meeting of the party in Mwanza in September 1961. After noting that the ANC and TANU were identical in striving for *uhuru*, Mkama enunciated the Mtemvu line that the ANC wanted *uhuru* for Africans only whereas TANU was a 'multi-racial' party. Mashamba questioned the retention of non-Africans in the Legislative Council. Another leader advocated a national election before independence, but wished chiefs to retain their positions after *Uhuru*. TANU was criticized for allegedly telling chiefs to instruct their people to join TANU, for threatening non-members with eviction from their land and expulsion from the country after independence and for improper intervention on behalf of the VFCU and against the Saidia Waafrika Company.[2]

Therefore, in addition to harboring those who chose to advocate a more militant black nationalism, the ANC served as an umbrella for some who wished to safeguard the position of traditional chiefs and for others who wanted opportunities to compete for the region's cotton market. There were many, too, who found themselves displeased with TANU's tendency to nominate, without much concern for local village sentiment, faithful party workers who, standing unopposed, then became 'representative' councillors to the District Council. Thus, the ideology of the ANC was not nearly as important in garnering support in parts of Sukumaland as was the simple fact that it offered an alternative for those who had for one reason or another become disenchanted with TANU.

---

[1] From 1953 to 1963 Ngalaiswa was a school supervisor for the Tanganyika Episcopal Conference of the Roman Catholic Church. He was elected to the Mwanza District Council in 1960 and served until his resignation in 1964.

[2] *Lumuli*, No. 200, 1 Oct. 1961.

Whether the malcontents first came to the ANC or whether the ANC first tailored its message to appeal to this miscellany of specific grievances is not altogether clear, but a *marriage de convenance* did take place. Like the leaders of TAA and of the Sukuma Union a decade earlier, the leaders of the ANC found it possible to begin the organization of a political movement by focusing a variety of discontents into a coordinated protest. The ANC grew, especially in Kwimba and Shinyanga, as various brands and degrees of popular discontent found it an available and therefore useful vehicle for expression.

Isolation of ANC Councillors

In Kwimba Samson Masalu, the disappointed organizer of the Saidia Waafrika Company, became by early 1962 outspoken in his criticism of TANU and open in his support of the ANC. Though he himself refrained from aggressive organizational activity, he apparently did sell ANC membership cards and hundreds of his Saidia Waafrika followers gravitated into political identification with the Congress. At the same time, Masalu continued as an independent to represent his home constituency in the Kwimba District Council. Surprisingly since all but a handful of the councillors had come into office as TANU candidates, Masalu was elected chairman of the council's Natural Resources Committee in early 1962.

That an independent known to be a member of the ANC should be a committee chairman struck TANU district leaders as intolerable. The chairman of the full council denounced the selection of Masalu and asked the Natural Resources Committee to vote again. Masalu was re-elected. The Executive Officer of the Council, Sylvester Lubala, ordered the committee to elect someone else or the committee would be closed down. Masalu was chosen a third time. TANU leaders then brought the matter before the full council which decided that it had no confidence in Masalu and could not 'permit him to serve as chairman of any committee whatsoever.' Lubala's case against Masalu, and that of the council majority, was that he had been 'elected independently, was a member of Congress and a prime opponent of the government's programs.'[1] That such strenuous efforts were required to dislodge Masalu from his post was a testament either

[1] Minutes of a meeting of the Kwimba District Council, 13–14 Apr. 1962; E.O. to Masalu, 21 July 1962, KWDF.

342 The New Regime

to Masalu's personal popularity with some members of the Council or to the extent to which Kwimba's TANU leaders had already succeeded in evoking recalcitrant responses from councillors who were not willing to be told what to do. It is not likely that the twice-repeated reaffirmation by members of the committee of Masalu's original selection was indicative of support for ANC *per se*, but the use of TANU's greater power to enforce the exclusion of Masalu from the chairmanship provided the sort of incident on which the ANC could build a case against TANU.

Outraged by the undemocratic treatment he was receiving, Masalu complained to the Area Commissioner and the Minister for Local Government: 'Since the Council is composed of people freely elected by the people, it cannot tolerate interference from one who is only a civil servant and who was not chosen by the people to represent them.' His somewhat lengthy defense is of interest as an example of the principles invoked by articulate opponents of TANU:

With regard to his accusations that I oppose the programs of the government, this is unadulterated nonsense. As a councillor, I understand completely my obligations to my government. Clearly a councillor is one who is charged with showing a good example to the people and doubtless the confidence of the people in choosing me to be councillor arose from my zeal for and obedience to my government...

That I am a member of Congress does not imply that I do not represent the people. As a councillor I represent everyone, be he TANU, Congress, or any other party in the country. As a councillor I work for the welfare of all people and of the entire country not for personal profit or a particular party. If the Executive Officer works only as a TANU member and for the benefit only of TANU, perhaps he does not understand his obligations to the District and to this country of Tanganyika.[1]

Masalu did not regain his committee chairmanship though discussion of the matter with the Ministry for Local Government dragged on into 1963. The record then states simply that the Regional Commissioner interviewed Masalu and that Masalu 'dropped the subject.'[2]

Ngalaiswa encountered similar difficulties in the Mwanza District Council, having been elected to the council unopposed in 1960 when TANU had failed to find a suitable and locally acceptable candidate to stand against him. Like Masalu, he was an independent known to be a member of the ANC and reportedly,

[1] Masalu to A.C. and Member for Local Government, 13, 24 July 1962, KWDF.
[2] A.C. to R.C., 31 Jan. 1963, KWDF.

therefore, subjected to intense pressure from TANU to resign. He found it difficult to get a hearing in the council where improper as well as proper procedures were used to by-pass him. At an April 1962 meeting of the council, for example, he noted that two councillors were in jail and suggested that they should not be allowed to continue to hold their official positions. In response to Ngalaiswa's suggestion, the council minutes record what is surely a most curious procedural move by the chairman on an item of business brought by a member:

This matter caused misunderstanding in the Council and the Chairman ruled that Mr. Ngalaiswa should leave the meeting. When he refused to do so, the Chairman adjourned the meeting.[1]

Customarily, TANU councillors met together in the TANU office before every council session; it was there under the supervision of TANU leaders rather than in the council chamber itself that important questions were decided. Likewise, if a dispute arose during the council session, the meeting was suspended so that difficulties could be ironed out in the TANU office during the recess. Councillors supported by TANU for election were, in practice, obliged to follow the instructions or suggestions of district party leaders. Ngalaiswa, of course, was excluded from these TANU caucuses but, despite his superior education and experience, he was also shunted aside within the council as being politically undesirable. He was not allowed, for example, to sit on the education committee which was his specialty. The only role he was able to play was that of gadfly: to call attention to certain abuses, to warn the council itself about 'the further spread of doubts and anxieties in the hearts of the people.'[2]

The ANC in Shinyanga, Maswa and Geita

In Shinyanga, meanwhile, the ANC, though without independent representatives in the District Council, made substantial headway in some important chiefdoms. As early as April 1960, before the ANC had even appeared in Mwanza or Kwimba, a district branch opened in Shinyanga town. Claiming 100 members at its inception, the Shinyanga branch was led by district chairman Hassani Makwaia, an elder step-brother of Chief Hussein Makwaia, and

[1] Minutes of a meeting of the Mwanza District Council, 12–16 Apr. 1962, MZDF.
[2] Ngalaiswa to Chairman of the Mwanza District Council, 28 Jan. 1962, MZDF.

by district secretary Idi Makwaia, a younger brother of Chief Hussein. By accident or design, the ANC office was located on Makwaia Street in the township.

According to some, Idi Makwaia had hoped to become chief of Usiha before Hussein was selected to succeed David Kidaha in 1954. When TANU opened in Shinyanga in 1958, Idi quickly joined and became a local leader. Apparently he hoped that TANU would support him in a bid for the chieftainship or eventually would provide for him a new route to power in Usiha. But Chief Hussein already worked closely with TANU's district secretary, Shabani Mohamed, and it may have appeaìed to Idi that there was nowhere for him to go politically. Eventually, he resigned from TANU to become secretary of the African National Congress.[1]

Under Idi Makwaia's leadership the ANC moved to build a basis of popular support to challenge the political hegemony of TANU in Shinyanga. At the end of 1960 the administration reported: 'The ANC is now attracting larger audiences. They appear to be exploiting the differences between the unofficial [TANU] councillors and traditional Native Authorities.'[2] Because the ANC was active in Shinyanga, the Provincial Commissioner asked that its office-bearers 'apply for registration without further delay.'[3] When the ANC's national officer, Omido, made his visit to Sukumaland in January 1961, he travelled with Idi Makwaia to various parts of the district. Makwaia, together with the new district chairmen, Ndugulile Malingila, an ex-chief and former secretary of the Shinyanga Tanganyika African Association, toured extensively in outlying areas from March to August 1961. At the public meetings the leaders discussed ANC policies, problems of economics and local government, and local council elections. Political touring followed the pattern set earlier by TANU, and the ANC unabashedly sought not only the permission but the active support of local native authorities.

The ANC was active also in parts of Maswa District during 1961 and 1962. A district branch office with fifty members and a committee of twelve opened at Nyalikungu following Omido's

[1] Another member of the family, Robert Mwinula Makwaia, remained a TANU supporter, served as a TANU branch leader, and was elected with TANU backing to the Shinyanga District Council. By 1964, however, he was in preventive detention—another indication that members of the Makwaia family were rightly or wrongly held in suspicion by other TANU leaders.
[2] District Team Report, 28 Nov. 1960, SHDF.
[3] P.C. to D.C., 14 Dec. 1960, SHDF.

visit in January 1961. Alex Abdalah served as district chairman and Francis Mwandu as secretary. By the end of February Chief Majebere's chiefdom of Mwagala reported 187 members. While not openly an opponent of TANU, Majebere seemed to lend his covert sympathy to the ANC and, under the leadership of Masanja Kija, the party gained considerable support in Mwagala during 1961 and early 1962. While local leaders in the district came from a variety of personal backgrounds, it is of interest that two, Chenge Mwanilanga and Longa Majebere, were respectively a former chief deposed by the colonial administration for unsatisfactory conduct and a former subchief dismissed for the same reason by the TANU-controlled District Council just before independence.

After registration of the Maswa branch was granted officially by the government in February 1962, ANC President Mtemvu visited Maswa during an up-country tour. Until July (when ANC meetings were banned by the government throughout the Lake Region), ANC leaders in Maswa held scores of meetings throughout the district. As elsewhere, the party combined in its appeal to the populace the radical proposition of government by and citizenship for Africans only, the conservative theme of respect for traditional native authorities, and a variety of grievances against TANU and the TANU-supported cooperatives.

In contrast to the other Sukumaland districts, the ANC made little if any headway in Geita where popular government was firmly based and TANU strong. When Mtemvu made a visit to Geita on behalf of ANC in early 1962, he found nowhere to stay because no one was willing to take him in. People were reasonably satisfied with their lives and there was therefore little political discontent. While covert identification with ANC was a recourse for some individual personalities who found themselves by-passed or otherwise disenchanted, the position of TANU in Geita had not weakened as much by 1962 as it had in the other Sukuma districts. Augustine Madaha, TANU's district secretary, and Hussein Majaliwa, the district chairman, undertook a TANU census and membership recruitment campaign in early 1962. In twelve days they collected nearly 5,400 shillings and registered 3,000 new members, bringing total TANU membership in the district to 28,000.[1] Thus, TANU membership rose in Geita at the same time that the ANC was creating a problem for an increasingly

[1] Press release, Provincial Information Office, 28 Mar. 1962, LPF.

embattled TANU in the other districts. While the pages of *Lumuli* registered in news reports and letters to the editor sentiment favoring the ANC among significant numbers in Kwimba and Mwanza districts, a letter written to *Lumuli* in May 1961 was indicative of the hostile reaction of the vast majority of Geita people to the ANC.

We do not like the Congress of [Mr. F. E.] Omido. When Nyerere was fighting with TANU for Uhuru these Congress people were silent. Today when there is no problem they start with their political parties. We Sukuma are not so stupid as to join. Surely these [Congress] people are clever like birds who eat the millet before the owner [gathers the grain]. So, Omido, you had better take your party back to Kenya where there would then be three parties: KANU, KADU, and Congress. We Sukuma will not accept such a party [as the ANC].[1]

While it may be an unwarranted generalization to say, as has Ngalaiswa, that any political party had to have the support of the local chief and headmen before it could make any headway, it is probably true that the ANC found support most readily in those areas where chiefs who still retained prestige and influence received it sympathetically. For the most part, Sukumaland's chiefs had finally accepted TANU in 1958 and 1959 together with TANU's assurances that chiefs would be respected during the transition from colonial rule to independence. By 1960 and 1961, however, they were becoming disabused of any thoughts they may have had of maintaining their positions of leadership in the face of the strong assault against them, waged in the district councils and elsewhere by local TANU leadership. The ANC, therefore, had an *entré*: it could make the same promises to the chiefs that TANU had made two years earlier but had failed to fulfil. In fact, an important part of the ANC's message in Sukumaland was that chiefs should be respected and their positions preserved in an independent Tanganyika. Especially in Shinyanga and Maswa, chiefs, their extended families and their sympathizers then provided an emotional and numerical core for ANC strength. Once launched, the opposition movement attracted a diversity of discontented elements—like those who initiated ANC activity in Mwanza and Kwimba—who were united principally by their distaste for political trends under TANU leadership. The rallying cry of the dissidents—'democracy' and 'freedom'—posed a perplexing question: should a movement opposed to TANU

[1] Letter from Julius Ubaga, *Lumuli*, No. 191, 1 May 1961.

be permitted to exist outside of TANU? After independence TANU answered in the negative: it criticized, restricted and eventually abolished organized opposition.

Shinyanga illustrated the pattern whereby sympathy for native authorities coalesced with disapproval of TANU to produce an opposition prepared to fight for its rights on grounds of political principle. In March 1962 the Shinyanga branch of ANC had been registered by the government as a political party. In May ANC's district chairman, Hassani Makwaia, wrote to TANU headquarters questioning and criticizing statements made by TANU leaders in public meetings. Countering a TANU accusation that chiefs and their families appropriated schools and hospitals for their own use during the colonial period, he argued that they were among the few who forced themselves and their relatives to take advantage of the opportunities made available to the people during the colonial era. He then moved on to the crux of the developing conflict in political philosophy between TANU and the ANC—which, of course, had to affirm the appropriateness of opposition as a rationale for its own existence:

> It is a very regrettable thing to say that TANU is the government. In this regard you deceive people. TANU is only a political party with its own flag. The government has a [different] flag which is the flag of our nation. The sum total of all Tanganyikans, even those of no political identification whatsoever, fought for Independence. Had it been TANU alone relatively few people would have been involved and we would not have succeeded...

Makwaia also charged that TANU used techniques of compulsion which was tantamount to a new colonialism:

> It is a very regrettable thing that TANU secretaries follow people to their homes to pressure them into buying membership cards on threat of being called out first for voluntary labor if they do not. I say that this is colonialism rather than self-help. TANU is a political party which had to procure registration. Others parties have the same right and obligation...

> It seems clear that any native authority who does not take out a TANU card will be dismissed from his position. Is this to build or to tear down? You leave aside, then embrace colonialism... [1]

He wrote to the District Commissioner lodging a formal complaint that people were being forced to buy TANU membership cards.

[1] Makwaia to TANU District branch headquarters, Shinyanga, 8 May 1962, SHDF.

While some chiefs undoubtedly helped to foster the ANC, others still openly identified with TANU. Makwaia Luhende, the sub-chief of Negezi in Usiha and another member of the Makwaia family, roundly criticized Hassani for his May letter criticizing TANU. He pointed out, quite correctly, that TANU was both the government and a political party. Hassani wrote back that a sub-chief's job was to serve all the people within his jurisdiction. If a subchief identified with TANU, should ANC supporters then elect their own subchief to take care of their needs? He angrily denounced the gratuitous suggestion of Luhende that he resign from the ANC, affirming that he had entered and would leave any political party he wished of his own free will.[1]

Other chiefs did not know what position to take but were clear that sympathy with the ANC could have unfortunate consequences. Officially, the ANC was a legal party and like TANU required only the permission of the local chief before applying to the police and the district office for an official meeting permit. The burden of decision, therefore, lay initially with the chief. During a post-independence transitional period when Tanganyika was rapidly becoming, but had not yet become, a one-party state, it was difficult indeed for chiefs—especially those who still reported to expatriate District Commissioners—to decide whether or not to grant permission for ANC meetings. Legally, the ANC had a right to meet, but politically the chiefs feared TANU might take strong steps against them if they gave their permission.

While the chiefs contemplated their dilemma or took one side or the other, competition between TANU and ANC supporters characterized the local scene wherever ANC established an outpost. Open conflict sometimes erupted. One ANC sub-branch, which had requested but had not yet received registration, raised the red and black flag of the party 'without permission.'[2] TANU supporters overran the ANC office and burned the flag. The ANC sub-branch chairman deplored the resort to violence and appealed to the District Commissioner and the police for protection.[3] The question of the ANC's right to fly its own flag arose also in Maswa, and ultimately the Regional Commissioner himself had to inform TANU district secretaries that no permission was required to fly the Congress flag since the ANC was a legally permitted political party.

[1] Luhende to Hassani, 16 May; Hassani to Luhende, 22 May 1962, SHDF
[2] Chief of Uchunga to Police Commander, 7 Aug. 1962, SHDF.
[3] Uchunga ANC to D.C. and Police, n.d. (Aug. 1962), SHDF.

Ban on the ANC

In early June 1962—four months before Tanganyika's first post-independence national election—ANC's regional chairman, Mzee Mkama, led a meeting in Mwanza which prompted a ban on the party's meetings throughout the region for most of the remaining campaign time. According to the government, ANC speakers at the meeting burned a 'TANU card, a TANU flag and a portrait of the TANU President, Mr. Nyerere.'[1] Other accounts say that Mkama had collected from the audience and had started to burn some TANU cards but had not yet burned Nyerere's picture (though he apparently indicated an intent to do so) when some in the audience threw sand and stones. A small riot ensued and Mkama was beaten before police restored order. Concerned about ANC activities in several of the districts of the Lake Region, Oscar Kambona, the Minister for Home Affairs, took the occasion 'to cancel any further meetings planned by ANC in the Lake Region or elsewhere until...satisfied that provocative conduct of the kind that took place in Mwanza will not be repeated.' The government statement said:

The rights of members of the public to hold meetings and to criticize Government Policy is not in question. Government is, however, determined that law and order shall be maintained. It has been a tradition in Tanganyika that politics of all kinds should be conducted in a peaceful and orderly fashion. Provocative acts of a nature likely to lead to breaches of the peace cannot be permitted to continue...[2]

The problem of provocative acts had always been a two-sided affair. Without in any way condoning Mkama's approach, fairness requires that it be pointed out that ANC meetings were sometimes subjected to organized harassment by TANU supporters. The untoward pressures brought to bear on ANC leaders and would-be candidates for public office are a matter of record. While the government may have been perfectly justified in its action from the point of view of maintaining law and order, one cannot but reflect that history echoes if it does not repeat itself. Kambona's rhetoric was nearly identical to the language the colonial administration used in suppressing irresponsible TANU activities in an earlier day. Beneath the language, too, was a similar intent. While extolling the virtues of free political expression, the colonial government found the pretexts it needed to quash political

[1] Press release, Provincial Information Office, 13 June 1962, LPF.   [2] *Ibid.*

expression which raised uncomfortable or embarrassing questions about British rule. Similarly, the TANU government of independent Tanganyika would tolerate no threat to its dominant position. While reserving judgment on the ideological and political commitment to the one-party democratic state which followed the formation of the Republic in December 1962, it must here be observed that, while speaking the language of free political expression at a time when a campaign between duly registered political parties was being waged, the TANU government nevertheless moved in mid-1962 to circumscribe the public activities of the only political opposition of any importance—the ANC.

And the ANC was making headway in mid-1962—the sort of headway which prompted the government to take the Mwanza incident as the occasion to suppress the entire party. Earlier, the Maswa District Council attempted on its own to ban the party in Maswa. The Kwimba District Council had written the Minister for Home Affairs requesting a ban on the ANC not only in Kwimba but in Sukumaland as a whole. The TANU-dominated council argued that Congress organizers in Kwimba 'misinterpreted' TANU policy with the result that TANU was given a 'bad reputation' in the district. The June issue of *Lumuli* reported that 600 people in Kwimba had renounced TANU and joined the ANC. P. C. Walwa, Kwimba's former TANU district chairman and Tanganyika's Junior Minister for Agriculture, told an audience in Kwimba that any government servant who wished to join the ANC would have to renounce TANU, turn in his TANU card, and face dismissal from his job. Affirming its unqualified support for TANU, the District Council made the same declaration with regard to servants of local native authorities. In a letter to the editor of *Lumuli*, a dismayed Congress supporter asked how the capability of a government servant would be deemed to change simply because of political identification? ANC's president, Mtemvu, told *Lumuli* he didn't see why, if the Congress had widespread support in Kwimba, it should be banned. He noted that even TANU members were turning to the ANC and said that if the government did not allow it to operate in the district, 'then it means that Tanganyika is not a democratic country.'[1]

The seriousness of the ANC's inroads in Kwimba—even after the ban had been in effect more than a month—became manifest

---

[1] *Lumuli*, No. 216, 20 June, 1962.

when a special high-level TANU delegation from outside the district made a tour through Kwimba in early September to counter ANC propaganda. A press release from the Regional Information Office stated:

As a result of the activities of some members of the African [National] Congress in Kwimba District recently leaders of TANU from all districts of Sukumaland have launched a direct campaign against this opposition political party in view of the forthcoming Presidential Election.[1]

Regional Commissioner Wambura and Isaac Munanka, Parliamentary Secretary in the Prime Minister's office, joined the delegation for major public meetings at Ibindo, the constituency represented in the District Council by Samson Masalu and at Bungulwa, the headquarters of Chief Francis Masanja of Usmao, who had been elected a Member of Legislative Council with TANU support in 1960 but by 1962 was considered to have drifted into sympathy with the opposition.

Rustication of Francis Masanja, Member of Parliament

By late 1961 Masanja had begun to run into difficulties with local TANU leadership in Kwimba—in particular with the district secretary, Robert Mamiro. He took exception to public statements by Mamiro attacking chiefs and privately questioned Mamiro's leadership capabilities. TANU leaders felt that Francis had supported the Saidia Waafrika movement (which had its strongest base of support in Usmao) and had encouraged independent candidates for election to the District Council. As early as October 1961 the TANU District Committee passed a resolution of no confidence in Masanja. Concerned about pockets of ANC sentiment in the district—particularly in Usmao—Mamiro blamed Masanja for allowing an anti-TANU psychology to develop. He accused him of doing a poor job as chief and Member of Parliament and of being against TANU.[2]

Wambura then openly criticized Masanja at a public meeting in the latter's chiefdom:

I have heard that you are being misled by some political agitators amongst whom your chief has been included. Your chief has joined the opposition political party called the African National Congress. Indeed you have become like the lost sheep of the Bible and I have come to look for you.

[1] Press release, Provincial Information Office, 22 Sept. 1962, LPF.
[2] Mamiro to Chairman of the Kwimba African Council, 27 Oct. 1961, KWDF.

Wambura asked all who were TANU members to raise their hands. According to a government press release 'all people raised up their hands in the air to prove that they were members and there was nobody who was a follower of Congress.' Wambura continued:

I expect your chief to be here in his capacity as a chief and also as M.P. but unfortunately he is not here. Although up to the time I am talking to you your chief is still a Member of Parliament on the TANU ticket he has found it fit to join the opposition party namely the African National Congress. This is a gross hypocrisy! I am also informed that he is abusing his responsibility as a chief by not working hard. However, the solution to this is not very far to seek.

For Wambura the solution was to prepare for the removal of Masanja from his position as chief and for his deportation from Kwimba District. Within a matter of days he was 'suspended by the Minister for Local Government and Administration...as a result of various allegations that have been made.' The government would allow Masanja to attend the September session of the National Assembly, but a 'formal inquiry into these allegations' would follow thereafter.[1]

Masanja arrived at the Bungulwa meeting after Wambura's departure. Angered by what was reported to him about the Regional Commissioner's speech, which he considered an unwarranted 'personal attack,' he announced to his constituents that he could no longer tolerate TANU and intended to resign forthwith.[2] While in Dar es Salaam Masanja sought the counsel of Chief Charles Masanja who advised him to try to clarify matters with senior TANU personnel before formally breaking with the party.[3] Francis felt that the breach could not be healed and he decided to resign before he was expelled. He joined the ANC, informed the press of his decision, and was thereupon deported by government order to Geita where he remained in rustication for several months. He was subsequently formally deposed, though this was a somewhat academic result since all chiefs in Tanganyika lost their executive and administrative powers at the start of the new year. Though estranged from TANU, he remained a Member of the National Assembly.

The People's Democratic Party

During 1962 a new political party joined the ranks of the opposition. C. K. Tumbo was the founder of the People's Democratic

[1] Press release, Provincial Information Office, 26 Sept. 1962, LPF.
[2] *Lumuli*, No. 218, July 1962.   [3] Chief Charles Masanja, interview.

Party. Like Zuberi Mtemvu, Tumbo began his political career as a TANU activist. A trade union leader, he was elected to the National Assembly with TANU support in 1960 but by early 1962 found himself disinclined to continue to follow the lead of Nyerere and TANU. On the floor of the National Assembly he struck a radical pose, suggesting after independence that Tanganyika was 'soft,' that it had not had a real revolution as had the Congo. The party's motto was 'Freedom, Equality and Unity.' The PDP was registered territorially in March 1962 and opened a Mwanza office in October.

Again, as with the ANC before it, specific items of principle and program—which in any case were far from clearly articulated—seemed less important in garnering support than the simple fact that the new party offered another alternative to TANU. Chief Francis Masanja joined and became vice-president of the PDP after his brief flirtation with the ANC. To those disenchanted with TANU, the ANC seemed by September 1962 to be losing ground whereas the PDP seemed untarnished and promising. Discontented elements repaired to the new banner.

One such was Shinyanga's ex-chief, David Kidaha Makwaia. One of Tanganyika's most important personalities in the early postwar period, he became estranged from TANU for a variety of reasons in the middle and late 1950s. He had a popular following, however, in his home chiefdom of Usiha and generally throughout Sukumaland. A member of the Legislative Council since 1945 and an Assistant Minister in 1957–58, he considered standing for the Legislative Council elections of February 1959 in opposition to the official TANU candidate, Paul Bomani, but Nyerere and John Rupia persuaded him not to. Nyerere argued that there was little point in Africans fighting against each other in the first territorial elections when only a few seats were open to them. Nyerere suggested that Kidaha wait until a later election when there would be more constituencies available.

Kidaha was not asked by TANU to run in the 1960 elections and he took no initiative himself. By 1962, however, he had become increasingly distressed with the abuses of people in power. He interpreted some of Nyerere's speeches as inviting constructive opposition. He had never joined the ANC, which he felt was 'basically the same as TANU' except for 'personality differences.' But the PDP appeared different, or at least, as he explained it: 'I felt it could be different in my area, . . . [that it would be possible]

BB

to work for democracy.' When he joined the PDP in October, he was offered a national office in the party but he refused it. He became an ordinary member and volunteered, as the first priority task for the party, to recruit members.[1]

Kidaha immediately embarked on an active recruitment campaign in Shinyanga, Kwimba and Maswa. Three sorts of grievances were widespread and provided the basis for his appeal to the people: criticism of the Victoria Federation, disenchantment with rigid TANU control of local government institutions and elections and disapproval of the denigration of chiefs. People felt the Victoria Federation had officious clerks, practiced nepotism and fed profits to the Bomani family rather than back to the growers—the last, a view that Regional Commissioner Wambura felt it necessary to counter publicly in Kwimba.[2] People were angered with TANU's sometimes arbitrary designation of candidates in local elections and its equally strenuous efforts to discourage anyone else from contesting an election once a TANU candidate had been designated. Kidaha did not make chieftainship itself explicitly an issue—it was academic since he had resigned as chief in 1954—but implicitly it could not help but be an important undercurrent with Kidaha himself recruiting actively for a dissident political party.

Deportation of the Makwaias

Thus, as had been the case with the ANC during the previous two years, the PDP in Sukumaland had the potential of rallying sometimes disparate, sometimes overlapping segments of anti-VFCU, anti-TANU and pro-chief sentiment behind a single opposition banner. If anything, the overt association of two outstanding and influential Sukumaland personalities—Francis Masanja and Kidaha—made PDP potentially more of a threat to TANU's position in Sukumaland than the ANC, which had suffered from outside foreign (Omido was from Kenya) and less distinguished local leadership. Some of Kidaha's supporters have said that if he had been allowed to continue his organizational activities on behalf of the PDP, he would have turned the balance in all of Sukumaland. While this may be an exaggeration, there is no question but that Kidaha had immense prestige and that an open challenge by him of TANU leadership would have had substantial impact.

---

[1] Chief David Kidaha, interview.
[2] Press release, Provincial Information Office, 22 Sept. 1962, LPF.

Kidaha's recruitment campaign lasted only a week. On 30 October the government announced that deportation orders had been served on Kidaha and on his brother Chief Hussein for 'using their position as ex-Chief and Chief not only to stir up opposition to Government's policy with regard to Chiefs but to inflame local feelings by conduct calculated to endanger peace and good order in Shinyanga District.' While the reason for Kidaha's deportation was clearly his activity on behalf of the PDP, Hussein seems to have been guilty only by association. The two were rusticated to Tunduru and Chunya respectively in southern Tanganyika where they were permitted to live a normal life, but with movement restricted and confined to certain areas.[1]

That the government was gravely concerned about the prospects for the organization and articulation of opposition sentiment in Sukumaland under the aegis of such prominent personalities as Francis and the Makwaias could not have been made more clear than by the stern steps of deportation taken against them. Nowhere else in Tanganyika did leading chiefs provoke or receive the application of such stringent prophylactic measures. The problem of opposition in Sukumaland was more acute, and regarded by the government as potentially much more troublesome, than elsewhere. The same geopolitical factors which made Sukumaland of such interest to the colonial government made it important to the new regime: Sukumaland was large, populous, wealthy. The Sukuma penchant for not wishing to be pushed around by outsiders—combined with the proven capability for concerted popular expression of discontent, civil disobedience and effectively organized opposition—made manifestations of disenchantment in Sukumaland especially worrisome. While Sukumaland's relation to Tanganyika was not comparable to that of Buganda to Uganda or Katanga to the Congo, Sukumaland was still of a size and importance to require special handling. It will be recalled that the new regime had decided against the continuation in any form of the Sukumaland Federal Council, that the conservative heartland area of Sukumaland was divided between separate regions in a special subsequent revision when new administrative boundaries were drawn up, and that Sukuma Area Commissioners—including a member of another important chiefly line in Makwaia's home district of Shinyanga—had been appointed to all the Sukumaland districts except Mwanza by late 1962. The

[1] Press release, Provincial Information Office, 30 Oct. 1962, LPF.

rustication of the several politically active Sukuma chiefs—at a
time when the popular reaction to the deposition of chiefs from
their positions of administrative authority was not yet clear and
when manifestations of opposition political sentiment were all too
clear—was but another move calculated to insure against increasing difficulties for the government in Sukumaland.

An End of Opposition

Nyerere's overwhelming victory over Mtemvu in the October
presidential election paved the way for the demise of the ANC
and for the formal and official commitment of TANU and Tanganyika to the formation of a one-party state. While Mtemvu
might have received a few more votes if the ANC had not been
victimized and banned in Sukumaland, it is also possible that he
might have received fewer. Either way, the few thousand votes
which he did receive rendered his challenge to Nyerere and TANU
at the territorial level, and in Sukumaland, insignificant. Meeting
in early January 1963, TANU's National Executive Committee
resolved, and the TANU Annual Conference subsequently approved the resolution, that Tanganyika should become a democratic
one-party state.

Consistent with this commitment, the National Executive
Committee decided to open TANU to non-Africans and to welcome back into the party all former members who had strayed to
opposition groups in previous years. Amir H. Jamal, an Asian
cabinet minister, became the first non-African member of TANU
on 21 January 1963. The following day Mtemvu—whose ANC
Executive Committee had decided on the party's dissolution in
November after the presidential election—rejoined TANU. The
Registrar of Societies announced that ANC was officially struck
from the register and the government made clear that any further
activity on behalf of ANC or any of its branches would be
illegal.[1]

Though other national officers of the PDP took the opportunity
to rejoin TANU in January 1963, Tumbo himself spurned the
offer. Eventually, he fled to Kenya and his party, though not
officially struck from the register, became moribund. In Sukumaland the rustications of the two most prominent PDP leaders had
crippled the party's efforts there as early as October 1962. Consistent with the new soft line toward past opponents or accused

[1] *Tanganyika News Review*, Feb. 1963, p. 4.

opponents of the party, Nyerere revoked in March the rustication orders against Kidaha and Hussein Makwaia 'in accord with the prevailing spirit of amity and national unification.'[1] Hussein— who had joined TANU in 1958 and never strayed officially into the opposition fold—became a civil servant and within a month of his release had become a staff officer at Morogoro. By February 1964 he had risen to the post of Area Secretary. Kidaha did not join the government; but the unusual style of Tanganyikan politics was illustrated by the fact that immediately after his release he was welcomed to the State House for dinner with President Nyerere. He joined TANU for the first time in January 1964.

While organized opposition in Sukumaland was all but dead by early 1963, a few intrepid individuals raised their voices from time to time. There were letters of complaint about specific abuses and an occasional illegal meeting. Citizens in one chiefdom of Shinyanga, for example, complained bitterly of intimidation and a rigged nomination procedure for a vacant seat on the District Council. Alleging that the only people who favored the candidate were TANU Youth League contingents and district TANU leaders, and that some citizens had been unlawfully seized, they wrote: 'This is Dictatorship and not Democracy.'[2]

Samson Masalu, the perennial independent, withdrew his candidature for re-election to the Kwimba District Council under government pressure in July 1963. He subsequently charged that people were intimidated by threats of arrest if they did not choose TANU-sponsored candidates and that some non-TANU members were denied ballots and others had their marked ballots destroyed by government officers after they voted. After TANU candidates won all thirty-six seats in the District Council, he compared the situation in Kwimba with that in Spain and South Africa.[3] In October he was accused in Mwanza of holding illegal night meetings of the PDP.[4] Later he sought government permission for yet another opposition group—the People's Convention Party (PCP)—an option which no longer existed, given Tanganyika's official commitment to a one-party state.

In 1963, too, the resignation from the cabinet of the nationally prominent Nyamwezi, Chief Abdullah Fundikira, stirred

[1] Press release, Provincial Information Office, 9 Mar. 1963, LPF.
[2] Letters to R.C., 14, 15 Apr.; 4 May 1963, SHDF.
[3] *Lumuli*, No. 240, Aug. 1963.
[4] TANU Branch Secretary, Bunegeji, to A.C., Mwanza, 24 Oct. 1963, MZDF.

uneasiness among TANU personnel in Sukumaland as elsewhere in the country. Fundikira's estrangement from TANU and the independent government—which he had served as Member of Legislative Council, Minister of Lands and Minister of Justice—had potentially serious political implications since it was based in part on his opposition to the one-party state. In addition to being one of Tanganyika's most powerful and influential chiefs, Fundikira was a leading Muslim religious figure. His brother-in-law was president of the All-Muslim National Union of Tanganyika (AMNUT)—a Muslim pressure group which periodically fell afoul of TANU.[1] Energetically pursued disaffection by Fundikira—and he eventually did break with TANU for a few months during 1964—might conceivably have focused a range of disparate groups, interests and sentiments into some sort of anti-TANU coalition. As a leading chief, Fundikira could have had the support of non-Muslim (predominantly Catholic) Sukuma who resented the denigration of chiefs and TANU's handling of local government, and who had earlier given their support to the opposition efforts of Francis Masanja and David Kidaha. As a prominent Muslim, he might have captured the imagination of anti-chief Muslim politicians who, like Fundikira himself, had joined with TANU but who now, because they were generally not as well educated as their Christian compatriots, felt forgotten and set aside during the early post-independence years when education and qualifications became more important for assignment to leading government posts than political battle scars.

Thus, interspersed with TANU's call to the positive program of nation-building and as part of its stress on unity, the campaign against dissidents continued through 1963 despite the lack of legal political opposition. In October 1963 a special delegation of the TANU National Executive Committee, appointed by the President, toured the country to look into 'problems facing the people,' 'explain government policies' and insist on loyalty to TANU. With opposition political parties defunct, dissent expressed as sympathy for Fundikira or focused through religious groups such as AMNUT became of great concern to the delegation. It 'gave stern warning to those irresponsible agitators who were hiding themselves under their destructive and selfish shield of religion in order to pervert the "bona fide" people and upset the peace of the country.' The delegation disclosed that

[1] Bienen, *Tanzania*, pp. 59, 69.

documents written by Muslim and Christian leaders 'who wished to overthrow the Government' had been discovered and that such agitators, unless they 'stop their nonsense and concentrate in the fight against disease, ignorance and poverty,' would be severely punished or deported. Sentiment favoring restoration of power to chiefs was also decried by the NEC delegation, especially in Shinyanga 'where there was a rumour and tendency of trying to restore the chiefs to their hereditary powers.' The delegation pointed out that chieftainship had been 'abolished forever in the Republic of Tanganyika,' but that qualified chiefs could apply for and be given suitable government posts.[1] That government press releases featured those portions of the delegation's speeches which attacked dissent indicated that the government was very sensitive to a lingering sense of disenchantment and subdued opposition in Sukumaland a year after the rustication of the three Sukuma chiefs, the formation of a Republic, the announcement of intention to form a democratic one-party state, and the abolition of legal political opposition.

In this context of continuing political uneasiness the mutiny of the Dar es Salaam-based First Battalion of the Tanganyika Rifles on 20 January 1964, profoundly shook Nyerere and his government. In a few brief hours it became clear to all how vulnerable the new independent government could be. Though the mutiny seemed limited in its aims—the mutineers demanded higher pay and the dismissal of their expatriate British officers—the government took the opportunity provided by the upheaval to detain scores of persons that attempted, or that it felt might be inclined to attempt, to capitalize politically on an unstable situation. Recalcitrant labor union leaders, noisome partisans of defunct opposition parties, dissident religious leaders, even government and TANU officials who for whatever reason too hastily revealed at the time of the mutiny an untoward sympathy to the possibility for change in national leadership, were arrested and imprisoned. While the number of persons detained was not known, the total national figure was probably not more than several hundred. In Sukumaland—which had been one of the principal breeding grounds for opposition over two years since independence—at least several score persons, including Samson Masalu, were detained.

In making political arrests beyond those justified strictly in

[1] Press release, Provincial Information Office, 12 Oct. 1963.

terms of the mutiny, the government had acted in line with its
standing belief that if it were to achieve its lofty aim of establishing
a democratic one-party state, it could not tolerate overt hostility
to this already determined national policy. But the mutiny made
Nyerere equally convinced that he should move quickly to set
machinery in motion to bring the substance of that goal closer
to realization. In January 1963 he had been empowered by the
NEC to appoint a Presidential Commission 'which would be charged
with the task of considering the changes in the Constitution of
Tanganyika and the Constitution of the Tanganyika African
National Union and in the practice of Government that might
be necessary to bring into effect a democratic One Party State
in Tanganyika.'[1] At the time of the mutiny, however, the commission had not yet been established. On 28 January 1964—
one week after the outbreak and three days after invited British
troops disarmed the mutineers—Nyerere appointed the commission and defined its terms of reference.

The mutiny and its immediate aftermath marked the end of an
initial phase of post-independence political consolidation which
had been marred by TANU's methods of compulsion and by
persistent opposition. If compulsion and resistance were not to
feed on each other, further changes in Tanganyika's political
institutions and procedures clearly would be necessary.

3   TOWARD DEMOCRACY IN A ONE-PARTY STATE

The appointment of the commission had earlier been delayed
because of governmental preoccupation with more immediately
pressing problems. After the establishment in 1962 of the Republic,
the deposition of chiefs, the proscribing or collapsing of opposition
political movements and the definition of national policy in matters
of local government—1963 had been a year of attempting to patch
up the wounds in the body politic and to establish a new administrative structure. As local government gradually became more
responsible and TANU became, both through pressure and by
default, more all-encompassing, open political conflict receded.
Grievances and rivalries continued to exist, however, and were
only ostensibly subsumed in the drive for national unity and the
campaign to build the nation. As 1964 opened, Tanganyika—
even in troublesome Sukumaland—had become in fact as well as

[1] Nyerere statement of 28 Jan. 1964, quoted in *Africa Report* (Oct. 1965), p. 21.

intention a one-party state; but it was not yet 'democratic.' The mutiny dramatized what the history of pre- and post-independence opposition had already demonstrated: that one of Tanganyika's most pressing problems was precisely how a one-party state could govern itself democratically. This was the problem which occupied the attention of the Presidential Commission during 1964.

Nyerere's Political Theory

In elaborating his ideological commitments to African socialism and one-party democracy, Nyerere had ruled out the two-party or multi-party system of the Western democracies on the grounds that: (1) a new state requires the combined efforts of all in building a unified nation and in maximizing economic and social development; (2) traditional African cultural attitudes and communal practices favor decision by consensus; and (3) multi-party systems themselves are either artificial luxuries which tend to make government into a game, or they are perversions of true democracy in that they represent and solidify class divisions and inequalities rather than eliminating them. Indeed, Nyerere argued that a one-party state could be even more democratic than one with two or more parties:

Where there is one party and that party is identified with the nation as a whole, the foundations of democracy are firmer than they can ever be where you have two or more parties, each representing only a section of the community.[1]

He rejected equally, however, the totalitarian organization of the Communist state in which 'the individual...is secondary to something called the state.'[2] The ideal of African socialism is communal and egalitarian, and its theoretical political corollary is government not by an elitist vanguard but by popular participation. In early 1962 Nyerere called for

[1] Nyerere, 'Democracy and the party system,' a speech delivered 14 Jan. 1963, reprinted in *Tanganyika Standard*, 16–18, 21, 22 Jan. 1963, and quoted in Harvey Glickman, 'Dilemmas of political theory in an African context: the ideology of Julius Nyerere,' Jeffrey Butler and A. A. Castagno, eds., *Boston University papers on Africa: transition in African politics* (New York: Praeger, 1967), p. 211. As Glickman indicates, the Nyerere speech appeared also as 'One Party System' in *Spearhead*, II (Jan. 1963), 1, 12–23. The Glickman paper, to which I am indebted in these paragraphs, provides an excellent explication and critical analysis of Nyerere's political ideology.

[2] Nyerere, 'Africa's bid for democracy,' *African and Colonial World*, VIII (July 1960).

a strong political organization active in every village, which acts like a two-way all-weather road along which the purposes, plans, and problems of the Government can travel to the people at the same time as the ideas, desires and misunderstandings of the people can travel direct to the Government. This is the job of the new TANU.[1]

At all levels within the party there would be disagreement on 'how to do things which we agree should be done.'[2] Because there could be no question as to overall goals and commitments, however, legitimate differences of viewpoint could usefully be expressed only within the single party of national unity, TANU. Given freedom of expression within the party which provided thus a two-way process of communication between the government and the people, the essence of democracy would be preserved, for 'basically democracy is government by discussion.'[3]

Difficulties in Practice: Elite vs. the People

I do not intend here to explore the subtleties of Nyerere's political theory but simply to point out that even his own definitions of democracy failed of fulfilment in the Tanganyika of the early 1960s. That a gap existed between the new political elite, exercising the power they had struggled to wrest from colonial predecessors, and the masses of the people was hardly surprising. Such a gap is common to all developing nations if not, indeed, to developed states as well. In Tanzania, the horizontal amalgamation of diverse tribal units into a coherent and functioning territorial political system has—for a variety of tribal, geographical, linguistic, economic and historical reasons—posed no serious difficulty. The key problem in national political integration therefore, has been the development of viable vertical links of communication and cooperation from national headquarters through regional and district party and governmental apparatus to the villages and homesteads of the individual citizen. The question has been whether President Nyerere's 'two-way, all-weather road' between the government and the people would become a functioning reality, whether TANU could succeed in its new and much more difficult role.

To discuss TANU's difficulties in the post-independence years

[1] Nyerere, press conference, *Tanganyika Standard*, 23 Jan. 1962, quoted in Glickman, p. 214.
[2] Nyerere, 'The challenge of independence,' *East Africa and Rhodesia* (7 Dec. 1961), 339-40.
[3] Nyerere, 'One party government,' *Spearhead*, i, (Nov. 1961), 7.

should in no way detract from two facts: (1) that TANU guided Tanganyika after independence with more overall success and less short-term strain and dislocation than many had predicted; and (2) that TANU under Nyerere's leadership has shown more persistence in attempting to transform theoretical political ideals into actuality than many another party in many another new state. To appreciate achievements, however, difficulties must first be described and understood.

Government policy has derived not from the mass of the population, which was still mostly uneducated and lethargic, but from a select elite whose members held the top government and TANU positions. In some respects, in fact, the administrative system of the new nation took on an appearance strikingly similar in structure and style to that of the authoritarian colonial regime. While, as Glickman has pointed out, Nyerere clearly 'desires a continuously self-governing society', it is equally true that he 'wants to make certain that self-government served the right purposes.'[1] This Rousseauist dilemma of his political theory is the dilemma of his administration: how to reconcile democratic popular participation and self-government by a predominantly unsophisticated citizenry with the requirements for unity and nation-building which are clearly perceived and understood in terms of specific policies only by the governing elite and which, therefore, seem to require a centrally directed effort that could only with difficulty not be described as authoritarian.

The new administrators are African rather than European and they are representatives of the same TANU which had widespread popular support during the struggle for independence. Yet, in important respects, the current governing elite are to the locality and people they serve very much as were the colonial administrators who preceded them. As Provincial and District Commissioners were the directly appointed representatives of the Governor and responsible only to him for the administration of their areas, so the Regional and Area Commissioners are the directly appointed representatives of the President responsible only to Dar es Salaam. Though Regional and Area Commissioners have been shorn of judicial and other powers formerly exercised by the Provincial and District Commissioners, they are alike in exercising what amounts to supreme political and administrative power in their areas (with the partial exception of the District Council, which is

[1] Glickman, p. 216.

now more independent of Regional and District administration). They are alike in their overall political–administrative style, which involves a combination of safaris for speech-making and inspection purposes; chairing a multitude of committees and boards; sorting out the continual tangles, jealousies and conflicts which are ever-present in the lower echelons of the administrative and political cadres; and listening to the daily *shidas* (problems) of those members of the population who are intrepid enough to call at the office. They are alike in their overriding concern for organizing and promoting development schemes while quietly removing economically and/or politically inspired opposition elements.

At local levels, too, the new pattern of administration is reminiscent of the old system and not replete with possibilities for an expression of views upward. Like chiefs and headmen before them, Divisional and Assistant Divisional Executive Officers and headmen collect taxes and enforce policies and regulations decided on at higher levels. Village development committees resemble the parish councils of colonial days in that they are less deliberative bodies than vehicles for the central government's efforts to move forward development policy at the local level. Thus, government and party officials—like their colonial predecessors—have had difficulty stimulating village committees into activity.

Ensuring popular participation has been further complicated by factors independent of distasteful correspondence with the colonial regime. Village development committees have tended to lack clear understanding and definition of their functions and responsibilities in relation to organs of government at higher levels and to the regime's over-all development plan. When committees did act, it was sometimes without sufficient regard for important contingent factors, as when classrooms were built without teachers available to staff them or roads which would vanish in the next rainy season. Such fruitless or abortive efforts, lengthy delays and bureaucratic red tape accompanying applications for approved development projects, and frequent refusal of permission for projects due to lack of funds, material or staff—such wilted the enthusiasm of committees which did initially indicate an interest in taking initiatives.[1]

The functioning of local committees has been marred, too, by role conflicts among individuals and committees within the villages

[1] See Joseph S. Nye, Jr., 'Tanganyika self help,' *Transition*, II (Nov. 1963), 35–39.

themselves. Village TANU committees, village development committees, local representatives on the district council, headmen and elders might all press overlapping claims to authority with regard to allocating land and settling disputes within the village, recruitment for and implementation of local self-help development schemes, levying fines and collection of taxes and fees, the general organization of community affairs and representation of the views of the people to higher levels of government and party. Partly to meet this problem, the government in 1964 merged village TANU and village development committees, with chairman and members elected locally to deal simultaneously with TANU and development committee affairs. Theoretically, the combined committee has absorbed most of the functions formerly exercised under the colonial regime by village councils, headmen and elders—as well as party tasks—but who exercises the real power in any given village today still depends very much on personalities and factors peculiar to each local situation.

National development plans have moved forward much more gradually than had been hoped. In addition to serious shortages locally of qualified political leaders and adequately trained development staff,[1] the authoritarian overtones and untried administrative structures and techniques of the new regime, the meagerness of any substructure of already developed resources, the relative unsophistication in things modern of the people, and the confusion of roles at the local level have dictated that, even in the 'young nation in a hurry,'[2] haste would be made slowly. In such a context, the maintenance at the village level of popular enthusiasm for and the encouragement of popular participation in the tasks of nation-building becomes a primary political—and *primarily* a political—problem.

The Problem of Meaningful Choice

Although the administrative organization of the new regime and even its development goals appear in important respects similar to those of the preceding colonial regime, the new political fact is independence and the new political reality is TANU. From the standpoint of Nyerere's political theory, the existence of TANU

---

[1] See above, pp. 321–3.
[2] Phrase taken from the title of Alexander MacDonald's, *Tanzania: young nation in a hurry* (New York: Hawthorn, 1966), a somewhat uncritical overview of Tanzania since independence.

should be the all-transforming qualitative difference. While administrators of necessity are charged with the inevitably 'authoritarian' task of administering, the authority for their exercise of power stems theoretically from the consent of the people expressed through TANU. The alien colonial regime, devoid of legitimacy, had given way to TANU which was identified with the nation as a whole and was to provide at every level from village upward the two-way road linking the desires of the people to the plans and purposes of their government.

The difficulty, however, was that though elections were held popularly at village, district and national levels, all candidates first had to be accepted as suitable by the appropriate TANU committees. The TANU committees then produced a slate of TANU candidates—one for each office—whose members were certain to be, except in the most unusual circumstances, elected to the vacant posts. In practice, therefore, while TANU triumphed over dissident elements, it disenfranchised the electorate through the virtually automatic endorsement at election time of single slates of candidates previously selected by TANU committees. This would not necessarily have been an undemocratic, unrepresentative procedure if the TANU committees themselves had been linked more securely to popular opinion; but in post-independence Sukumaland the gap between TANU leaders and the people had not yet been bridged successfully within the party any more than through the administration—a weakness which made the one-party state, in the absence of any meaningful opportunity for citizens to express at least their preferences as between opposing candidates, undemocratic.

While perhaps well over half the adult population had at one time joined TANU, most did not regularly pay their dues and participate personally in party activities. Political rallies and public meetings gave leaders a chance to speak to the people, but they did not give the people much chance to express their real feelings to their leaders—any more than did the public *barazas* of the colonial era. More than a few citizens—members of TANU and non-members alike—have felt themselves, especially since independence, to be on the outside looking in. Some characterize TANU as a set of professional politicians and semiprofessional local activists who, though talking the language of building the nation, go about the business of consolidating wealth and exercising power.

It is recalled today that during the struggle for independence—especially during the 1959–61 period after people came to understand the purposes of the party and when TANU achieved its greater popular support—people offered their houses to be used as TANU offices, their cattle and food for TANU leaders and public feasts, their money to pay for transportation costs of TANU personnel, their time to work as clerks without being requested. TANU was held in such high regard that anyone who then opposed TANU was likely to be regarded as a laughing stock, or ostracized and even fined by the community for not attending TANU meetings.[1] While most people still have generally the finest things to say about Nyerere, about the work of TANU in achieving independence with all its benefits (no discrimination, high posts for Africans, elections, etc.), about the unity and strength and hard work characteristic of the people before independence and even on occasion about some local TANU leaders, many have been very critical of the party or disenchanted altogether. They give expression to some or all of a number of widespread complaints:

1. TANU has not fulfilled its promises to the effect that Africans will receive first consideration in employment, in trading and business, and in all the public and private bureaucracies which organize and operate the affairs of the nation and the people. Why do whites and Asians still have special privileges and greater riches than Africans?

2. Taxes, fees, and levies of all kinds are too numerous, too frequently assessed, and too costly to the average person, who does not really understand what such monies are used for and who, if he objects to paying, is likely to be warned severely or punished by the government.

3. Local TANU leaders interfere in all aspects of local affairs and worry the people because they behave like investigators always looking for wrongdoers. The TANU Youth League in particular is a law unto itself; its members harass people from homestead to homestead for payment of TANU dues, take unecessary matters before the courts, and generally pry into matters with which they should have no concern. People are confused by the sometimes conflicting directives of and frightened by the seemingly arbitrary powers exercised by local government and party personnel, including at times elected district councillors.

4. People are forced to become members of TANU because one must have a TANU card and pay the TANU fee before one can pay the government tax, before receiving one's wages if employed, before one's

---

[1] Thus, to some extent, traditional social controls and political institutions were harnessed to service the TANU cause—especially after chiefs switched from hostility to support for TANU.

case will be heard in a local court or complaint discussed by the ADEO, before one can sell his cotton at a buying post, before one can get a job or open a business, before one can move to another subdivision or village, and in some instances before one can travel on a public bus. But joining a political party should be voluntary for the individual, not the result of constraint.

5. Self-help schemes for nation-building should be voluntary and people should be paid some money at least for their labor. Before independence TANU opposed the colonial government's unpaid labor requirements, but now TANU insists on the same thing and people who do not participate are sometimes even fined.

6. Even people's land is being used without their consent for government projects. They are asked to move their homes and are given only two acres of land in the project where they might previously have cultivated four or six acres. Even if they receive compensatory land elsewhere, the best land has been taken.

7. Changes in customary tribal law and in court organization and procedures are objectionable. Sometimes TANU party personnel even disrupt the orderly procedures of the courts.

8. Elections do not permit people to express their preferences freely. TANU leaders select the candidates—one for each office—and others who might also wish to stand are urged or coerced into not standing.[1]

It is clear that the above complaints arise partly from misunderstandings of the programs and requirements of a modernizing government, but also partly from coercive techniques which, whether or not condoned at high levels, have helped to shape negative popular reaction to TANU's operations at the local level.[2] Repeatedly, interviews with cross-sections of village people in all parts of Sukumaland revealed 'great misunderstanding between the ordinary people and the government and TANU officers.'[3]

---

[1] Distilled from scores of interviews in selected parts of Sukumaland.

[2] In October 1964, a Ministry of Local Government circular warned all E.O.s that some D.E.O. and A.D.E.O.s had been abusing their powers by detaining persons without due cause simply to demonstrate their authority. One D.E.O., for example, locked up nineteen parents because they prevented their children from attending school. An A.D.E.O. jailed one man five days without any reason. The Ministry warned that officers who 'use their power illegally will be arrested and severely punished' (LG. 39/1964, 7 Oct. 1964).

[3] A song known throughout Sukumaland symbolized the feeling of many that government and TANU leaders—who owed their positions to the support given TANU by ordinary people—enriched themselves while forgetting about the poor citizenry tied to the land:

> We Tanzanians rule ourselves
>   But only some enjoy the fruits of the independent people.
> Those with high positions in the government
>   Receive high salaries,

That ample grounds existed for some of these complaints make the more comprehensible the manifestations of political opposition which appeared in Sukumaland in the early 1960s. It also made the more necessary—after the proscribing of legal opposition—improvements in the political process which would reduce to a minimum the validity of such complaints. As one ordinary citizen put it:

The one-party state is good, in fact it is best when the country is as poor as Tanzania, but the leaders must do it the right way. Ever since independence, it has not been done the right way because leaders are unqualified but all-powerful, all decisions come from the top, and people can only agree or accept the consequences. Therefore a two-party or multi-party system would be better.[1]

The decision that Tanzania was to be a one-party state, however, had been made. Tanzanians would have to come to understand that there existed no real choice about whether or not to be a member of TANU. TANU was the foundation of the government itself; and the government was the 'result of,' the 'branches of,' the 'property of,' the 'child of' TANU.[2] To be a member of TANU was like being a citizen of Tanzania. To pay the annual fees to TANU was no less obligatory in principle than to pay an annual tax to the government. TANU was not a political association among several to be selected or rejected; it was the original and all-inclusive political association of which everyone 'must' be a part. Such reasoning lay behind the customary derisive denunciation at TANU public meetings of any persons who opposed or even failed to become members and actively support TANU. TANU leaders have been fond of the phrase that such persons 'will not be tolerated' and have often suggested that they will find themselves more at home in some country other than Tanzania.

> But the cultivators shall not profit;
>   Bondage remains.
> The rainy season approaches
>   And we cultivate the cotton:
> We shall see that the cotton price goes down.
>
> Gents, we are enriching others,
>   Making them fat and prosperous.
> Look at their wrist watches
>   And the way they use handkerchiefs to wipe their noses!
>   (trans. from the Sukuma)

---

[1] Interview, anonymous.

[2] Statement by Paul Bomani to the Mwanza District Council, press release, Provincial Information Office, 27 July 1963, LPF.

But political oratory and coercive techniques for enrollment of membership have, understandably, not sufficed to convince people that they will have the opportunities they obviously desire for discussion, debate, constructive criticism *and expression of free choice* within the framework of the single party whose local operations have often, since independence, appeared in such questionable guise. Improvements in the political process were a necessity if the one-party state was to attain a reality based on more than grudging acquiescence.

Even before the important elections of 1965, attempts at modification and improvement were under way. Local government and party officials were enabled to increase their understanding and capabilities in special seminars and courses. More able and enlightened administrators and party officials began to address themselves more sensitively to the complaints of local people.[1] In quiet discussions rather than in the inhibiting context of public meetings, people began to respond with more honest expressions of their problems and desires. While election contests for seats in district councils remained dominated by TANU-selected candidates who ran unopposed, greater scope was given in some localities for consultation of the people about who the TANU candidate should be. The combined TANU–village development committees were elected in open balloting at village meetings arranged for the purpose. Candidates had to be literate (in Swahili) and party members, but the voters themselves, instead of local TANU leaders as in the past, were permitted to choose between a number of candidates from each group of homesteads.

By early 1965 in some areas local TANU chairmen were selected by popular vote rather than in party caucuses. Again, candidates had to be TANU members but proof of TANU membership was not required for voters and anyone from the locality who was present at the election meeting could cast a ballot. At village level the same individual was often returned without opposition if he had done a satisfactory job, but at subdivisional levels a

---

[1] I am greatly indebted to Edwin Nyamubi, Area Commissioner of Geita District in 1964, for having permitted me to join him and other government and party officials on a four-day safari to outlying areas of the district in March 1964. Nyamubi was most impressive in the way he confronted openly and honestly the problems of the party and of ordinary people, without pretension or arbitrariness, very much in the style of Nyerere himself. He is, I believe, one of Tanzania's finer young administrators; I was gratified to learn of his election to the National Assembly from his home area of Ngara in 1965.

multiplicity of candidates began to compete for the posts. In 1964 and 1965 efforts to resuscitate local participation in party activities —which had lagged severely since independence—were entrusted to groups of elders in each village, each of whom was to be responsible for enlisting the membership and participation of the householders from ten homesteads. It was hoped that these elders would be more acceptable to the ordinary citizen than the militant and often tactless Youth League contingents, who in turn were told that they would work only under the guidance of senior personnel.

Elections 1965

In spite of earlier difficulties—and perhaps in part from what had been learned because of them—Tanzania's first post-independence national elections in September 1965 brought a significant measure of reality to the 'democratic' part of President Nyerere's conception of the democratic one-party state. As Ruth Schachter Morgenthau observed:

Rarely in any century is an original contribution made to the art of democratic government. Tanzanians accordingly take pride in the political and electoral innovations introduced in their presidential and parliamentary elections...Based on universal suffrage, the elections were honestly run and offered the voters genuine choices between two rival candidates in more than a hundred single-member constituencies... Barely a quarter of the incumbent members were reelected as a result of decisions not imposed from above, but freely taken by the voters... Tanzania's system...lifts to a new level the debate on the possibility for democracy in single-party states...[1]

In the parliamentary elections of 1958–9 TANU candidates had decisively defeated opposing candidates from the United Tanganyika Party and from the African National Congress. In the 1960 elections, however, TANU candidates ran unopposed in most constituencies. In submitting its report in March 1965, the Presidential Commission on the Establishment of a Democratic One-Party State made the oversimplified observation that opposition to TANU 'has simply disintegrated' in the face of the outstanding support and clear mandate given to TANU by the people and that Tanganyika had, since 1959, been a *de facto* one-party state. Against this background, the Commission, with greater perception, argued:

[1] Ruth Schachter Morgenthau, 'African elections: Tanzania's contribution,' *Africa Report*, x (Dec. 1965), p. 12.

One Party government operating within the context of a constitution intended for two or more parties inevitably results in the disenfranchise-ment of the voter. So long as the law permits the establishment of alter-native parties TANU must continue to fight elections, both national and local, on a party basis. This means putting forward a single candidate in each constituency or ward. In Tanganyika in most cases such candidates have been unopposed and the people have, in consequence, the right to vote but no opportunity to do so. In the rare cases where a candidate has stood in opposition to TANU his chance of succeeding at the polls has been so meagre that the election itself has been a matter of small signifi-cance. The real choice has been made at an earlier stage when TANU adopted its candidate. By a paradox the more support the people have given to TANU as a party the more they have reduced their partici-pation in the process of government.[1]

The Commission therefore proposed that Tanzania be made in law, as well as in fact, a one-party state and that the institutions of the one-party system of government be adjusted 'to permit wider democratic participation and fuller discussion of national issues.' Specifically with regard to elections to the National Assembly, the commission recommended that voters be given a choice between three candidates in every constituency. While all aspiring candi-dates would be required to be members of TANU, and while the number of candidates to stand in each constituency would be narrowed to three through pre-selection by district and national TANU Executive Committees, the voters would make the final determination as to which of the several TANU-approved candid-ates would best represent their interests in the National Assembly.

The government accepted most of the recommendations of the Commission though it was decided that two rather than three candidates should stand in each constituency. Also TANU district conferences (which included a substantial number of delegates from throughout the district) rather than district committees (which were restricted to district TANU officers and a few commit-teemen) would make the initial selections. In preparation for the September campaign, each aspirant first collected the twenty-five supporting signatures required to submit his name to the TANU conference of his district. Each district conference then met to vote its preference from among the names submitted and transmitted the results to TANU's National Executive Committee in Dar es Salaam for final approval of candidates to stand in each constituency.

[1] *Report of the presidential commission on the establishment of a democratic one party state* (Dar es Salaam, 1965), p. 14.

In most cases the TANU National Executive Committee accepted the choices of the district conferences, rejecting only four first choices and twelve second choices. The reasons behind the NEC's decisions remain secret, though the main criteria are thought to have been a candidate's TANU record and his adherence to TANU principles.[1]

Once the rival candidates had been designated, the campaign could begin—but all candidates had to observe certain ground rules. Candidates were 'formally forbidden to discuss race, tribe, or religion, to use languages other than Swahili' or to organize their own meetings or engage in electioneering activities independent of the officially sponsored and supervised campaign functions. Also outside the realm of permissible campaign discussions were such policy issues as allocations under the five-year development plan, the role of the military, the position of Asians, Arabs and other middlemen in the economy, the 1964 union with Zanzibar, the replacement of the East African common currency with a national one and the question of nonalignment in foreign policy. The government and TANU covered all election expenses and arranged for the printing of electoral manifestos for each constituency. These bore 'the pictures and names of the two candidates, their assigned symbol of house or hoe, and a biographical summary written in Swahili.'[2] District TANU committees— in cooperation with Regional and Area Commissioners, specially appointed election supervisers, and the candidates themselves— arranged public meetings at which the candidates shared a common platform in taking their message to the people. With so many controversial topics explicitly excluded from campaign debate, most candidates emphasized their personal qualifications (education and vocational experience), their role in the struggle for independence, their identification with TANU and their closeness to the problems and desires of the people whom they were seeking to represent.

The election results were startling—at least for anyone who had underestimated either the extent to which popular disaffection with existing TANU leadership was present in many areas, or the extent to which President Nyerere—despite what must have been at least his partial awareness of this disaffection—was committed to the realization of democratic principles in practice as well as in theory. The results found two ministers and six junior ministers defeated, less than a fourth of the incumbent members reelected,

[1] Morgenthau, p. 15.   [2] *Ibid.*

and local TANU party stalwarts often beaten by candidates whom
the voters judged more capable and attractive.[1]

The Results in Sukumaland

To those for whom the results nationally were startling, the
results in Sukumaland must have appeared especially so. Not one
of the area's seven incumbent members returned to the National
Assembly. The two who did face the voters—Paul Bomani,
Minister of Finance, and John Rupia, a former national vice-
president of TANU—were defeated by very substantial majorities
in their home constituencies in Mwanza and Shinyanga. The
Maswa Area Commissioner, Sylvester Lubala, suffered a crushing
defeat in a Maswa constituency by a margin of ten to one. In the
two Kwimba constituencies the district chairman and the district
secretary of TANU were both resoundingly defeated by their
challengers. Even in Geita, where indigenous political feeling had
been most closely identified with TANU's rise and opposition
groups such as the ANC and PDP had been virtually nonexistent,
three newcomers made a clean sweep against candidates who had
been closely identified with Geita's protest politics in the late
1950s.[2]

The two non-African members from Sukumaland—Barbara

[1] 'The victories of five non-Africans (two of whom were appointed Ministers)
demonstrated that TANU's nonracial policies are more than a slogan...
Four women won against men...The defeat of Oscar Kambona's brother,
and the failure of one of President Nyerere's brothers to gain the NEC's
endorsement of his proposed candidacy, indicate that nepotism was not a
factor...On the whole, the new members have solid roots in their constituencies, are younger (their average age is under thirty-five) and better
educated than their predecessors. Some studied in the U.S., the U.K., Israel,
or Leipzig, and at Makerere; most have had experience in the cooperative or
labor movements, or in the youth, student, or TANU party organizations.
Quite a few distinguished themselves in the civil service' (Morgenthau, p.
16).

[2] Election results and biographical notes on the winning candidates were
published in the *Tanganyika Standard*, 2 Oct. 1965. I am indebted to Professor Margaret Bates for more extended biographical information on all the
contesting Sukumaland candidates: she returned from a 1965 visit to Tanzania with a collection of the election manifestos from nearly all constituencies
and generously shared them with me. For the lists of applicants in each
constituency and the tallies in district conference voting, I am indebted to
Martin Lowenkopf, formerly of the University College, Dar es Salaam.
The statistical materials on this and the following pages are drawn from
these sources. For another very interesting analysis of the election in Sukumaland, see Ganja Geneya, 'Sukumaland: Traditional Values and modern
leadership,' in Lionel Cliffe, ed., *One-party democracy: the 1965 Tanzania
general elections* (Nairobi: East Africa Publishing House, 1967), pp. 186–207.

Johansson and N. K. Laxman—did not seek re-election. Reserved seats for Europeans and Asians had been abolished and Johansson and Laxman, for different reasons, decided not to stand.

Bomani's Defeat in Mwanza

The most stunning defeat of a top leader in Sukumaland—and perhaps the most stunning of all nationally—was that of Bomani in the Mwanza East constituency. The founder of the cotton cooperative movement and for fifteen years the most prominent African political figure in Sukumaland, Bomani had moved quite naturally to national leadership. The most well known, most important, and the most powerful Sukuma in all of Tanganyika, he had progressed from General Manager of the Victoria Federation of Cooperative Unions to become Minister of Agriculture in 1960 and Minister of Finance in 1962. After submitting his name for the Mwanza East constituency, he received forty-four of the fifty-five votes cast at the Mwanza District TANU conference. The NEC selected Zacharia Madilla, who had tied for fourth place with a single vote in the district conference poll, to stand against Bomani.[1] Madilla was a fifty-four-year-old farmer who had been a member of TAA in Mwanza in the early 1950s and subsequently a local TANU leader.[2] Madilla won the election with 14,146 votes to Bomani's 9,639.

The question, of course, is why. Madilla was a respected local citizen but no more active nor well known than many another. Bomani was one of Tanzania's greatest leaders. The best explanation is probably one which is almost tautological: the voters of

[1] Lameck Bogohe, the former leader of the Sukuma Union and of TANU, placed second with five votes. The reasons for his elimination from the ballot by the NEC are not known. In spite of his leadership role in TANU in 1954 and his educational qualifications, Bogohe had an independent bent which did not endear him to TANU regulars. He would also have seemed a natural selection for a post as Area Commissioner, but he was passed by. While some may have had doubts about his suitability, it was known that he enjoyed strong support in his home area of Nassa and he may have been regarded as more of a threat to Bomani (since dissatisfaction with Bomani was apparent, though its extent was not anticipated) than Mr Madilla. Apparently, Bogohe was detained for a while during the campaign. It is possible that the treatment Bogohe received created additional protest votes for Madilla.

[2] Madilla was among those who petitioned the government in mid-1958 to permit the opening of TANU in Sukumaland and who brought membership cards from Dar es Salaam to sell secretly before TANU was reopened. At the time of the election in 1963, he was TANU chairman of a subdivision, a member of the district TANU committee, and chairman of a local cotton cooperative society.

Mwanza East felt Bomani would represent what they conceived to be their best interests less well than Madilla. The evidence suggests that the voters of Mwanza East decided that Bomani had become too important and had gone too far away to be truly *their* representative. It was felt that he rarely visited the constituency, and as Minister of Finance he was thought by many to be responsible for the unpopular taxes and fees levied by the government.

In addition, more specific dissatisfactions with the monopoly exercised by the Victoria Federation may have contributed to Bomani's defeat. The rise of Masalu's Saidia Waafrika movement in 1961 and 1962 had dramatized the feeling of an increasing number of cotton growers that the VFCU absorbed for the Bomanis and their friends, and for those who drew substantial allowances as officers and committeemen, entirely too much of the return on cotton, a greater portion of which they felt should go to the farmer himself. Saidia Waafrika was suppressed by the government in cooperation with the VFCU and TANU, and many watched with jealousy and anger as the Bomanis continued to enjoy what appeared to be an overly generous share of the material perquisites accruing from their positions. The feeling against Bomani may have been reinforced by traditional tribal restraints—which Bomani implicitly violated by the very fact of his remarkable successes in economics and politics—designed to assure that no individual be permitted to overachieve.[1] At any rate, the view that Bomani could be defeated by an attractive opponent in open balloting was shared by a significant number of Sukumaland residents in the two or three years before the 1965 elections. For many, Madilla's defeat of Bomani was not entirely a surprise.

The same can be said of Rupia's defeat in Shinyanga. Though originally from Shinyanga, Rupia had moved permanently to Dar es Salaam many years earlier. He played an active role nationally as TANU's vice-president, but he had only the most tenuous relationship with his Shinyanga constituency where he had been TANU's unopposed nominee for the National Assembly in 1960. In the 1965 balloting in the Shinyanga TANU District Conference he led his nearest challenger, Shaban Msonde, by sixty-one votes to ten. However, Msonde, an Assistant Divisional

---

[1] See R. E. S. Tanner, 'Law enforcement by communal action in Sukumaland, Tanganyika Territory,' *Journal of African Administration*, IV (Oct. 1965), 159–65.

Executive Officer employed by the District Council, won the election by a margin of better than three to one. As in Mwanza East, the voters clearly preferred someone who had discernible ties with the constituency, not someone who—however important he may have been nationally—seemed to have come to them from afar. Moreover, both Rupia and Bomani may have suffered to some extent in 1965 because the voters had had no choice in 1960.

Rejection of other TANU Leaders

The voters expressed dissatisfaction also with local TANU leadership, most notably in Kwimba and Maswa. It will be recalled that Chief Francis Masanja of Kwimba had been relieved of his chiefship and rusticated after a clash with Wambura and Kwimba TANU leaders in 1962. Though he continued as a member of the National Assembly, he was *persona non grata* with TANU. Incredibly, then, in balloting for nominees for the Kwimba North constituency, the District TANU Conference gave Masanja twenty-eight votes—a very close second to the thirty-one votes polled by Titus Mpanduji, TANU's District Chairman. The closeness of this vote revealed a deep split in Kwimba between the local leadership of TANU—which often seemed more adept at antagonizing many with its strong-arm tactics than at working constructively for the good of TANU and the district—and another collection of quite different individuals which, though loyal to TANU, was partly identified with Kwimba's traditional ruling families and more responsive to popular disenchantment with TANU's past excesses than were those who had helped personally to perpetrate them.

In spite of his excellent showing, however, Masanja was eliminated from consideration by TANU's National Executive Committee. Given his outspoken criticism of TANU and his past association with the opposition ANC and PDP parties, TANU's national leadership apparently was not prepared to acquiesce in a possible political comeback for him even if he were once again nominally within the TANU fold. The expectation, then, was that TANU chairman Mpanduji would win against the less well-known Marco Mabawa, the district conference's third choice. Mabawa, however, defeated Mpanduji by a majority of almost four to one. The NEC's elimination of Masanja from the contest must have sharpened existing resentment against Mpanduji, a leader of TANU'S local hard-core group. People may also have responded positively to Mabawa, whom they saw as a man like themselves rather than a politician interested in his own advancement.

Disenchantment with local TANU leadership was borne out in the other Kwimba constituency. In the district conference voting for Kwimba South, Michael Malebo, TANU's district secretary, outpolled Mageni Musobi by a thirty-five to fourteen vote. Musobi was a younger member of the Nera ruling family who had served the Kwimba District (Native Authority) Council as secretary–treasurer and executive secretary in the late 1950s. Despite the fact that Musobi had resigned his post with the Kwimba District Council after disagreements with the TANU leadership of the council in 1962, the NEC in this instance endorsed Musobi as well as Malebo. In the election itself Musobi reversed the district conference tally, defeating Malebo by better than a two to one majority. Like Mabawa, Musobi could claim that he was a farmer who was close to the people at the time he was elected. In addition to his years of local government service, he had improved his credentials by earning a Diploma in Economics and General Principles of English Law by correspondence from the British Tutorial College in Nairobi—though this probably had less influence on the electorate than Musobi's known reservations about past TANU operations in Kwimba and his own strong basis of indigenous support.

It is noteworthy that both Mabawa and Musobi were born and raised in Kwimba, whereas the defeated candidates, Mpanduji and Malebo, though they now lived and worked for TANU in Kwimba, were both originally from Mwanza District. After several years of TANU activities conducted sometimes very insensitively by outsiders, and of the suppression of indigenous feelings expressed through dissident groups which coalesced first around Samson Masalu and later around Chief Francis Masanja, Kwimba citizens made clear in the election of 1965 that they wanted their representatives and political leaders to be their own.

Maswa voters expressed a similar dissatisfaction with district TANU leadership in their all-but-unanimous rejection of Area Commissioner Sylvester Lubala. Mwanga Kulwa—a widely known and respected ex-subchief who managed also to earn credentials with TANU while not estranging himself from the pulse of popular sentiment and opinion—won the election by 20,914 votes to 2,226, handing Lubala one of the most thoroughgoing defeats of any candidate in the whole of Tanzania. Like

Musobi in Kwimba, Kulwa was a member of one of the prominent traditional ruling families. Unlike many other native authorities, however, he worked openly in behalf of the cotton cooperatives and of TANU and was rewarded with a post as Divisional Executive Officer after 1963. Lubala's home was in Kwimba District, and he probably made a tactical error in submitting his candidature in a part of Maswa which knew him only in his role as a somewhat authoritarian Area Commissioner.

Youth in Geita

In Geita a number of those who had been leaders in the protest against *Mseto* (the multi-racial district council) in 1958 and who had themselves played active roles in Geita's District Council in the following years placed their names in nomination for the National Assembly from Geita's three constituencies. Hezeroni Mpandachalo and Wilson Mwihendi joined the Geita incumbent, Bartholomew Mwiza, in the contest in Geita North; Wilson Bunuma and Ernest Kizimba were among those seeking a place on the ballot from Geita South; and Tito Budodi submitted his name for Geita East. Not one of these well-known figures, however, became a Member of Parliament. Faithful to their reputation for volatility and avant-garde–ism, the people of Geita registered a decided preference for new and younger faces—and, in one case, for a lady.

Balloting in the district conference for the Geita North seat resulted in three votes for the incumbent M.P. Mwiza, four votes for Mpandachalo, nine for Mwihendi, and fifteen for a twenty-nine-year-old, Alphonse Rulegura, who had earned a Bachelor of Science degree in Economics in the United States in 1963. Rulegura had joined TANU on his return to Tanganyika in 1964 and, after a few months of work with the Geita District Council, had become an administrative officer in the central government's Treasury Department in Dar es Salaam. Despite Mwihendi's longer record of political activity, Rulegura won a very close election with a sixty-two vote margin over Mwihendi out of nearly 14,000 votes cast.

In Geita East twenty-five-year-old Fortunatus Masha—the recipient of a Bachelor of Science Degree in Journalism from Southern Illinois University—defeated the more widely known and established political figure and chairman of the Geita District Council, Tito Budodi, polling 10,320 votes to Budodi's 4,442.

Like Rulegura, Masha had worked briefly with the Geita District Council—as a public relations officer—and, while in the United States, had served as a leader of African and foreign student organizations.

Thus, the young, dynamic figures, Masha and Rulegura, triumphed against the seasoned leaders, Mwihendi and Budodi. The latter may have suffered from reservations expressed in some quarters that Mwihendi had not really risked himself during the campaign against *Mseto* in 1958 as some others had, and that Budodi was a late-comer to the district who had never really participated in the most trying days of the anti-administration struggle. By contrast, Masha and Rulegura were exciting new personalities who, in addition to having been born and raised in Geita, had returned to the district as the first university-educated aspirants for political office.[1] Youth and attractiveness triumphed also in Geita South where a twenty-nine-year-old leader of the Union of Tanganyika Women, Salome Kisusi, defeated an artisan and teacher, Hassani Saalum, who had played an active political role in Msalala chiefdom and Geita in the 1950s and become a district TANU leader in the early 1960s. Two other well-known political activists from the 1950s, Wilson Bunuma and Ernest Kizimba failed to secure a place on the ballot. Kisusi won the election by a handsome majority.

Thus, of Geita's three new Members of the National Assembly, not one was yet thirty years old, two had university-level training abroad, and the third was an enterprising young woman.

Council Chairmen Elected

Budodi had lost in Geita, but in three other districts chairmen of district councils catapulted successfully into the National Assembly. In Mwanza West, twenty-nine-year-old Joseph Kasubi—a primary-school teacher and cooperative society secretary who joined TANU in 1959 and was elected to the district council in 1960—defeated M. I. Kitenge, Mwanza's perennial political

---

[1] One final imponderable was the fact that Mwihendi and Budodi were Sukuma immigrants like some 50 per cent of northeast Geita's population. Rulegura and Masha were, like most of the Geita-born portion of the population, Hima or Zinza. To what extent the tribal identification of the candidates constituted a factor in the elections of 1965 is impossible to ascertain; but one may surmise that, since Budodi lost so heavily in a predominantly Sukuma constituency and Rulegura won where Sukuma outnumbered Zinza, tribe was less important than youth, general attractiveness, qualifications, and the feeling that perhaps it was time for a change.

gadfly who had worked with TAA and TANU since the early 1950s. In Maswa South, Saidi Salum, the twenty-eight-year-old chairman of the district council, won the election comfortably against a prominent opponent, Jacob Mbutu—who, in fact, had been chairman of the district council from 1962 until 1964. In Shinyanga the council chairman, Kiariro Phillipo—at forty-nine years of age one of the more elderly of the winning candidates and one of the few TANU 'old pros' to be returned—won election by a margin of more than two to one.

Democracy in a One-Party State

The elections, then, were remarkable for the diversity and unpre-dictability of the results—probably the best possible witness to the fact that, within the framework of specific substantive limitations already described, they were truly democratic. Voters had a real choice and they exercised that choice freely. Even as powerful a figure as Bomani had to run the gauntlet of constituency sentiment and, like any newcomer, let the chips fall where they might. The rejection of Bomani and Rupia and Lubala, of TANU's two top officials in Kwimba, of well-known local political activists like Budodi, Mwihendi, Saalum and Kitenge, dramatized a decided voter preference for change. Clearly, the practices, the slogans, and the credentials drawn from past skirmishes with the colonial regime no longer sufficed in and of themselves to galvanize political support.

Yet the pattern for the future was not entirely clear. If change was the nearest common denominator of the election results, the results still expressed a diversity of tendencies and preferences on alternative possibilities for the future. While some TANU leaders were crushingly defeated, some more youthful—and in some cases very powerful—TANU stalwarts were successful: Kasubi in Mwanza, Salum in Maswa, Kisusi in Geita. In some consti-tuencies, attractive newcomers like Masha and Rulegura won without the benefit either of activist histories of personal involve-ment or strong connections with TANU. In other areas men who had, through family connection and previous service, been identified to some extent with traditional rulers during the colonial era were winners: Nzingula in Shinyanga, Kulwa in Maswa, Musobi in Kwimba. While Mabawa himself had no such connec-tion, his decisive defeat of Mpanduji in Kwimba North probably derived in part from voter dissatisfaction with the NEC's elimination from the ballot of the popular incumbent, Chief Francis Masanja.

The district TANU conferences, of course, exercised the very important function of pre-selection. First, the NEC seldom took exception to conference preferences. Secondly, the very lengthy and diverse lists of candidates considered by the conferences suggested that most hopefuls succeeded in reaching this stage of the process. Apparently, intimidation of potential candidates and the related reluctance of many potential candidates to face the consequences of opposition to TANU's preferred candidates (both important factors in earlier elections) had all but disappeared. In these circumstances, the nature of the selecting process by the conference necessarily became—in addition, of course, to free and secret balloting by the voters themselves—a most important determinant of the extent to which the electoral process could be considered democratic.

In six of Sukumaland's thirteen constituencies the candidate who received the highest number of votes in the district conference balloting won the election—indicating that at least between the two candidates finally on the ballot in these contests, the voters agreed with the TANU conference as to which candidate was the better. In the other seven constituencies the voters endorsed the one who had received the lesser number of votes in the conference tally; and in six of these instances the conference had voted decisively, in some cases overwhelmingly, for the first of the two candidates. These results indicated substantial variance at least half the time between the preferences of TANU conference delegates and the voters. This gave substance to the feeling of many that the wishes of the people at large were not always given expression through the party apparatus. It gave validity to the argument that, even in a one-party state, it was necessary to have more than one candidate face the electorate if the popular will were truly to be democratically represented.

But should there have been more than two candidates for each constituency—perhaps three as originally suggested by the Presidential Commission—to reduce the possibility that a truly deserving and popular figure would be excluded in the pre-selection process? While it is certainly possible that one or even both of the most qualified and widely supported candidates in a given constituency might be rejected for arbitrary reasons by the district TANU conference, there is little reason to suppose that this actually happened in Sukumaland in 1965. Former chiefs and relatives who submitted their names in various constituencies received few or relatively few votes; but they should not necessarily have finished in a more impressive manner in the conference balloting—either on their merits or on grounds of popularity. Indeed, the substantial votes received in district conferences by Chief Francis, Musobi and Kulwa suggest that men with traditional ties, but with high qualifications, need not be counted out— even when subjected to expressions of preference in a local TANU party conference. Also, while prominent men in Geita like the incumbent Mwiza, and once-popular activists Mpandachalo, Bunuma and Kizimba, did not do as well in the conference voting as they might have liked, it seems clear that their qualifications— if indeed not also their popularity—were less extensive than those of the candidates selected by the district conference for each of the constituencies in question. Previous overt identification with an opposition political party, however, was admittedly more of a problem. Idi Makwaia, previously of the ANC, received only one vote in the conference voting for the Shinyanga Central constituency. Chief Francis, formerly of the ANC and the PDP, was of course eliminated by the NEC—though he received astonishingly strong support, nevertheless, from the TANU conference in Kwimba.

In general, the evidence suggests that the conference pre-selection system provided no more of a stumbling block to the democratic process, and perhaps less, than party nominating conventions in the United States. The NEC, of course, could act as an occasional corrective in case a conference had chosen unwisely. And the voters could—and did—frequently reverse conference rankings as between the two final candidates.

Thus, while separate parties did not vie for power, the Tanzania national election of 1965 was, in its conception and in its implementation, democratic. It constituted a most unusual and promising development on the African political scene and a constructive and novel contribution to democratic theory generally. It provided the needed antidote to the stultification and resentment which authoritarian TANU party and government operations had widely engendered in Sukumaland and elsewhere in the nation in the early 1960s.

One problem, of course, is that able men like Paul Bomani may sometimes be rejected by the voters for insubstantial reasons. To place decisions about a nation's leaders truly in the hands of the people is, however, to take this risk. No alternative system of government is without a similar risk that able men will sometimes be excluded. As Nyerere has pointed out, Tanzania can afford such exclusions less than other nations which have more talent available, and under the Tanzanian system Nyerere can still appoint those he needs—like Bomani—to important posts. And he has done so. With time the voters, too, may distinguish more carefully between substantial and insubstantial reasons for approving or rejecting a particular candidate.

The elections of 1965, however, indicate that Tanzanian voters may already count themselves among those few electorates in the world who truly have a choice. That the choice is theirs, and that they have exercised it fully, are impressive achievements for the Tanzanian nation.

Selected Bibliography

PUBLIC DOCUMENTS

Great Britain. *Development of African Local Government in Tanganyika*, Col. No. 277, 1951.
——. *Reports by H. M. G. in the United Kingdom and Northern Ireland to the Trusteeship Council of the United Nations on the Administration of Tanganyika*, 1947–59.
Tanganyika. *Annual Reports of the Provincial Commissioners*, 1945–59.
——. *The County Council in Tanganyika: 1951–1956*, 1956.
——. *Development of (African) Local Government in Tanganyika*, 1955–59.
——. *Laws.*
——. *Local Government Memoranda*, No. 1, Part 1, 1954.
——. *Proceedings of the Legislative Council*, 1945–59.
——. *Report of the Committee on Constitutional Development*, 1951.
——. *Report of the Special Commissioner Appointed to Examine Matters Arising Out of the Report of the Committee on Constitutional Development*, 1953.
——. *Second Interim Report on the County Council in Tanganyika: 1956–1957*, 1957.
——. *Some Comments on Mr. Nyerere's Speech at the Fourth Committee of the United Nations*, 1957.
Tanzania. *Report of the Presidential Commission on the Establishment of a Democratic one Party State*, 1965.
United Nations. Trusteeship Council, Official Records. *Petitions from Tanganyika* (T/Pet. 2 series). New York: 1948–58. (Mimeographed.)
——. Trusteeship Council, Official Records (Supplements). *Visiting Mission to Trust Territories in East Africa: Report on Tanganyika*, 1948, 1951, 1954, 1957, 1960 (T/218, T/1032, T/1169, T/1401, T/1550). New York: 1948–60.

BOOKS AND ARTICLES

Abrahams, R. G. *The political organization of Unyamwezi*. London: Cambridge University Press, 1967.
Apter, David E. *The political kingdom in Uganda: a study in bureaucratic nationalism*. Princeton: Princeton University Press, 1961.
——. 'The role of traditionalism in the political modernization of Ghana and Uganda.' *World Politics*, XIII (Oct. 1960), 45–68.

Austen, Ralph A. 'Notes on the pre-history of TANU,' *Makerere Journal*, No. 9 (1964), 1–6.
——. *Northwest Tanzania under German and British rule: colonial policy and tribal politics, 1889–1939*. New Haven: Yale University Press, 1968.
Austin, Dennis. *Politics in Ghana: 1946–1960*. London: Oxford University Press, 1964.

Bailey, F. G. *Politics and social change: Orissa in 1959*. Berkeley: University of California Press, 1963.
Bates, Margaret. 'Tanganyika,' in Gwendolyn Carter, ed., *African one-party states*. Ithaca: Cornell University Press, 1962.
Bennett, George. 'The development of political organisations in Kenya,' *Political Studies*, v (June 1957), 111–30.
——. 'An outline history of TANU,' *Makerere Journal*, No. 7 (1963), 1–18.
Bienen, Henry. 'National security in Tanganyika after the mutiny,' *Transition*, v (Apr. 1965), 39–46.
——. Tanzania: *Party transformation and economic development*. Princeton: Princeton University Press, 1967.
——. 'The party and the no-party state: Tanganyika and the Soviet Union,' *Transition*, III (Mar.–Apr. 1964), 25–32.
Brown, Roland. 'Tanganyika and Northern Rhodesia: recent repressive legislation,' *Venture* (Apr. 1956).
Burke, Fred. *Tanganyika: Preplanning*. Syracuse: Syracuse University Press, 1965.

Chidzero, B. T. G. *Tanganyika and international trusteeship*. London: Oxford University Press, 1961.
Cliffe, Lionel, ed. *One party democracy: the 1965 Tanzania general elections*. Nairobi: East African Publishing House, 1967.
Cole, J. S. R. and W. N. Denison. *Tanganyika*, Vol. XII of *The British commonwealth: the development of its laws and constitution*, ed. G. W. Keeton. London: Stevens, 1964.
Coleman, James S. 'Nationalism in tropical Africa,' *American Political Science Review*, XLVIII (June 1954), 404–26.
——. *Nigeria, background to nationalism*. Berkeley: University of California Press, 1958.
——. 'The politics of Sub-Saharan Africa,' in Gabriel A. Almond and James S. Coleman, eds., *The politics of the developing areas*. Princeton: Princeton University Press, 1960.
Cory, Hans. *The indigenous political system of the Sukuma and proposals for political reform*. Kampala, Uganda: Eagle Press, 1954.
——. *The Ntemi: traditional rites of a Sukuma chief in Tanganyika*. London: Macmillan, 1951.
——. *Sukuma law and custom*. London: Oxford University Press, 1953.

Delf, George. *Asians in East Africa*. London: Oxford University Press, 1963.

de Wilde, John C. assisted by Peter F. M. McLoughlin, Andrew Guinard, Thayer Scudder and Robert Maubouche. *Experiences with agricultural development in tropical Africa.* 2 vols. Baltimore: Johns Hopkins Press, 1967.

Dudbridge, B. J. and J. E. S. Griffiths. 'The development of local government in Sukumaland,' *Journal of African Administration*, III (July 1951), 141–6.

Emerson, Rupert. *From empire to nation.* Cambridge, Mass.: Harvard University Press, 1960.

Fallers, Lloyd A. *Bantu bureaucracy.* Cambridge, Eng.: Heffer, 1956.
——. 'The predicament of the modern African chief: an instance from Uganda,' *American Anthropologist*, LVII (Apr. 1955), 290–305.

Friedland, William H. 'Co-operation, conflict, and conscription: TANU–TFL relations, 1955–1964,' in Jeffrey Butler and A. A. Castagno, eds., *Boston University papers on Africa: transition in African politics.* New York: Praeger, 1967, pp. 67–103.

Geneya, Ganja. 'Sukumaland: traditional values and modern leadership,' in Lionel Cliffe, ed., *One party democracy: the 1965 Tanzania general elections.* Nairobi: East African Publishing House, 1967, pp. 186–207.

Glickman, Harvey. 'Dilemmas of political theory in an African context: the ideology of Julius Nyerere,' in Jeffrey Butler and A. A. Castagno, eds., *Boston University papers on Africa: transition in African politics.* New York: Praeger, 1967, pp. 195–223.
——. 'One-party system in Tanganyika,' *The Annals of the American Academy of Political and Social Science*, CCCCLVIII (Mar. 1965), 136–49.
——. *Some observations on the Army and political unrest in Tanganyika.* Pittsburgh: Institute for African Affairs, Duquesne University, 1964.
——. 'Traditional politics and democratic institutions in mainland Tanzania,' in *Asian and African Studies Annual*, IV. Jerusalem: Hebrew University Institute of Asian and African Studies, 1968.

Hailey, Lord. *Native administration in the British African Territories.* Vol. I: *East Africa.* London: H.M. Stationery Office, 1950.

Hodgkin, Thomas. *Nationalism in colonial Africa.* New York: New York University Press, 1957.

Ingham, Kenneth. *A history of East Africa.* London: Longmans, 1962.

Kandoro, S. A. *Mwito wa Uhuru.* Dar es Salaam: Thakers, 1961.

Kilson, Martin. 'Sierra Leone,' in James S. Coleman and Carl G. Rosberg, eds., *Political parties and national integration in tropical Africa.* Berkeley: University of California Press, 1964.

388   *Selected Bibliography*

Kilson, Martin. 'Authoritarian and single-party tendencies in African politics,' *World Politics*, xv (Jan. 1963), 262–94.
——. *Political change in a West African state: a study of the modernization process in Sierra Leone.* Cambridge: Harvard University Press, 1966.
Klerru, Wilbert. *One-party system of government.* Dar es Salaam: Mwananchi Publishing Company, Ltd, 1964.

Lang, Gottfried O. and Martha B. 'Problems of social and economic change in Sukumaland, Tanganyika,' *Anthropological Quarterly*, xxxv (Apr. 1962), 86–101.
Leys, Colin. 'Tanganyika: the realities of independence,' *International Journal*, xvii (Summer 1962), 251–68.
Liebenow, J. Gus. 'Responses to planned political change in a Tanganyika tribal group,' *American Political Science Review*, i (June 1956), 442–61.
——. 'The Sukuma,' in Audrey I. Richards, ed., *East African chiefs.* London: Faber, 1959.
——. 'Some problems in introducing local government reform in Tanganyika,' *Journal of African Administration*, viii (July 1956), 132–9.
——. 'The chief in Sukuma local government,' *Journal of African Administration*, xi (Apr. 1959), 84–92.
Listowel, Judith. *The making of Tanganyika.* New York: London House and Maxwell, 1965.
Lowenkopf, Martin. 'The meaning of Arusha,' *Africa Report*, xii (Mar. 1967), 8–10.

MacDonald, Alexander. *Tanzania: young nation in a hurry.* New York: Hawthorn, 1966.
Maguire, G. Andrew. 'The emergence of TANU in the Lake Province,' in Robert I. Rotberg and Ali Mazuri, eds., *Protest and Power in Black Africa.* New York: Oxford University Press, 1970.
Malcolm, D. W. *Sukumaland: an African people and their country.* London: Oxford University Press, 1953.
Marsh, Z. A. and G. W. Kingsnorth. *Introduction to the history of East Africa.* Cambridge, Eng.: Cambridge University Press, 1961.
Moffett, J. P., ed. *Handbook of Tanganyika.* Dar Es Salaam: Government Printer, 1958.
Morgenthau, Ruth Schachter. 'African elections: Tanzania's contribution,' *Africa Report*, x (Dec. 1965), 12–16.

Nye, Joseph S. Jr. 'Tanganyika's self help,' *Transition*, ii (Nov. 1963), 35–9.
——. 'TANU and UPC: the impact of independence on two African nationalist parties,' in Jeffrey Butler and A. A. Castagno, eds., *Boston University papers on Africa: transition in African politics.* New York: Praeger, 1967, 224–50.
Nyerere, Julius. 'Africa's bid for democracy,' *African and Colonial World*, viii (July 1960), 3.
——. 'Tanganyika today: the nationalist view,' *International Affairs*, xxxvi (1960), 43–7.

——. 'The challenge of independence,' *East Africa and Rhodesia* (7 Dec. 1961), pp. 339–40.
——. 'Democracy and the party system,' *Tanganyika Standard* (16–18, 21, 22 Jan. 1963).
——. 'One party government,' *Spearhead*, I (Nov. 1961), 7.
——. 'One party system,' *Spearhead*, II (Jan. 1963), I, 12–23.

Paulus, Margarete. *Das Genossenschaftswesen in Tanganyika und Uganda: Möglichkeiten und Aufgaben.* Berlin: Springerverlag, 1967.
Perham, Margery. 'The psychology of African nationalism,' *Optima*, X, No. 1 (1960), 27–36.
Pratt, R. C. 'Multi-racialism and local government in Tanganyika,' *Race*, II (Nov. 1960), 33–49.
Pye, Lucian W. 'The non-western political process,' *Journal of Politics*, XX (1958), 468–86.

Rotberg, Robert I. *The rise of nationalism in Central Africa: the making of Malawi and Zambia, 1873–1964.* Cambridge, Mass.: Harvard University Press, 1965.
Roth, Warren J. 'The Wasukuma of Tanganyika, an annotated bibliography,' *Anthropological Quarterly*, XXXIV (July 1961), 158–63.
Rounce, N. V. *The agriculture of the cultivation steppe.* Cape Town.: Longmans, 1949.

Segal, Aron. 'Where is Tanzania heading?' *Africa Report*, X (Oct. 1965), 10–17.
Shaw, J. V. 'The development of African local government in Sukumaland,' *Journal of African Administration*, VI (Oct. 1954), 171–8.
Shils, Edward. *Political development in the new states.* New York: Humanities Press, Inc.
Sutton, Francis X. 'Authority and authoritarianism in the new Africa,' *Journal of International Affairs*, XV (1961), 7–17.
Sywulka, Marie. *Workers together with him: a short history, Africa Inland Mission—Tanganyika Territory.* Rethy, Irumi, Belgian Congo: Africa Inland Mission Press, 1952.

Tanner, R. E. S. 'Law enforcement by communal action in Sukumaland, Tanganyika Territory,' *Journal of African Administration*, IV (Oct. 1955), 159–65.
TANU. Sheria na Madhumuni ya Chama. Dar es Salaam: Mwananchi Publishing Company, Ltd, n.d.
Taylor, J. Clagett. *The political development of Tanganyika.* Stanford: Stanford University Press, 1963.
Tordoff, William. *Government and politics in Tanzania.* Nairobi: East African Publishing House, 1967.
Twining, Lord. 'The last nine years in Tanganyika,' *African Affairs*, LVIII (Jan. 1959), 15–24.
——. 'Tanganyika's middle course in race relations,' *Optima*, VIII (Dec. 1958), 211–18.

'United Tanganyika party's statement of policy,' *East Africa and Rhodesia*, XXXIV (3 Oct. 1957), 142–3.

Who's Who in East Africa. Nairobi: Marco Surveys, 1964.
Wicken, Joan. 'Tanganyika tightrope,' *Socialist Commentary* (April 1958), 14–16.
——. 'What next in Tanganyika?' *Venture* (Sept. 1958).

Young, Roland and Henry Fosbrook. *Smoke in the hills: political tensions in the Morogoro district of Tanganyika*. Evanston: Northwestern University Press, 1960.

Zolberg, Aristide R. *Creating political order: the party states of West Africa*. Chicago: Rand McNally, 1966.

NEWSPAPERS AND PERIODICALS

Ilaka (Sukumaland Federal Council, Malya) (Swahili).
Lake Province News (Office of Information, Mwanza).
Lumuli (Roman Catholic Diocese, Mwanza) (Sukuma).
Mwafrika (Dar es Salaam) (Swahili).
Sauti ya TANU (Dar es Salaam) (Swahili).
Spearhead (Dar es Salaam).
Tanganyika News Review (Government of Tanganyika, Dar es Salaam).
Tanganyika Notes and Records (Dar es Salaam).
Tanganyika Standard (Dar es Salaam).
Transition (Kampala).
Venture (London).
What's the Answer? (Government of Tanganyika, Dar es Salaam).

UNPUBLISHED MATERIAL

A. Official Sources
Tanganyika. District Books of the Geita, Kwimba, Maswa, Mwanza and Shinyanga District administrations of the Government of Tanganyika. (Copies in Roland Oliver collection, vol. VI, School of Oriental and African Studies, London.)
——. Files of the Geita, Kwimba, Maswa, Mwanza and Shinyanga District administrations of the Government of Tanganyika, 1945–1959. (Transferred from the districts to the National Archives, Dar es Salaam, in 1965.)
——. Files of the Lake Province administration of the Government of Tanganyika, 1945–1959. (Transferred from Mwanza to the National Archives, Dar es Salaam, in 1965.)
——. Files of the Tanganyika Territory Secretariat, 1920–55. National Archives, Dar es Salaam.

B. Dissertations and Papers
Abrahams, Raphael G. 'The political organization of Nyamweziland.' Unpublished Ph.D. dissertation, Cambridge University, 1962.

Austen, Ralph A. 'Historical research in Sukumaland.' Paper prepared for Sukumaland Research Conference, Philadelphia, Pa., Oct. 1965.
——. 'Native policy and African politics: indirect rule in north-west Tanzania, 1889–1939.' Unpublished Ph.D. dissertation, Harvard University, 1965.

Bates, Margaret L. 'Tanganyika under British administration, 1920–1955.' Unpublished Ph.D. dissertation, Oxford University, 1956.
Burke, Fred. 'Some implications of the applications of the English committee system to local government in Uganda.' Paper read at the Conference held at the East African Institute of Social Research, Kampala, Uganda, July 1956.

Cliffe, Lionel. 'Nationalism and the reaction to enforced agricultural improvement in Tanganyika.' Paper prepared for discussion at Kivukoni College, Dar es Salaam, 1964.
Cory, Hans. 'Destocking in Sukumaland.' Paper prepared for the Government of Tanganyika, 1956.

Geneya, Ganja. 'Political adaptation in Sukumaland.' Unpublished B.A. thesis, Makerere University College, Kampala, 1968.
Glickman, Harvey. 'Traditional pluralism and democratic processes in Tanganyika.' Paper delivered at the annual Meeting of the American Political Science Association, Chicago, Illinois, Sept. 1964.

Hatfield, Colby R. Jr. 'The Nfumu in tradition and change: a study of the position of religious practitioners among the Sukuma of Tanzania, East Africa.' Unpublished Ph.D. dissertation, Catholic University of America, 1968.

Lang, Gottfried O. 'The evolution of a research project.' Paper prepared for Sukumaland Research Conference, Philadelphia, Pa., Oct. 1965.
Liebenow, J. Gus. 'Chieftainship and local government in Tanganyika: a study of institutional adaptation.' Unpublished Ph.D. dissertation, Northwestern University, 1955.
——. 'Modernization in East Africa through cultural continuity: the case of the Sukuma.' Unpublished essay prepared for Lang and Peter F. M. McLoughlin, eds., *Recent research in Sukumaland: essays in social, economic and political development* (in preparation).
Lowenkopf, Martin. 'Political parties in Uganda and Tanganyika.' Unpublished Master's dissertation, London University, 1961.

McLoughlin, Peter F. M. 'Some aspects of Sukumaland's economic development problem.' Paper prepared for Sukumaland Research Conference, Philadelphia, Pa., Oct. 1965.
Mecer-Wright, Justin. 'Notes for instructors.' A field manual for agricultural instructors, Ukiriguru, Tanganyika, 1957.

Nicholson, Mary Read. 'Legal change in Tanzania as seen among the Sukuma.' Unpublished Ph.D. dissertation, University of Minnesota, 1968.

Noble, Charles O. 'Voluntary associations and their milieu in Sukuma-land.' Unpublished manuscript.

Petro, Joseph K. 'Political history of TAA [Tanganyika African Associa-tion] Shinyanga.' Paper prepared for Kivukoni College, Dar es Salaam, 1964.
Purvis, John T., B. J. Dudbridge and J. B. Clegg. 'The mechanisation and capitalisation of peasant agriculture.' Paper prepared for the Government of Tanganyika, 1952.

Roth, Warren J. 'The intercultural individual: two examples of change among the Sukuma.' Paper prepared for Sukumaland Research Conference, Philadelphia, Pa., Oct. 1965.
——. 'Three cooperatives and a credit union as examples of culture change among the Sukuma of Tanzania.' Unpublished Ph.D. dissertation, Catholic University of America, 1966.
Rounce, N. V. 'Technical considerations in the economic development of Sukumaland.' Paper prepared for the Government of Tanganyika, 1952.
Wright, A. C. A. 'Political and economic considerations arising in relation to economic development in Busukuma.' Paper prepared for the Government of Tanganyika, 1952.
——. 'The transition from "Native Administration" to Local Govern-ment.' Paper prepared for the Government of Tanganyika, 1952.

OTHER SOURCES

Bogohe, L. M. Selected papers, privately held. Nassa, Tanzania.
Cory, Hans. Collected papers. University College Library, Dar es Salaam.
Fabian Colonial Bureau. File on Tanganyika. London.
Historical surveys of politics in selected villages in Sukumaland, by Pastor Balele, research assistant to the writer, 1964. Occasional research by Francis Madoshi, William Simba and Joseph William, 1964.
Kitenge, M. I. Selected papers, privately held. Mwanza, Tanzania.
Labour Party. File on Tanganyika. Transport House, London.
Leadership questionnaires. Distributed by the writer in cooperation with the Mwanza Regional Office of the Tanzania Information Services, 1964.
Personal interviews. England and East Africa.
Roth, Warren J. Field notes of research in Sukumaland, 1962–3. Nyegezi Social Research Institute, Mwanza, Tanzania.
Sagala, Yakabo. Selected papers, privately held. Nassa, Tanzania.
Sukuma Union. Files, minutes of meetings, and correspondence, pri-vately held. Mwanza, Tanzania.
Walden, S. A. Selected papers, privately held. London.

Index

Abbreviations used in the index may be found on page xiv or, alternatively, under the appropriate index headings themselves, as in 'African National Congress, ANC'.

Kaseko, Stanley, 171, 176–8, 185, 290, 327
Kasubi, Joseph, 380
Kaswende, Jacob A., 326
Kawawa, Rashidi, 182, 194, 226, 281
Kerewe, 78
Kibaja, Eustace, 32
kibanda, 1 n, 316–17
Kidaha, see Makwaia, Chief David Kidaha
Kija, Masanja, 345
Kilala, Philip, 122, 166
King, R. S., 293–4
Kipondya, Dominick, 128
Kirilo, Japhet, 150–1
Kisenge, E. A., 226, 250–1, 256
Kisesa, Kasim, 85–6
Kishiba, Kipande, 76
Kisusi, Salome, 380–1
Kitenge, M. I., 138, 153, 189, 219, 380
Kizimba, Ernest, 208, 215, 379–80
Kulwa, Mwanga, 378
Kwimba, district, 242, 247, 297–8, 377–8
Kyaze, Christopher, 97

Labour Party, British, 168
Lake Province Africans General Trading Company, 182
Lake Province African Tailors Union, 140
Lake Province Council, 18, 32–3, 35, 154; see also Bomani, Paul
Lake Province Growers Association, LPGA:
 cooperative, 63, 91, 97
 political aspects of, 98, 104, 107–8
 grievances of, 100–1, 106–8, 111, 153
 see also Bomani, Paul
Lake Province Local Tribes Union, 78
Lake Victoria, 3
land usage/utilization, 20, 27, 29, see also Sukumaland Development Scheme; Sukumaland Federal Council
Laxman, N. K., 215, 272–3, 375
League of Nations, 8, 11
Legislative Council:
 of 1945 (members appointed) xxiv, 13–14, 33–4, 45, 57, 106, 132, 172, 193; legislation of, 172, 206
 of 1959 (members elected), 267–9
 of 1960, 270–3
Lennox-Boyd, Alan, 195

Lint and Seed Marketing Board, 91, 98, 102, 300
liwali, 72
local government:
 Native Authority system (Chiefs), 21, 30, 47, 50, 122, 131, 141, 157–8, 167, 170, 202, 203; see also Sukumaland Federal Council; Sukumaland Development Scheme; Native Authorities
 hierarchy of representative councils, (NAs and African Councillors—1954–61), 22–6, 31–2, 274, 291; position of NAs in, 274; TANU opposition to, 276–7; replaced in 1963, 325, 332; see also Cory, Hans
 multi-racial councils (African, European, Asian—1955–8): administration arguments favouring, 32, 202, 204; pilot project in Geita, 196–3; see also Geita crisis; opposition to, 34, 108, 199–200, 276–7; weaknesses: lacked popular consent, 237; artificial, ineffectual, 236–7; diminution of NA power, 202, 232, 236–7, 292; protest against, see Geita crisis, civil disobedience; administration response to protest, 233; see also Geita crisis; South East Lake County Council; Legislative Council; Lake Province Council
 African district councils (elected majorities—1959–61): TANU control of, 269–71, 278–9; status of NAs in, 277–8, 290–1, 296–7; election of subchiefs, 291–2; Geita successes, 292–4; administration strategy, 293–4, 296–7; problems of, 270, 294–7
 District Councils (fully elected—1962–), 274, 297, 311, 331–3, 335, 341–3, 365, 370, 380–1; see also Tanzania government, development committees
Loughborough College, 105
Lubala, Sylvester, 281, 327
 case against Masalu, 341–2
 1965 defeat, 374, 378
Lugaila, John, 76, 122
Lugard, Lord, 6
Luhende, Makwaia, 348
Luhende, Chief Shoka, 32
Lumuli (Sukuma newspaper), 129,

racial councils, 217–19
jailed, 219
proposed boycott, 221
'Kenyatta' of Geita, 221
importance of, 216, 218
see also Geita crisis
Mpanduji, Titus, 337–8
Mseto (multi-racial district council),
218–19, 221, 231, 379–80
Msonde, Shaban, 376
Msowoya, Isaac, 66, 84
Mtemvu, Zuberi, 270, 300, 338, 345,
350, 356
Muhaya, Albert, 215, 217
multi-racialism:
British policy of, 32–3
Kidaha's theory of, 55–6
TAA's attitude toward, 154
multi-racial councils, *see* local
government, multi-racial councils
problems with NAs, 199
problems with non-Africans, 203–4,
207
breakdown of, 196
see also Legislative Council; Lake
Province Council
Munanka, Isaac Bhoke, 136–7, 152,
168, 174, 179, 181–2, 189, 195
Musobi, Mageni, 378
Musoma, district, 82, 111, 220; *see
also* Bomani, Paul
Mwafrika (Geita Swahili publication),
214, 254–5
Mwandu, Francis, 345
Mwanilanga, Chenge, 345
Mwanza, town:
administrative headquarters, 63
commercial entrepôt, 5
educated elite, 63, 65
center for voluntary associations, 61–
3; *see also* associations, voluntary
beginning of Sukuma Union, 75–7;
see also SU
beginning of cooperatives, 83; *see
also* Mwanza African Traders Cooperative Society
beginning of Lake Province
Growers Association, 91; *see also*
LPGA
founding of PAFMECA; *see*
PAFMECA
Lake Province TAA headquarters,
67
Lake Province TANU headquarters,
250

Town Council, 154
Township Authority, 71, 136
protest march to, *see* Geita crisis
see also TAA; TANU
Mwanza African Traders Cooperative
Society, 63, 78, 83–5, 87
Mwanza Federation of Chiefs, 157
Mweli Farmers Union, 104; *see also*
VFCU
Mwihendi, Wilson, 212, 217, 379
Mwiza, Bartholomew, 273–4, 379

Nassa, chiefdom, 85, 89–90, 114, 125,
198
nationalism, xxii, xxiv, xxvi–xxviii, 74,
113; *see also* UNVM, Shinyanga
Petition; SU
Vox Populi vox Dei, 189, 197; *see
also* Geita crisis
Native Authorities, Chiefs/NAs:
traditional role of, 1, 2, 48, 124
role in British administration, 6, 30,
45, 50–2, 122, 124–5, 131, 134,
147, 157–8, 167, 170, 177–8,
201–2, 279, 285–6
protest against administration
policies, 25–6, 49–50, 199, 202–4
conflict with politicians, 41, 169–71,
177, 290–1
politicians' support of, 204, 208,
285–6, 288
petitions of grievance: to PC,
49–50; to UNVM, 133; to
Colonial Office, 50
strength of, in Shinyanga, 100–1,
193; in Kwimba, 297–8
weakness of, 61; in Geita, 198–203
pass.; 207–8, 298
decline of, 41, 59, 131–2, 134, 202,
282–3, 289, 311, 323, 330–3, 336
eligibility in new government,
330–4, 359
see also grievances, African; SU;
British administration
Native Authority Ordinance, 28, 171
natural resources legislation: *see* grievances, African; British administration, compulsory legislation
revoking of, 196
Ndaturu, Chief, 170, 176, 280, 286,
290, 339
Ngalaiswa, Fabian, 76–8, 270, 339–40,
343
Ngogeja, J. B., 281
Ngusa, Simon, 223, 225–6